On Jean-Jacques Rousseau

For Joan,

    with my most heartfelt thanks
for all you have done to make
this book possible,
and above all for honoring me
with your friendship,

            Jim

          March 2000

PHILOSOPHY   POLITICAL THEORY   AESTHETICS

Judith Butler and Frederick M. Dolan

EDITORS

On Jean-Jacques Rousseau

CONSIDERED AS ONE OF THE FIRST
AUTHORS OF THE REVOLUTION

James Swenson

Stanford University Press

Stanford, California 2000

Stanford University Press
Stanford, California

© 2000 by the Board of Trustees of the Leland Stanford Junior University

Printed in the United States of America
CIP data appear at the end of the book

Contents

Preface

This book is about reading as a historical problem. It is not a history of reading, but a study of the historical role and political efficacy of reading, in the strong sense that literary criticism gives to the term. The example is canonical: Jean-Jacques Rousseau and the French Revolution. My concern is not to arrive at some final determination of relations of "influence," but rather to examine the role that the difficult and problematic nature of reading an author like Rousseau—a brief glance at the history of Rousseau criticism is enough to show just how difficult and problematic—plays in a concrete historical situation with dramatic political consequences. Rousseau is so important, at least in part, because he pursues multiple lines of argument in a single work and often seems to contradict himself. Understanding how these lines of argument relate to one another is neither easy nor evident, but the beauty of Rousseau's language, the urgency of his rhetoric, and the force of his arguments compel us to try. As it compelled the generation of the Revolution. But people did, and do, disagree passionately about the interpretation of Rousseau.

This concentration on the problematic character of reading, and thus "influence," allows for the formulation of a new interpretive framework for old questions concerning the relation between the Enlightenment and the French Revolution. I hope not so much to resolve these questions as to understand why they are so thorny, and so necessary. In 1791, Louis-Sébastien Mercier (from whom I have taken the title of this book) proclaimed Rousseau to be "one of the first authors of the Revolution." The pamphlets and speeches of the revolutionary decade are full of similar statements, and they have often been seconded by the historiographical tradition. Nevertheless, a persistent set of difficulties haunt this filiation. First of all, the prerevolutionary reception of Rousseau's political work appears inconsequential when compared with the reception of his literary texts. Prerevolutionary devotion to Rousseau is a poor predictor of political radicalism during the Revolution; Rousseauists are to be found in all political camps. Finally, "readings" of Rousseau during the Revolution, as embodied in pamphlets, speeches, laws, and even insurrections, are often contradictory and highly partial. There seems to be no single revolutionary understanding of Rousseau—perhaps no understanding at all. Jean-Joseph Mounier, a leading figure in the National Assembly in 1789, provided what is to my mind the most succinct formulation of the paradoxical structure of the link between Rousseau and the Revolution when he remarked, "It was not in the least the influence of these principles that produced the Revolution; on the contrary, it was the Revolution that produced their influence."

Now, I do not feel, as some critics have argued, that these facts should lead us to minimize Rousseau's "influence" on the Revolution. Nor do I wish to minimize the importance of these facts (although recent research leads to a more nuanced view of some of them than may have been prevalent before). To the contrary, my fundamental contention in these pages will be that these paradoxes stem from the structure of Rousseau's discourse itself, and that they are indicative of a profound Rousseauism that goes beyond subjective choice. Rousseau is "one of the first authors of the Revolution" not because he was one of its causes but because he provided the terms in which the logic of events could be interpreted.

Rousseau's two *Discours*, together with his autobiographical and fictional texts, provide a model for understanding the narrative discontinuities and causal reversals that so bedevil the historiographical tradition. Indeed, given the structure of those texts, their "influence" could occur only in such a paradoxical, nonlinear form. Rousseau's texts generate a division in their own reading. This can occur sequentially, in the form of the discontinuities and reversals characteristic equally of narratives such as *Julie* or the second *Discours*, and narratives about the reception and effects of those texts. Such acts of division can also occur simultaneously, in the form of incompatible attempts to apply the lessons of a single text to an urgent historical moment. That, I will argue, was the fate of the *Contrat social* between 1789 and 1794. The structure of debate over the proper reading of the text, at a moment when readings occurred as political programs, is grounded in the rhetorical structure of the text itself. That does not make correct interpretation any easier; far from it. But it does allow us to see that we must not short-circuit the moment of reading if we wish to understand what it might mean to be the author of a Revolution.

Reading in this sense is necessarily procedure as well as theme. I apply the techniques of literary criticism to domains for which they were not intended, taking in the constitutional discourse of the Revolution together with Rousseau's major texts, both literary and political, the contemporary historiography of the Enlightenment alongside the Enlightenment tradition of universal history. I attempt to read not only texts but also problems in historiography and political theory—even, perhaps, to read events. The historiographic texts subjected to this treatment are chosen on account of my admiration for them; close reading of this sort is possible only on the basis of a deep respect. The stronger a text is, I believe, the more interpretive pressure it not only will sustain but indeed reward. What this implies is that one learns most from a text by pushing its arguments to their limits and by probing its contradictions. A synthetic understanding that stops short of this, that has not fully taken apart ("deconstructed") a text's arguments, does not pay its full measure of respect. And while I may not subject historians' texts to quite the same specifically linguistic interpretive pressure applied to Rousseau in later chapters, the principle is the same. Just as reflection on the problem of the place of reading in historical analysis is a constant preoccupation in these pages, it also represents, in my view, a major part of the particular contribution that a literary critic such as myself can make to historiographic debate. I therefore do not claim to show something that my predecessors have misunderstood or overlooked. Rather, my sense of what I am doing here is that it is precisely in *reading* their texts—taking as full a measure as possible of their coherence but also of the contradictions they generate—that a significant pattern can be seen to emerge.

This book is based entirely on printed sources. The field is a well worked one, distinguished for the intensive archival research, extensive documentary publications, and admirable critical editions that we owe to several generations of scholars. I hope to have made good and full use of their work. My notes and bibliography reflect the paths by which I built my own argument; there are many worthy books I know, and doubtless even more I do not know, that I have not cited. I have used a short title system in the notes; full details are reserved for the bibliography. I have used English translations for secondary materials when available. As for primary materials, I have generally opted for the most recent scholarly edition in the original language, cited together with translations for languages other than French or English. Rarer items were consulted at the Beinecke Library at Yale, the New York Public Library, and the Réserve at the Bibliothèque Sainte-Geneviève in Paris. Dates given are usually those of first publication rather than composition. With occasional exceptions, translations of French sources are my own. I have checked my translations of Rousseau against the fine translations now available in the *Collected Writings of Rousseau,* as well as Victor Gourevitch's renderings of the political works. I have in particular adopted a number of readings from the spectacular translation of *Julie* by Philip Stewart and Jean Vaché in the *Collected Writings.* References to works by Rousseau are given parenthetically in the text, with volume and page numbers from the Pléiade edition; details are given in the bibliography.

This project began as a dissertation, and it took many years to emerge into its current form. It has been with me through a number of institutions. Parts of the initial research were supported by grants from the Yale Council on International and Area Studies and the Center for West European Studies; much of the final draft was made possible by a sabbatical leave from the Faculty of Arts and Sciences at Rutgers. The French departments at Johns Hopkins and Berkeley provided some shelter during my time of wandering, and I feel I have found a home at Rutgers. A crucial impetus to a new conception of Chapters 1 and 2 came from a National Endowment for the Humanities seminar on "Institutions of Enlightenment," directed by Keith Baker and John Bender, at Stanford University in the summer of 1996. Portions of the text were presented at meetings of the American Society for Eighteenth-Century Studies and the Eighteenth-Century Scottish Studies Society, and I learned much from discussions in those contexts. I would like to offer my thanks to the faculty and staff of the School of Social Sciences of the Institute for Advanced Study, who quite gratuitously and most gracefully provided me with a place to work.

Many people have been involved in this project in one way or another: professors, fellow students, and now colleagues. I first remember Brian, Rena, Mary, and Maggy. My thanks for their care, concern, and contributions go to Wilda Anderson, Roger Blood, Ellen Burt, Judith Butler, Joseph Chaves, François Cornilliat, Uri Eisenzweig, Paul Friedland, Neil Hertz, Denis Hollier, Jennifer Jones, Rick Lockwood, Kirstie McClure, Jan Mieszkowski, Thomas Pepper, Suzanne Roos, Margery Safir, Peter Sahlins, Viviana Santos, Haun Saussy, Michael Shae, Mary Shaw, Michael Syrotinski, Kathleen Tobin, and Jack Undank. Special thanks go to Cathy Caruth, my dissertation director, and Joan Scott, who played mentor to me for three years.

My parents and sisters have been unwavering in their support.

I dedicate this book to my wife and companion, Debra Keates, who is full of love and good ideas.

And to Nicolas and Lucinda, for whom I am full of amazement.

J.S.

On Jean-Jacques Rousseau

1. Intellectual, Cultural, and Ideological Origins

> Je ne considère pas qu'il soit d'aucune façon légitime d'avoir écrit que les
> structures ne descendent pas dans la rue, parce que, s'il y a quelque chose
> que démontrent les événements de mai, c'est précisément la descente
> dans la rue des structures. Le fait qu'on l'écrive à la place même où s'est
> opérée cette descente dans la rue ne prouve rien d'autre que, simplement,
> ce qui est très souvent, et même le plus souvent, interne à ce qu'on
> appelle l'acte, c'est qu'il se méconnaît lui-même.
>
> —*Jacques Lacan*, FEBRUARY 22, 1969[1]

History of Enlightenment and Enlightenment History

The question of the "intellectual origins of the French Revolution," and in
particular of the influence of the Enlightenment, has a long and illustrious
history. Well before it became a consecrated object of study or a song in a
novel, it provided a framework within which many contemporaries understood—or at least attempted to understand—the events through which they
had lived, both before, during, and immediately following the Revolution.
Since then it has provided the crucial test case for the philosophy of history,
for all attempts to endow the course of European (or even world) history
with a meaning. It is not simply one problem among many for intellectual
history. With respect to the historiography of the Revolution in general,
François Furet has noted that the event is "not so much a topic in modern
history as one of its chief manifestations, in that it embodies a mode of
change and human action that is fundamental to its significance. . . . All the
histories of the Revolution deal with a topic far vaster than the history of the
Revolution; they are actually constructing a meaning for time itself."[2]

Much the same could be said of the problem of the intellectual origins of
the Revolution. The possibility of a filiation between a current of thought
and a set of political or historical events takes on meaning, for us, beginning
from this problem. That such a filiation played a large role in the way con-

temporaries experienced the event is doubtless important. The *philosophes* saw themselves as spreading, precisely, light; the orators of the Revolutionary assemblies, from the Constituent to the Directory, saw their actions as the application of reason and truth to politics. Ever since, for the right as for the left, the Revolution has been the child, in some sense, of the Enlightenment. The difficulties of interpreting that "sense" have provided the most consistent matrix for thought about the place of ideas in history, and above all about the relation between our political concepts, such as democracy, and our political institutions.

The very metaphor of "enlightenment," *les lumières*, necessarily leads to concepts of diffusion and influence. *Lumières* designates first of all the property of an individual: an enlightened person "has" *lumières*. In this sense it can be identical with natural reason, but it can also be tied to faith.[3] At the same time it designates—increasingly as the century progresses—an objective, societal fact that is ultimately not dependent on individuals, however much they may fight for or against it. In 1782, Jean-Antoine-Nicolas Caritat, marquis de Condorcet, addressing the Académie française, declared the progress of enlightenment to be irreversible. "These first truths, these methods spread through all Nations and carried to both Worlds, can no longer be annihilated; the human Race will see no more these alternatives of darkness and light to which it was long believed to be eternally condemned by Nature. It is no longer within the power of men to put out the torch lit by Genius."[4] For Condorcet as for many of his contemporaries, it is the invention of the printing press that bears the burden of this autonomization of enlightenment. "Thanks to printing, this Art which conserves human Reason, a principle useful to public happiness has no sooner been discovered than it becomes part of the patrimony of all Nations."[5] It is the fundamental characteristic of *lumières* in this sense to spread, and enlightened individuals tend to become its agents rather than its possessors. Finally, the term comes to denote a certain body of thought in eighteenth-century France (which may or may not be particularly coherent), more frequently termed *philosophie*. The metaphorical range of the term extends from peaceful (and often agentless) images of the sun or other celestial bodies rising in the sky to dissipate gently the darkness of the night,[6] to the more active "torch" of philosophy penetrating into dark, hidden recesses. This imagery can even become violent when this torch sets fire to the idols of obscurantism, a conceit literalized in the revolutionary festivals of 1794.[7]

The relations between these different senses of the term *lumières* constitute the series of problems that any study of the intellectual or ideological origins of the Revolution must deal with. How widely spread does enlightenment need to be (what percentage of individuals need to be enlightened, what sorts of institutions must they be organized in, etc.) for enlightenment to become a social force? What agency spreads it, and is this action pacific or turbulent? Is there a determinate relationship, on either an epistemological or simply on an empirical level, between a substantive definition of Enlightenment philosophy—what Condorcet refers to as "first truths," for example, sensationist epistemology, religious tolerance, or advocacy of free trade—and a more formalist definition of Enlightenment, such as Immanuel Kant's "the human being's emergence from his self-incurred minority [*der Ausgang des Menschen aus seiner selbst verschuldeten Unmündigkeit*],"[8] or, more simply, the habit of critical thought? While advocacy of a critical attitude with respect to metaphysics, religion, and politics is an important component of Enlightenment philosophy, that philosophy is not the only possible source of such an attitude.

AN INTERPRETIVE UNITY?

The model of influence, whether valorized as progress or demonized as conspiracy, dominated nineteenth-century historiography of the Revolution. Whether their work was oriented toward narrative or toward analysis, toward celebration or toward condemnation, the great nineteenth-century historians all gave this model a central place in their accounts. Jules Michelet said of François-Marie Arouet de Voltaire and Jean-Jacques Rousseau that "when these two men passed, the Revolution was already accomplished in the high realm of the mind."[9] Michelet's narrative account of the Revolution seldom makes an explicit place for the consideration of such questions of influence. But his central question and explicative schema, the relation of the Revolution to religion, depends upon his interpretation, as laid out in the Introduction, of the Enlightenment as the reawakening of justice.

Hippolyte Taine's history is generally more sober than Michelet's, although his treatment of the role of the Enlightenment is just as lyrical—albeit as elegy rather than encomium. "When we see a man of weak constitution, but of healthy appearance and peaceful habits, greedily drink a new kind of liquor, then suddenly fall to the ground and foam at the mouth, become delirious and wrestle in convulsions, we can easily guess that there was a dangerous substance in the pleasant drink."[10] Taine goes on to describe the two components of this insidious beverage, the progress of science and the abstractness of the *esprit classique* (particularly the reduction of the literary vocabulary of French to what he calls *expressions générales* and *lieux communs*, which render it a marvelous instrument for analysis but incapable of capturing the detail and life of individuality).[11] Separately they may be "salutary," but they become poisonous when combined. Taine summarized his argument in the following terms:

> I hope to show that Boileau, Descartes, Lemaistre de Sacy, Corneille, Racine, Fléchier, etc., are the ancestors of Saint-Just and Robespierre. What had held them back had been the intactness of monarchical and religious dogma; once this dogma had been worn out by its own excess and overturned by the scientific world view (Newton as presented by Voltaire), the *esprit classique* necessarily [*fatalement*] produced the theory of natural, abstract man and the social contract.[12]

Taine's explanation, based entirely on literary evidence, is fundamentally culturalist in form. The *esprit classique* for him characterizes the whole society—or at least the whole of society that counts. (The peasants are not part of it, but they are not civilized; the political awakening of the Third Estate is subsequent to—or coincident with—its introduction into this way of thinking.) This "spirit" functions as the unconscious presupposition of thought: Taine describes what he is looking for as "the structure of their internal eye, by which I mean the settled form of their intelligence, that they carry with them, unwittingly and unknowingly."[13] As such it is imposed by the oratorical culture shared by the educational system, the sociability of the salons with their *bienséances* and *convenances*, and literature. The *esprit classique* therefore can be considered to be what a later generation of French historians called a *mentalité*: a given of political culture.[14] His characterization of the *esprit classique*'s "fault"—its abstraction, its focus on "man" as such rather than Frenchmen, Englishmen, peasants, bourgeois, etc.—is also fundamentally a culturalist argument, which can be found in just about every other counterrevolutionary screed from Edmund Burke and Joseph de Maistre on. It is therefore a necessary part of this argument that he defend particularity and tradition as such.[15] The strength of the explanation, moreover, also seems to me to lie in its treatment of abstraction: abstraction appears not only as part of the ideological content of the *esprit classique* and its daughter (or manifestation) the Enlightenment but also as one of the most important factors ensuring its "propagation" and popular success. In Taine's account Enlightenment arguments are easy to understand, and were therefore widely adopted, precisely because they are abstract, and this abstraction was already the fundamental characteristic of French *mentalité* at the dawn of the eighteenth century.

Alexis de Tocqueville may be the most sober of all the great nineteenth-century historians, but his judgment is not fundamentally different:

> The philosophy of the eighteenth century has rightly been considered to be one of the principal causes of the Revolution. . . . All the new or rejuvenated opinions relating to the principles of civil and political law, such, for example, as the natural equality of men, the abolition of all privileges held by castes, classes, and professions which is its consequence, the sovereignty of the people, the omnipotence of societal power, the uniformity of rules . . . are not only the causes of the French Revolution but are, so to speak, its substance; they are, in the passing of time, what is most fundamental, most durable, and most true in its works.[16]

The fundamental question of the coming of the Revolution, for Tocqueville, is why the single point of departure that underlies the various political systems of the eighteenth century, the substitution of "simple and elementary rules, drawn from reason and natural law, for the complicated and traditional customs which then regulated society," instead of having "come to a halt, as it had so often done in the past, in the heads of a few philosophers, descended into the crowd and took on the consistency and fire of a political passion."[17]

Tocqueville's account stages two primary actors: the centralizing administration and the men of letters. On the one hand, there is an enormous gulf between the two. The creation of an "abstract and literary politics" in the last forty years of the Old Regime was based on the separation of writers from the sphere of power and government, leaving them entirely ignorant of the constraints of practice. "In the almost infinite isolation from practice in which they lived, no experience was available to temper the ardor of their character; nothing warned them of the obstacles that existing facts could bring to bear against even the most desirable reforms; they had no idea of the perils that always accompany the most necessary of revolutions."[18] This ignorance was itself the product of the absence of political freedom and the discussion of affairs that it entails. Thus politics in France "was as if divided into two separate provinces, with no communication between them," a realm in which real society was governed and administered and a realm in which the ideal reconstruction of society could proceed unimpeded by practicalities. "Above real society . . . was thus slowly built an imaginary society, in which everything appeared simple and coordinated, uniform, just, and in agreement with reason."[19] This abstractness and desire to abolish everything existing in order to build that second, heretofore imaginary society was the hallmark of the revolutionary spirit.

On the other hand, the fundamental lesson for Tocqueville of the study of how the Old Regime gave birth to the Revolution lies not in eighteenth-century philosophy, which he sees as having lost most of its attractiveness, but rather in the continuity of the centralizing administration, which is both what the Revolution shares with the Old Regime and the most durable product of the revolutionary experience. Centralization loves what *philosophie* loves—the equality of conditions and the uniformity of laws and regulations—and hates what *philosophie* hates—diversity, tradition, and countervailing powers (in a word, feudalism).[20] Administration and enlightenment (practice and theory) thus have the same content for Tocqueville. When he writes that "political life was violently repressed [*refoulé*] into literature,"[21] we can see a strictly, if anachronistically, Freudian identity between repression and the return of the repressed.

Michelet, Taine, and Tocqueville have markedly different ideas of the significance of the Enlightenment and the Revolution. But each of them gives a single interpretation of the unity Enlightenment-and-Revolution. A certain selection within the Enlightenment occurs for this to be possible: Michelet emphasizes the concepts of freedom and justice and the struggle against fanaticism and for religious tolerance; Taine blames the abstraction of both the political theory of Rousseau and the psychology of Étienne Bonnot de Condillac; Tocqueville, who equally emphasizes abstraction, is led by his interpretation of the role of administrative centralization to give a particular privilege to the physiocrats.[22] In each case the spirit (the culture) of the Enlightenment turns out also to be the spirit (the fundamental significance) of the Revolution.

KINGS AND MEN OF LETTERS

Within the Enlightenment itself the question was already pressing. The Academy of Dijon put the inquiry thus: "Whether the restoration of the arts and sciences has contributed to the purification of morals." But the problem is by no means confined to Rousseau's *Discours sur les sciences et les arts* and the polemical literature surrounding it. In one form or another, the basic question of the relation between enlightenment and politics is omnipresent. The fundamental problem of Enlightenment historiography—and it is a problem as much as a theme—is the relation between intellectual history and political history, understanding and practical reason, knowledge and action. In the "Discours préliminaire" to the *Encyclopédie* (1751), for example, Jean Lerond d'Alembert writes, "The object of human history is either man's actions or his knowledge; consequently it is either civil or literary, that is, divided between great nations and great geniuses, between kings and men of letters, between conquerors and philosophers."[23] D'Alembert's choice is clear: Enlightenment history will be the history of enlightenment rather than of politics. Defending himself in the "Avertissement des éditeurs" to the third volume against attacks on what had been omitted, d'Alembert writes, "One will not find in this work . . . the *conquerors* who have devastated the earth, but the immortal geniuses who enlightened it; nor will one find the crowd of *sovereigns* that history should have banished."[24]

Nevertheless, even if politics is relegated to this sort of historical limbo on the theoretical level, it continues to play an important role in practical terms. Progress in the arts and sciences, d'Alembert argues in the *Essai sur la société des gens de lettres et des grands*, does not occur in opposition to or in spite of absolutism but precisely because of it, under its tutelage. "At last Louis XIV appeared," writes d'Alembert, "and the esteem he expressed for men of letters soon set the tone for a nation accustomed to receiving it from its masters. . . . Above all philosophy, animated by the monarch's regard, finally emerged, if slowly, from the sort of prison to which idiocy and superstition had confined it."[25] Protestations that philosophy forms no threat to the tranquillity of the sovereign and public order are, of course, numerous. But these protestations, which could seem to have a purely defensive function, frequently prescribe a positive role for the monarch.[26]

The same basic conception of history can also be found in Voltaire's *Le Siècle de Louis XIV*, with its listing of some 360 authors. The project, as announced in the prefatory letter to the abbé Jean-Baptiste Dubos, presumes that what counts in human history is not the chronicle of political events but the catalogue of intellectual attainments. "It is not simply the life of this prince that I write; neither is it the annals of his reign; it is rather the history of the human spirit, drawn from the century most glorious to it."[27] The reasons for this philosophical *gloire* can be summarized as the beginning of an age of enlightenment. "Human reason in general was perfected. Healthy philosophy has only been known since this time, and it is correct to say . . . that the general revolution that has occurred in our arts, our minds, our morals and our government will forever be a sign of the true glory of our country."[28] If over half of the book is dedicated to politico-military history—the *gloire* of Louis XIV in a very unphilosophical sense—and only four short chapters to the development of the arts and sciences, Voltaire is very clear about the relative worth of each. He is clear enough, in fact, that it sometimes seems that the political and military history is there, like the ecclesiastical history that occupies the final chapters, only to be exposed to ridicule. (Voltaire does still seem to be, however, somewhat under the spell of military glory, which renders these chapters rather dull in comparison with the religious ones, in which his sarcasm gives itself full rein.) "We have sufficiently insinuated in the course of this history that the public calamities of which it is composed, and which succeed upon one another almost without a break, are in the end effaced from the registers of time. The details and machinations of politics fall into oblivion. Wise laws, institutions, monuments produced by the arts and sciences subsist forever."[29] This theme can of course be stated with less prudence, and become the occasion for aggressive declamations. Louis-Sébastien Mercier, dedicating his *L'An 2440* to the year named in the title, foresaw the judgment of posterity.

> The kings who today are seated on their thrones will be no longer; their posterity will be no longer; and you, you will judge both these deceased monarchs and the writers who lived subjected to their power. The names of the friends and defenders of humanity will be brilliant and honored: their glory will be pure and radiant. But the vile rabble of kings who will have tormented in every sense the human race, buried in an oblivion deeper than the land of the dead, will escape opprobrium only thanks to nothingness.[30]

The Enlightenment's historical discourse about itself is doubtless characterized by a large amount of polemical tub-thumping, but certain hesitations remain. This is due, above all, to the fact that the Enlightenment is not one thing. It contains conflicting strategies and goals, rhetorics and doctrines. But the debates of the mid-eighteenth century on the relation of the arts and sciences to political developments already provide an outline for the entire problematic of the "intellectual origins of the revolution." The major themes of both classical and contemporary historiography can all be found there: the movement from religious to political critique, the institutions devoted to the diffusion of ideas and the concept of public opinion, the contradiction between political liberty and the economic liberalism promoted by the centralizing monarchical administration.

FIRST AUTHORS

From the very beginning, the Revolution had a powerful sense of its own intellectual origins. As early as August 21, 1789, one could read in the *Journal de Paris*, "French liberty has only existed for a month. . . . Philosophy itself was the instrument that Providence used to work this miracle. It was Philosophy that implanted ideas of liberty in [our] souls, fired [our] hearts and animated [our] courage."[31] Jean-Paul Marat, summarizing his understanding of the early stages of the Revolution (and his own role in it) at the beginning of his *Appel à la nation* (February 1790), wrote that the "time had come for the French to throw off the cruel yoke under which they had trembled for so many centuries. . . . If they know their rights, they owe this advantage to Philosophy, which removed the blindfold of error with which despotism had crowned their brow."[32] A Revolutionary catechism from 1793 proposed the following list of heroes:

Q.   Who are the men whose writings prepared the Revolution?
A.   Helvétius, Mably, J. J. Rousseau, Voltaire, Franklin.

Q.   What are these great men called?
A.   Philosophers.

Q.   What does this word mean?
A.   Wise man, friend of humanity.[33]

The remains of both Rousseau and Voltaire were transferred to the Pantheon during the course of the Revolution. Voltaire's pantheonization on July 11, 1791 (three weeks after the king's flight and a week before the Champ de Mars massacre), was attended by large crowds despite bad weather. The massive sarcophagus (probably designed by the painter Jacques-Louis David) featured a winged Immortality crowning the recumbent figure of the philosopher with laurels. On the sides the following words were inscribed: "He combated atheists and fanatics, He inspired toleration, He demanded the rights of man against the servitude of feudalism," and "Poet Historian Philosopher, He enlarged the human spirit and taught it that it must be free."[34]

Rousseau's remains stayed in Ermenonville until the fall of 1794 (vendémiaire Year III), but their transfer to the Pantheon was first demanded in August 1791 in a mass petition written by Pierre-Louis Ginguené.[35] Ginguené, addressing the Assembly, cited Rousseau's political theory as the fundamental inspiration for the revolutionary constitution:

> With what sovereignty were you invested in order to regenerate a great empire, to give it a free constitution? With the inalienable and imprescriptible sovereignty of the people. On what base did you found this constitution, which will become the model for all human constitutions? On the equality of rights. Well, Messieurs, Rousseau was the first, under the very eyes of despotism, to systematically establish the equality of rights among men and the sovereignty of the people.[36]

These principles are described as having "taken root and grown [*germé*] in the souls of the French" as a result of "meditation on [Rousseau's] writings," making him "incontestably" the *premier fondateur* of the constitution. But equally important for Ginguené and his cosigners was Rousseau's work of moral regeneration, his condemnations of the artificiality of Old Regime culture and his propagation of simple tastes, as well as the élan and enthusiasm that characterize his writings and that they in turn inspired. It is only this sort of interior and moral reform, the petitioners argue, that can make the new political system lasting. Charles-Louis-Victor de Broglie's response as president of the Assembly to this petition took up a similar linkage of the moral and political aspects of Rousseau's influence.

> Every day the French feel more strongly how much they owe to he who, in his *Contrat social*, reduced to its true value the specious right of the strongest, gave back to men their equality of rights and to peoples their usurped sovereignty, he who, in all his works, taught not only to be virtuous but also to love virtue; not only to shake off the chains of despotism and superstition but also those of vice; he who, ceaselessly recalling us to natural sentiments, prepared us so powerfully for the sentiment of freedom, the first and most powerful of all.[37]

The actual ceremony was strongly marked by its date, shortly after Thermidor, and the shifting ideological burdens of the emergence from the Terror.[38] But the speech given by Jean-Jacques-Régis de Cambacérès as president of the Convention continues the theme of a total—moral and political—regeneration as the hallmark of Rousseau's influence. "It is to Rousseau that we owe the salutary regeneration that has produced so many happy changes in our morals [*mœurs*], in our customs, in our laws, in our minds, and in our habits."[39]

One of the most extensive examples of this sort of invocation can be found in Louis-Sébastien Mercier's *De J. J. Rousseau considéré comme l'un des premiers auteurs de la Révolution.* Mercier's text is wide ranging, even inchoate: he discusses now *La Nouvelle Héloïse*, now Rousseau's life, now the *Confessions*; he devotes long sections to his own views of current controversies and attempts to reconcile the doctrine of the *Contrat social* with the Constitution of 1791.[40] The constitution, Mercier expostulates, that "temple raised to freedom, bears the mark of Rousseau's genius," and "Rousseau's maxims have thus formed most of our laws, and our representatives have had both the modesty and the loyalty to declare that the *Contrat social* was for them the lever with which they were able to shake and eventually overthrow the enormous colossus of despotism."[41]

But Mercier's central claim, and the reason why I have taken my own title from it, is contained in the use of "author" in the title. Rousseau is only one example of this structure. Indeed, exactly the same claim—that of being the "first author of the revolution"—was also made for Voltaire. Reviewing Condorcet's *Vie de Voltaire*, the *Mercure de France* argued,

> It seems at least that it was still possible to further develop the eternal obligations that the human race owes to Voltaire. The present circumstances have furnished a fine opportunity. He did not live to see all that he created, but he created all that we see [*Il n'a point vu tout ce qu'il a fait, mais il a fait tout ce que nous voyons*]. . . . The first author of this great Revolution which astonishes Europe, and which spreads, in all directions, hope among the peoples and fear in the courts, is, without question, Voltaire. . . . The human spirit can no more be stopped in its independence than in its servitude, and it is Voltaire who freed it, by accustoming it to judge from all sides those who enslaved it. It is he who made reason popular, and if the people had not learned how to think, it never would have used its force. It is the thought of the wise which prepares political revolutions, but it is always the arm of the people which executes them.[42]

At the core of Mercier's book is the claim that the Enlightenment as a whole is the inspiration of the Revolution, and thus its fundamental cause. When he presents the most general version of this argument, Mercier refers not to *auteurs* but to *écrivains* and *gens de lettres*. Describing what defended the old order as merely a "military mass," which cannot think and merely follows orders, Mercier writes:

> Happily the general disposition of minds was opposed to [this military mass]. This disposition was due solely to the magnanimous writings, courageous speeches, unfettered thoughts, and profound reasonings of writers [*aux généreux écrits, aux courageux discours, aux fortes pensées, aux profonds raison-nements des écrivains*] who have for the past twenty years devoted . . . all their faculties, all their talents, and all their forces to combating despotism. The formidable current revolution is not due to a few hands and a few muskets; it is due to the works of men of letters [*aux ouvrages des gens de lettres*].[43]

This terminological shift refers to the contemporary debate concerning the social status of intellectuals, a debate in which Mercier was a major participant. Although these distinctions are tendencies rather than fixed meanings, it would seem that the key term of social consecration in the Enlightenment was not *auteur* but *homme de lettres* (*gens de lettres* in the plural). *Auteur* refers specifically to the activity of publication,[44] whereas *gens de lettres* is primarily a social category, whose usefulness as a vehicle for social promotion depends on its refusal of an exclusively professional definition. Like the Académie française, it sets professional writers side by side with grandees who cultivate letters. Refined aesthetic judgment rather than publication is what defines the *homme de lettres*. In the article on "Gens de lettres" that he wrote for the *Encyclopédie*, Voltaire recalls that the Greek or Roman grammarian, the direct ancestor of the modern man of letters, was not a specialist but a generalist, who approached geometry, philosophy, and history through his knowledge of poetry and eloquence. Rather than being specialists defined by particular branches of knowledge, "true *gens de lettres* are those who make themselves capable of walking through all different fields, even if they cannot cultivate each one [*se mettent en état de porter leurs pas dans ces différents terrains, s'ils ne peuvent les cultiver tous*]."[45] Their fundamental activity is thus not the production of knowledge but criticism or judgment. Critical philology has given rise to criticism of prejudices and a general *esprit philosophique*.

> There are many men of letters who are not authors, and they are probably the happiest; they are sheltered from the distasteful situations that the author's profession sometimes leads him into, from the quarrels born from rivalry, from the

animosity of parties, and from false judgments; they are more closely united and enjoy society; they are judges, and the others are the judged.[46]

Mercier, in *De la littérature et des littérateurs*, takes up this same limitation of the term *auteur* to those who publish, when, counseling those who do not feel a true vocation to avoid the career of letters, he distinguishes between the *sentiment généreux qui anime l'écrivain* and *la rage d'Auteur*.[47] But for Mercier the term to be opposed to *auteur* is not the social category *homme de lettres* but rather *écrivain*, which does indeed denote professional specialization.

> In order to cast off the heavy burden of recognition, we hear people call out on all sides: *there are an immense number of Authors*. Yes, of those who usurp the name or who have put out a single brochure in their whole lives to prove they are not complete idiots. But in fact there are in France no more than thirty Writers who habitually follow this career and are continually dedicated to their art. [Mercier continues in a note:] I put in the list of Writers I have in mind only those who publish [*donnent au Public*] works of imagination or Philosophy, and who fulfill the Public's expectations by successive productions every year, or at slightly greater intervals, relative to the importance and extent of their subject.[48]

Thus when Mercier attributes the coming of the Revolution to the influence of *écrivains*, he is referring to those who had consistently demonstrated a true vocation for philosophy and literature. It is certainly the case that, for Mercier, Rousseau is one of the foremost among those writers, based not only on the quality of his production but also on the wide diffusion of his works. He is also the "*first author* of the Revolution" in a more fundamental, indeed, theological sense. Eighteenth-century dictionaries list the primary meaning of *auteur* as cause, and its literary sense as second and derived. The *Encyclopédie*, for example, gives the following definition:

> AUTHOR, in the proper sense signifies he who creates or produces something. The name is eminently applicable to God, as first cause of all beings; thus He is called author of the world, author of the universe, author of nature. See CAUSE, GOD, NATURE. The word is Latin, and derives, according to some, from *auctus*, participle of *augeo*, "I increase [*j'accrois*]." Others derive it from the Greek *autos*, "self," since the *author* of something is understood to produce it by himself [*parce que l'auteur de quelque chose que ce soit est censé la produire par lui-même*]. . . . In Literature, an author is a person who has composed some work.[49]

The history of the term, derived from the medieval sense of *auctores*, the authoritative texts of both the sciences and liberal arts, makes it difficult to accept, today, the assertion that the theological meaning is literal and the literary meaning metaphorical. But the question of which sense is primary and which secondary is less important than their shared assumption, the ground of the metaphor that passes between them: the explanation or understanding of something, be it a text or the world (the "book of Nature") is to be found in its cause, the presumed source of its meaning and therefore the guarantee of its intelligibility.[50]

The fact that the Revolution claimed to be the heritage of the Enlightenment does not, of course, decide the question in and of itself. Citations such as these from the Revolutionary period can be interpreted either as testimony to the influence of *philosophie*, or as speech acts that are part of the retrospective construction of a legitimizing ancestry for the Revolution. Hans-Ulrich Gumbrecht, in his study of the evolution of the social figure of the *philosophe*, has argued that "only as precursors who had retreated into the past were the *philosophes* able to preserve their glory and legitimizing function in the Revolution." The various declarations of fidelity by the revolutionaries, according to Gumbrecht, share "a gesture of causal linkage," but also insist upon a "qualitative distinction between Enlightenment and Revolution."[51] The distinction is drawn between the preparatory work of clearing the terrain (a fundamentally destructive, at least critical labor) and the properly revolutionary task of constructing new institutions. Gumbrecht argues that the philosopher must become a figure of the past because the social conditions that had made his existence (or more properly his triumph) possible were in fact tied to the Old Regime and have ceased to exist. "Critique" could no longer be practiced in the same way once the separation between rulers and ruled had been torn down and theories had to be applied.[52]

In a similar vein, Roger Chartier has recently proposed, on much the same evidentiary basis, that the traditional formulation is perhaps reversed, and that rather than philosophical books having "made" the Revolution, "it was the Revolution that made the books and philosophy—that is, that it was on the basis of the revolutionary event that a corpus of works was constituted and authors selected who were held to have prepared and announced it."[53] This sort of reversal of the more traditional pattern of cause and effect is a seductive hypothesis, which, as we shall see, allows for an understanding of certain difficulties in the chronology of reception of Rousseau's political texts. A particularly cogent statement was given as early as 1801 by Jean-Joseph Mounier, who argued that the celebrity of the *Contrat social* during the Revolution was an effect rather than a cause. "It was not in the least the influence of these principles that produced the Revolution," wrote Mounier. "On the contrary, it was the Revolution that produced their influence [*Ce ne fut point l'influence de ces principes qui produisit la révolution, ce fut au contraire la révolution qui produisit leur influence*]."[54]

Even if no one read the *Contrat social* before 1789—and Mercier himself describes it as "formerly the least read of Rousseau's works"[55]—its emergence as a key reference in public discourse at that point remains significant. The metaphorical interpretation of the phrase "first author of the Revolution," as the ground and guarantee of the intelligibility of the Revolution, would remain valid. The substitution of the relation between author and text for that between cause and effect is not without consequences, and may well allow for a disturbance of the relation between temporality and causality such as that described by Mounier. The shift proposed by Chartier toward "cultural" rather than intellectual origins, as we shall see, is precisely designed to move the debate from questions of causality to questions of intelligibility. "Attributing 'cultural origins' to the French Revolution," Chartier writes, "does not by any means establish the Revolution's causes; rather, it pinpoints certain of the conditions that made it possible because it was conceivable [*possible parce que pensable*]."[56] The interest and challenge of Mercier's claim for Rousseau as "first author" of the Revolution, however, is precisely that it holds together causality and intelligibility.

The following two sections present an extended analysis of debates in the historiographical tradition concerning the relation between the Enlightenment and the Revolution, with a particular focus on current arguments in the field, in order to trace a set of variations on Mounier's paradox. The problem Enlightenment-and-Revolution, I will argue, is structured around a fundamental discontinuity, one that can be displaced in a variety of ways but that never goes away. It can appear, as it does in Mounier, as an involution of temporal sequence; it can also take the simpler form of an abrupt discontinuity in narrative logic—for example, a sudden shift in the grounds of explanation. In the most recent debates it seems to me to manifest itself in terms of a growing incompatibility between the form and content of Enlightenment sociability. In another ten years debate will no doubt have shifted, perhaps dramatically. The implication of my argument here is that this discontinuity will have shifted with it. Perhaps the simplest way to state this is to recall that, as a radical transformation of ideas, the Revolution needed to negate its own origins even as it constructed its legitimacy on their basis.[57]

My further contention is that this discontinuity inevitably leads us to the "example" of Rousseau. I say "example" here to call attention both to the fact that this reference tends to occur as empirical illustration, and that the problem involves the relation between a more general structure and a particular, if unavoidable, figure. It is the burden of this book's central chapters to show that there are reasons internal to Rousseau's texts for this to be the case. For the moment, we can simply remark that we still do not know whether Rousseau was the most central or the most marginal figure of the Enlightenment.

Counting Books and Reading Texts

THE TWO HISTORIES

If the Enlightenment predominantly saw itself as a process of diffusion of rationality that would lead to the creation of a better world, and if the Revolution often thought of itself as putting into practice Enlightenment precepts, it nevertheless remains an open question whether these assumptions were correct: did the Enlightenment and the Revolution understand or misunderstand their own actions? In this century, the tendency to write a single history of the Enlightenment and the Revolution has often been challenged. Most frequently, this challenge has proceeded as an attempt to measure the breadth and depth of the diffusion of enlightenment—what Tocqueville calls "descending into the crowd" and Taine "what is repeated in the streets"[58]— and to determine the extent to which members of the various social classes or groups that appear as actors in the Revolution—in the events of 1789, for instance, the alliance of liberal nobility and upper bourgeoisie that held sway in the National Assembly, or the *petit peuple* of Paris that assembled in front of the Bastille—can be assumed to have been exposed, directly or indirectly, to the influence of Enlightenment thought. The methods and even the questions possible within this field of inquiry have been largely determined by the book that founded it as a scholarly field, Daniel Mornet's *Les Origines intellectuelles de la Révolution française*. Robert Darnton has described the transformation of the field as being due to Mornet's having, for the first

time, posed a very simple question: "What did eighteenth-century Frenchmen read?"[59]

Mornet was primarily concerned with the diffusion rather than the content of the Enlightenment. He expresses this orientation, in his introduction, as the difference between "the history of the intellectual origins of the
Revolution" and "that of revolutionary ideas."[60] The ideas we identify with
the Revolution have a long and complex history of their own, which, for
Mornet, does nothing to explain why this Revolution occurred in 1789. He
thus proposes to study "the role of intelligence in the preparation of the Revolution."[61] This notion of intelligence is fairly general and, indeed, formal:
it does not depend upon any particular content. The analysis and understanding of texts thus enters Mornet's history only at a secondary level, to
the extent that it may be necessary to determine which ideas are being dif-
fused. The abstraction of the concept of intelligence implied by this approach inevitably shows up in the conclusions that Mornet draws. If for
Mornet, as for his nineteenth-century predecessors, the fundamental link
between the Enlightenment and the Revolution is a certain hostility to religion in general and to the link between the Church and the absolutist state
in particular, the fundamental importance of this critique is the habit of critical thought:

> Whatever the diffusion of incredulity and political discontent may have been,
> it seems to us to be less important than a more general and more easily demon-
> strated evolution of opinion. . . . When the habit of "observation" and "experi-
> mentation" is acquired; when the sciences are asked to constantly demonstrate
> their explanations; when it is not systems of agriculture that are wanted but
> a knowledge of what will grow and how much it will cost; at the same time
> people will acquire the habit of believing that politics should not be any differ-
> ent from physics, chemistry, or the growing of wheat; that mysteries, secrets,
> and reasons of State must be abolished, and that one has the right to observe,
> discuss, and demand real and practical reforms.[62]

The primary characteristic of this critical spirit is thus a refusal to accept, as
Descartes had done, a distinction between a realm of reason and a realm of
authority. Mornet sums up his discussion of a variety of examples drawn
from the period from 1748 to 1770, which he characterizes as "the decisive
struggle," by saying that "all are avid to know and to learn; all want not simply to know but also to understand; all refuse to distinguish between what
one has the right to discuss and what one accepts blindly."[63]

A crucial consequence of this concentration on the diffusion of enlightened habits of thought rather than Enlightenment ideas is that it is precisely
the Estates General and not the course of the Revolution that is prepared or
precipitated by this diffusion. The progress of religious indifference and political discontent, Mornet says at one point, "explains, if not the Revolution,
at least its point of departure, the Estates General and their spirit."[64] From
the point of view of an understanding of enlightenment as the spread of critical thought, the difference is essential. The Estates General came to an end
(becoming the National Assembly) when the location of sovereignty in the
nation was asserted as a positive doctrine. As doctrine, this is a "revolutionary idea" rather than a product of the critical spirit. Mornet is thus led, as a
matter of principle, to separate the Revolution from its own origins. If the
concept of "intellectual origins" would seem at first to posit a continuity between ideas and events, Mornet's study is in fact predicated upon a discontinuity between Revolution and Enlightenment, between an action and the
idea presumed to be its cause. "The origins of the Revolution are one story;
the history of the Revolution is another."[65]

On the methodological level, this separation is expressed in the limits
Mornet imposes on his inquiry. "I have studied the purely intellectual origins," he writes in his Introduction. "It is for this reason that I stopped in
the year 1787. Until 1787 everything occurs as discussion; ideas do not act directly or they act only on points of detail. But from 1788 on the action begins, and once it begins it dominates."[66] But this separation is not simply a
contingent one or the scope of a particular inquiry, which might be overcome by a broader, more synthetic treatment. Arguing against Taine, Mornet notes that "one cannot make an argument about the origins of the Revolution while keeping the development of the Revolution constantly in
mind. . . . It must be repeated that the directions taken by the Revolution
are not necessarily those people thought of when, in 1788–1789, they wanted
to reform France."[67]

This is not merely a necessary caution against the dangers of teleological
historiography, of assuming that if the Revolution occurred it must have
been the goal of all that preceded it. Only a separation or discontinuity between the Revolution and its origins can define the former as in fact revolutionary. On the level of historical explanation, such a separation makes misunderstanding into a central category. If the two histories of which Mornet
speaks are not one, it can only be because "intelligence" did not in fact un-

derstand its own action, and did something different and perhaps even the opposite of what it intended to do. Commenting on the relatively limited diffusion of the Enlightenment among the popular classes, Mornet notes that "the immense majority of the common people were certainly able to accept, follow, and then precipitate the Revolution, but they never conceived of its doctrine nor even conceived of the idea of it."[68] Indeed, the "idea of the Revolution" never appears in Mornet's study. Whenever he encounters a text that hints at such an idea, he dismisses it as a *discours de collège*—that is, a purely "academic" or "rhetorical" exercise without any effect in the real world. Thus Mornet can only conclude that "it was intelligence that drew and organized the consequences [of the political problems of France in 1787–1789], and came to desire the Estates General. And from the Estates General, without intelligence even suspecting it [*sans d'ailleurs que l'intelligence s'en soit doutée*], would come the Revolution."[69]

If the empirical aspects of much of Mornet's research have been surpassed (most frequently by being confirmed with greater precision), and his "trickle-down" model of diffusion much contested on a theoretical level, this separation between the history of the Revolution and the history of its origins has remained a persistent and doubtless inevitable feature of subsequent research. The problem remains fundamentally that of the relation between the development of enlightened habits of thought—as they can be traced in the history of the book trade and in that of cultural institutions, both domains pioneered by Mornet—and the effect of "revolutionary ideas," which remains largely undeterminable. This division can also be seen, it seems to me, in the relations between the historiographical procedures that dominate each of these subfields, statistical bibliography and the cultural or sociological determination of context, respectively, and the more properly literary activity of reading texts. I hope to show that the absence of a bridge between the determination of which books were available, or what context conditioned their reception, and how individual works were actually interpreted, is structurally coincident with the gap between origins and event.

STATISTICS

Recent historical studies with a quantitative orientation have certainly confirmed,[70] at the level of generality at which it is posed, Mornet's sense of the spread of "intelligence"—today we would be more likely to call it access to culture—in the eighteenth century. Male literacy rates for France as a whole grew from 29 to 47 percent during the course of the eighteenth century,[71] and urban literacy rates were undoubtedly higher. In the case of Paris, Daniel Roche's research reveals strikingly high figures for many social categories. At least potentially, Parisians of all but the lowest class had some access to written culture.[72]

Even more spectacular than the growth of literacy was the growth of the book trade in France in the eighteenth century. Henri-Jean Martin, the doyen of *l'histoire du livre* in France, has estimated that the number of books published yearly in French tripled between 1700 and 1770, and his graphs indicate (although he does not himself hazard this) that production had further doubled by 1789.[73] But this massive expansion of print culture does not yet answer any questions about the spread of enlightenment. The overall growth rates of literacy and the book trade tell us nothing about the relative proportions of tradition and innovation, of *livres de dévotion* and *livres philosophiques*.

The fundamental analysis of the book trade in France in the eighteenth century is the two-volume study carried out by a group from the École pratique des hautes études: *Livre et société dans la France du XVIII⁰ siècle*. This collection of monographs on various aspects of publication and consumption is centered around François Furet's study of the registers kept by the Chancery, which held authority over the direction of the book trade, of both *privilèges* (which gave the legal monopoly of a title to a publisher) and tacit permissions to publish. The former register extends over the entire century and can be considered as representing the official written culture of the realm. The register of *permissions tacites* dates from 1718 but was little used until the nomination of Malesherbes as director of the book trade in 1751. After that point it quickly comes to hold as many titles as the official register. Tacit permissions, in Malesherbes's words, were used in "circumstances in which we did not dare publicly authorize a book, but in which we nevertheless felt that it would not be possible to prohibit it."[74]

Furet's statistics for the realm of privileges show a strong continuity across the entire century in the domains of law, history, and belles-lettres, whose respective shares varied little in his samplings (totaling almost half of privileged production) and whose internal divisions also show the permanence of classical literary, legal, and historical culture. However, Furet notes, "two bibliographical categories exchanged their respective dimensions between 1724 and 1789: 'theology' and 'arts and sciences.'"[75] Theology declined from a third of the first sample to a tenth of the last one; the arts and sciences moved from about a fifth to about a third. In the registers of the tacit permissions, by definition a realm of innovation, theology and law almost entirely disappear; figures there are dominated by belles-lettres and the arts and sciences. Once again, the largest gain is made by the arts and sciences, which come to occupy more than 40 percent of the total in 1780–1784.[76]

These figures leave Furet with a somewhat contradictory set of conclusions. The overall movements that can be traced across both sets of figures, the decline of theology and the growth of the arts and sciences, are interpreted by Furet as corresponding to "the attempt by the *philosophes* to eliminate the supernatural from the human world" and "the desacralization of a society and a culture."[77] Even if he quibbles with his predecessor's periodization, Furet's conclusions confirm those of Mornet. A general detachment from religious authority would seem to have occurred during the course of the century, accompanied by a growing interest in political questions toward the very end of that century. These trends—or rather, this trend, for the decline of theology and the growth of the arts and sciences appear as the two sides of a single coin—can easily be taken to constitute the "Enlightenment" in the most general sense of the term.

As Furet himself is the first to recognize, however, there are important limitations to the use of the permissions registers for calculating the relative proportions of books published in Old Regime France. First of all, provincial publications are not necessarily included. During most of the eighteenth century once-prosperous publishers in the provinces languished, but in 1777 they were given a shot in the arm by the creation of the *permissions simples*—a category of permission not included in the registers studied by Furet. This category allowed the republication of books that had fallen into the newly created "public domain," and in the provinces those were overwhelmingly religious books, 63 percent by volume.[78] Similarly, an inventory of the stock of one of the major publishers of the *bibliothèque bleue de Troyes*, Garnier, taken in 1789, showed 43 percent religious works by volume.[79] As, according to Furet, "the main types of religious books to disappear [between the first and last of his samples] were liturgical and devotional works,"[80] and almost the entirety of the provincial production of religious works after 1777 falls into that subcategory, it is entirely possible that the decline of religious titles in Furet's study is due to their leaving his source rather than their leaving the marketplace. This puts into question of notion of "desacralization" as measurable at this level.

On the other side, books that were too "philosophical" even to risk applying for a tacit permission (whether they received an assurance of toleration or whether they were outrightly clandestine) are equally beyond the reach of his permissions registers. That group included, of course, the most virulent attacks on religion, whether Voltaire or the *Histoire de Dom Bougre portier des Chartreux*, as well as much of what we now consider to be the high Enlightenment. (Both *De l'esprit des lois* and *Émile* are famous examples of the practice Malesherbes refers to as publication with the "connivance" of the authorities.)[81] An indication of the extent of the total publication that escapes Furet's statistics can be found in a study by Jacqueline Artier of the surviving literary production of the year 1764. Only 22 percent are books graced with an official privilege. A further 18 percent were published with a tacit permission, meaning that some 60 percent of books published in French in 1764 that survive could not have been included in Furet's study. It is notable, then, that the proportion of works that could be considered to be part of the Enlightenment in a narrower sense would appear to be substantially higher than in Furet's figures: the sum of theology, history, and law reaches only 35 percent; almost half of the theology section is composed of controversial works refuting the deism of such pernicious tracts as Rousseau's *Profession de foi*. Finally, the subcategory of philosophy occupies 38 percent of the arts and sciences.[82] However, working from existing collections is handicapped by the intermediate selection of what later generations thought was worth preserving, with the Revolution itself having doubtless destroyed a large number of religious works. The precise place of truly clandestine literature, and with it the Enlightenment in the strict sense, remains impossible to integrate with any of the figures that have been proposed to this point.

COUNTING AND READING

The most detailed studies of the clandestine book trade are those by Robert Darnton in his collection of essays *The Literary Underground of the Old Regime* and his recent synthesis *The Forbidden Best-Sellers of Pre-Revolutionary France*. Because *The Forbidden Best-Sellers* is also one of the few works in the historiography of the field to combine an extensive use of statistical bibliography with careful and sensitive close reading of particular texts, it has a special importance for my attempt to understand how these procedures interact, and the relation between its incontestable successes and its limitations has much to teach. Darnton has often criticized the study of *mentalités* in the *Annales* tradition for an excessive reliance on statistics, most notably in the conclusion to *The Great Cat Massacre*, in which he contends that cultural objects "need to be read, not counted."[83] But he is equally prone to criticize intellectual history for an excessive concentration on the interpretation of great texts and an ignorance of the social dimension of the production and diffusion of ideas. In practice he regularly plays the two poles off against each other, the statistical approach providing a sort of guarantee for the cultural-hermeneutic one.[84]

As much of Darnton's argument is a polemic directed against Roger Chartier's *Cultural Origins of the French Revolution*, it might be best to begin with a brief description of the primary point of conflict. As we have already noted, Chartier's essay reverses the traditional understanding of the relationship between Enlightenment and Revolution, arguing that the former is a retrospective construction by the latter. From this point of view it is understandable that when he comes to the question of the specific effects of Enlightenment discourse in the form of books, Chartier is particularly concerned with refuting the idea, common to Tocqueville, Taine, and Mornet, that "reading is endowed with such power that it is capable of totally transforming readers and making them into what the texts envisage."[85] Drawing on Mercier, he argues that not everything that is read is taken seriously, and, using the example of Rousseau, that readers of a given text go on to make "contradictory choices" about how to understand and apply it to their lives. "These facts," Chartier concludes, "make it impossible to attribute too direct a role to books. The new representations that they proposed did not become imprinted on the readers' minds, and in all cases they were open to varied use and multiple interpretations."[86] Thus for Chartier what matters is not what books were read (the "content" of those books) but rather how they were read (what sort of cultural practice "reading" was). Drawing on the model proposed for Germany by Rolf Engelsing,[87] he suggests that eighteenth-century France may have seen a "reading revolution," a movement from an intensive and often communal reading of a small number of texts invested with authority, to a freer, more extensive, individual and critical mode of reading. Enlightenment, after all, may well consist in not believing everything you read.

> In this way, a new relationship between reader and text was forged; it was disrespectful of authorities, in turn seduced and disillusioned by novelty, and, above all, little inclined to belief and adherence. The new manner of reading

was accompanied by the exercise—both on a large scale and in the immediacy of practice—of Kant's "public use of one's reason" on the part of "private persons." Thus the crux of the matter is not the content of "philosophical" books, which quite possibly did not have the persuasive impact generously attributed to them, but rather a new mode of reading that, even when the texts it took on were in total conformity with religious and political order, developed a critical attitude freed from the ties of dependence and obedience that underlay earlier representations.[88]

This argument can be said to give a certain prominence to statistical study, at least on the broadest level, in that the increase in total numbers of texts available is one of the most important indexes of the possibility of "extensive reading." But, in spite of Chartier's own sophisticated readings of secondary texts, it denies any real role to the activity of interpretation—that is, in this context, to any attempt to identify specifically *textual* modes of diffusion of "revolutionary ideas" (in Mornet's terms). "Extensive reading" is another term for the "habit of critical thought." Darnton's project in *Forbidden Best-Sellers*, on the other hand, is to attempt to hold these two procedures together as far as possible: to use statistical study of book sales to identify which texts might have had the greatest influence, and textual interpretation to specify how that influence might have operated.

Darnton's argument begins with the identification of *livres philosophiques* as a publishing category in the Old Regime, which shows up as the denomination for forbidden books in all aspects of the trade (printing, pricing, distribution, etc.). The reason for taking over this category as it is found in the trade jargon and practices of eighteenth-century publishing is that it allows us to avoid the anachronism of "beginning with modern notions of what should have threatened the orthodoxies of the Old Regime."[89] The implicit assumption is that if the French state and its various agents found these texts threatening enough to ban them and invest a great deal of time pursuing them and the people who trafficked in them, it must have been with good reason. Darnton's primary evidence against the objection that *livres philosophiques* might have been merely a form of trivial amusement that readers never took seriously is how seriously the police took them. As one provincial official cited by Darnton warned, "Reading these bad books produces a disturbed spirit among the citizens and provokes them constantly to shake the yoke of submission, of obedience, and of respect."[90]

The orders for forbidden books conserved in the archives of the Société

Typographique de Neuchâtel allow Darnton to give a statistical breakdown of what the realm of philosophy understood in this sense looks like. Perhaps the most surprising thing about the list, particularly given Darnton's iconoclastic rhetoric, is just how much like the canonical Enlightenment it looks.[91] However, Darnton argues, systematic thought had only a small place in this version of "philosophy," which, as for Mornet, is primarily characterized by an "omnipresent . . . critical spirit."[92] The largest subcategory is what Darnton terms "general philosophic books" (he specifically refers to Mercier's *L'An 2440*, the abbé Guillaume-Thomas-François Raynal's *Histoire philosophique des deux Indes*, and Voltaire's *Questions sur l'Encyclopédie*), encyclopedic compendiums of critique that "contained something to offend practically everyone in authority under the Old Regime and at the same time appealed to the broadest range of readers."[93] But this tendency is very much part of the canonical Enlightenment, whose central text is still most often thought to be the *Encyclopédie* and whose key word, from Pierre Bayle to Kant, was "critique."[94]

Darnton next proceeds to provide three exemplary readings of texts taken from the top of his best-seller list: *Thérèse philosophe*, a piece of "philosophical [i.e., antireligious] pornography" attributed to Jean-Baptiste de Boyer, marquis d'Argens (1748?, fifteenth on the list); Louis-Sébastien Mercier's "utopian fantasy" *L'An 2440* (first on the list); and the *Anecdotes sur Mme la comtesse du Barry* by Mathieu-François Pidansat de Mairobert, a "political slander" (1775, second on the list). In this set of readings Darnton is much concerned to avoid anachronistic assumptions about how eighteenth-century readers actually interpreted the texts, as the moment of "inner appropriation" remains beyond historiographical research. Nevertheless, he argues, "it should be possible to steer clear of anachronisms while studying the way the texts work. Like all others, the texts of 'philosophical books' operate within generic and rhetorical conventions peculiar to their time. They develop implicit strategies for evoking responses from readers. So, even if the actual responses elude us, we can learn enough by examining texts and contexts to make some well-informed inferences about what the books meant to readers of the Old Regime."[95]

This appeal to the possibility of interpreting the texts based on the way in which they attempt to program their reception occurs repeatedly in all three readings, and in fact it is used successfully to produce compelling rhetorical interpretations. Each text can be shown to stage within its narra-

tive the action of readers by the sort of *mise-en-abîme* so dear to literary criticism of the last thirty years, and thereby to provide a script or at least a
model for its own reception. *Thérèse philosophe* presents Thérèse herself,
reading and masturbating in response, as a model for the reader's own relation to the pornographic text. Eroticism provides not only the text's content
but also its rhetorical model of persuasion. Likewise, Mercier's rhetoric in
L'An 2440 "anticipated and directed [readers'] responses." Reading and writing play a vital role in Mercier's representation of a new, morally regenerated
polity. A large part of the rhetorical appeal of Mercier's shift from the sort of
utopia set in a land beyond the seas to a future state set in Paris itself, Darnton argues, is that this narrative "made the reading of the book seem to be
part of the historical process whose outcome it revealed."[96] The *Anecdotes
sur Mme la comtesse du Barry* stage within their own narration the process by
which rumor circulates between court and town, accretes commentary, gets
published, and becomes "public opinion." Commentary on the news becomes in turn a new object of commentary, since what people are thinking
and saying now counted as a political factor. Thus the *Anecdotes* "can be read
not merely as an attempt to influence public opinion but also as an account
of how public opinion came into being."[97] Darnton's readings of these three
texts are careful, attentive to detail, and frequently subtle. As a literary critic
working in a field normally considered the preserve of historians, I cannot
help but salute a professional historian who has taken the canons and re-
quirements of my own field so much to heart.

The final section of *Forbidden Best-Sellers* attempts to move from these
rhetorical prescriptions of reading to an account of how such reading contributed to the outbreak of the Revolution. Darnton argues that it is necessary to move away from the sort of "trickle-down" model of diffusion found
in Mornet; instead he posits the existence of a communication network open
to influence from a variety of directions. The model he proposes for the circulation of news, drawing on his account of the *Anecdotes*, links together a
variety of media (rumors, gossip, songs, *mauvais propos*, poems, *nouvelles à la
main*, prints, posters, graffiti, printed pamphlets, and books) and sites of interaction (streets, markets, cafes, salons, circles, bookstores, libraries, etc.).
The polyvalency of this circuit, Darnton argues, illustrates that the "connection between the circulation of illegal literature and the radicalization of
public opinion" was "not simply one of cause and effect" but can be more
accurately described in terms of "mutual reinforcement, feedback, and am-

plification." The particular importance of books in the midst of this flow of information is linked, Darnton continues, to the way it gives disaffection a fixed, permanent, and diffusible form in print, and fits it into narratives, thereby "transforming loose talk into coherent discourse."[98] Such a conceptualization implies that we must reject as overly rigid an either/or formulation of the question as to whether forbidden books formed public opinion through their wide diffusion and rhetorical strategies, or on the contrary owed their success to the fact that they reflected that opinion. Darnton is thus willing to admit that the "desacralization" of the monarchy was the result of "a series of shocks and a long-term process of erosion," in which the monarchy's own actions played as important a role as the *libellistes*, and in which each trauma was marked by the simultaneity of "*libelles* and *mauvais propos.*"[99]

Darnton's account of the role of clandestine literature in the formation of public opinion as a feedback system is eminently plausible, but it is so plausible precisely because it seems to retreat from any strong argument as to determining causal factors. The problem here is that Darnton, with his detailed focus on specific texts, has committed himself to an attempt to go beyond a vague critical spirit and instead show that particular themes, set forth in particular books by means of particular rhetorical procedures, had a determinable effect on the outbreak of the Revolution. He presents such an argument for only one genre, the political *libelles* exemplified by the *Anecdotes*. Not only did the pornographic aspects of that genre play a role in the long-term desacralization of the royal body,[100] they also, and more fundamentally, provided a "folkloric" framework that "helped contemporaries make sense" of the political situation in 1787–1788 by fitting it into a "master narrative" of the degeneration of the monarchy into ministerial despotism. The *libelles* thus provided the crucial model for the development of the vocabulary, narrative forms, and rhetorical strategies of the anti-Calonne and anti-Brienne pamphlet literature of the prerevolution. In its reduction of the complexities of policy to the denunciation of despotism, that literature both polarized public opinion and also expressed it.[101]

Once again, this is plausible. But it will not work for the other two texts he discusses in detail. Neither despotism nor the quasi-sacral status of the king is in question in *Thérèse philosophe*. *L'An 2440* does indeed mobilize a concept of despotism (as do countless other texts, including *De l'esprit des lois* and *Du contrat social*), but it operates in a completely different register than the *Anecdotes*. Both texts may have a relation to the formation of pre-revolutionary or revolutionary mentality, but this relation is necessarily different in each case. The introduction of close reading as a procedure provokes a deep division within the argument, necessitating a separate argument for the effect of each genre if not each text. The argument for the particular pertinence of the *libelles* is no longer based on their statistical place within the corpus of illegal literature, which was prominent but not preponderant (the number of *libelles* slightly trails that of "general social, cultural criticism," although it becomes the largest category if combined with "topical works" and *chroniques scandaleuses*). The argument that actually connects the *libelles* with the outbreak of the Revolution is an interpretive one, based on the resemblance of themes and rhetorical structures. Darnton himself characterizes it as "unproven" but convincing,[102] which is exactly correct: in the end it is a literary argument that operates in the realm of persuasion rather than proof.

To ask, as both Chartier and Darnton do, "How did eighteenth-century Frenchmen read?" seems to me a fundamentally disingenuous question. All available evidence indicates that the literate elite read in more or less the same way we do (for example, we know that silent reading was the norm for this group),[103] and the debate between Darnton and Chartier actually has very little to do with anything specific to the eighteenth century in this regard. In particular, the question of how to understand the reading process in its hermeneutic and cognitive structure (what Darnton calls the "moment of inner appropriation") puts into play the same fundamental opposition that can be found in contemporary reader-response criticism: between textual determinacy and its corollary of an ideal reader, on the one hand, and the empirically observable, if never fully legitimated, indeterminacy of individual response on the other.[104] Chartier's version of a "reading revolution," however, in fact describes a domination of the cultural (i.e., of the reproduction of *mentalités*) over the textual. The change is in not taking texts too seriously, rather than in taking them seriously enough to risk stable identities in the process of reading. Darnton correctly points out, in his critique of Chartier's use of a notion of "appropriation" drawn from Michel de Certeau and Richard Hoggart,[105] that examples of creative rereading do not in fact oppose the reception of official culture to the idiosyncrasy of readers, but rather to the reproduction of another culture. "Other research on reader response [the references are all to studies by historians rather than literary critics or theorists] has confirmed this tendency. It does not demonstrate the prevalence of passivity on the one hand or of indeterminacy on the other. Instead, it suggests that readers found meaning in texts by fitting them within a preexisting cultural frame."[106]

Within the field of reader-response criticism in literary theory, the tendency for the critique of textual determinism to shift into a form of cultural determinism is best illustrated by the work of Stanley Fish on "the authority of interpretive communities."[107] To put it bluntly, if it is not the text that tells the reader what to think, it is the culture. The opposition can thus be seen to resolve into one between two forms of determinism, textual and cultural. The reader is to be found somewhere in between. For today's readers as for eighteenth-century Frenchmen, it is (and was) simultaneously true that readers' minds are not soft wax, and therefore that reading is a processing of a new discourse through an established framework—and that people's opinions are often changed by what they read, occasionally, if rarely, to the point of provoking a fundamental reordering of their whole mental framework. If there exists or has existed a truly "premodern" society in which a fully sacralized text prohibits this dual relation, eighteenth-century France was not it. (And if medieval France had been one, the creation of this possibility would indeed be the fundamental "cultural origin" of the Revolution.) Neither of these poles is more "modern" or "enlightened" than the other; indeed, enlightenment requires a controlled balance between open-mindedness and credulity.

The name for the techniques that writers use to mediate between these two poles is rhetoric. Historically, this discipline has often been castigated as the teaching of a set of rules and clichés (that is, the repetition of a traditional framework),[108] but its goal remains persuasion. What constitutes effective rhetoric changes over time, but the vocation of rhetoric to persuasion remains, and in a descriptive sense it is therefore a reflection on what makes a discourse effective. It is in this sense that the term remains relevant today, however often it is conjugated with "mere." The more relevant (and less intractable) question therefore seems to me to be: what sort of rhetoric did eighteenth-century Frenchmen find convincing? There will not be a single answer to this question. Different rhetorics appeal to different groups within a society, and individuals often have positive responses to more than one rhetorical strategy, even if their social and epistemological presuppositions are radically incompatible. In terms of the field with which we are dealing, it is possible to be swayed one day by Voltairean wit, the next by Rousseauian sincerity.

In most historical periods, reading is doubtless dominated by the pole of assimilation of texts to existing mental frameworks. Indeed, most texts are dominated by those same frameworks (this is what allows us to speak of a culture). But the simple fact of the Revolution, which involves at the very least a substantial discontinuity of consciousness, whatever other continuities it may involve, encourages us to look for the possibility of forms of reading that may have radically changed people's minds. The examples are few in number.[109] To a great extent, this recalls the fundamental fact that the great changing of minds occurred in the process of the Revolution itself, and not beforehand. Nonetheless, it seems to me to be significant that our most important examples of life-changing reading in the eighteenth century involve Rousseau: Jean Ranson, Marie-Jeanne Roland, Jacques-Pierre Brissot de Warville. Ranson remained an obscure merchant in La Rochelle through the Revolution;[110] Brissot and Roland were more active participants. But even at this level, where the reactions of individual readers to particular texts can be traced in their own writings documenting their experience, determinism breaks down. The example of Marie-Jeanne Roland shows clearly the extent to which the interaction of the poles can make them in fact indiscernible. It is impossible to say whether her experience of reading Rousseau was a revolution in her mental framework or a reconfirmation of it.[111] The young Manon Phlipon had read both widely and carefully in both modern and classical literature and philosophy. In particular, her account of her study of Enlightenment philosophy (in a fairly technical sense) shows a mode of reading that was "extensive" in that many, often discordant, texts were read with an open (but by no means frivolous) mind. Her encounter with Rousseau's *La Nouvelle Héloïse* after her mother's death, however, had the effect of a revelation. But it is experienced more as a self-revelation, bringing into the light of consciousness a truth long experienced but never fully understood.

> I was twenty-one years old, I had read a great deal, I knew a large number of writers on history, literature, and philosophy; but Rousseau made on me at that time an impression comparable to the one Plutarch had made on me at the age of eight: It seemed that he was the nourishment that I needed and the interpreter of sentiments that I had before reading him, but that he alone knew how to explain to me.[112]

In an account of reading experience such as that of Roland, effective rhetoric in the text and individual choice become imperceptible, precisely to the extent that the rhetoric is effective. Thus Darnton's focus on the rhetoric of the texts in question—that is, the means that they deploy to persuade and convince their readers—is a procedure that I can only endorse. In its assumption that this rhetoric is indeed effective, however, it remains a form of textual determinism, as is necessary if one wants to maintain a connection between the *livres philosophiques* and the Revolution. But like Mornet's set of examples from the period between 1771 and 1787—including Brissot, Mme Roland, and Lucy and Camille Desmoulins—this particular connection with the Revolution abandons the high ground of serial analysis of diffusion, of attempting to answer the question "What did eighteenth-century Frenchmen read?" on the widest possible basis; it returns to the story of the origins of the revolutionaries. It is only at this anecdotal level that any influence of the Enlightenment on the Revolution would seem to be actually demonstrable.[113] But it is not demonstrable in reverse. Once again, Rousseau is the key example. As is noted in almost every study of the topic, prerevolutionary devotees of Jean-Jacques ended up in every ideological grouping of the period.

Theory and Practice of the Public Sphere

INSTITUTIONS OF ENLIGHTENMENT

The other sector originally explored by Mornet in which our knowledge has been greatly increased by recent research is that of the new forms of sociability characteristic of the eighteenth century, which both allowed for the diffusion of enlightened ideas and embodied Enlightenment practices. The vast majority of this work has been articulated around Jürgen Habermas's proposal, in his early work on *The Structural Transformation of the Public Sphere*, that the eighteenth century in Europe saw the creation of a "bourgeois public sphere" opposed to the traditional representational public sphere of the court. In this new sphere "private people come together as a public"—that is, to make a "public use of their reason" about matters of general concern.[114] One of the major reasons why Habermas's thesis has proved so popular and so productive of further research is the conceptual ambivalence of his "public sphere," the fact that it can be understood either as a discursive analysis of

a new principle of legitimacy or as a sociological analysis of a historical formation particular to Enlightenment Europe.[115] This two-sided proposal is
particularly attractive in that it brings into view the possibility of a truly cultural history, an understanding of the Enlightenment not merely as a set of
philosophical discourses but more fundamentally as the set of institutions
and practices that support those discourses. Our major concern here will
thus be with the relation between an institution and its "implicit" ideology,
or, as this relation appears from the point of view of scholarly procedures, between the determination of contexts and the reading of texts.

Habermas's account begins with the creation of a new sphere of domestic
intimacy, fostered by economic changes in the status of the family and bol-
stered by new ideals of domestic relations. As Dena Goodman has pointed
out in a perceptive review essay, Habermas's "public sphere" is congruent
in many ways with the new history of "private life" proposed by Philippe
Ariès, in which the movement from the medieval lack of distinction between public and private domains to the creation of a new realm of privacy
toward the end of the seventeenth century "comes down to a change in the
forms of sociability."[116] In Habermas's terms, "the public's understanding of
the public use of reason was guided by such private experiences as grew out
of the audience-oriented subjectivity of the conjugal family's intimate domain."[117] The differentiation of the space of the household from that of economic necessity and social reproduction allowed for the creation of an ideal
of family life that

> seemed to be established voluntarily and by free individuals and to be main-
> tained without coercion; it seemed to rest on the lasting community of love
> on the part of the two spouses; it seemed to permit that noninstrumental
> development of all faculties that marks the cultivated personality. The three
> elements of voluntariness, community of love, and cultivation were conjoined
> in a concept of the humanity that was supposed to inhere in humankind as
> such.[118]

A first crucial role is thus given to literary or aesthetic experience in Habermas's argument insofar as literature, in a broad sense, appears as the realm of
cultivation and expression of this new "audience-oriented subjectivity." Letters, diaries, and above all novels became the sites in which subjectivity developed and came to conceive of itself as common humanity. "The relations
between author, work, and public changed. They became intimate mutual

relations between privatized individuals who were psychologically interested in what was 'human,' in self-knowledge, and in empathy."[119]

The first avatar of the bourgeois public sphere was thus the "public sphere in the world of letters," and it is on the basis of the psychic and institutional structures evolved in this domain that a "public sphere in the political realm" becomes possible. In the first instance the *public* designates the audience for works of art and literature, most particularly the audience of a play. This public can be considered "bourgeois" insofar as the very end of the seventeenth century and the early eighteenth century saw the greater separation of "court" and "town," whose conjunction had been the traditional designation for the agency of judgment in matters of taste,[120] and the growing independence of the latter.[121] What Habermas calls "the predominance of the 'town,'" marked in France by the Orléans regency, was characterized by the development there of a series of institutions of sociability that "were centers of criticism—literary at first, then also political—in which began to emerge, between aristocratic society and bourgeois intellectuals, a certain parity of the educated."[122] This new sociability was centered in institutions that allowed participation in and discussion of an increasingly commodified cultural and artistic sphere: the periodical press, coffee houses, salons, theater and concerts, the painting exhibition at the biennial Salon sponsored by the Académie de peinture, provincial academies, masonic lodges, and private educational and literary societies known as *lycées* or *musées.*[123]

There are important distinctions between these various institutions. The press had an ambiguous relation to sociability: reading of new journals could be at the center of social gatherings, where it was often used to start conversation, but it could also be a substitute for social interaction, particularly for provincial readers. Cafés such as the Foy, Caveau, Procope, or Régence were sites of promiscuous social mixing where police spies were constantly on the lookout for subversive gossip. Concerts and particularly the theater were open to whoever could afford to buy a ticket (which is to say, most of the Parisian population); the Salon de peinture was free. The "public" of these institutions had some money and some leisure, but there could be no formal criteria for membership. The great Parisian salons were distinguished by being centered around a female host—Marie-Thérèse Geoffrin, Julie de Lespinasse, Suzanne Curchod Necker (the exception being the "coterie d'Holbach")—and by the informal but highly selective nature of "membership," based on fidelity on the part of the guests and discernment on the part of the hostess. The provincial academies, officially recognized by royal letters patent and usually under the patronage of a provincial governor, bishop, or intendant, were dominated by local elites, particularly office-holding nobility, and they devoted their activities to the ideal of useful knowledge. *Musées* had a more "open" (that is, commercial) structure of membership and more explicitly pedagogical ambitions. Masonry, with the most socially diverse recruitment and largest membership (estimates range from thirty-five thousand to fifty thousand in 1789), was distinguished by the "secrecy" of its proceedings, the complex interplay between the principle of equality and grades of initiation (more developed and diverse in France than elsewhere), and the moral-civic character of its discourse.

Nonetheless it is possible to discern a number of key shared characteristics. Some are sociological in character. All of these institutions were more or less exclusively urban phenomena.[124] Participation presupposed (and membership regulations often explicitly required) the possession of literacy and leisure; the "public" of the public sphere is not the "people." Most, but not all, of these institutions were predominantly if not exclusively masculine.[125] But most important for us here are a number of shared characteristics relating to the principles of association. The first and most important is that they were voluntary, participation being an expression of individual choice. No one was "naturally" a member of salon, academy, or lodge; participation in these forms of sociability had a totally different basis from membership in family, church, or the various corporate bodies around which so much of Old Regime life was organized. They therefore took as their operative model reciprocal relations between individuals freed from relations of economic dependence and abstracted from their social statuses. In practice most of these institutions were very respectful of external status hierarchies and reproduced them in their governance, but this was justified in terms of an ideology of merit or virtue, rather than birth, and was often confirmed by formally egalitarian procedures such as elections. In nonformalized groupings the rules of politeness governing debate would seem to have excluded reference to status. No one in eighteenth-century France would ever forget who was a marquis and who the son of a provincial cutler, but the operative fiction underlying social interaction in the "public sphere" was that such determinations did not matter. All were presumed to participate equally in debate on the basis of the autonomy of their reason. Thus while in practice there were also many exclusions (and a certain exclusivity was certainly part of the attraction for joining such groups), the public was "in principle inclusive." The way in which this unrealized claim to universality was nonetheless a functional principle marks the public sphere as, in Habermas's words, simultaneously "ideology . . . and more than ideology."[126]

From their beginnings as forums for the discussion and judgment of new cultural products, Habermas argues, the institutions of the public sphere in the world of letters became a sphere of political critique. New objects of debate were introduced into an already-formed structure of judgment. "The process in which the state-governed public sphere was appropriated by the public of private people making use of their reason and was established as a sphere of criticism of public authority was one of functionally converting the public sphere in the world of letters already equipped with institutions of the public and with forums for discussion."[127] The public sphere thus constituted is almost necessarily oppositional in the context of an absolute monarchy. In particular, the principle of publicity is fundamentally opposed to the practices of baroque politics, with its dual emphasis on the display of power and the secrecy of the king's cabinet ("reason of state"). The structure of debate in the public sphere stipulates the existence and legitimacy of a reason that, far from being restricted to the royal cabinet, is available to all. This right of the "public" to judge was not only increasingly asserted by its self-proclaimed spokesmen but also more and more recognized by the monarchy itself. Throughout the reign of Louis XVI the administration attempted to justify itself in print to a reading public in a way that would have been not only unnecessary, but incomprehensible to Louis's predecessors. A key moment pointed to by Habermas is Jacques Necker's publication of his *Compte rendu* shortly before his dismissal from the post of controller general in 1781. From that time on, writes Habermas, "this public sphere in the political realm could only be suppressed; it could no longer be effectively put out of commission."[128]

The expression of this rational critique of political authority took the name of "public opinion." Until well into the eighteenth century, in Habermas's account, "opinion" continued to have the dominant meaning of *doxa*—that is, uncertain and variable judgment. The conjugation of opinion with "public" can only designate the importance of the reputation of "public figures"—that is, the king and *les grands*—in the eyes of the population, which Jean-Armand du Plessis, cardinal duc de Richelieu's *Testament politique*, describes as "all the more necessary to a prince in that he who enjoys a good reputation [*celui duquel on a bonne opinion*] can do more with his name alone than those who are not esteemed can do with armies."[129] This emphasis on the reputation of kings, princes, and ministers remains an essential component of Necker's use of the term, not to mention his political practice. Nonetheless, by the second half of the eighteenth century the term had undergone a substantial rationalization.[130]

> Only when the physiocrats ascribed it to the *publique* [*sic*] *éclairé* itself did *opinion publique* receive the strict meaning of an opinion purified through critical discussion in the public sphere to constitute a true opinion. . . . *L'opinion publique* was the enlightened outcome of common and public reflection on the foundations of social order. It encapsulated the latter's natural laws: it did not rule, but the enlightened ruler would have to follow its insight.[131]

Public opinion would therefore no longer express the inconstancy and vagary of popular enthusiasms, but would instead be founded upon the universality of reason. The law itself ought to be an expression of reason, and be open to the sight of all, and not simply the will of the monarch. In a striking reversal of Hobbes's formulation, Habermas proposes that it is no longer authority but truth that constitutes the law: *veritas non auctoritas facit legem.* "Just as secrecy was supposed to serve the maintenance of sovereignty based on *voluntas,* so publicity was supposed to serve the promotion of legislation based on *ratio.*" What is more, such a law no longer designates the diverse acquired rights and privileges of subjects, corporations, and provinces, but "general and abstract norms"—that is, "rational rules of a certain universality and permanence."[132] Such norms of universal applicability presuppose the abstract humanity of the subject in the same way as the conditions of debate in the public sphere do. The relation between the structure of the public sphere and its content—that is, the critique of absolutist politics in the name of rationality—appears in Habermas's argument as a relation of implication. As Keith Baker puts it, the "rational criteria of generality and abstractness . . . simply restated and expanded upon the norms of openness and inclusiveness by which the bourgeois public sphere was in principle accessible to all individuals regardless of their statuses."[133] This relation of ideological implication can be seen as the trace of the slippage in Habermas's argument between normative (or philosophical) and descriptive (or sociological) modes, but it also points to the fundamental question at stake in the shift from an "intellectual" to a "cultural" approach to the problem of the ideological origins of the Revolution: did this practice have, need, imply, or lead to a theory?

SITUATING DISCOURSES

When Roger Chartier describes the "cultural origins" of the Revolution (which, again, he distinguishes from causes) as lying in long-term trends of dechristianization and desacralization of the monarchy, he stipulates that neither trend can be understood as the result of intellectual developments as such. Drawing on the work of Michel de Certeau and Michel Foucault, Chartier poses discontinuities and discordances between and among practices and discourses as the primary object of his inquiry, putting into question the concord of the practice of sociability and the ideology it produces that Habermas's argument highlights. "To move from the 'intellectual' to the 'cultural' is thus, to my mind, not only to enlarge an inquiry or change its object. Fundamentally, this movement implies casting doubt on two ideas: first, that practices can be deduced from the discourses that authorize or justify them; second, that it is possible to translate into the terms of an explicit ideology the latent meaning of social mechanisms." This perspective implies that the Enlightenment consists less in "a corpus of self-contained, transparent ideas or . . . a set of clear and distinct propositions" than in "multiple practices guided by an interest in utility and service that aimed at the management of space and populations and whose mechanisms (intellectual or institutional) imposed a profound reorganization of the systems of perception and of the order of the social world."[134]

Chartier thus wants to locate the opening up of a distance between French society and the monarchy and church not on the level of formal discourse but on that of everyday practices. He sees dechristianization largely as a result of conflicts internal to the practices of the post-Tridentine church (greater social separation between parish priests and the faithful, mutations in treatment of sexual morality, Jansenist sacramental rigorism and contestation of episcopal authority, etc.). "More than the 'enlightened' denunciations of Voltaire and the materialists," Chartier argues, "it was religious discourse, turned inside out by the faithful in their inability to live up to its demands, that produced the most massive abandonment of Christianity."[135] Similarly, his account of the "desacralization" of the monarchy focuses primarily on the changing practices of the monarchy itself, particularly in the public royal rituals that symbolically articulated the link between the king and God, his dynasty, and his peoples. The relation of both peasants and urban laborers to politics was transformed by the channeling (often, it would seem, encouraged by the monarchy) of their contestations with *seigneurs* or guild masters into lawsuits whose "formalities" and "vocabulary" accustomed them "to think of their disputes with the masters according to mental categories—those of civil law and natural law—that universalized and politicized every individual lawsuit."[136] Finally, as we have already seen, he sees the transformation of the practice of reading as having a far more profound impact than the content of what was read. In all of these cases a crucial role is played by specific aspects of social or cultural practices that are discordant with, if not entirely separate from, the discourses that surround them.

Chartier's essay also gives pride of place to Habermas's public sphere and the research concerning intellectual sociability that derives from it, devoting one whole chapter and half of another to it.[137] The placement of these discussions toward the beginning and again toward the end of the book gives Habermas's notion the function of a framing hypothesis. In his conclusion, Chartier writes,

> By taking for themselves the ethical imperatives denied by the reason of state, practicing free exercise of the faculty of judgment, and annulling obligatory obedience to a society of orders and corps, the institutions and forms of sociability founded on the rights of private persons created a sphere of discourse within the fabric of the absolute monarchy that undermined its principles.[138]

The question that must be posed here is where exactly this subversion is to be located? Does it exist entirely at the level of practice, as a sort of "unconscious" of sociability? Or is the "content" of that social interaction, the discourse that occurs within that sphere, involved in a more essential way?

The first of these possibilities is characteristic of the school of thought that begins with Augustin Cochin (if not with the abbé Augustin Barruel), which has been taken up more recently by François Furet and his followers. This tradition sees "democratic" sociability as secreting an ideology, which may never become conscious in the majority of participants, but which still determines the historical significance of their practice. Cochin proposes to look at *philosophie* as no more than the "necessary and unconscious result of certain material conditions of association."[139] Chartier clearly wishes to distance himself from this view, which he sees as relying on the second methodological proposition he criticizes, the "translat[ion] into the terms of an explicit ideology [of] the latent meaning of social mechanisms." But he himself wishes to "reinvest the intellectual sociability of the century with a political content."[140] His frequent use of Kant to explicate Habermas (he even speaks of a "Kant-Habermas model") suggests that the sociability of the public sphere can indeed be understood in terms of a genuinely philosophical discourse. This discourse may in fact be simply a formal model for the operation of that sphere, but it might also have implications for the content of the speech and publication that occur there. What, indeed, are the relations of connection or disconnection that exist between the form and content of the public sphere understood as a historical phenomenon in prerevolutionary France?

The interaction between the interpretation of discourses and the description of cultural contexts can perhaps be clarified by looking at a study of one particular institution. Dena Goodman's *Republic of Letters* focuses attention on the Parisian salon, which she describes as "by all accounts . . . the social base of the Enlightenment Republic of Letters."[141] The salons led by Geoffrin, Lespinasse, and Necker were indeed distinguished, among all the institutions of the public sphere, by the consistent participation of prominent *philosophes* of every generation between the 1750s and the Revolution. Unlike the Académie française, the only other institution that could claim the membership of men like Voltaire, d'Alembert, and Condorcet, the salons seem to have often functioned as working spaces within which new ideas could be tried out, texts in progress read aloud, and constructive discussion occur. But the most important feature distinguishing the salons from other spaces of intellectual sociability in Old Regime Paris was the presence, at their center, of a woman. A long historiographical tradition, which Goodman traces to an unreflected adoption of Rousseau's polemics, has identified this feminization of discourse with frivolity.[142] But in Goodman's account, the *salonnière* had a serious, necessary, and active role to fulfill, that of the "governance" of discourse. While the women who ran the salons may have had "selfish" motivations of their own, the attraction of these feminocentric spaces for the *philosophes* was that feminine governance of discourse saved them from the anarchy and chaos that the disputatious and combative intellectual style fostered by their educations (largely in Jesuit and Oratorian *collèges*) threatened to produce. Order in the Republic of Letters, Goodman writes, "could be established only through voluntary submission to the rules of polite discourse and the female governors who enforced them."[143] Goodman's account of the seriousness of purpose with which *salonnières* approached this function is borne out by extensive analysis of the development of their careers and their practices of preparation. The notes published after her death in Suzanne Necker's *Mélanges* confirm Goodman's contention that "her purpose in life was not to distract men from their serious business but rather to discipline herself and her guests so that business might be carried out."[144] Further testimony to the effectiveness of the *salonnière's* role is provided by the tributes that *philosophes* such as Diderot, Jakob Heinrich Meister, Jean-François Marmontel, and André-Antoine Thomas wrote in their honor.

The concept of sociability thus operates at two levels in Goodman's argument. On the one hand, the practice of polite (or *policée*)[145] sociability becomes the defining characteristic of the Enlightenment understood as a cultural phenomenon. On the other hand, the account of society as the result of a civilizing process in which martial or combative models are replaced by commercial or collaborative ones becomes the central doctrine of Enlightenment thought. "Women played a central role both in the representation of history upon which the convivial ideal of sociability was based and in the practice and representation of polite conversation in the Parisian salons in which French men of letters experienced sociability. The French Enlightenment was grounded in a female-centered mixed-gender sociability that gendered French culture, the Enlightenment, and civilization itself as feminine."[146] The idea and social practice of sociability existed in a mutually reinforcing relation. In many ways, this unity is best figured by a negative example, Rousseau's rejection of Parisian sociability coming together with his theoretical critique of natural sociability.

A more positive version of this unity of an intellectual construct and the social practice that supports it can be found in Goodman's discussion of the abbé Ferdinando Galiani's *Dialogues sur le commerce des blés* (1770) and the polemics surrounding it. Goodman describes Galiani's antiphysiocratic defense of government regulation of the grain trade as a challenge to "French public policy and the physiocratic economic principles on which it was based" (even though these principles had ceased to underlay government policy by the time the text actually appeared)[147] as well as to the physiocrats' intellectual style, based on dogmatic argument. The form and content of the *Dialogues* embody the "discursive values" of salon conversation and politeness against "the pedantic, enthusiastic, and disputatious spirit of the physiocrats."[148] The key concept here is that of *police*, translated by Goodman as "government."

The word *police* begins its career in French as a direct translation for the Greek *politeia*. But toward the end of the seventeenth century, it becomes gradually associated with practices of administration. As Daniel Gordon puts it, "Urban security and prosperity became the principal meanings of *police* in both its descriptive and normative senses."[149] Now, it is possible to distinguish between a purely absolutist vision of this regulation, such as that found in Nicolas Delamare's *Traité de la police*, where the natural lawlessness of human nature needs to be continually held in check by the exercise of firm and unquestioned authority, and a more characteristically Enlightenment vision such as that found in Jacques Peuchet's *Encyclopédie méthodique* volumes on *Police et municipalités*. There the concept of a *peuple policé* designates the result of a process of internalization of regulation that has rendered the constant application of force unnecessary.[150] But throughout the period and across this semantic movement, *police* maintains a privileged relation not only with the city (as the site of urbanity, pure language, freedom from serfdom, commerce, and government, it is the motor of the civilizing process in Peuchet's account), but also with the place within the city where civilized behavior, always represented as fragile among the *populace*, was most likely to break down completely: the bread market. As Steven Kaplan puts it,

> Police and provisioning formed an inseparable couple in old-regime society. Police embodied a conception of social organization that valued order above all else and a conception of social relations that made order contingent on an adequate food supply.[151]

It is in this context that we must understand Galiani's assertion that "bread . . . belongs to *police* and not to commerce."[152] As Goodman points out, this notion operates both on the level of style and on that of substance.

> Galiani was a champion of *police* as the key to politeness, to a civil society, as the basis of order in matters of grain and of language. . . . If we understand *police* as Galiani and many of his enlightened contemporaries did, as the basis of an "orderly liberty" and the necessary defense against anarchy and chaos, then it is easy to see his reaction here, as well as his approach to the problems of the grain trade, as entirely consistent with the values and practices of the salon-based Republic of Letters.[153]

Now, it may well be that the physiocrats are both dogmatic and boring, and that their style of argumentation was characterized by *esprit de système* and *esprit de parti* rather than the open and critical examination of received ideas. Their tendency to welcome an authoritarian imposition of policy was much criticized by figures otherwise sympathetic to their economic thought, such as Anne-Robert-Jacques Turgot and Adam Smith. And it may also be that Galiani was primarily concerned to promote open, critical discussion of grain policy in a manner both nondogmatic and appealing to a nonspecialist audience. I would not want to make "freedom of commerce" into a litmus test for inclusion in the Enlightenment; policy regarding the market in subsistence goods was a continual and often acrimonious subject of debate within the Enlightenment (as it was to be during the Revolution). But a symmetrical exclusion of the doctrine of freedom of commerce from the Enlightenment in the name of *police* and politeness strikes me as equally troubling.

Galiani's publication was attacked not only by physiocrats but also by his oldest friend in Paris, the abbé André Morellet (writing, it would seem, on behalf of the ministry). Morellet is one of the central figures in Goodman's story, where he appears as both the major theorist of salon sociability and as the *mauvais sujet* of this republic on account of his combative and disputatious character.[154] Goodman interprets this episode as illustrating the fact that

> the polite discourse of Enlightenment could not be sustained in the public world of print, where the royal policing of the book trade was a poor substitute for the republican governance of salonnières. Despite the honest efforts of the philosophes to free the search for truth from the divisive personal relations of the age and to embrace the practice of public debate, the movement from controlled salon discourse to the public world of print destroyed their dreams of harmony and unity every time. The Republic of Letters was falling into anarchy and discord as surely as would the monarchy itself in 1789.[155]

This treatment of print as a realm of disputation and anarchy reinforces the extent to which Goodman conceives of Enlightenment sociability as founded in governance or *police*. Even if royal censorship is ineffective, the role it aspires to (particularly insofar as it prohibits personal attacks) is seen as all the more legitimate and necessary. The comparison between the fall of the monarchy and the decline of the Enlightenment is by no means accidental. It is in fact central to Goodman's argument that the Revolution is the child not of the Enlightenment but rather of the deterioration and masculinization of its characteristic mode of sociability, marked by the creation of a new set of institutions, the *musées*, in which women were marginalized, decentered, and displaced. Even when women were allowed into *musées* they were conceived of as window-dressing and were given neither an active nor a necessary role. "The revolution that transformed the Republic of Letters," Goodman writes, "began not in 1789 but in 1778, when men began to meet without the supervision of women."[156] The phenomenon of the *musées* is linked to "the apotheosis of public opinion" in its "objective" and "rational" form in the 1780s. "Both developments can be understood as attempts to actualize a fantasy of masculine self-governance whose obvious correlate was the myth of female despotism and whose greatest manifestation was the French Revolution."[157] Another, and particularly provocative, corollary is Goodman's suggestion that Kant's philosophy be seen as a further manifestation of this fantasy.[158] Like the doctrine of the freedom of commerce, the autonomy of reason becomes part of a falling-away from the true practice of Enlightenment.

Goodman presents her work as a "cultural history of the Enlightenment," which for her does not simply indicate a broadening of the field of intellectual history to include materials beyond the traditional canon of great texts. Rather she sees it as a decentering of those texts and their authors (Kant, Rousseau, et al.) in order to make the relation between practice and discourse the center of attention. "Unlike intellectual history," she writes, "cultural history does not assume that ideas, or even those who articulate them, are the primary subject matter of historical inquiry. Rather, cultural history focuses on social and discursive practices and institutions: both the ground on which particular discursive actions take place and the actions themselves."[159] Culture in this sense (and I believe this is entirely characteristic of the current adaptation of the anthropological use of the term in history and literary criticism) plays a simultaneously unifying and limiting role.[160] Here it primarily designates a continuity between the theory and practice of the Republic of Letters, which in turn leads to an exclusion of those discourses that conflict with the social practices on which they are based.

Here it is probably the exclusion in principle of Rousseau rather than the physiocrats that is most revealing. Rousseau presents a virulent critique of the feminocentric sociability of the salons, most notably in the *Lettre à d'Alembert* and Saint-Preux's letters on Paris in book II of *La Nouvelle Héloïse*. But in those same texts, he promotes single-sex *cercles* as a foundation of Genevan republicanism. In what seems to me to be a related way, he was clearly uncomfortable with a fully commercialized vision of authorship and often seemed to prefer a patronage model.[161] But Rousseau's activity as a writer (and even more, the public reception of that activity) participated in and presupposed a Habermasian public sphere *in print* to as great a degree as any other author of the century. Not only do his works address a public sphere audience, the epistolary exchange that structures *La Nouvelle Héloïse* reproduces one of its most characteristic practices (a point on which Habermas and Goodman are in complete agreement).[162] But the readers of a novel, unlike theater spectators, constitute a public dispersed in private, domestic spaces in both city and country; print culture addresses both men and women (Rousseau is quite conscious and accepting of women's preponderant place in the audience for novels), but separately. Far more women participated in the public sphere through the circulation of print culture than did through the salons (indeed, there were probably more women novelists than *salonnières*). Kant, too, constitutes the public as a "reading public" addressed through the universality of print.[163] If this vision of print is a masculine fantasy, it is one characteristic of the Enlightenment as a whole, particularly in its doctrinal contradictions. It seems to me that it is necessary to account for the circulation, within a public sphere whose institutions are only partially homogeneous, of a number of discourses, some of which justify and others of which contest their own cultural presuppositions.

One possible approach to this problem is suggested by the classification of late eighteenth-century political discourses proposed by Keith Baker. If politics, as Baker defines it, is a process of making, negotiating, and enforcing claims, then "political culture . . . is the set of discourses or symbolic practices by which these claims are made." It can thus be said to include the legitimated positions that subjects can occupy, particularly as they define membership and status in the community, the meanings of the terms recognized as relevant by participants in debate, and the constitution of agencies that resolve conflicts between claims. "Thus political authority is in this view essentially a matter of linguistic authority."[164] The concepts of both culture and discourse, in my view, designate some form of constraint and attempt to think limitation and possibility together. If it makes sense to speak of a political *culture* in this sense, it means first of all that not all discourses are possible (and within any given discourse not all things can be said), not because some are forbidden but rather because they are simply inconceivable.[165] The amount of unity that such a limitation implies is one of the major sticking points of any theory of culture. But the idea of a *political* culture may give the problem of unity even higher stakes. While Baker's definition speaks of a "set" of discourses, the introduction of linguistic authority that closes the definition necessarily singularizes these discourses, or more accurately hierarchizes them, the point being that only one discourse can be authoritative. In a version of this text published as the Introduction to the first volume of *The French Revolution and the Creation of Modern Political Culture*, Baker suggests that heterogeneity is the normal condition of political culture in complex societies, whereas it is precisely in a "revolutionary" situation that "the terms of many of the political games being played out in a society seem (often quite unexpectedly) to align themselves in a unitary and coherent lexical field."[166] But the more general trend of his analyses in *Inventing the French Revolution* seems to me to go in the opposite direction. There—if only to establish a stable point of contrast—it would seem to be absolutist politics as it was inherited from Louis XIV, Richelieu, Jean-Baptiste Colbert, and Jacques-Bénigne Bossuet that was marked by the unity of its discourse and particularly of the site to which discourses were addressed and where they were evaluated. The coming of the Revolution is marked precisely by the coming apart of this unitary discourse. Baker sees late eighteenth-century political discussion in France as analyzable in terms of "three basic strands of discourse," which he designates as administrative, judicial, and political.

> These strands represent a disaggregation of the attributes traditionally bound together in the concept of monarchical authority—reason, justice and will—and their reconceptualization as the basis of competing definitions (or attempted redefinitions) of the body politic. . . . In the second part of the eighteenth century, this cluster of attributes seems to separate into three strands of discourse, each characterized by the analytical priority it gives to one or the other of these terms.[167]

Baker gives the least attention in *Inventing the French Revolution* to what he calls the "judicial discourse," although this may be because it is already well known. Represented in Baker's programmatic essays "On the Problem of the Ideological Origins of the French Revolution" and "French Political Thought at the Accession of Louis XVI" by Malesherbes's 1775 *Remontrances*, written for the Cour des Aides, this defense of the traditional constitution of the state has its roots in what is often called the *thèse nobiliaire*.

First articulated by the group around Louis, duc de Bourgogne, at the beginning of the century (the group consisting of Louis de Rouvroy, duc de Saint-Simon, François de Salignac de la Mothe-Fénelon, and Henri, comte de Boulainvilliers) and given definitive form by the discussion by Charles de Secondat, baron de la Brède et de Montesquieu, of the relation between nobility and monarchy in *De l'esprit des lois*,[168] the emphasis on the necessity of intermediary institutions, and particularly of instances of justice that are independent of administration, provided parlementary resistance to the extension of administrative competencies throughout the century with its most compelling arguments.[169]

The "political" discourse emphasizing will is represented by Gabriel Bonnot de Mably and the radical Bordeaux parlementarian Guillaume-Joseph Saige, but lurking behind them is clearly the figure of Rousseau, and on the revolutionary horizon, the abbé Emmanuel-Joseph Sieyes. Baker sees Mably, for example, as representative of a "specifically political mode of thinking," by which he means "a representation of the social field that emphasizes will, contingency, choice, participation." All forms of society, in their contrasting organizations and different degrees of legitimacy, are seen in this perspective "as the expression of will, whether exercised unilaterally by a sovereign power (de jure or de facto) or multilaterally by the conflict or concurrence of any number of competing bodies."[170] The discourse of will drew extensively on classical republicanism, both through the Latin texts that continued to dominate education and through English sources. It gives prominent play to the dominance of the passions over reason in human action. Finally, in Baker's account, political discourse privileges the rights of the nation over the rights of the individual.[171]

The discourse closest to Baker's heart is clearly what he calls the administrative discourse of reason, represented by Turgot and other reforming administrators, Condorcet, Necker, and the physiocrats. In this discourse, both the particularistic and corporative social order and the grounding of sovereignty in (arbitrary) will as such appear as irrationalities and atavisms that have become incompatible with the progress of enlightenment and of civilization. Rather than opposing one will to another, and countering the contingent character of the royal will with that of the nation, reason and enlightenment must come to be exercised in its place. This reconstruction of political legitimacy implies that "the social order must be reconstituted on the basis of nature—which is to say, property and civic equality—in order to transform political contingency into rational order, arbitrary government into rational administration, law into education, and representation into an institutional means for the expression of rational social choice."[172] The substitution of rationality for these anachronistic discourses is particularly clear in Turgot's proposition for consultative representative assemblies, formed on the basis of property ownership rather than social status, that would enlighten administrators but could not claim the power to block reforms. For Turgot and his followers, Baker writes, "the nation is to be reconstituted on the basis of universalistic norms, as embodied in the doctrine of the rights of man; legal-rational authority is to be exercised with the support of an enlightened public opinion, as expressed in representative assemblies. Reason, not will, is to be the hallmark of public authority."[173]

In Baker's account the theory of public opinion falls squarely into the discourse of reason. This theory was particularly prevalent in administrative and physiocratic *milieux*, and it presented itself as a distinctly modern phenomenon. The "public" thus conceived is modeled neither on the population of the ancient city assembled in the *agora* or forum, nor on privilege and corporative solidarity. Since the public is above all a reading public, it is dispersed, anonymous, and egalitarian. Most important, as we saw in Habermas, public opinion is no longer seen as the inconsistent, shifting, and stormy voice of the populace, but rather as the stable, durable, and peaceful expression of general enlightenment. As Jacques Necker put it, what must be listened to is "that public opinion whose characteristics are all authoritative [*imposants*] and which reason, time, and the universality of sentiments alone have the right to consecrate."[174] The conception of reforming administrators such as Necker, Baker argues, "ascribed to public opinion—understood as the rational consensus achieved by open procedures of public discussion and criticism—the universality and rationality, order and objectivity, that absolutist theorists had once claimed as the hallmark of monarchical rule."[175] Thus while the deployment of a notion of public opinion as a new locus of legitimation occurs within a "politics of contestation," it somewhat paradoxically presents an "image of a rational consensus untroubled by the passions of willful human action,"[176] that is, a pacification of contestation in the name of what is universally accepted.

Baker is careful (and quite correct, in my view) to define public opinion as "a political or ideological construct, rather than as a discrete sociological referent."[177] But if it is true, as he also argues, that "one can understand the conflicts of the Pre-Revolution as a series of struggles to fix the sociological referent of the concept in favor of one or another competing group," then the control of the construct does not necessarily coincide with its elaboration. If there is a real competition in the public sphere to occupy the position of "public opinion" (and all three of Baker's "strands of discourse" participated in this competition), there is no guarantee that the "content" of this notion will be as rationalistic as its theory. It thus seems to me that Baker is entirely correct to insist, against Habermas, that there is a very marked difference between the physiocratic or administrative use of the term "public opinion" and that found in Rousseau, where it designates the inertia that *mœurs* and accepted prejudices oppose to change, what Baker calls "a social rather than a political category . . . , a challenge to the legislator's art rather than an expression of political will."[178] Even if it is true, however, that "the rationalist conception of public opinion and the voluntaristic conception of the general will belonged to radically different political discourses,"[179] this does not mean that "political" discourses such as those inspired by Rousseau did not compete, perhaps quite successfully, in the arena of public opinion. Indeed, Baker himself sees this competition ending in the triumph of the discourse of will in the summer of 1789. The destruction of "feudalism" and the creation of a formally egalitarian social order based on property and the rights of man correspond to a certain fulfillment of the claims of the discourse of reason, and the establishment of a constitution subjecting the exercise of authority to representational control responds to magisterial constitutionalism. But these accomplishments, Baker concludes, were "construed as an act of [political] will"; the discourses of reason and justice were "bracketed, in short, within the discourse of will."[180]

VIRTUE IN THE PUBLIC SPHERE

The attempt to describe a correlation between the ideology and the sociology of the public sphere thus can be sustained only at the cost of serious restrictions. What this has forced us to consider is the possibility that discourses that did not espouse an ideology congruent with the epistemological basis of the public sphere were in fact able to compete within it effectively for the approbation of the public. Or, since I think that Baker is correct in seeing the "public" as an ideological construct in search of a sociological referent, when a public did come into existence it was around a discourse of neither administrative rationality nor polite conversation and wit. Indeed, the two most convincing accounts of the coalescence of a public sphere in a sociological form that goes beyond a very restricted elite domain are those provided by Sara Maza in her study of *mémoires judiciaires* and Thomas Crow in his analysis of debates around the painting Salon. In both cases, this formation of a public occurs around an ideology of sentimentalized (and strongly gender-coded) virtue, derived in large part from Rousseau. One of the major reasons, to my mind at least, that they are so convincing is that they give detailed demonstrations of one of the most important aspects of Habermas's argument, namely the interaction of aesthetic and political modes of discourse.[181]

Maza shows how the legally uncensored and avidly read legal briefs of the last twenty years of the Old Regime appealed above the courts to the tribunal of public opinion by drawing on rhetorical strategies developed in contemporary literary genres such as the sentimental novel, the *drame bourgeois*, and autobiography. Maza calls attention to three major themes, each of which is germane to our argument here.

First, Maza describes the formation in cases contemporaneous with the "Maupeou Revolution" (particularly the Véron-Morangiès affair) of a discourse that "drew upon and brought together the two major (and competing) ideological currents of the age, 'magisterial' opposition to 'despotism' and 'ministerial' attacks on 'aristocracy.'"[182] While this case did involve a conflict between commoners and an aristocrat, the imagery survives in later cases where two noble parties compete for the strategically superior position of virtue persecuted by uncontrolled power. These two currents were indeed usually opposed before the Revolution (they are, respectively, variants of Baker's "judicial" and "administrative" discourses), but their connection is typical in many ways of the discourse of the Revolution itself (it marks the admittedly fragile equivalence of liberty and equality). Maza sees the production of this translation of "political tensions into social imagery" as the result of a "symbiosis of political concerns (about 'despotism') and new literary forms." In these briefs, politics is seen through the lens of melodramatic emplotting, characterized by "extreme moral polarization, hyperbolic expressions and gestures, sketchy characterization, complicated plotting, and emphatic moral didacticism." This prefiguration of what Baker calls the "bracketing" of discourses of reason and justice occurs, in the prerevolutionary setting, primarily in terms of a discourse of virtue.[183]

The second theme that Maza sees emerging from the *mémoires judiciaires* is a persistent emphasis on "issues of gender, and especially concerns about the public role of women that had been articulated most forcefully in the previous generation by Rousseau."[184] This rewriting of the politics of gender roles appears most prominently in the feminization of "despotism" in publications concerning the diamond necklace affair, but it also plays a determinant role in the two great "domestic" cases of the later 1780s, the Sanois and Kornmann affairs, both of which turned on analogies between domestic and social order. Maza summarizes Rousseau's influence on these cases in the following terms:

> Rousseau's works spoke to all aspects of his reader's lives, clarifying the connection between private experience and public ideals. His political works set up a model of healthy masculine republicanism as an antithesis to the over-civilized decay of monarchical France; his educational and fictional writings popularized new ideals of domestic life, of marital and parental happiness; his *Confessions* and other autobiographical writings introduced readers to a man of courageous integrity, a self-proclaimed outcast who shunned the cultural and intellectual fashions of his day and dared to reveal in print his most shameful thoughts and actions.[185]

In other words, despite all the antifeminist themes in his work, we can see in this adaptation of Rousseau one of the most important sources of the grounding proposition of modern feminism: the personal is the political. But this connection is made at least as much in terms of a rhetoric of virtue (and of the separate ideals of masculine and feminine virtue) as in one of rights.[186]

This model of connection between public and private derived from Rousseau also underlies the third of Maza's major themes. For it was precisely the turn to a rhetoric of *sensibilité* and the use of first-person confessional narrative that allowed the articulation of an increasingly political message in legal briefs. Maza describes how the *mémoires* of the 1780s "began to address problems of social iniquity in impersonal, structural terms." The judicial system replaces the malicious individual grandee as the great villain of these dramas, suggesting, in Maza's words, "a shift from a preoccupation with the *abuse* of social and political power to a critique of the very *bases* of that power—from a reaction against a sociopolitical tyranny to a reflection on the nature of the social contract."[187] But this process of generalization continues to occur in terms of a rhetoric of persecuted virtue, given more force here by the persistent self-dramatization of the lawyer as a champion of the oppressed and an *homme sensible.*

The authors of trial briefs began to adopt techniques aimed at fostering the ideal of Rousseauan (and revolutionary) "transparency": by bringing to the fore the personality and reactions of the barrister-author and inviting their readers to share the intimacy of the *sensible* protagonist, the authors of mémoires sought to create an unmediated connection between the presumed virtue and sensibility of their client and that of their readers; this intimate connection between reader, lawyer, and client was then pressed into the service of the political argument spelled out in the mémoire.[188]

The major lesson of Maza's book seems to me to be that, in the competition to represent "public opinion," neither the discourse that did the most to define the term (that of administrative rationality) nor the discourse that grounded polite sociability between intellectuals and aristocrats (that of wit) was victorious. The rhetorically strongest position in this competition seems to have been the discourse of virtue, defined in terms of an opposition between *sensibilité* and sincerity, on the one hand, and arbitrary persecution and decadent artifice on the other. Perhaps most important, the language of passion and sincerity seems to have been sufficiently powerful to override other factors (such as the actual facts of the case) in determining which side was able to occupy the position of persecuted virtue and which was relegated to that of decadent and self-interested abuse of power. And, as Carol Blum has demonstrated, the strongest vector propagating this discourse was subjective identification with the character of "Jean-Jacques."[189]

In following recent developments in the debate on the intellectual, cultural, and ideological origins of the Revolution, we have been guided by a concern to reconcile two statements contemporary with the Revolution itself. Louis-Sébastien Mercier, stating what we might call the classical position, called Rousseau "one of the first authors of the Revolution." Jean-Joseph Mounier responded in a revisionist spirit that "it was not in the least the influence of these principles that produced the revolution. On the contrary, it was the revolution that produced their influence." The problem, fundamentally, is not to choose between these two positions or their variants, but to understand how both of them can be true at the same time.

The debate between Robert Darnton and Roger Chartier on "how eighteenth-century Frenchmen read" provides a fairly immediate transformation of this dilemma. I have tried to stake out an intermediate and, I hope, commonsensical position between Darnton's emphasis on the transformative power of clandestine literature and Chartier's provocative reformulation of the idea of a retrospective construction of the Enlightenment. We operate within inherited cultural frameworks whose transformations are most often a relatively impersonal process. It is no less true that what we read can change what we think. Combining Mercier's and Mounier's statements suggests that the transformation provoked by the reading of new texts is always also an activity of reconstruction, that is, that influence is always retrospective. Such "influence" does not always happen right away, and when it does happen it rewrites its own history and often erases its own presuppositions. Mounier, after all (and this is to my mind the great virtue of his formulation), does indeed say that the Revolution produced the influence of Rousseau's texts, not that it produced the illusion of their influence. Putting into question the linear or unidirectional model of influence does not require us to abandon any notion of the historical agency of texts. What it does demand is rather that we rethink the link between causality and intelligibility contained in Mercier's use of the notion of "author." It is at this point that we might seek the possibility of a genuinely literary history.

The cultural-sociological approach inspired by Habermas displaces this temporal discontinuity into a synchronic mode, where it appears as a growing incompatibility between the form and content of Enlightenment sociability, between the theory and the practice of the public sphere. In this case the challenge is posed by the presence or even the dominance of recognizably Rousseauian motifs within a cultural context that is both theoretically and sociologically inimical to them. This suggests that such relations of discontinuous and retrospective causality were already present within what we call the Enlightenment. These disturbances were most often, and above all most forcefully, signified by the name, person, and work of Jean-Jacques Rousseau. The subsequent chapters will attempt to show that this is also where they were given their most important theoretical elaborations.

2. The Unnatural Order of Enlightenment Universal History

Barbarus hic ego sum quia non intelligor illis.

—*Ovid, 'Tristia'* 5.10.37[1]

The Debate on the Arts and Sciences

On 18 floréal year II, at the height of the power of the government of the Committee of Public Safety, Maximilien Robespierre addressed the National Convention "Sur les rapports des idées religieuses et morales avec les principes républicains." In this, the most famous of his discourses, Robespierre proposed the institution of the Festival of the Supreme Being as a way to go beyond the debilitating conflict between the dechristianization associated with the recently executed *hébertistes* and the manifest residual religiosity of a large part of the population. The major theme of the discourse is thus the social and moral unification of the nation around a shared, if minimal, religious consensus that rejects both atheism and clerical charlatanism. Moreover, it is precisely the unifying power of religious sentiment that makes it a necessary component of republican virtue in Robespierre's conception. "Bring men together," he exclaims, "and you will render them better."[2] But characteristically, this movement toward unity and reconciliation was accompanied by a ferocious drawing of lines and denunciation of enemies. Among those denounced by Robespierre in this case was Jean-Antoine-Nicolas Caritat, ci-devant marquis de Condorcet, formerly a member of the Académie française and perpetual secretary of the Académie des sciences ("a great geometer in the judgment of men of letters [*littérateurs*], and a great man of letters according to the geometers" was Robespierre's biting dismissal),[3] who had since had an important revolutionary career, first as a journalist and later as a member of the Convention, where he had been associated with the Girondins. Condorcet had been in hiding since the previous summer, following the proscription of the Girondins, and one month before Robespierre's speech he had left his hiding place, been arrested, and died in prison.[4] Here, however, he is denounced not primarily for his Girondin sympathies but for his prerevolutionary association with the encyclopedists, who are presented by Robespierre as the model of antireligious cynicism and fanaticism.

The question of religion is the occasion for Robespierre to raise the issue of the intellectual origins of the Revolution, which he does in terms that provide a striking prefiguration of the debates we examined in the preceding chapter.

> For a long time enlightened observers had been able to glimpse a few symptoms of the current Revolution. All important events tended in its direction. . . . Famous men of letters, by virtue of their influence on opinion, began to have an influence on politics [*les affaires*]. The most ambitious among them then formed a sort of coalition that increased their importance. . . . The most powerful and illustrious [group] was that known under the name of the *encyclopedists*. It contained a few estimable men and a larger number of ambitious charlatans. Several of its leaders had become considerable figures in the state; anyone ignorant of its influence and its policy would have a very incomplete idea of the preface of our Revolution.[5]

But if the encyclopedists played an important role in the origins of the Revolution, they do not truly express its spirit. Robespierre's attack on the encyclopedists, after underlining the theoretical egoism of their philosophy and the practical hypocrisy of their conduct, ends with a denunciation of their persecution of Jean-Jacques Rousseau.

> Among those who, at the time I am speaking about, showed their talent in the career of letters and philosophy, a man, by the elevation of his soul and the greatness of his character, showed himself worthy of the ministry of preceptor to the human race. He attacked tyranny with frankness; he spoke with enthusiasm of the Divinity; his male and forthright eloquence painted the charms of virtue in fiery brush strokes; he defended the consoling dogmas that reason gives to the human heart for support. The purity of his doctrine, drawn from nature and a profound hatred of vice, as much as his invincible contempt for the intriguing sophists who usurped the name of philosophers, earned him the hatred and persecution of his rivals and false friends.[6]

What is at stake here, among other things, is the relation between two possible visions, represented by Condorcet and Rousseau, of the origins of the Revolution and its relation to the Enlightenment. This opposition functions both on the level of content (here, primarily the contrast between irreligion and natural religion) and, equally important, on the level of models of historical causality. If for Condorcet the Revolution can be described as the inevitable result of the progress of the arts and sciences and the diffusion of knowledge and truth, the other vision, in which Robespierre declares his fidelity to Rousseau, insists on the question of virtue.

In an earlier section of his discourse, Robespierre had explicitly placed this question in the framework of debates on universal history, a debate in which Condorcet and Rousseau clearly represented two poles. Robespierre begins by describing a contrast between the lessons of nature and the lessons of history. "Nature tells us that man is born for freedom, and the experience of the centuries shows us man as a slave; his rights are written in his heart, and his humiliation in history."[7] The moments when the lessons of nature have appeared in history are only brief illuminations. "Sparta shines like a lightning bolt amidst immense shadows." Nonetheless there has been historical progress, the history of civilization, the history of the arts and sciences. "The civilized nations have followed savages wandering in the desert; fertile harvests have taken the place of the ancient forests that covered the globe." Progress in language, geography, science, and the arts has rendered the moderns incomparably greater than the ancients. But that progress is merely external; it represents only what Robespierre calls the "physical order" in opposition to the "political and moral order." This means that the task is only half accomplished. "Man's reason still resembles the globe he inhabits; half of it is plunged in darkness while the other half is in light. The peoples of Europe have made astonishing progress in what are called the arts and sciences, and they seem completely ignorant of the first notions of public morality; they know everything except their rights and their duties." Robespierre's framework thus produces a violent dissociation within the doctrine of the unity of progress associated with Condorcet's thought. Progress in the natural sciences has no effect on progress in the moral sciences. Robespierre denies the presence of any causal connection whatsoever between the two fields. They would seem to work on different principles. In fact, Robespierre's explanation for this disparity is that the two domains have opposite relations to the passions. To cultivate the arts and sciences, argues Robespierre, "one need only follow one's passions, whereas to defend one's rights and respect those of others, it is necessary to conquer those passions."[8] The historical opposition between barbarism and civilization is admitted, but only in order to be disqualified in the name of an opposition between vice and virtue that is not in the least historical.

An examination of the Revolution's conceptualization of its relation to the Enlightenment thus cannot presume a unity either in the Enlightenment or in the Revolution on this point. In particular, it is necessary to recognize and examine the presence in Enlightenment historical discourse of a number of models of historical causality, particularly with respect to the role of ideas in history. Our study of this problem will begin with the contrast between Condorcet and Rousseau suggested by Robespierre, before widening to a broader context that will include Scottish as well as French writing. Because Condorcet's *Esquisse d'un tableau historique des progrès de l'esprit humain* specifically addresses the origins of the Revolution, and thus can be read simultaneously as a document of the Enlightenment and of the Revolution, it will serve as our point of departure, although our constant and final concern will be to determine the specificity of Rousseau within the constellation of Enlightenment thought on this topic.

CONDORCET'S REVOLUTION

It is often described as one of the ironies of history that Condorcet should have written the *Esquisse* while in hiding during the Terror, devoting his last days to the composition of the most complete declaration of faith in the infinite progress of human knowledge and perfectibility of human society that the Enlightenment produced. Posthumously published by his widow and given wide distribution by the Thermidorian convention, the *Esquisse* has a reputation for being a monumental and triumphalist version of the ideology of progress, a reputation that is not entirely unmerited. Condorcet's history, he says at the beginning, will demonstrate "the links by which nature has indissolubly united the progresses of enlightenment and those of freedom, of virtue, of respect for the natural rights of man; and how these, the only worldly goods worth having, so often separated that they have been believed to be incompatible, must on the contrary become inseparable."[9] Three factors account for the monumental character of this history. First, Condorcet attributes to what he calls the moral sciences both a degree of certainty and a cumulative effectivity more frequently reserved for the natural sciences. Secondly, he argues that humankind has passed a point of no return in the career of enlightenment, and a second version of the Dark Ages has been rendered impossible. Thus a tenth epoch can be confidently devoted to the future progress of the human mind. Finally, a single dynamic and a single battle is waged throughout the course of history: the confrontation between truth and error, enlightenment and ignorance, philosophy and superstition. The good guys do not always win, at least in the short term. But they never die, so to speak, lose their identity, or do harm by mistake. Because truth is eternal there is no such thing, for Condorcet, as a premature truth. Minds may not be ready to accept it (or more to the point, to discover it), but in itself truth is always beneficial. Condorcet is radically antihistoricist in this respect, which explains the relative absence in his account of a theory of types of society, such as the "four-stages" model to be found in his mentor Anne-Robert-Jacques Turgot's *Deux discours sur l'histoire universelle*, which is his primary inspiration.[10]

The basic themes and even the tone of the *Esquisse* can already be found in a number of Condorcet's prerevolutionary writings. The "Discours préliminaire" to his *Essai sur l'application de l'analyse à la probabilité des décisions rendues à la pluralité des voix* of 1785, for example, begins with a eulogy of Turgot: "A great man . . . was convinced that the truths of the moral and political sciences are susceptible of the same certainty as those that form the system of the physical sciences. . . . This opinion was dear to him because it leads to the consoling hope that the human race will necessarily [make] progress toward happiness and perfection, as it has in the knowledge of truth."[11] This ability to transfer principles from the exact to the social sciences will remain the primary resource of Condorcet's argument. In the tenth epoch of the *Esquisse*, "Des progrès futurs de l'esprit humain," he will specifically found the hope for continual progress on the concept of regularity upon which the functioning of all scientific laws is based. "The only foundation for belief in the natural sciences," he writes, "is the idea that the general laws, known or unknown, that regulate the phenomena of the universe, are necessary and constant; and for what reason would this principle be less true for the development of the intellectual and moral faculties of man than for the other operations of nature?"[12] This argument can be stated only as a rhetorical question because it contains its only possible proof. If the concept of scientific law is universally valid—that is, if the fundamental characteristic of nature is its regularity—then the intelligence that discovers that law cannot be excluded from its application. Regularity must apply to man, and in particular to his intellectual development, insofar as he is part of nature. Because human intelligence and its objects are both parts of the same whole, namely nature, an exchange of certain basic properties and principles becomes possible. The relation between two fields of human inquiry, the physical and moral sciences, is mediated by the concept of nature: intelligence discovers regularity in nature, but it is itself part of nature and therefore must be regular. The key element that must be transferred from physics to politics is its teleological orientation, so that the ever-increasing number of truths known about nature (and consequent technological control of the natural world) is doubled by an ever-increasing understanding and mastery of moral and political phenomena. The very irreversibility of this model can then be counted among those truths.

As Catherine Kintzler has emphasized, Condorcet's concept of progress as indissolubly scientific and moral stands in distinct opposition to the other great synthesis of the Enlightenment at the end of the century, Kant's *Critiques*.[13] The keystone of the critical system is the disjunction (which is not, for Kant, an incompatibility) of cognition and morality. Condorcet's concept of "moral sciences" (a term that it would be impossible to use today) would be, in Kantian terms, an aesthetic concept, one that attempts to bridge the gap separating the *Critique of Pure Reason* from the *Critique of Practical Reason*. It could even be described as mysticism (*Schwärmerei*) in that, from the Kantian point of view, it is a symbol (a concept of reason for which no corresponding intuition is possible) that presents itself as a schema (a concept of the understanding for which corresponding intuitions can be supplied a priori).[14] The teleological orientation of this system will not surprise readers of the *Critique of Judgment*.

The establishment of this exchange between the physical and moral sciences is more the goal of the text than its point of departure. But similar exchanges regulate the entire functioning of the argument. The most important of these is set forth by Condorcet at the beginning of the *Esquisse*, where he establishes a metaphorical link between the basis of Enlightenment epistemology, from John Locke to the *Encyclopédie* by way of Étienne Bonnot de Condillac, namely, the genealogy of the development of the faculties of the individual taken in isolation, and the development of the species as a whole. This continuity between social and individual development appears most explicitly as the foundation of the conjectural argument presented by Condorcet in the first epoch, but it underlies the movement of the whole argument. "If this same development is considered in its results, relative to the mass of individuals who coexist in a given time and place, and if it is followed from generation to generation, it then presents the *tableau* of the progresses of the human mind. This progress is submitted to the same general laws as are observed in the individual development of our faculties."[15] The laws of history are grounded in the laws of individual psychology; just as each individual becomes progressively more knowledgeable and reasonable, so can the species, with the added advantage that the progress of the species is not limited by mortality. In an early draft, Condorcet stated this portion of his argument in a clearly developmental form:

> In the midst of events governed by the hazards of wars, subject to the influence of physical revolutions, the human species has become what the necessary development of human faculties demanded that it become; . . . its present state, and those through which it has passed, are a necessary consequence of the moral constitution of man.[16]

It is important to note, however, that this continuity expresses an isomorphism rather than an identity, and that Condorcet must therefore still make his argument on several levels at once. If the developmental paths of individuals, of individual sciences, and of the species as a whole follow the same laws, they do not occur at the same pace. Each has its own rhythm and its own measure. Condorcet thus must distinguish between "the progress of science itself, whose only measure is the number [*somme*] of truths that it contains," and "that of a nation in each science," measured in terms of the number of citizens who know these truths as well as by the number of truths they know.[17]

This distinction presents Condorcet's argument with its first important difficulty, which it will convert into a major dialectical resource. The problem is that it is possible that what aids science as such does not aid its spread, or conversely that doctrines that are not themselves true can contribute to the spreading of truth. Scholastic logic, for example, "did not lead to the discovery of truth," but the sharpening of intellectual faculties that it entailed "was the primary origin of philosophical analysis, which since has been such a rich source of our progress."[18] Likewise, "the very audacity of [Descartes'] errors served the progress of the human race."[19] Finally, the use of Latin for scientific communication makes it easier for scientists themselves to keep abreast of recent developments but renders it nearly impossible for the public to do so. Thus the use of the vulgar languages "made the sciences more popular," but at the price (at least in the short run) of their absolute development. But, Condorcet goes on to argue, this popularization is ultimately necessary to their continued absolute progress.

> The existence of a sort of scientific language, the same in all countries, while the people of each spoke a different one, would have separated men into two classes and perpetuated prejudices and errors among the people . . . ; in thus holding back the progress of the mass of the human race it would have finished, as in the Orient, by putting an end to those of the sciences themselves.[20]

Social ills in general and violence in particular are always presented by Condorcet as the product of ignorance and error. "All errors in politics and ethics are based on philosophical errors," Condorcet insists, "which themselves are linked to errors in physics. There exists neither a religious system nor a supernatural extravagance that is not founded on an ignorance of the laws of nature."[21] Partially this is due to Condorcet's optimistic anthropology, which refuses to give evil a positive character of its own: evil is simply ignorance, the absence of enlightenment. But equally important is the "sociology of error," as Keith Baker calls it,[22] in terms of which this dynamic plays itself out historically. The key event of the first epoch, determinant for the rest of human history, is the formation of a priestly class that transforms knowledge into a secret and institutes "the separation of humanity into two parts, the first destined to teach and the second to believe."[23] An interest in ignorance and falsehood is thereby created, and the priests and their various avatars will figure as the villains throughout the rest of the story. Condorcet's interpretation of the decadence of the sciences in China, for example, is based on a critique of allegorism as the characteristic of a clerical caste that attempts to monopolize knowledge.[24] More than error itself, which can be corrected, it is religion, which transforms error and the ignorance of the many into an interest and a source of power for the few, that is the fundamental figure of social evil for Condorcet. Thus it is of crucial importance to Condorcet to insist on an equal right of all to the truth as the most fundamental of the rights of man. The distinction between the progress of a science and the progress of a nation in that science is thus only provisional; in the end progress must regain its unity. It is this overall identity of human progress toward which the argument constantly tends. Progress is a totality; the development of philosophy, and the development of science, politics, and morals, are completely interdependent.[25]

With respect to the specific question of the influence of the Enlightenment on the Revolution, Condorcet's explanation is extremely clear, and it presents a number of features that, as we have seen, have since become unavoidable topoi. While other causes contributed to the form of the Revolution, philosophy is the ultimate cause, the principle at stake. Condorcet summarizes the origins of the Revolution as follows: "The incompetence of the government precipitated this revolution; philosophy directed its principles; the people's force destroyed the obstacles that could have halted its movement."[26] Intellectual causes are everything here, from the lack of necessary enlightenment on the part of the monarchy to the fundamental conformity of *la force populaire* with the principles of philosophy.

Condorcet's analysis of this conflict between two forces, one enlightened and the other obscurantist, begins by positing three degrees of enlightenment operative in modern society: that at which philosophy has arrived, that reached by the cultivated public, and that of the government. The key central term, the enlightenment of the cultivated classes, mediates between philosophy as such and the actions of the government. The formation of common enlightenment, "a new kind of forum [*tribune*]" or "public opinion,"[27] is largely due to the appearance of the *philosophes*, "a class of men less concerned with discovering or with exploring the truth than with spreading it; who . . . placed their glory in the destruction of popular errors."[28] Opinion always lags behind philosophy, and the government lags even further behind opinion, but an influence is definitely present. If there was always, in absolutist Europe, a considerable distance between the truth and public opinion, and an equal or greater distance between public opinion and the government, still they followed one another, and public opinion formed the means by which philosophy could have some effect on public affairs.[29] Nevertheless, truth was continually forced to do battle with prejudice, and absolutism, even if occasionally enlightened, remained despotic and as such tied to religion and obscurantism generally. In the end it would necessarily rediscover its opposition to public opinion. "Despotism too," writes Condorcet, "has its instinct; and this instinct had revealed to kings that men, after having submitted religious prejudices to the examination of reason, would soon extend this examination to political prejudices; that being enlightened with respect to the usurpations of the popes, they would end by wanting to be enlightened with respect to the usurpations of kings."[30]

The approach of the Revolution is described by Condorcet as an acceleration of this influence, which "suddenly ceases to be slow and imperceptible."[31] The first step is the closing of the gap between philosophy and opinion. This represents not only an advance in the truth-content of opinion but also an increase in the number of men and women to whom such a degree of enlightenment is available. Condorcet's summary of the basic contents of this public opinion on the eve of the Revolution can be taken as a list of the basic doctrines of the Enlightenment:

> [A] general knowledge of the rights of man, even the opinion that these rights are inalienable and imprescriptible, a strongly pronounced wish for the freedom of thought and of the press, for that of commerce and industry, for the relief of the people, for the abolition of any criminal law against dissident religions, for the abolition of torture and of barbaric punishments; the desire for a softer criminal legislation, for a jurisprudence that would give complete security to innocence, for a simpler civil code, more in conformity with reason and nature; indifference toward religions, at last placed among superstitions and political inventions; hatred of hypocrisy and fanaticism, contempt for prejudices, zeal for the propagation of enlightenment.[32]

This advance in opinion makes the distance between it and the government increasingly problematic. An equilibrium between opinion and government must be established and the gap closed—and rapidly. If reform did not come quickly, the people would be forced to take matters into its own hands. "Either the people itself was going to establish these principles of reason and nature, which philosophy had been able to endear to it, or governments would have to make haste to render this unnecessary, and would have to regulate their course upon that of opinions."[33] The government therefore found itself faced with a choice between reform and revolution. The revolutionary option would be faster and more complete, but it would also necessarily be "stormy" and would require what Condorcet calls, in a substantial understatement given the circumstances under which he was writing, "passing ills [*maux passagers*]." It is important to note that in Condorcet's conception the entire responsibility for these ills falls upon the government, which chose the revolutionary path—it "precipitated" the Revolution—on account of its "ignorance and corruption."[34] The revolution is therefore violent because it must overcome the prior violence of despotism. Because despotism is a system, "the revolution had to embrace the whole economy of society, change all social relations, and penetrate to the last links of the social chain."[35] This radicality (going to the roots) gives the French Revolution a degree of universality—that is, of truth—that the American Revolution did not have, inasmuch as, in Condorcet's view, it was based on the identity of interests rather than the equality of rights. But this radicality also meant that the French experience could not be peaceful. Not only did it have to change everything but it also had to do it at one time.

This same emphasis on speed is to be found in the key texts of the following fall that "institutionalize" revolutionary government. The decree of October 10, 1793, making "the provisional government of France revolutionary until peace," states in particular that "revolutionary laws must be executed speedily" and that "since the inertia of the government is the cause of reverses, the periods for execution of decrees and measures of public safety are fixed. Violation of such periods shall be punished as an attack on liberty."[36] The report proposing this decree, presented by Louis-Antoine de Saint-Just, criticizes bureaucratic inertia and the proliferation of paperwork, arguing that it is necessary to govern "laconically." Further, the report justifies the suspension of the constitution by arguing that it "would lack the necessary violence" to protect itself from attack; instead, "the sword of the law must go forth everywhere at once [*il faut que le glaive des lois se promène partout avec rapidité*]."[37] The need for revolutionary government is consubstantial with the war, both internal and external; Robespierre defines revolutionary government as "the war of freedom against its enemies" or as "the war of freedom against tyranny."[38]

It will come as no surprise to say that the difference between reform and revolution is one of speed. Violence would seem to be a function of the velocity of history. When Karl Marx, for example, described violence as the "midwife of every society that is pregnant with a new one," he like Condorcet represents revolutionary violence as the acceleration of the inevitable. In "so-called primitive accumulation," writes Marx, we can see "the concentrated and organized force of society [i.e., state power]" employed in order to "hasten, as in a hothouse, the process of transformation of the feudal mode of production into the capitalist mode, and to shorten the transition."[39] The day before the expulsion of the Girondins from the Convention, Condorcet published an article entitled "Sur le sens du mot révolutionnaire." In it he accepts the increasingly prevalent distinction between revolutionary and ordinary periods of government. By revolutionary laws, he writes, "are understood those laws . . . that are not among those appropriate for a peaceful society, but that have the distinguishing characteristic of being proper only to a time of revolution, even though they would be harmful or unjust in another time."[40] Obviously it is better to have only laws whose justice is eternal and unconditional, but it is permissible, for example, to restrict the freedom of commerce in subsistence goods in times of need, even though freedom of property is a basic right. Such measures are specifically justified by the state of war and the existence of a counterrevolution that falsely speaks the language of rights. The key point, however, is speed: "Let us make revolutionary laws," he concludes, "but in order to hasten the moment when we will no longer need to. Let us adopt revolutionary measures, not in order to make the Revolution longer or bloodier [*prolonger ou ensanglanter la Révolution*] but to complete it and precipitate its end."[41]

Obviously this text is written under the pressure of circumstances, but the emphasis on problems of temporality is clearly in agreement with the discussion of the role of haste in the *Esquisse*. Elsewhere, Condorcet writes that the application of the universally valid rules of social science to particular historical circumstances must be adjusted following temporal criteria: "Reason must be firm without being abrupt, systematic without being dogmatic, inflexible and rigorously precise in all that is permanent, indulgent and moderate in everything that must last only as long as it is necessary to achieve a new order."[42] Because Condorcet's conceptual system is fundamentally based on the development of continuously operating causal factors, revolution can appear only as a question of acceleration.

THE ENIGMA OF VIRTUE IN ROUSSEAU'S FIRST 'DISCOURS'

When Condorcet summarizes his argument by asserting that "the progresses of enlightenment and those of freedom, of virtue, of respect for the natural rights of man . . . , so often separated that they have been believed to be incompatible [*qu'on les a crus incompatibles*], must on the contrary become inseparable,"[43] the impersonal *on* of this sentence is necessarily translated into English by an agentless passive. In fact, however, it has a precise reference: Rousseau's *Discours sur les sciences et les arts*. Condorcet explicitly praises the *Contrat social*,[44] but the first *Discours* is strictly inassimilable:

We will prove that these elegant declamations against the arts and sciences are based on a false application of history; and that on the contrary the progress of virtue has always accompanied that of enlightenment, as the progress of corruption has always followed or announced its decadence.[45]

In many ways, the first *Discours* is one of the simplest and most straight-forward of Rousseau's works. The brevity of the text, imposed by the structure of the academic prize competition for which it was written, combined with an unwavering concentration on the polemic, gives it a clarity that, at least on first reading, many of Rousseau's later texts refuse to yield. It has accordingly attracted much less critical attention than a text such as the *Discours sur l'origine de l'inégalité*, which operates at a significantly higher level of complexity. Whereas the argument of the latter text can be difficult just to paraphrase, there are no such problems in the case of the first *Discours*. Rousseau responds in the negative to the question posed by the Academy of Dijon. He accuses the arts and sciences (understanding "arts" in a modern sense, as including literature, and not as restricted to the liberal and mechanical arts of eighteenth-century bibliography) of having contributed, wherever they have flourished, to the degradation of morals. Their cultivation produces a misplacement or reversal of values. Aesthetics has displaced morality in our judgments of both men and their actions. "We no longer ask about a man whether he has probity, but whether he has talents; nor about a book whether it is useful, but whether it is well written" (*Discours sur les sciences et les arts*, p. 25). Not only does this displacement distract men from pursuing virtue; more fundamentally, the psychic dispositions that make it possible, and that it fosters in turn, are incompatible with those necessary for the cultivation of virtue. In the first half of the text, the logic used to establish this claim is purely inductive; Rousseau limits himself to establishing, by means of historical examples, a constant relation between the two phenomena. In the second half, Rousseau presents a more deductive (or conjectural) approach, based on a consideration of the arts and sciences "in themselves," or rather, of their origins, their objects, and their effects.

Against Condorcet, but in exactly the same manner, Rousseau claims for his thesis the regularity of a law of nature. "The daily rise and fall of the Ocean's waters have been no more regularly subject to the course of the Star which lights our night sky than the fate of morals and probity has been to the progress of the Arts and Sciences. Virtue has been seen to flee just as their light [*lumière*] has risen on the horizon, and the same phenomenon has been observed at all times and in all places" (p. 10). What is most important to Rousseau at this stage of the argument is primarily the inevitability of the connection between the two phenomena, not the precise order of causality. Indeed, the order of causality is fundamentally reversible, as can be illustrated by considering the crucial role attributed to mediating third terms such as luxury, which participate to some extent in both the arts and the degradation of morals. In a single paragraph Rousseau will present several possible constructions of the position of luxury in relation to the arts and moral corruption. "Worse evils yet follow upon arts and literature. One such is luxury, born like them of the idleness and vanity of men. Luxury is rarely found without the arts and sciences, and they are never found without it [*D'autres maux pires encore suivent les Lettres et les Arts. Tel est le luxe, né comme eux de l'oisiveté et de la vanité des hommes. Le luxe va rarement sans les sciences et les arts, et jamais ils ne vont sans lui*]" (p. 19). If the first sentence implies that the arts are the cause of evils such as luxury, the second one places the arts and luxury on the same level, as the common effects of a single cause. The third and last sentence, by establishing at least the possibility of luxury without the arts (but not of the arts without luxury), would seem to reverse the initial proposition and make luxury itself the causal agent.[46] A confirmation of this point can be seen in the critique offered by Jean-François de La Harpe of Rousseau's causal reasoning, which inadvertently ends up restating Rousseau's major point.

> Rousseau's first work is the most elegantly written and least estimable of all. . . . The erroneous principle that reigns in this *Discours* consists in the supposition that the progress of the arts and sciences and the corruption of morals, which ordinarily go together, stand in the same relation as cause and effect. Nonsense. Man is not corrupted because he is enlightened; but when he is corrupted he can, in order to add to his vices, use the same enlightenment that could have added to his virtues. Corruption follows upon power and riches, and power and riches produce at the same time the arts that embellish society.[47]

La Harpe's final statement could in fact stand as a summary of Rousseau's entire argument. Once the regularity of the connection is granted, the precise order of causality is not necessary. What this indicates is that we are not dealing with a linear ("billiard ball") sort of causality, but with an expressive causality in which each element of a system expresses the system as a whole, and therefore any given element can equally well be described as the cause (or ground of intelligibility) of any other.[48] The relation between the decline of morals and the progress of the arts and sciences is mediated by the totality of which they are both parts, in this case culture rather than nature.[49]

Rousseau begins the critique of the arts and sciences as a critique of hypocrisy. This theme is announced by the second epigraph, drawn from Horace: *Decipimur specie recti* (We are deceived by the appearance of right).[50] Everyone in modern society is polite, but that does not mean they are virtuous. Politeness is a "uniform and perfidious veil" that renders it impossible to tell the good man from the wicked one. Hypocrisy is thus a lack of connection between inner and outer, between "exterior countenance" and "the dispositions of the heart." It is an antiexpressive system. Rousseau does not leave us in this state of uncertainty for long, however. Clarity is restored as soon as the opposite, expressive principle—namely, virtue—is introduced. Virtue is indeed defined precisely as the correspondence of inner and outer, that is, as expression.

> It is in the rustic garb of a plowman, and not the gilded clothes [*la dorure*] of a courtier, that one can find the force and vigor of the body. Adornment [*la parure*] is no less foreign to virtue, which is the force and vigor of the soul. The good man is an athlete who prefers to fight in the nude: He despises all those vile ornaments that would interfere with the use of his forces, most of which were invented only to hide some deformity. (p. 8)

Virtue is a moral force that can be recognized by the simplicity and directness with which it is necessarily expressed ("necessarily" meaning both that it cannot be expressed by other, more roundabout paths, and that it does not exist if it is not expressed). What this definition implies, in turn, is that politeness—which begins as indirect, ambiguous behavior that does not necessarily express anything in particular—can never be the outer appearance of virtue and therefore invariably hides treachery. This means, precisely, that treachery can never really hide. The metaphorical system therefore functions, in the end, with complete clarity on both sides. On the side of the simplicity of morals, virtue is necessarily recognized by its expression. On the side of luxury, the movement is converse: the *oisiveté* and *mollesse* of the body is a sure sign, and cause, of that of the soul. The hermeneutical and moralistic problem from which Rousseau begins is thus easily solved, as can be measured by the movement from the "foreigner" who, looking at our arts and manners, "would guess our morals [*mœurs*] to be exactly the opposite of what they truly are" (p. 9), to the "barbarians" who, seeing civilized morals, have consciously decided to reject the arts and sciences: "They were not ignorant of the fact that in other countries idle men spent their lives arguing about the supreme good, about vice and virtue . . . ; but they considered their morals [*mœurs*] and learned to disdain their doctrines" (p. 12). This quest for clarity is particularly well expressed in a passage of the "Réponse à Stanislas," in which Rousseau takes to task La Rochefoucauld's maxim that "hypocrisy is an homage that vice renders to virtue."[51] My adversary, he writes, "asks if I would prefer that vice show itself openly. Most assuredly I would. Confidence and esteem would be reborn among good men, one would learn to be wary of the wicked, and society would be more secure" (p. 51).

This denunciation of hypocrisy is not particularly original. As Jean Starobinski has noted, the thematics of being and appearance that form the vehicle for so much of the argument had wide and deep roots in the literary and rhetorical culture of the time. One of the clearest ways to measure this is simply to note how heavily Rousseau relies on Michel de Montaigne's *Essais* in the *Discours*, referring to him directly half a dozen times and drawing equally many examples from him. The concept of Spartan or early Roman virtue used by Rousseau is no more of an innovation.[52] Indeed, these borrowings did not pass unnoticed. In a version of what Sigmund Freud called the logic of the kettle, Rousseau describes himself as being simultaneously accused of having said things that no one, himself included, could believe, and of having said nothing that had not been said before.

> You say that I am reproached for my paradoxes. Well, Madame, so much the better! Be sure that I would be much less reproached for paradoxes if I could be reproached for errors. Once it has been proven that I think differently from the multitude [*le peuple*], lo and behold, I stand refuted? A very saintly monk named Cajot, on the other hand, has just published a fat book proving that my books contain nothing that is my own and that I have said nothing that others haven't said before. I think that my only response will be to let his Reverence fight it out with those who reproach me so loudly with wanting to think differently from everyone else.[53]

This points us to the central paradox of the reception of the first *Discours*, which was universally praised for the power of its rhetoric but which seems to have actually convinced almost no one. If it was true that, as Denis Diderot wrote to Rousseau, "everyone is completely overwhelmed by it [*Il prend tout par dessus les nues*]; there has never been a success like it" (*Confessions*, p. 363), this success would seem to have been limited to the establishment of literary celebrity and a reputation for "paradoxical" brilliance. Diderot's account of the origin of the *Discours*, in which Rousseau asks Diderot which side of the question to take, reinforces this image of Rousseau as a *rhéteur* who could have just as easily defended the *pour* as the *contre*.

> The Academy of Dijon proposed as the subject for its prize, *Whether the arts and sciences are more harmful than useful to society*. I was then in the chateau of Vincennes. Rousseau came to see me and used the opportunity to consult with me about which side of the question he would take. "Don't hesitate," I said to him. "You'll take the side no one will take." "You're right," he responded; and he went to work accordingly.[54]

The discomfort with Rousseau's argument, or perhaps with his way of advancing it, is most frequently expressed by the conviction that he does not sincerely believe the point of view he has taken. This reaction groups the first *Discours* with the second, along with the *Lettre sur la musique française* and the *Lettre à d'Alembert sur les spectacles*, all of which are perceived as "paradoxes" designed to bring Rousseau celebrity rather than to advance a serious philosophical argument. Samuel Taylor's extensive study of the polemical literature surrounding Rousseau's early writings indicates that "dominating all the individual refutations of Rousseau's paradoxes was a growing belief that these paradoxes did not at all represent Rousseau's private beliefs. . . . In fact, not one commentator has been encountered in over 200 works of the period who accepted the discourse paradoxes as Rousseau's sincere belief."[55] Thus Stanislas of Poland wrote, "It is clear to see that he does not believe what he feigns to want to persuade the reader of," and the *Journal encyclopédique* described Rousseau as a man "not in the least persuaded by what he wanted to maintain."[56]

Although Rousseau's sincerity has ceased to be a pressing question for criticism, his contradictions have not. And this perplexity on the part of his contemporaries can easily be seen to be the transposition, into a vocabulary of intention, of the more fundamental question of whether or not we are meant to take the first *Discours* literally. In particular, the question that this poses is that of the referential status of Rousseau's historical examples. In this respect, the contemporary tendency to associate the two *Discours* is particularly interesting.[57] As is well known, the state of nature in the *Discours sur l'inégalité* is explicitly characterized as a methodological fiction, "a state which no longer exists, which perhaps never existed, and which probably never will exist, but of which it is necessary to have a correct understanding in order to properly evaluate our present condition" (*Discours sur l'inégalité*, p. 123). The state of nature in the second *Discours* provides a regulative ideal that serves as a point of comparison allowing us to measure the denaturalizations produced by the development of society.[58] This implies that Rousseau's fiction in that work is hypothetical, that is, explanatory, without being conjectural in the strict sense, that is, an account of what "most likely" happened. Can the various periods of virtue described by Rousseau in the *Discours sur les sciences et les arts* be taken in the same way? There certainly are moments in the earlier text that seem to approach this sort of fictionality by way of the vocabulary of nostalgia and the elegiac tone that, in Rousseau, are invariably associated with it.

> It is impossible to reflect on morals without taking pleasure in recalling the image of the simplicity of the earliest times. It is a fair riverbank [*un beau rivage*], adorned by the hand of nature alone, toward which we incessantly turn our eyes and from which we take leave with regret. When men, virtuous and innocent, loved to have the Gods as witnesses of their acts, they lived together under the same primitive roofs. (*Discours sur les sciences et les arts*, p. 22)

This image, which ties together simplicity of morals and transparency of hearts in a specifically rustic natural setting, forms one of the generative matrices of Rousseau's imagination; it prefigures *La Nouvelle Héloïse* as much as the *Discours sur l'inégalité*.

If we were to consider the periods of virtue to be fictions like that of the state of nature, the element that would at first seem to be affected would be the correspondence between being and appearance, between the "dispositions of the heart" and the "exterior countenance" whose separation Rousseau denounces in order to begin his critique. In this case the "ease of reciprocal penetration" that, by contrast, marks the ages of virtue, would not be false but rather ideal. That is, it would have (only) a normative value, allowing us to see the opacity of our social relations as factitious and unnatural. What would be deceptive, on the other hand, would be the historical narration of the *Discours*, for it would serve only as a tool for denouncing the separation between "doing good [*bien faire*]" and "speaking well [*bien dire*]" (p. 30), which would have in fact existed at all times and in all places. The historian would then be nothing more than a mask for the most traditional—and unhistorical—of moralists.

However, there are important differences between the periods of virtue in the first *Discours* and the state of nature in the second that should not be overlooked. First of all, the relative concreteness of the former—that is, the use of proper names (Sparta, Athens, Rome, etc.), which can be correlated with dates, maps, and other historical documentation—confers on them a certain degree of referentiality that can never be entirely vacated. But in and of itself, the description of an ideal through a historically attested example does not deprive that example of regulative value. Perhaps even more important, then, is the simple fact of the plurality and particularity of these examples, in contrast with the unity or even universality of the state of nature. Fragmented and dispersed in space and time, the state of virtue, rather than preceding all history, would have to enter into the narrative of universal history at a number of points. While Rousseau states in very explicit terms at the end of the first part and again in the opening lines of the second part of the *Discours* that he is shifting from empirical to conjectural modes of analysis,[59] this is reflected in the text more by an increased prominence of causal linkages than by an abandonment or even change in register of the historical examples adduced.

Nevertheless a consistent pattern is established in which the state of virtue always stands at the beginning of a historical development. This pattern would lead from simplicity of morals to virtue, from virtue to military prowess, and from military prowess to conquest and glory. At this point the downward trend of the cycle begins, for the elements that favor the development of the arts and sciences appear, leading to the decadence of morals. This decadence in turn results in subjugation to another people, one presumably still engaged in the upward movement of the cycle.

> The Romans confessed that military virtue was extinguished among them as they began to verse themselves in paintings, engravings, gold-worked vases and to cultivate the beaux-arts; and as if this famous land was destined always to serve as an example to the other peoples of the earth, the rise of the Medici and the restoration of letters caused the repeated and perhaps irreversible loss of the military reputation that Italy seemed to have recovered a few centuries ago. (p. 23)

This is in fact the history of all great powers as recounted by Rousseau. They owed their greatness to their virtue, but lost that virtue when they began to cultivate the arts and sciences. History—the history of nations—would thus be, fundamentally, the repetition of a single error.

Disengaging this cycle clarifies some issues. Rousseau's treatment of the classical notion of a historical cycle of the rise and fall of states (an idea to which he will return more explicitly in the *Contrat social*), combining as he does the internal cycle with the idea of a (potentially repeatable) migration of virtue, and exemplified by the relation between Rome and Florence, draws most directly on Niccolò Machiavelli's adaptation of Polybius in the *Discorsi sopra la prima deca di Tito Livio*.[60] Machiavelli would also be the likely source for Rousseau's continual insistence on the importance of military virtues and the critique of "the renowned valor of all these modern warriors, so knowledgeably disciplined," in the name, presumably, of citizen militias (p. 23). For Rousseau as for Machiavelli (although probably for different reasons), civic virtue is thoroughly militarized and conquering. As the force of the soul, virtue must seek expression as literal force. While he would later renounce any glorification of military aggression, the logic of Rousseau's argument here necessarily leads him to identify virtue with a desire for conquest. "The only talent worthy of Rome," exclaims Rousseau's Fabricius, "is that of conquering the world and making virtue reign in it" (p. 15). Indeed, Machiavelli's liberation of *virtù* from the Christian virtues would appear to be the major historical precondition of the first *Discours*.[61] The restatement of this position by Charles de Secondat, baron de la Brède et de Montesquieu, in the Avertissement to *De l'esprit des lois* is one that Rousseau will remain faithful to in *Du contrat social*: "What I call *virtue* is the love of the fatherland, that is, the love of equality. This is neither a moral virtue nor a Christian virtue; it is *political* virtue."[62]

But this Machiavellian cycle poses questions that are more fundamental. In Polybius and his modern followers (including, with important differences, both Machiavelli and Montesquieu), the idea of cyclical instability gives rise to a quest for stability in the form of a theory of mixed constitution.[63] Sparta, whose legendary durability was attributed by Machiavelli, following Polybius, to both the *virtù* of Lycurgus and the mixed character of her institutions, is also the one state mentioned by Rousseau whose decadence is not discussed. But Rousseau does not attribute this to anything but virtue; institutional solutions of this sort are never mentioned in the text. Indeed, nothing could be further from Rousseau's later political thought, as expressed in the *Contrat social*, than the doctrine of the mixed constitution, whether in the form of perpetual class warfare to which Machiavelli attributes the maintenance of Roman institutions and virtue or the system of checks and balances described by Montesquieu in his discussion of England.[64] The traditional patterns for conceiving the possibility of republican stability would seem to be ruled out. Nor, on the other side, is any real role given to a concept like *fortuna*. The explanation of corruption can be given only in terms of the self-relating activity of virtue itself. The question would then become, is the cultivation of the arts and sciences intentional and therefore a mistake that could be avoided, as Rousseau often seems to present it, or is it in fact a necessary consequence of virtue? How does this cycle relate to the overall structure that regulates the argument, namely, the opposition between interior and exterior or doing and saying?

The historical aspect of the *Discours*, instead of simply opposing virtue and hypocrisy, links them within a single narration (however often it may be repeated, it remains the same story) that cannot be understood without the intervention of causal connections. Thus each half of the narration presents a stable metaphorical system within which causality is expressive, but the narrative transition from one half of the system to the other (the moment when corruption begins) can no longer be described in metaphorical or expressive terms. This moment, which we have called the repetition of an error, is not at all mimetic. Effect does not resemble cause; end does not resemble origin. Thus it is not finally intentional. The famous prosopopeia of Fabricius—"Fools, what have you done?" (p. 14)—is fundamentally a disavowal of the possibility that a virtuous intention could recognize itself, or be recognized, in the cultivation of the arts and sciences. Nor can it be understood as a structural consequence of virtue insofar as virtue has been described as a metaphorical system of expression. The moment of transition can be considered only as the breakdown of any metaphorical system. Virtue suddenly ceases to express itself in a natural way and turns instead to the arts and sciences, which cannot in the least be understood as its expression. Instead of occurring according to the metaphorical model of force and expression, or the homologous development of the parts of a totality, the history of the loss of virtue is based on a fundamental discontinuity between cause and effect. This discontinuity can be translated into intentional terms only as an error. But the repetitive pattern of this error as the inevitable fate of nations shows that it is not a mistake that could have been avoided, or that might be avoided in the future now that its threat has been noticed. It is the breakdown of historical progress as such, of the narrative of cause and effect. Rousseau does not describe an error that has occurred repeatedly in history, but history as the repetition of an error.

In later years Rousseau was to express his dissatisfaction with his first book, calling it "completely lacking in logic and order" (*Confessions*, p. 352). It represents a negative moment in the development of Rousseau's thought, being, as Rousseau put it in the *Dialogues*, "more concerned with destroying the illusory prestige that gives us a stupid admiration for the instruments of our miseries" than with the construction of his own system (*Dialogues*, p. 934).[65] Rather than constructing a theory of the discontinuity of political history, the *Discours sur les sciences et les arts* merely states and restates the breakdown of linear or metaphorical narratives.

The full development of these problems will thus have to wait for later texts. But two important points can be asserted based on our preliminary argument here. The first concerns the location of the incompatibility between Rousseau's system and Condorcet's. If the theme of persecution allowed Condorcet's model a certain amount of dialectical flexibility, in the long run the system depends upon a homology between political and intellectual history, supported by the fundamental unity of human progress and ultimately by a synecdochal continuity between individual development and that of society. In a first moment, Rousseau seems to have maintained this homology and simply inscribed it in an inverse ratio: As knowledge increases, virtue decreases. But in a second moment, Rousseau destroys the homology without, however, allowing political and intellectual history simply to go their separate ways. In the *Dialogues*, Rousseau described the fundamental insight of his earliest works in the following terms: "While admiring the progress of the human mind he was astonished to see public calamities grow in the same degree. He caught a glimpse of the secret opposition that exists between the constitution of man and the constitution of our societies [*En admirant les progrès de l'esprit humain il s'étonnait de voir croître en même proportion les calamités publiques. Il entrevoyait une secrète opposition entre la constitution de l'homme et celle de nos sociétés*]" (p. 828). What is important is not that Rousseau asserts this "secret opposition" as a premise of his political system but that the *Discours sur les sciences et les arts* installs this discontinuity within the main causal articulation of political history, which then appears as a repeated failure of understanding.

Secondly, and as a consequence of this point, any possibility of considering Rousseau as the "author of the Revolution," to return to Louis-Sébastien Mercier's phrase, has become significantly complicated. Any narrative articulation of Rousseau and the Revolution would have to be marked by a constitutive moment of misunderstanding or negativity. In the speech by Robespierre with which we began, it is the familiar and quintessentially Rousseauian motif of persecution that marks this function. It prevents Robespierre from actually attributing any influence to Rousseau as he does to the encyclopedists, even if it is the solitary victim rather than the influential philosophers who was truly in sympathy with the Revolution. But this adoption of the motif of persecution is merely the stand-in for a deeper problem. If we are to argue that the revolutionaries understood Rousseau's critique of genetic narrative, could they have claimed him as an origin? And if the Revolution failed to understand this critique, how could we consider him to be its author?

Scottish Gradualism and French Impatience

PERIODIZATION AND THE PROBLEM OF TRANSITION

The construction of narratives of universal history, recounting the movement of mankind from primitive barbarism to the civilized state of modern commercial society, played an equally prominent role in the development of Enlightenment thought in both France and Scotland, and without doubt constitutes the most important philosophical genre to be shared by the two nations. Although in France it may provide the overall organization for texts less often than in Scotland, the developmental narrative tends to insinuate itself everywhere and informs every sort of question, in part on account of its formal isomorphism with the genetic narratives of sensationist psychology and epistemology as developed by Locke and codified for France by Condillac.

I have chosen to take the term "universal history" from Turgot, rather than "conjectural history," which has been the most frequently used term in English-language scholarship since Dugald Stewart's comments in his *Ac-*

count of the Life and Writings of Adam Smith,[66] in order to emphasize problems raised by the integration of conjectural and empirical aspects of world history. In particular this allows for inclusion of texts such as book III of Adam Smith's *Wealth of Nations* (which Stewart considered closely related to the conjectural history problematic) and William Robertson's "Progress of Society in Europe," neither of which has anything properly conjectural about it. But we can best begin by looking briefly at two canonical statements of the distinctly conjectural "four-stages" theory, one French and one Scottish, in order to see what we can learn about the structure of the conceptual field from their differences. They are the two examples that Ronald Meek, in *Social Science and the Ignoble Savage*, claims are the earliest in each country, Smith and Turgot.[67]

Smith introduces the question at the outset of the *Lectures on Jurisprudence* (1762–63 text) as a way of accounting for different modes of acquisition of property. He begins with a simple statement of what the four stages are—the age of hunters, age of shepherds, age of agriculture, and age of commerce. He accounts for the transition from one age to another in terms of the pressure of expanding population. Thus, of the transition from hunters to shepherds he says, "In process of time, as their numbers multiplied, they would find the chase too precarious for support. They would be necessitated to contrive some other method whereby to support themselves."[68] Their first effort would be to "lay up" any surplus, but in the case of game that would have a limited efficiency; the best way to store meat is on the hoof: "The most naturally [*sic*] contrivance they could think of would be to tame some of those wild animals they caught." Domestication of animals requires less knowledge than does agriculture and therefore must precede it. The same principle is used to account for the subsequent transition: "But when a society becomes numerous they would find a difficulty in supporting themselves by herds and flocks. Then they would naturally turn to the cultivation of land." Agriculture is gradually learned through a process of observation of natural processes: seeing that a seed reproduces the plant it comes from, which kind of ground it grows best in, which kinds of plants are useful and worth cultivating. This leads, in the text of these lecture notes, very directly into the fourth stage.

> And by this means they would gradually advance in to the age of agriculture. As society was farther improved, the several arts, which at first would be exercised by each individual as far as was necessary for his welfare, would be sepa-

rated. . . . They would exchange with one another what they produced more than was necessary for their support. . . . This exchange of commodities extends in time not only betwixt the individuals of the same society but betwixt those of different nations. . . . Thus at last the age of commerce arises.[69]

We should note that in the case of the transition from agriculture to commerce there is no need to appeal to the principle of population growth. Once the division of labor has been introduced, this is both unnecessary and impossible, since the fact of exchange implies a certain form of surplus.

Turgot introduces his conception of the stages of society in two manuscripts dating from the 1750s, the "Plan d'un ouvrage sur la géographie politique" and the "Plan de deux discours sur l'histoire universelle."[70] Both of these texts are projects: at points they are very detailed, but fundamentally they provide a list of topics to be discussed rather than extended arguments. Most explicitly in the "Géographie politique," but also in the "Histoire universelle," Turgot gives a great deal of attention to the making and unmaking of empires, which seems to me to reflect a lingering element of the theological background of Turgot's project.[71] The mixture of different peoples is part of the same theme, which concerns the creation of a real universality (or catholicity) in the course of history, capable of serving as a support to the diffusion of universal ideas. The text of "Géographie politique" presents seven *mappemondes*, which are defined as cross-sections (*coupes*) of universal history. The majority of these cross-sections deal with known rather than "conjectural" history, mostly ancient. The third section begins with the formation of the first known civilizations in China, the Near East, and Greece, followed by sections on the age of Alexander and the Roman republic and empire. The seventh and final *mappemonde* presents a schematic movement from the barbarian invasions to present-day Europe. Thus only the first two sections are "conjectural," and as the second deals entirely with the formation of government, the classification of modes of subsistence takes place entirely within the first *mappemonde*. In much the same way, when Smith reintroduces the question of stages later in the *Lectures on Jurisprudence* to account for the development of government, he in fact uses the theoretical model only for the first two stages. When he reaches the point where he should discuss agriculture he shifts to an empirical, if exemplary, discussion of the history of ancient Greece. From this point onward his discussion remains focused on strictly European (and in the end British) developments.[72]

The stadial model likewise occupies a restricted place in the "Plan de deux discours sur l'histoire universelle." The second of the two planned discourses is entirely devoted to intellectual history; as it takes its point of departure in a genetic account of sensationist psychology, it is parallel to rather than integrated within politico-economic history. Commerce, for example, appears as a way in which new discoveries and truths are universalized, but there is no question of the influence of the economic basis of society. And much of the first discourse is still devoted to the rise and fall of empires. Nevertheless this text is worthy of our attention not only on account of the early date for a stadial theory but also because of the analysis of the movement between stages. In Turgot as in Rousseau, the original state is one of dispersal of mankind in the forests.

> Without provisions, in the midst of the forests, men could only be concerned with subsistence. The fruits that the earth produces without culture are of too little account; it was necessary to have recourse to the hunting of animals which, being few in number and incapable of supplying food for a large number of men in any one district, thereby accelerated the dispersion of peoples and their rapid diffusion.[73]

The inefficiency of hunting as a means of subsistence thus functions first and foremost as a limit to population growth in a given area. The causality here is the reverse of what we saw in Smith. Rather than population growth necessitating a change in the mode of subsistence, a change in the mode of subsistence is necessary for population growth. Turgot proposes what amounts to a theory of the unequal distribution of nature's gifts, in which it is availability or ease that allows for a new mode of subsistence.

> There are animals who allow themselves to be domesticated by men, such as cattle, sheep, and goats, and men find it more advantageous to bring them together into herds than to chase after wandering animals. The pastoral way of life did not take long to be introduced wherever these animals were to be found. . . . The way of life of hunting peoples was preserved in the parts of America where these species are lacking. . . . Pastoral peoples, having more abundant and more certain subsistence, were more numerous.[74]

This moment marks for Turgot the introduction not only of property but also of a social surplus and therefore of a class not directly engaged in the production of subsistence. The movement to the next stage follows much the same logic. "The pastoral peoples located in fertile lands were doubtless the first to pass to the agricultural state." Agriculture produces an even greater social surplus, to such an extent that everything that Smith separated as a stage of commerce is already contained, for Turgot, in the invention of agriculture.

> Moreover, among [agricultural peoples], the land nourishes many more men than are required to cultivate it. Whence come idle men; whence come cities, commerce, and all the useful and merely agreeable arts; whence comes the most rapid progress of every sort, for everything follows the general progression of the mind [*la marche générale de l'esprit*].[75]

Turgot's account emphasizes the relative ease with which these transitions are made when nature provides the opportunity by underlining the factor of speed, which can be seen in each of the above citations (*n'a pas tardé, ont passé les premiers, les progrès les plus rapides*), in striking contrast with the idea of gradualism associated with the Scottish school.

This brief comparison allows us to disengage three major problems. First, the nature of the motive force in the transitions between the first three stages can be characterized in terms of an alternative between the necessity of population pressure and the opportunity of natural abundance, with the explanatory advantages and disadvantages of each thesis primarily concerning the relations between the universality of the concept of human nature and the observable differences between human societies. Second, the transition between agriculture and commerce seems to be of an entirely different nature than the two preceding transitions. Finally, the integration (or the absence thereof) of "conjectural" and "empirical" history presents in both cases an important difficulty in the continuity of argument.

In the case of the first problem, the explanations given by Smith and Turgot are mirror reversals of one another. Smith's position, if only because of the tremendous influence his lectures seem to have had on other Scottish writers, is generally taken to be the orthodox view. Some sort of appeal to hunger as a universal motive force is inevitable in an account of subsistence. The strong version of such an argument, which sees a firm link between population growth and diminishing natural resources, is particularly well illustrated by Claude-Adrien Helvétius, and it can also be found in Hugo Grotius and Samuel Pufendorf, John Dalrymple, Henry Home, Lord Kames, and Smith himself.[76] David Hume's use of this sort of argument in "Of Commerce" is perhaps the boldest in that it completely reverses Turgot's argument by claiming that nature's bounty discourages civilization, and thus that it is only in regions where subsistence is difficult that progress occurs. Hume attributes the greater poverty of the French, Italian, and Spanish peasantry, in comparison to the English, precisely to the greater fertility of their soil. Where agriculture is easy there is no need to accumulate stock in order to improve the land. Generally speaking civilization is lacking in the tropics and present throughout the temperate zone. "It is probable that one cause of this phenomenon is the warmth and equality of weather in the torrid zone which render clothes and houses less requisite for the inhabitants, and thereby remove, in part, that necessity, which is the great spur to industry and invention. *Curis acuens mortalia corda.*"[77]

Thus the primary advantage of the argument presented by Turgot is that if population growth is posed as universal and inevitable, more or less a part of human nature, it becomes difficult to account for why some societies have not left the earlier stages. The thesis that changes in mode of subsistence occur because of population pressure requires, in order to explain Amerindian societies, something like the speculations of George-Louis Leclerc, comte de Buffon, on hairless chins as indicative of low sex drive.[78] Placing the difference in the gifts of nature allows for a flexible argument that maintains a concept of the universality of human nature developing differently in various geographical and climatic situations. This advantage can be clearly seen in Adam Ferguson's use of a similar thesis in the *Essay on the History of Civil Society*: "The circumstances of the soil, and the climate, determine whether the inhabitant shall apply himself chiefly to agriculture or pasture."[79] In both Turgot and Ferguson, we thus find what is as much a typology as a succession of social forms.

NATURAL SOCIABILITY, RECIPROCAL NEED, AND THE DIVISION OF LABOR

The lack of bounty in nature can function in a universal history of mankind only if it is understood not as a statement concerning physical nature itself but as the expression of an essential penury or indigence in human nature. This inscription of need as an original and enduring constituent of humanity can proceed, it seems to me, in two basic but closely related fashions. The first is to dynamize the concept: to recognize that the content of the notion of "need" is historically variable. We can see this sort of argument, once again, in Ferguson's *Essay*: "But even the increase of mankind which attends the accumulation of wealth, has its limits. The necessary of life is a vague and relative term: it is one thing in the opinion of the savage; another in that of the polished citizen: it has a reference to the fancy, and to the habits of living."[80] In Ferguson this argument goes hand in hand with the positive redeployment of the Augustinian critique of *divertissement*, so that happiness is to be found in striving itself rather than in a peaceful enjoyment of its results.[81] The implication, of course, is that no level of material culture can be considered to be intrinsically "happier" than another. We might also note that Ferguson's argument on this point is very close to the dialectic of need and passion developed by Rousseau in the second *Discours* after society has awakened *amour-propre* (again part of the vocabulary of seventeenth-century Augustinianism). Each man's estimation of his own "need" is determined comparatively based on what his peers enjoy. The key term in the Ferguson passage just cited is "fancy," echoed in Rousseau by "imagination." Need is no longer a physiological fact, but the infinity of desire regulated only by the imagination (which is to say, not regulated at all). For Ferguson this dialectic is at work from the beginning and is part of human nature, while for Rousseau it needs to be set in motion by "fortuitous" factors and is thus part of a peculiarly human drift away from nature. In both cases, however, the possibility of an assurance of a real progress in satisfaction or happiness disappears. Smith also gives a central place to a process of infinitization of desire, but introduces a crucial sectorial distinction between desire for foodstuffs and desire for manufactured goods. While the rich may desire and seek out ever more refined and delicate comestibles, it is not possible, beyond a certain limit, to continually desire, and especially not to actually consume, an ever-greater quantity of food. No limit, either quantitative or qualitative, however, can be placed on the desire for clothing, housing, and "conveniencies" (particularly "baubles and trinkets"). Thus agricultural surpluses must be shared in some form. "Those, therefore, who have the command of more food than they themselves can consume, are always willing to exchange the surplus, or what is the same thing, the price of it, for gratifications of this other kind. What is over and above satisfying the limited desire, is given for the amusement of those desires which cannot be satisfied, but seem to be altogether endless."[82]

It is also possible to make need an originary part of human nature—not dependent on nature's bounty in any empirical sense—by defining it as *mutual* need, a need for the assistance of others rather than for particular natural goods, and thus as a form of originary sociability.[83] This is the tack taken by Smith in the opening pages of the *Wealth of Nations*, when he founds the division of labor, which he has already characterized as the specific difference between "savage nations of hunters and fishers" and "civilized and thriving nations."[84] "The division of labor . . . is the . . . consequence of a certain propensity in human nature . . . , the propensity to truck, barter and exchange one thing for another." This propensity is immediately related by Smith to the lack of self-sufficiency of the adult human in contrast to all other adult animals. Man is continually in need of "the help of his brethren." He needs to persuade them to give him this help, and this persuasion takes the form of exchange: the necessity of appealing to the butcher's, brewer's, or baker's self-interest in order to gain his help.[85] Istvan Hont has usefully pointed to Pufendorf's discussions of the state of nature as an important source for Smith's argument here. Whereas animal life is characterized by uniformity of the species, limitation of needs, and a close match between those needs and the ability to satisfy them, human needs are neither finite nor uniform but rather insatiable, infinitely variable, and marked by a fundamental disparity with individual capacities for fulfillment. "The contrast between animal and human nature," writes Hont, "made co-operation between men an absolute necessity," and this cooperation (or sociability) expresses itself as *commerce*—that is, in Smith's words, "a mercenary exchange of good offices according to an agreed valuation."[86] This argument is formally almost identical to that made by Rousseau in the *Discours sur l'origine de l'inégalité*, with the crucial difference, as we shall see, that for Rousseau "natural man" is in fact an animal, that is, his needs are limited and their satisfaction lies within the reach of his individual capacities. In every case there is a key link between the diversity of human wants, the infinite and fundamentally unfulfillable character of desire, and sociability understood as interdependence. Interdependence and cooperation are thus rendered necessary less by any natural weakness as by the dynamic of emulation or mimetic desire, what Rousseau, in a passage translated by Smith in his "Letter to the Editors of the *Edinburgh Review*," calls living "in the opinion of others" (*Discours sur l'inégalité*, p. 193).

It is difficult to give a precise content to this need qua intersubjective in the earliest stages. But I would suggest that the rarity of subsistence goods as a function of competition can be seen as the projection of this intersubjective need back into the most primitive state. It would be useful to consider, in this regard, the passage in the *Lectures on Jurisprudence* where Smith describes the rarity of game as the effect rather than the cause of the institution of private property in the form of herds: "The appropriation of flocks and herds renders subsistence by hunting very uncertain and precarious. Those animals which are most adapted for the use of man, as oxen, sheep, horses, camels, etc., which are also the most numerous, are no longer in common but are the property of certain individuals."[87] More generally, we can say that the extension of the division of labor, while it increases opulence, reduces physiological need, but it simultaneously and essentially increases intersubjective need in the form of interdependence. If it solves one kind of need it is by replacing it with another. This somewhat "virtual" status of rarity makes it of crucial importance to see how the division of labor is operative at least in principle from the beginning of universal history, so that the progress of society and the progress of the division of labor are at every stage strictly identical. In the passage of the *Wealth of Nations* under consideration, Smith places the first steps of the division of labor in the age of hunters, where the first separate profession was that of armorer ("in a tribe of hunters or shepherds a particular person makes bows and arrows, for example, with more readiness and dexterity than any other"), followed by the carpenter, the smith, and the tanner.[88]

Furthermore, the noncontractual origin and nature of government, one of the other great themes of Scottish conjectural history,[89] can also be accounted for in terms of the extension of the division of labor. On the one hand, it is this process, in the form of the inequality of property from which it is inseparable, that makes government necessary.

> The age of shepherds is where government first commences. Property makes it absolutely necessary. . . . Certain individuals become very rich in flocks and herds . . . while others have not one single animal. . . . Laws and government may be considered in this and indeed in every case as a combination of the rich to oppress the poor, and preserve to themselves the inequality of goods which would otherwise be soon destroyed by the attacks of the poor, who if not hindered by the government would soon reduce the others to an equality with themselves by open violence.[90]

The institution of justice as a distinct social function permanently confided to certain individuals is also, in itself, a form of the division of labor. The increase in property and arts and manufactures operates a sort of pincers movement upon democratic justice, both increasing the number of cases of dispute and decreasing the amount of time individuals can devote to such matters.[91]

Most fundamentally, it seems to me that we can see this action of the division of labor as an expression of the definition of humanity in terms of intersubjective rather than physiological need in the status of the division of labor as the privileged, indeed essential example in Scottish conjectural history of the law of unintended consequences as a historical principle of gradualism. By "historical principle of gradualism" I mean to differentiate this use of the idea of unintended consequences from, on the one hand, the simple observation that the intentions of historical actors and the actual results of their actions seldom coincide, and, on the other, from the more providentialist notion of the "invisible hand," in which the self-seeking actions of individuals result in the good of all.[92] As a historical principle, gradualism asserts that the development of civilization(s) is not the result of great actions intending that effect (thus the critique of the adulation of law-givers such as Solon, Lycurgus, etc., as the founders of states that are ever after marked by the spirit of their foundation);[93] rather, it is the result of the accumulation of an infinity of particular actions. This can be clearly seen in the passage from the beginning of the *Wealth of Nations* cited above, which reads in full, "The division of labor, from which so many advantages are derived, is not originally the effect of any human wisdom, which foresees and intends that general opulence to which it gives occasion. It is the necessary, though very slow and gradual, consequence of a certain propensity in human nature which has in view no such extensive utility; the propensity to truck, barter and exchange one thing for another."[94] Smith emphasizes the importance of the technical rather than the social division of labor (i.e., the specialization of tasks within the production process) in his account of the increase in productivity that makes possible the progress of opulence, on account of increasing dexterity, time saved in moving from task to task, and, most important, inventions created by specialized workmen to economize on their own labor.[95] The entire debate over the relation between the primary causal factors of need sharpened by population growth and opportunity provided by natural abundance can thus be seen as resolving, in Smith, into the question of the status of the division of labor, which, even as it is grounded in an innate and original disposition of man, depends upon the extent of the market and the accumulation of capital. Need is originarily social (or, need is only natural to the precise extent that society is natural).

This puts us in a position to resolve our second question, concerning the difference between the transitions that occur between the first three stages and the transition between stages three and four. The birth and gradual extension of the division of labor (and the accompanying inequality of property) give rise to two qualitative changes in the form of society, from hunting and gathering to pastoral and from pastoral to agricultural. Even if these changes are slow and gradual, they are genuinely qualitative, that is, they involve a certain discontinuity or "revolution" in the kind of society in question. From this point on, however, change occurs as a purely quantitative extension of the division of labor, accumulation of capital, refinement of the arts, and so forth. The difference between agricultural and commercial societies is one of degree, not of kind, even though the principle of explanation has not fundamentally changed. Indeed, the relation between commerce and agriculture is perpetuated within all commercial societies, not merely as the atavistic survival of a previous mode of subsistence that continues to characterize certain "backward" or "underdeveloped" regions. It is instead the fundamental dialectic driving the economy: the commerce between town and country. "The great commerce of every civilized society, is that carried on between the inhabitants of the town and those of the country, [and] consists in the exchange of rude for manufactured produce."[96] The relations between agriculture and commerce must therefore be considered to be simultaneously historical and structural.

THE "UNNATURAL AND RETROGRADE ORDER"

This overlay of history and structure means that we have in fact reached the final problem posed by our initial comparison of Turgot and Smith, namely, the integration of conjectural with empirical history. In French texts this problem is most frequently played out in terms of intellectual history. In this case the fundamental problem is the Middle Ages considered as a period of obscurantism, in which scholastic philosophy tends to play the heavy, with respect to which it is necessary to account for the regression of enlightenment. As Bertrand Binoche has shown, Jean Lerond d'Alembert tries to avoid this problem in the "Discours préliminaire" to the *Encyclopédie* by beginning the empirical section with the Renaissance, providing no articulation with the genetic narrative of sensationist psychology and the logical development of knowledge that began the text. Binoche likewise describes Turgot as being torn between genetic and historical points of view, arguing that Turgot's project remained unfinished because it was unfinishable within the French problematic of the 1750s; the "Histoire universelle" indeed becomes increasingly sketchy with the fall of the Roman Empire.[97] The second problem posed by the Middle Ages to French universal history is how to guarantee against a new "barbarian invasion." This concern can be found in prerevolutionary texts like the *Encyclopédie*, which conceives of itself as a monument to civilization after its future demise. "A revolution may even now be burgeoning in some remote region of the world, or be smoldering in the center of a civilized country," wrote Diderot in the "Avertissement des éditeurs" to volume VIII. "Should it break out, destroy the cities, scatter the nations anew, and bring back ignorance and darkness, all will not be lost, if a single copy of this work survives."[98] This theme was to become a veritable obsession with thinkers after Thermidor who described the intervention of the Parisian populace into the Revolution in precisely those terms.[99]

Even while remaining within the sphere of economics, the historical sections of the *Wealth of Nations* confront a strictly analogous problem, which can be designated as the unnatural character of feudal economics (while Smith does not use the term "feudalism" here because he maintains a juridical, but not political or economic, distinction between the feudal and allodial forms of land ownership, it remains the best shorthand for us). In the "natural order of things," agriculture should precede commerce, for two reasons. The first concerns the satisfaction of genuine human needs taking a necessary priority over indulgence in luxury goods, which implies that agriculture must precede manufactures. "As subsistence is, in the nature of things, prior to conveniency and luxury, so the industry which procures the former, must necessarily be prior to that which ministers to the latter. The cultivation and improvement of the country, therefore, must be prior to the increase of the town, which furnishes only the means of conveniency and luxury."[100] The town subsists on the surplus production of the country. This priority is seconded by a theory of the natural order of capital investments, based on the degree of security of that investment, so that capital should flow first to agriculture (the most secure as well as the most aesthetically satisfying), then to manufactures, and lastly to foreign commerce, the most risky.[101] But in modern Europe, Smith says, this natural order has "been, in many respects, entirely inverted."[102]

What follows is a familiar account (one can find versions of it, most notably, in Hume's essay "On Commerce" [1752] and Robertson's Introduction to the *History of the Reign of the Emperor Charles V* on "The Progress of Society in Europe" [1769]) of the revival of the European economy beginning with the stimulation provided to the foreign commerce of the cities of Italy by the Crusades.[103] What is unnatural about this history in Smith's account is not the barbarian invasions themselves but the complications their results introduced into the European economy's recovery from them. The agricultural sector, in particular, was struck with a complete immobility, characterized by large properties, unimproved and often uncultivated, whose division was prevented by noneconomic factors (ownership of land as a basis of political power, perpetuated within families by primogeniture and entailment). The revival of the economy began with the foreign commerce of the Italian cities, which stimulated a taste for luxuries, which in turn provided a market for domestic manufactures. The increasing wealth of the towns stimulated agriculture by introducing freedom and good government, always favorable to economic growth, and providing an expanding market for subsistence goods. But most important, it offered trinkets and baubles to the great feudal lords, allowing them to dissipate their fortunes and leading eventually to the breakup of their estates. The part of this story that is specific to Smith concerns the role of luxury goods in the division of the great landed estates characteristic of feudalism. In the absence of manufactures, Smith argues, a great landed proprietor must maintain a large number of dependents—he literally has nothing else to do with his surplus, most of which must be consumed on the spot (and which, since it consists of foodstuffs, he physically cannot do himself). But with the introduction of luxury goods he can consume his surplus himself, and in so doing maintains manufacturers who no longer have a relation of direct dependence upon him. This same analysis, we should note, can be found in the *Lectures on Jurisprudence*, where it characterizes the great inequality of wealth of pastoral societies.[104]

When, in 1790, an abridged translation of the *Wealth of Nations* appeared under Condorcet's direction, Smith's account of the "unnatural and retrograde order" was summarized in an editorial addition forming a transition between chapters three and four of book III:

> Such are the principal causes that led, against the natural order of things, to the prosperity of the towns preceding that of the countryside. If the country had been cultivated by free men, this natural order would not have been inverted; the progresses of agriculture would have preceded those of commerce and manufacturing. But all of Europe was then covered with the hideous feudalism that France has just ripped out by the roots, and which seemed to have the goal of striking the ground upon which it was established with an eternal sterility. However deplorable its consequences may have been, they could not but be transitory, for sooner or later nature must recover her rights. When violence is

done to nature she withdraws into herself, so to speak, and takes a retrograde path in order to arrive at her goal.

[Telles sont les principales causes qui firent, contre l'ordre naturel des choses, que la prospérité des villes devança celle des campagnes. Si les campagnes avaient été cultivées par des hommes libres, cet ordre naturel n'eût pas été interverti; les progrès de l'agriculture auraient précédé ceux du commerce et des manufactures; mais la hideuse féodalité, dont la France vient enfin d'arracher les dernières racines, couvraient alors toute l'Europe, et semblait s'être proposé de frapper d'une éternelle stérilité, le sol sur lequel elle s'était établie: quelque déplorables qu'en aient été les suites, elles ne pouvaient être que passagères; car il faut tôt ou tard que la nature reprenne ses droits. Quand on lui fait violence elle se replie, pour ainsi dire, sur elle-même, et prend, s'il le faut, une marche rétrograde pour arriver à son but.][105]

In certain respects this passage captures the movement of Smith's thought quite accurately: the way in which nature reasserts itself against violent intervention is indeed one of the fundamental lessons of book III. And Smith certainly would have been happy to see the remnants of feudalism disappear. But given the form of his critique of François Quesnay, it is almost impossible to imagine Smith as approving the idea of ripping anything out by the roots.

Smith's own use of "unnatural" to characterize this order is clearly based on economic rather than historical principles.[106] The idea of nature here draws much of its force from Smith's advocacy of the "obvious and simple system of natural liberty." This liberty is above all that of capital investments; it is defined in opposition to those systems that try to direct capital investments to a particular sector either by "extraordinary encouragements" or "extraordinary restraints." From the perspective that concerns us here, the particular importance of this argument is that it is addressed to the relation between agricultural and manufacturing sectors, and argues that the growth of agriculture is in fact most effectively encouraged by the existence and growth of manufacturing.[107] This argument is directed against physiocratic policies aimed at diverting investment away from the "sterile" manufacturing sector, but it also has two important implications with respect to the "unnatural and retrograde order," which we can consider as reflecting the overlay of history and structure.

The first implication is that even if the situation were created by unnatural (illiberal) policy, the recovery from it was perfectly natural in that it was noninterventionist. Smith's paradoxical history in book III can thus be seen as the story of the way in which the natural order is in the course of re-asserting itself without the necessity of violent state intervention. For Smith, as Istvan Hont puts it, "the art of economy was not in superimposing the natural order on the actual one, but rather in discovering how natural prog-ress asserts itself, in an imperfect but nonetheless forceful way, through the complex development of unintended consequences."[108]

The second implication is that the logical (capital-investment) priority of agriculture is largely relativized. In a two-sector economy, the dearness of the products of one sector implies the cheapness of those of the other, meaning that high agricultural prices and encouragement to agricultural improve-ment come from the plenty of manufactured goods, and low agricultural prices and discouragement to agricultural investment result from the scar-city of manufactures.[109] The question of whether the availability of manu-factured goods (therefore presuming the existence of a substantial nonagri-cultural population) calls forth improvements in agriculture, or whether the generation of agricultural surpluses renders the development of a manufac-turing sector possible, has exactly the same logical form as the question with which our comparison of Smith and Turgot began—that regarding the rela-tion between population growth and changes in the mode of subsistence. Movement on either side presupposes movement on the other, a potential paradox that Smith resolves by insisting on the incremental, and therefore mutually supporting, nature of this movement. This situation, in which no definitive priority can be ascribed to either of two factors in a relation of re-ciprocal causality, seems to me to be paradigmatic for the "social sciences," where there is no effective means of isolating dependent and independent variables. The cautionary gradualism that Smith here opposes to Quesnay represents a response to this dilemma, a determination not to let either of the two factors be given too much priority, whether it be on the theoretical level of universal history or on the pragmatic level of economic policy. Rous-seau, as we shall see, responds to similarly structured problems by insisting on the impossibility of logical resolution.[110]

INTELLECTUAL COMMERCE

The priority that the "unnatural order" places on commerce as the location of this exchange between town and country allows for a thoroughgoing iden-tification of commerce and sociability itself. Most prominently in French—but in eighteenth-century English as well—"commerce" refers not only to trade but also to social interaction in general, as Albert Hirschman remarked in his influential discussion of the theme of *le doux commerce*.[111] In Robertson's version of the story, it is commerce as communication or interaction between nations rather than as a specifically economic process that accounts for its civilizing effects.

> The progress of commerce had considerable influence in polishing the manners of the European nations, and in leading them to order, equal laws, and humanity. . . . Commerce tends to wear off those prejudices which maintain distinction and animosity between nations. It softens and polishes the manners of men. It unites them, by one of the strongest of all ties, the desire of supplying their mutual wants. It disposes them to peace, by establishing in every state an order of citizens bound by their interest to be the guardians of public tranquillity.[112]

As Daniel Gordon has shown in a study of Jean-Baptiste Suard's French translations of Robertson, this orientation, identifying commerce with communication and feudalism with insularity—that is, the lack of communication—was crucial for an integration of his thought into preexisting French concerns. "Robertson treated commerce as a form of sociability rather than a selfish pursuit," Gordon argues. "The emphasis was on communication as a distinctive aspect of the commercial life. . . . By representing commerce as a particular species of *interaction* and by insisting that interaction in general was the motor of civilization, Robertson created a conceptual space into which urbane French men of letters could insert their own conversational ideals."[113] I would further suggest that insofar as it tends to imply such an approach, the "reversal" of natural order identified by Smith is necessary to integrate the results of Scottish thought into the orientation toward intellectual history characteristic of the French school.

I think that a particularly clear example of this form of integration can be seen in Jacques Peuchet's "Discours préliminaire" to the *Encyclopédie méthodique* volumes on "Police et municipalités," written in 1789 (and rendered immediately obsolete, and therefore doubtless without influence, by the events of that year).[114] This text, one of the most extensive and exhaustive if not original examples imaginable of the *doux commerce* thesis, cannibalizes—literally transcribes—large sections of Robertson's "Progress of Society in Europe" from Suard's translation, together with parts of the third book of the *Wealth of Nations*. Peuchet directly cites Smith's description of the rustic hospitality of the barons and his account of their downfall without ever mentioning the question of the unnatural order. Peuchet cites at length paragraphs five (the unimaginable extent of rustic hospitality), six (tenants in the same position of dependence as retainers), ten (diamond buckles), eleven (direct versus indirect maintenance), thirteen and fourteen (the relation between growing personal expenses, rents, and lease conditions), and seventeen (how this process illustrates the idea of unintended consequences) of chapter 4. Peuchet's version of this last paragraph considerably softens Smith's judgmental language:

> Voilà comme une révolution d'une grande importance pour le bonheur public, s'est faite par deux sortes d'hommes, qui n'avaient pas la moindre intention de rendre ce service à la société. Le seul motif des propriétaires était de satisfaire leur luxe et leur vanité; les marchands et les artisans agirent uniquement par des motifs d'intérêt, et ni les uns ni les autres ne prévoyait sûrement pas la suite qu'aurait ce nouvel ordre de choses introduit parmi nous.[115]

Peuchet thus stops his compilation of Smith just short of the restatement of the idea of the unnatural order in paragraph eighteen. The one mention of an unnatural order in Peuchet's text concerns intellectual rather than economic history. In a part of the text drawn directly from Robertson, he argues that as imagination precedes reason, for both nations and individuals, so should poetry precede philosophy; the premature efflorescence of scholastic philosophy in medieval Europe thus represents a perversion of this natural order.[116] Peuchet in fact finds nothing "unnatural" about the economic progression; he is, after all, concerned with *municipalités* and not agriculture. Civilization always begins in and is most advanced in the city (home of the *civis*): site of the market, seat of government, and birthplace of good manners (urbanity). "An active consultation of history," writes Peuchet, "reveals that great capitals, commercial states, and sea-going peoples have always been ahead of their time in civilization and enlightenment."[117] This priority given to commerce and urbanization leads Peuchet to a direct critique of stadial theory:

> This is a common fault of a great many writers on the origin of society, into which the *economists* in particular, even the most intelligent among them, are particularly prone to fall. They claim that peoples were first *hunters*, then *fishermen*, and finally *agriculturalists*, and that in this final state entire nations, spread out over a vast expanse of territory, gave themselves laws and calculated and then adopted a system of government favorable to the right of property.

But history gives the lie to this philosophical construction. All the civilized peoples that exist were formed from the union of tribes [*peuplades*] each living under a municipal discipline [*discipline de cité*], a particular municipal police, owing its origin to the coming together of brigands for the purpose of war, and subsequently civilized by the need for order and subordination, even in the midst of their rustic and barbarian manners [*mœurs agrestes et barbares*].[118]

The most interesting part of the text is the theory of public opinion elaborated in the opening pages (here Peuchet pillages Jacques Necker's *De l'administration des finances*). Unlike the *morale publique* of the ancients, which was directly expressed in their "hard and ferocious" manners and institutions and could therefore never generate a critique or reform, modern public opinion is characterized by the irreducible gap between it and existing customs and institutions. In contrast to modern public opinion the *morale publique* of the ancients allowed for no gap between customs and ideas. "The *morale publique* of the ancients was never in contradiction with their manners [*mœurs*]; on the contrary, their more or less hard and ferocious manners were its expression and its practice. Among us, to the contrary, public opinion very often castigates usages, laws or customs that are stubbornly maintained contrary to the sentiment of the nation."[119] It thus allows for a process of reform, not only of institutions but also of the manners of the people. It also has a strong conservative tendency, due primarily, it seems to me, to the slow character of its action. On the one hand, it is "the strongest pillar of order, the guide and guardian of *police* and manners."[120] Moreover, its political effectiveness can be most clearly seen in its opposition to the "precipitous operations" of overambitious reforming ministers. Because it works slowly, it is better suited to temperate monarchies than to the tempestuous character of republican liberty.

The most important French version of this understanding of the slow movement of public opinion can be found in Benjamin Constant's attempt, in a series of texts written beginning from the Thermidorian period, to formulate a republican critique of revolution, focusing particularly on the temporality of revolutionary change.[121] The most famous aspect of Constant's political thought centers on the opposition between ancient and modern forms of liberty, which is based in turn on an opposition between martial and commercial societies and the associated critique of the Rousseauian enthusiasm for participatory democracy. Because modern societies are based on commerce rather than on war, the sacrifice of individual liberty demanded by the public liberty of the ancient city-state is profoundly anachronistic. "We can no longer," writes Constant, "enjoy the liberty of the ancients, which consisted in an active and constant participation in collective power. Our own liberty must consist of the peaceful enjoyment of private independence."[122] Seduced by the resurrection of the ideal of ancient liberty in the works of Gabriel Bonnot de Mably and Rousseau, the Revolution attempted to violently impose a form of liberty that was neither desirable nor possible. Constant's opposition between ancient and modern liberty is historical as well as historicist. It is not simply the opposition between two political ideals, but rather between two states—the two states—of society. Despite the fact that Constant refers most frequently to the seductive ideal of the ancient city-state, precisely because it is the attractive face of antiquity, the system on which it is based includes all precommercial societies. Not only Greece and Rome but also the savages of the New World, the barbarian legions, and the feudal Middle Ages were or are societies of conquest.

With respect to the four-stages model of the civilizing process, Constant has exercised a radical simplification. He does not consider the mode of production. Rather, his classification is based on the mode of exchange, specifically foreign exchange. Commerce and conquest are two modes of getting goods and services from foreigners. "War and commerce are only two different means of reaching the same goal, that of possessing what one desires. Commerce is simply a tribute paid to the strength of the possessor by he who aspires to possession. It is an attempt to gain by mutual agreement what one can no longer hope to obtain through violence."[123] Commerce arises as a lesson of experience, of learning that war is as easily lost as won. The opposition between ancient and modern liberty is thus subtended by one between civilization and barbarism, which places the key transitional moment in European history at the end of the Middle Ages. It should therefore come as no surprise to see Constant adopt the Thermidorian vision of the intervention of the Parisian populace in the French Revolution as a barbarian invasion.[124]

More interesting for our purposes here is Constant's attempt to establish an equilibrium theory of revolution and counterrevolution. One of Constant's earliest attempts to understand the temporality of revolutionary violence is the pamphlet *Des réactions politiques*. This pamphlet was written during the Thermidorian period as part of a campaign to rally support to a conservative republicanism—that is, to a consolidation of the gains of the Revolution and a refusal of both counterrevolution and further revolution.

Constant begins this work with a theory of the origins of revolutions as the need to reestablish an equilibrium between government and public opinion that closely resembles that proposed by Condorcet, for whom, as we have seen, the operation of public opinion was a major factor in accounting for the outbreak of the Revolution.[125] Constant's account shares the same basic vision of the causal relation between enlightenment, public opinion, and political institutions that Condorcet presented, but he is seeking to elaborate a course of political action that will establish republican principles without recourse to revolutionary measures. This requires approaching the question of public opinion as one of the management of the velocity of change.

> In order for a people's institutions to be stable, they must be at the same level as its ideas. Then there are no revolutions in the proper sense of the term. There may be shocks, individual reversals, men dethroned by other men, parties beaten by other parties; but as long as ideas and institutions are on the same level, the institutions subsist. When the harmony between institutions and ideas has been destroyed, revolutions are inevitable. They tend to reestablish this harmony. This is not always the goal of revolutionaries, but it is always the tendency of revolutions.[126]

It is possible, Constant argues, for a revolution to achieve this balance immediately, the Dutch and American revolutions being the examples he gives. But revolutions are also prone to go on too long and to go too far, to establish institutions that are "beyond" public opinion and to destroy institutions that are still in conformity with it. In this case what Constant calls a reaction is produced, a counterrevolution that is also trying to reestablish harmony but that is also prone to go too far. "The French Revolution, which was made against privilege, having gone beyond its goal by attacking property, a terrible reaction made itself felt."[127] Violence can thus be described as the result of either prematurity or anachronism, a failure to be of the age. It is not at all a question of the truth of the reigning ideas, only of the consequences of being out of step. The revolution can thus be said to have tried to go too fast, and precisely on this account to have lasted too long.

De l'esprit de conquête et de l'usurpation develops this analysis of the role of public opinion in the context of the opposition between ancient and modern forms of society. The bulk of the book is often described as showing the influence of Edmund Burke. But in a chapter added to the fourth edition, Constant makes a plea not for respect for tradition as such and presumption of its higher rationality but for the virtues of slowness. Public opinion has become more or less totally divorced from truth and has regained the fickleness that characterized "her" before the late Enlightenment. Constant notes that

> Public opinion appeared to have long demanded several of the improvements that the [Constitutional] Assembly attempted to enact. Too eager to please it, that gathering of enlightened but impatient men did not think that they could go too fast or too far. Yet public opinion was infuriated by the haste of its own interpreters. It drew back, because those interpreters wanted to drive it forward. Delicate to the point of capriciousness, it is irritated when its vague aspirations are taken for orders.[128]

Scottish gradualism, it would seem, is translated into the French context as a theory of the slow, or even slowing, action of public opinion as the form in which enlightenment acts on politics. It is important to note that such a theory is based on a modernist vision of history—it is neither traditionalist, nor, I think, prudential. Going slowly is not a precaution dictated by uncertainty about the content of reforms but rather by an understanding of the specific negative effects brought about by haste. For Constant's moderns, liberty is to be found not only in the formal independence from the government but also in a substantial independence that is expressed by the constant presence of a disequilibrium between the principles of government and public opinion. Such a disequilibrium will inevitably appear as a sort of oscillation, meaning that what Constant calls "reactions" are a constitutive feature of modernity. The desire for the liberty of the ancients expressed above all the desire to stop this oscillation and produce a definitive identity between public opinion and political practice. It can therefore be described as a more or less inevitable ideological production of the liberty of the moderns. By an identity of extremes characteristic of revolutionary thought, the way to stop the oscillation is to speed it up absolutely.

The Problem of Historical Causality in the 'Discours sur l'inégalité'

THE STATE OF NATURE

Rousseau has a catastrophic—which is to say, discontinuous—view of historical progress. The problem of causal discontinuity can be most easily illustrated by the *Discours sur l'origine et les fondements de l'inégalité parmi les hommes*. Rousseau's second *Discours* is structured around a formidable internal opposition that often appears as a contradiction. The first half of the text describes the state of nature as one that natural man had neither the means nor the motive, on his own, to leave; since nothing in this state can explain its end, an appeal must be made to external, "fortuitous causes." The second half, on the other hand, relates a hypothetical account of how natural man did indeed become civilized, and does so with great narrative continuity in that the primary explanatory factor would seem to be the slow development of man's moral and intellectual capacities. The key to this apparent contradiction then lies in the fact that these moral and intellectual capacities, among which are perfectibility and freedom, reason, pity, love, and all the passions, are at the beginning merely potentialities. In the state of nature they are latent or virtual. Civilization, understood as a process, consists primarily in the activation or awakening of latent faculties, giving rise to a concurrent development of the passions, reason and enlightenment, technology and social structure, in which the development of each factor reinforces and encourages that of each of the others.

Rousseau's argument that this process was not necessary (and thus that the transition from nature to culture is not inscribed in human nature) is based on his definition of the state of nature in terms of a postulate of individual self-sufficiency. Natural man is strong and healthy; his needs are few in number and easily satisfied. The immense forests through which he wanders alone, far from his fellow man, provide an inexhaustible bounty. Infirmities such as childhood, sickness, and old age affect him no more than other wild animals and much less than civilized man. His robust temperament (those who are born without one die young) implies, on the one hand, an insensibility to both physical discomfort and the refinements of the senses, and on the other, highly developed abilities in combat and flight and acute senses wherever they are useful in the procuration of food or in self-defense. He thus needs neither clothing and shelter to protect him from the elements, nor does he need tools: his body is his "only instrument." Natural man depends on no thing outside himself. He always has "all his forces at his disposal" and "always carries his entire self around, so to speak, with himself [*se port[e] toujours . . . tout entier avec soi*]" (*Discours sur l'inégalité*, p. 136).

Moreover, and more important, natural man depends on no one outside himself. The satisfaction of these needs implies neither repeated conflict nor lasting cooperation with other individuals. The combination of natural bounty and human dispersal (which are logically interdependent, indeed functionally equivalent concepts in Rousseau's argument)[129] remove both the occasion and the need for such "sociability." Even more important than his nonreliance on tools is his nonreliance on his fellows; natural needs are always within the capacity of the individual. Rousseau formally excludes the foundation of natural sociability on man's originary need for what Smith was to call the "help of his brethren." His needs never give rise to any form of dependence. As Rousseau repeatedly insists, the situation of natural abundance implies that the ability of the strong to amass more food, or to deprive the weak of food or shelter, cannot prevent the weak from seeking more food or another shelter elsewhere. As long as we remain in the state of nature, "natural inequality" (differences in strength, intelligence, or beauty) cannot develop into relations of dependence or servitude.

> The bonds of servitude being formed only upon men's mutual dependence and the reciprocal needs that unite them, it is impossible to subjugate [*asservir*] a man without having first made him unable to do without [*se passer de*] another man; and as this situation does not exist in the state of nature, everyone remains free from the yoke, and the law of the strongest is rendered vain. (p. 162)

This adequation between the needs and capacities of natural man depends not only on the bounty of nature and the dispersal of men; there are also key mental (or "moral," as Rousseau more often says) limitations that are necessary for this circular relation to be maintained. If natural man feels "only his true needs" and has "only the sentiments and the enlightenment necessary to [his] state," as Rousseau writes in a summary passage at the end of the first part of the *Discours*, it is because he is "subject to few passions" (p. 160). If the passions are born of need, they also are always going beyond it, reaching toward previously unnecessary objects. Natural man has no passions in the true sense; he desires only according to the "impulsions of nature." "His desires do not go beyond his physical needs," namely, nutrition, sex, and rest (p. 143). He has no knowledge of, and is incapable of imagining, any greater goods. This limitation of desire to necessity is what allows desire to remain focused upon what natural man is capable of accomplishing alone. And this is why he is happy. As the *Émile* puts it, "A sensitive being whose faculties were equal to his desires would be an absolutely happy being" (*Émile*, p. 304).

Natural man's fear is as limited as his desire. Like every animal, he fears pain and hunger, but not death, which he cannot conceive of because he has no imagination. Living entirely in the present, in a world of pure sensation, with neither projects nor foresight, he is incapable of change on his own. "His imagination paints nothing to him; his heart demands nothing of him. . . . His soul, agitated by nothing, yields itself to the sole sentiment of his present existence, without any idea of a future, however close it may be, and his projects, as limited as his views, hardly stretch as far as the end of the day." One of the most important and repeated goals of Rousseau's argument about natural man's mental life is to dampen the action of any principle internal to the state of nature that might account for leaving the state of nature. "Who does not see," he asks, "that everything seems to distance savage man from the temptation and the means of ceasing to be savage?" (*Discours sur l'inégalité*, p. 144).

This does not mean that such principles do not, in some sense, exist. Natural man has a number of faculties which, while an essential part of his humanity (one cannot define the difference between man and beast without reference to them), are nonetheless merely virtual or potential (*en puissance*)—that is, inactive—in the state of nature. When Rousseau defines natural law, he insists that what is paradoxical in the conjunction of the two terms be taken with full seriousness.

On the one hand, he refuses to admit Montesquieu's definition of law as "the necessary relations that derive from the nature of things,"[130] and insists that the term be restricted to the sense of the prescription of a rule. This implies that law is necessarily addressed to a "moral being" characterized by intelligence and freedom: men have laws but the beasts do not, because the former have freedom where the latter have instinct. If all animals, including man, have a principle of self-conservation, the difference lies in the fact that

> Nature alone does everything in the operations of the beast, whereas man participates in his own operations in his capacity as a free agent. The first chooses and rejects by instinct, and the second by an act of freedom, which means that the beast is unable to depart from the rule that nature has prescribed for him, even when it would be to his advantage, while man often does so to his prejudice. . . . It is thus not so much the understanding that constitutes the specific distinction of man among the animals as the quality of being a free agent. Nature commands every animal, and the beast obeys.

Man feels the same impression, but he recognizes that he is free to acquiesce or to resist. (pp. 141–42)

The proof of freedom is always to be found, for Rousseau, in negative examples, in the ability to defy Nature and go against one's own best interest. While formally distinct from freedom (Rousseau introduces it as "another quite specific quality"), "perfectibility," the one among the virtual faculties that "with the aid of circumstances, successively develops all the others," is established according to identical arguments (p. 142). The specificity of natural as opposed to civilized man can in this way be described in terms of his appearing to be an animal like any other. Perfectibility distinguishes him, but the distinction remains potential, and because perfectibility remains merely potential, because it has not yet been awakened, natural man acts as if he had instinct.

This "as if" indicates the other side of Rousseau's argument concerning natural law, his insistence that it be truly natural. The error of all previous writers on the subject, Rousseau argues, is that they have assumed that man in the state of nature is capable of deducing natural law through a complex series of reflections; they have thereby made of him a "great reasoner and a profound metaphysician." On the contrary, insists Rousseau, if a law is to be considered natural it must be addressed to men who have not yet learned how to reason. "Not only, for it to be a law, must the will of he who is obligated by it be able to submit to it knowingly; but it is also necessary, for this law to be natural, that it speak immediately with the voice of nature." Rousseau proposes "two principles anterior to reason" that meet this test and therefore form the basis of natural law, namely, *amour de soi*, or self-conservation, and pity, "a natural repugnance to see any sensitive being [*être sensible*], and in particular one of our kind, perish or suffer" (pp. 125–26). The combination of these two principles allows one to found natural law without any recourse to the notion of natural sociability.

Rousseau shared this interest in the action of pity with most of his contemporaries. The entire current of eighteenth-century thought classified under the rubric of "sensibility" is characterized by a shift away from a moral dualism in which the passions need to be restrained or suppressed by the agency of reason, and a concomitant promotion of the passions in general, and pity or compassion in particular, as a natural foundation or motivation for moral action. Because their impulsion is so strong, a doctrine of virtue founded on this rehabilitation of the passions promises to be substantially more efficacious, in any case much more optimistic about the possibility of virtuous action in this world. New analyses of the moral import of the passions can be seen in certain schools of sermonizing in both France and England beginning in the last two decades of the seventeenth century,[131] and in the course of the eighteenth century they appear in such diverse sites as the sentimental novel and the materialist epistemology and psychology of thinkers such as Diderot and Helvétius.[132] One of the clearest examples of Rousseau's participation in this current can be found in his argument in the *Émile* that, as the passions were given to us as part of our nature by God, they cannot be considered corrupt.[133]

> Our passions are the principal instruments of our conservation: Destroying them is therefore a project as vain as it is ridiculous. If God were to tell man to do away with the passions He had given to man, He would both will and not will something; He would contradict himself. Never did God give such a senseless command; nothing of the sort is inscribed in the human heart. What God wants man to do, He does not have announced by another man; He announces it himself by writing it in man's heart. (*Émile*, pp. 490–91)

Indeed, in this passage from *Émile*, Rousseau presents pity primarily as a social virtue. Émile begins to feel it only as he enters adolescence, and even though pity is the "*first* relative sentiment that touches the human heart in the order of nature," it is indeed a relative sentiment, one that depends on a certain degree of knowledge, reflection, and comparison (p. 505). The passion of pity would seem, in some measure, to represent the social within nature and the natural within society.[134]

Rousseau most often refers to pity not as a passion, or even a virtue, but more simply (less specifically) as a "sentiment" or an "impulsion." It is prerational and prereflective in its origin. It is first and foremost an expression of our sensibility, that is, the fact that we are subject to pain and pleasure. Since this is a feature that we share with all other animals, it is part of our animal nature. Indeed, the beasts participate in pity in two ways: not only do we feel pity for animals, who like us are capable of suffering, but even animals show occasional signs of pity for one another (*Discours sur l'inégalité*, pp. 126, 154). On the other hand, this "pure movement of nature" survives the end of the state of nature and continues to exist, if in an attenuated form, in the social state. Even "the most depraved manners [*mœurs*] can hardly destroy it." It is even characterized by Rousseau in the *Discours* as the source of all "*social* virtues":

> Indeed, what is generosity, clemency, or humanity but pity applied to the weak, to the guilty, or to the human species in general? Even benevolence and friendship are, properly understood, the products of a constant pity, fixed upon a particular object.

The socialization of pity thus involves a certain transformation of its action. Rousseau characterizes this transformation with a set of carefully chosen, and carefully balanced, adjectives. For the savage, pity is an "obscure and lively sentiment," whereas for civilized man it is "developed but weak." Natural pity is purely reactive: it occurs only in the present, at the sight of the current suffering of a fellow-being. Even if it does not result in any action (in many of Rousseau's examples the pathetic character of the scene is heightened by giving the spectator who feels pity no way of remedying or even meliorating the suffering to which he reacts), the sentiment itself is imperious. Social pity, however, is reflective rather than reactive. Reflection develops the sentiment, applies it to events that are not currently under our eyes, brings in analytic categories that have nothing to do with the scene of suffering itself (the weak, the guilty, the species), fixes it permanently on particular individuals and, in its noblest expression, turns repugnance at suffering into a continual and active concern to prevent it. None of this development would be possible without a reflective use of the imagination. But at the same time reflection weakens pity by allowing the spectator to feel his difference and distance from the sufferer.

> Commiseration will be all the more energetic as the spectator identifies more intimately with the suffering animal. But it is evident that this identification must have been infinitely closer in the state of nature than in the state of reasoning. It is reason that engenders *amour-propre*, and reflection that fortifies it; it is reason that turns man back upon himself, that separates him from everything that bothers him and afflicts him. (pp. 155–56)

Reflection is what allows man to resist the voice of nature. The philosopher can sleep tranquilly while murder is committed outside his window because his reason can arm his *amour-propre* with arguments against identification, above all by turning the movement away from the suffering individual and toward the good of humanity as a whole.[135] Because natural man is incapable of this sort of argument he is incapable of resisting the impulsion to identify with the sufferer and, if possible, to come to his aid.

This difficulty for natural man to distance himself from his own feelings returns us to the fundamental problem of the definition of natural law. It is pity, Rousseau writes in the conclusion to this discussion, "that, in the state of nature, takes the place [*tient lieu*] of laws, morals [*mœurs*], and virtue, with the advantage that no one is tempted to disobey its gentle voice" (p. 156). Rousseau must say that pity "takes the place" of law because the fundamental characteristic of law, in the sense that he gives to it, is that it can be disobeyed. Pity, in the state of nature, functions *as if* it were an instinct, that is, a law expressive of "necessary relations" rather than a commandment that requires a free act of acceptance or rejection in response. It may be the case that the instinct of self-preservation will be stronger and will silence pity, but this is a matter of the relative strength of two impulsions and not of rational deliberation leading to a free choice. The example of pity demonstrates that natural man remains ignorant of his own freedom. This ignorance stems from the absence of a number of crucial mental operations that allow pity to develop: in particular imagination, which alone allows for a relation to the future, and comparison, which allows for the movement outside of ourselves that identification implies to be perceived as such.

Immediately following the section on pity, and extending its analysis, is a treatment of the difference between love in the natural and civilized states. Need in its natural form is indifferent to the specific object that satisfies it. Just as food is food and shelter is shelter (and as long as there is more, being deprived of this food or that shelter is a matter of no real consequence), for natural man, Rousseau writes in a fairly brutal formulation, "any woman will do [*toute femme est bonne pour lui*]." Jealousy is therefore impossible and cannot give rise to any conflict. The "moral" aspect of love, in opposition to this purely physical level, is "what determines this desire and fixes it exclusively upon a single object." This fixation is a "factitious sentiment," created by women in a reversal of the one order of domination that Rousseau appears to regard as natural. This sort of durable attachment that excludes other attachments—that is, a passion—is based, writes Rousseau, "on ideas of merit and beauty that a savage is incapable of having and on comparisons that he is incapable of making" (pp. 157–58).

The closed circle of needs and capacities that defines primitive man's physical nature is maintained by the closed circle of needs and desires that defines him on the moral level. It is only when natural desire is replaced by passion that new, artificial "needs" are created that are not immediately within natural man's capacities. Needs, like "impulsions" such as physical love and natural pity, relate to objects primarily in terms of their generic qualities. Passions, on the other hand, simultaneously specify and multiply their objects. This double movement is that of comparison, which allows for the particular qualities of individual objects to be distinguished from those of other objects that are similar with respect to fulfilling needs, but it also introduces a relativization of desire. Civilized man, that is, not only compares objects but also compares himself as desiring subject to other desiring subjects; he has an "ardent desire to raise his relative fortune, less out of veritable need than to place himself above the others" (p. 175).

For Rousseau as for the whole eighteenth century, comparison (of sensations, or of the compounded sensations that are ideas) is the fundamental intellectual operation. In the case of love, the inability to make comparisons is specifically identified with an absence of imagination. "The imagination, which causes such disorders [*ravages*] among us, does not speak to savage hearts; everyone peacefully awaits the impulsion of nature, gives in to it without choice and with more pleasure than furor, and once need is satisfied, all desire is extinguished" (p. 158). But comparison is also the fundamental operation of reason. It is, for example, the major factor in Rousseau's description of concept-formation as a linguistic process in the digression on the origin of languages in the *Discours*, as well as in the longer treatment of that topic in the *Essai sur l'origine des langues*. As we shall see, comparison plays a key role in the development of civil society in the second half of the *Discours*. Most important at this moment in our analysis, comparison constitutes the fundamental difference between *amour de soi* and *amour-propre*, which is in turn the fundamental difference between natural and civilized man.

Amour de soi is in fact merely the principle of self-conservation, and hence another name for the adequation of needs, means, and desires that defines the state of nature. *Amour-propre*, on the other hand, "is only a relative and factitious sentiment, born in society, which impels every individual to consider himself more important than anyone else [*faire plus de cas de soi que de tout autre*]." *Amour-propre* represents the socialization of desire, the investment of objects in terms of the value placed upon them by others. Because it is comparative it is infinite; it knows no lasting satisfaction and no rest. Rousseau excludes the passion of *amour-propre* from the mental life of primitive man based on exactly the same argument by which he excluded "moral" love: he is incapable of making comparisons.

> I claim that in our primitive state, in the true state of man, *amour-propre* does not exist; for since each man in particular looks on himself as the only specta-tor observing him, as the only being in the universe who takes an interest in him, as the only judge of his own merit, it is impossible for a sentiment whose source lies in comparisons that he is not capable of making, to take root and grow in his soul. (note XV, p. 219)

The distinction of civilized from primitive man can thus be described in terms of the addition of the mental operation of comparison, that is, the transition from *amour de soi* to *amour-propre*. Insofar as the passions are dis-tinguished from needs by *amour-propre*, and *amour-propre* in turn is funda-mentally a rational calculation, this transition is what allows for the simul-taneous development of reason and the passions. It therefore makes man aware of his freedom precisely in the moment that it subjugates him to the opinion of others and creates the possibility of his economic and political subjugation. "Such is, in fact, the true cause of all these differences: the sav-age lives within himself; sociable man only knows how to live in the opin-ion of others, and it is, so to speak, from their judgment alone that he draws the sentiment of his own existence" (p. 193). The analysis of the transition from the state of nature to civilization must therefore begin with the ques-tion of the birth of comparison.

TRANSITIONS

The second half of the *Discours*, we have said, shows how man did "in fact" leave the state of nature. This "in fact" designates merely the irrefutable fact that we today find ourselves, irreversibly, outside of the state of nature. Rous-seau is quite willing to admit that the details of the narrative he tells are con-jectural and, as such, uncertain. But, he argues, this uncertainty (or mere probability) of detail does not affect the conclusions he draws. Once his def-inition of the state of nature has been admitted, the basic character of any imaginable path from it to civilization will be the same.

> Beyond the fact that these conjectures become reasons when they are the most likely that can be drawn from the nature of things, and the only means that are available to discover the truth, the consequences that I intend to deduce from mine will not themselves be at all conjectural, since, on the basis of the princi-

ples that I have just established, one could not form any other system that would not give the same results, and from which I could not draw the same conclusions. (p. 162)

If the state of nature is indeed the closed circle of self-sufficiency that Rousseau has described, any narrative of civilization will necessarily be a story of denaturalization rather than development. If we agree that the state of nature contains no principles that account for its end, then the causal factors that must be introduced will necessarily be external and fortuitous with respect to the state of nature itself. This is what leads Rousseau to characterize every major narrative articulation in the second *Discours* in some way as the crucial moment of denaturalization. That is, the principle of external causality seems to operate continuously, even if the claim is often (if not always) made that a single intervention would suffice.

Perhaps the most famous, and certainly the most dramatic (that is, polemical) moments are the denunciations of intentional frauds perpetrated by the rich upon the poor. It is in fact with such a moment that the second half of the *Discours* begins. "The first man who, having enclosed a plot of land, took it into his head to say, *this belongs to me*, and found other men simple-minded enough to believe him, was the true founder of civil society" (p. 164). This initial moment clearly shares a formally identical structure, in addition to the large overlap in content, with the description, later in the text, of the institution of civil government. It is precisely in order to protect his property against attacks by the poor that the rich man proposes laws and government. Since his wealth has no foundation in natural right and does not provide him with strength sufficient to overcome the superior numbers of the poor, the rich man "at last" conceives of "the most carefully considered project [*le projet le plus réfléchi*] that ever entered a human mind"—that of making his natural adversaries into his defenders by substituting property right for natural right. "Let us unite," says the rich man, "in order to guarantee the weak from oppression, to contain the ambitious, and to assure to each man the possession of what belongs to him." Rousseau characterizes the discourse of the founder of civil society as "specious," that is, both attractive and false. The institution accomplishes the opposite of what it promises and therefore is founded upon a fraud (and the credulity that makes fraud possible). "Everyone rushed into their chains, believing to assure their freedom" (p. 177).

Such was, or must have been, the origin of society and laws, which gave new fetters to the weak and new power to the rich, irreversibly destroyed natural freedom, forever fixed the law of property and inequality, made an irrevocable right of an adroit usurpation, and for the profit of a few ambitious men subjected forever after the entire human race to labor, servitude, and misery. (p. 178)

Both these passages clearly show a complete discontinuity, in which a radically new (revolutionary) institution changes an entire way of life. But this discontinuity is in turn limited by the explanatory weakness of the paradigm, for such events pose more questions than they answer. They have both material and mental presuppositions that are not to be found in the state of nature itself; in particular, the origin of the idea of such a fraud still needs to be accounted for. The foundation of civil society comes at the very end of the state of nature, when it has already lost its true character and degenerated into a Hobbesian state of universal war. It is only after the state of nature has ceased to have any positive existence that such a *projet réfléchi* becomes possible. As Rousseau puts it with respect to the idea of property, "Every appearance leads us to believe that things had by then arrived at a point where they could no longer go on as they had been before, for this idea of property, as it depends upon many prior ideas that could only have been born successively, was not formed all of a sudden in the human mind" (p. 164). Such ideas thus depend above all on the prior development of the passions and of knowledge.

It is also important to note that, while denounced here as fraudulent in origin, the institutions of private property and government are elsewhere praised by Rousseau (in other sections of this text and in other texts) as both necessary and legitimate. Rousseau even characterizes property right as "the most sacred of all of the citizens' rights" in *Économie politique* (p. 263). The legitimacy of the social contract is, of course, the subject of what is today considered Rousseau's most important work, where "the social order" is equally characterized as "a sacred right that serves as the foundation of all the others" (*Contrat social*, p. 352). In the second *Discours* itself, Rousseau in fact almost immediately reverses his perspective and begins to consider this contract as legitimate.[136] He defends the contractual origin of government by refuting theories that locate legitimacy in conquest and paternal authority, a procedure he characterizes as "examining the facts in the light of right" (*Discours sur l'inégalité*, p. 182). This reversal allows Rousseau to trace a history of the degeneration of governments, from freedom to servitude, that mirrors the progress of inequality; wealth is now the end point rather than the motivation of the founders (pp. 187–91).

Now, if this movement of degeneration corresponds to a valorization of the origin that is one of the strongest and most persistent motifs in Rousseau's texts, here at least as strongly as anywhere else, it does not follow, in my opinion, that we should regard the account of the first foundations of property and government as fraud as merely a rhetorical flourish. What this account in fact establishes is an essential distinction between the historical origin and the legitimate foundation.[137] The social contract, in its legitimate form, is not a historical event, even in a conjectural mode. It is a presupposition of a logical rather than genetic kind, which, while necessarily represented as preceding any act of law, must nonetheless be continually reaffirmed. Rousseau constantly reminds us not to mistake fact for right (as he accuses Grotius, for example, of doing), and it is this distinction that allows him to call arbitrary governments illegitimate. But the critique cuts equally well in the other direction. The account of legitimate foundations is in fact a different story, built on different principles and occupying a separate narrative space and time.

The articulations showing the greatest amount of apparent genetic continuity, on the other hand, are doubly grouped together: thematically, they concern the concurrent growth of the passions and enlightenment; chronologically, they run from the end of the "pure" state of nature (which in important ways occurs right at the beginning of the second part of the text) through what is commonly referred to as the golden age, or patriarchal society. Rousseau describes the formation of families with fixed dwellings as a "first revolution" that marks the beginning of the golden age. This *juste milieu*, precisely balanced between the brutality and idleness of nature and the vice and activity of civilization, should have been "the happiest and longest lasting . . . the least subject to revolutions" (p. 171). At the heart of this stability is a scene that is both the object of Rousseau's most powerful pastoral nostalgia (and thus of his most eloquent description), and the moment when the moral transformation of natural into civilized man occurs in a definitive way: the birth of the passions, and particularly that of love. Rousseau's description carefully balances the positive and negative sides of this development, the possibility of tenderness and moral feeling with the propensity of these sentiments toward degeneration.

Young people of different sexes inhabit neighboring huts; the passing commerce that nature demands soon leads to another, no less sweet and made more
permanent by mutual frequentation. They grow accustomed to considering
different objects, and to making comparisons; little by little they acquire ideas
of merit and beauty that produce sentiments of preference. . . . They grew
accustomed to gathering in front of their huts or around a great tree: song
and dance, true children of love and leisure, became the amusement or rather
the occupation of men and women gathered together in idleness. Everyone
began to watch the others and to want to be watched himself, and public
esteem became prized. He who sang or danced the best, the most handsome,
strong, adroit, or eloquent became the most esteemed [*considéré*], and this was
simultaneously the first step toward inequality and toward vice. (pp. 169–70)

Love itself, in agreement with Rousseau's earlier remarks, is described here as
the result of comparison between objects leading to "ideas of merit and
beauty" and "sentiments of preference." But this comparison of objects is inseparable from self-comparison; that is, love (*amour*) is inseparable from
amour-propre. The possibility of love is comparison, but it immediately implies both the desire to be loved and thereby the necessity to compare oneself. This process of self-comparison is the fundamental feature of social existence. "As soon as they are united in a single society, [men] are forced to
compare themselves to one another [*se comparer entre eux*], and to take into
account the differences that they find in the continual use they must make
of one another" (pp. 188–89).

Now, insofar as the story of the golden age is that of the awakening of virtual faculties, it can be recounted with a great deal of genetic continuity as
the development (the unfolding) of potentialities that are fully present
within human nature from the beginning. The verbs used by Rousseau in
this passage (*s'accoutumer, s'insinuer, se succéder*), together with adverbs such
as *insensiblement* ("little by little"), mark the slow passage of time and the
cumulative effect of small changes. But insofar as Rousseau indeed takes the
notion of virtuality seriously, this awakening can be provoked only by an external factor. The virtual faculties, we recall, "could never have developed of
themselves" but rather required the "fortuitous concurrence of several foreign causes that could never have been born [*concours fortuit de plusieurs
causes étrangères qui pouvaient ne jamais naître*]" (p. 162). This causal externality is represented by Rousseau in two ways.

The first representation of external causality in this passage of the *Dis-*

cours is discrete, almost imperceptible; one might call it an intimate externality. In the first half of the text, nature seemed to give itself to primitive man and was never genuinely opposed to him. At the very beginning of the second part, however, "difficulties soon [*bientôt*] presented themselves, and man had to learn to overcome them." The extent to which nature appears as an obstacle itself depends on the multiplication of the species. This is true not only in situations where increased population leads men to live in greater proximity but also in the movement of human populations into regions where nature is not quite so giving as she is in the tropics. The necessity of effort implies the use of rudimentary tools. "The natural weapons that are tree-branches and rocks soon found their way into his hands. He learned to overcome the obstacles of nature." Despite the formal declaration that natural man's body is his "only instrument," there are at least references to his use of stones.[138] Earlier such objects were interpreted as the pure extension of his hand, whereas in the second part they become fully external objects. Because they are external, their use can lead to reflection. "This reiterated application of diverse objects [*êtres*] to himself, and to one another, must have naturally engendered in the mind of man the perception of certain relations. These relations, which we express with the words big, small, strong, weak, fast, slow, fearful, brave, and other like ideas, compared at need, and almost without thinking about it, in the end produced in him some sort of reflection" (p. 165). This possibility needs to be developed. The form of comparison that counts for Rousseau is comparison between other people, and particularly between others and oneself, and that really comes into play when we begin to use others as tools. But the list of comparative ideas given by Rousseau in this first moment is already a set of comparisons between men.

The crux of the interpretation of this text seems to me to lie in the adverbs marking temporal relations, from *bientôt* at the beginning to *naturellement* at the end. We should recall that Rousseau is careful to distinguish between narrated time and narrative time ("the longer events took to follow upon one another, the faster they are to relate" [p. 167]), and it is not clear on which level this "soon" should be situated. Some degree of temporal lapse is certainly implied by population growth. But the vast forests of the first half of the text seemed capable of supporting indefinite populations. In an important note Rousseau follows Montesquieu in arguing that the modern world is becoming depopulated as a result of the cultivation of the arts and commerce, whereas barbarian nations are characterized precisely by the swarms of men they produce. There seems, rather than a gradual and continuous growth of population leading to minute increases in the difficulty of providing for subsistence, to be a sudden reversal in the interpretation of the relations between man and nature.

Rousseau marks this sudden change with another form of external causality, accounting in a highly dramatic passage for the end of the dispersal of natural man in the primitive forest by appealing to geological "revolutions" that created an artificial proximity. "Great floods or earthquakes surrounded inhabited regions with water or precipices; revolutions of the globe detached portions of the continent and cut them into islands." The men who lived in these transformed regions were thereby forced to live together. "It is at least plausible [*vraisemblable*] that society and languages began in islands, and were perfected there before being known on the continent" (pp. 168–69). A similar sort of geological externality appears in a particularly elegant form in the *Essai sur l'origine des langues*, where Rousseau opposes the languages of the arid south (accentual, energetic, expressive of passion) to those of the frozen north (articulated, clear, communicative of need). In each case language, love, and society are born in a festival that takes place around the presence of the opposite principle at the heart of the emerging community. In the south the scene strongly resembles that described in the *Discours*; it is the cool water of rivers and springs that brings together young men and women and gives birth to love and language.

> Beneath ancient oaks, conquerors of the years, ardent youth gradually [*par degrés*] forgot its ferocity; bit by bit [*peu à peu*] they tamed one another. . . .
> Here were held the first festivals, where the feet jumped with joy, where the urgent gesture was no longer sufficient, so that the voice lent to it its passionate accents. . . . Here finally is the true cradle of peoples, and from the pure crystal of fountains came the first fires of love." (*Essai*, p. 406)

In the cold of the north, however, the people "gather around a common hearth where they make merry and dance; the sweet ties of habit bring man closer to his kind" (p. 403). In addition to the purely geographical opposition (hot and arid versus cold and icy), this principle of externality appears on the moral level as well. Fire is of course the most standard metaphor for passion (*les premiers feux de l'amour*), while water is characterized by Rousseau in this text as a need ("springs and rivers are all the more necessary meeting points in that men can do without water even less easily than without fire" [p. 403]). Indeed, the very possibility of this geographic contrast is represented by Rousseau not as an original state of the climate (which was a "perpetual springtime") but as due to the intervention of an external force, a presumably divine finger that changes the inclination of the globe and creates seasonal change (p. 401).

This final example, in which the origin of language and the origin of society are explicitly identified, points us to another form of narrative articulation, one that cannot be conceptualized in genetic terms because it is impossible to assign a cause that does not presuppose the existence of its effect. The long digression on the origin of language in the first half of the text seems to have been written, as Jean Starobinski puts it in the notes to the Pléiade edition, "less to formulate a coherent theory of the origin of languages than to expose the difficulties that the problem raises" (vol. 3, p. 1322). Starobinski's interpretation emphasizes the factor of slowness in resolving this problem; Rousseau, he claims, multiplies intervals and obstacles in order to extend the temporal distance between prereflective (or prelinguistic) and reflective states. The passage ends, however, with Rousseau declaring the problem simply insoluble in a genetic framework:

> For my own part, frightened by the multiplication of difficulties, and convinced of the almost demonstrated impossibility for languages to ever have been born and become established by purely human means, I leave for whoever might wish to take it up, the discussion of the difficult problem of whether already formed society was more necessary to the institution of languages, or already invented languages to the establishment of society. (*Discours sur l'inégalité*, p. 151)

The discussion of language thus primarily provides a model demonstration of a conceptual dead end. Neither term of the historical sequence is thinkable without the preexistence of the other, a logical paradox that Rousseau formulates repeatedly in these pages, whether in terms of the relation between language and society or language and thought. The relation to society is posed in terms of the conventional nature of human language, which therefore requires the prior existence of the possibility of consensus (which can be expressed as the prior existence of society, or of language itself), while the relation to thought emphasizes the process of conceptualization as being fundamentally comparative and ultimately linguistic in nature. The most aggressive form of this denunciation of circular logic thus poses that language presupposes language. "Speech," writes Rousseau, "appears to have been entirely necessary in order to establish the use of speech" (pp. 148–49).[139]

These various forms of causal discontinuity all come together at a moment that Rousseau calls a "great revolution," namely, the invention of agriculture. The passage that introduces this question was singled out by Smith in his "Letter to the Editors of the *Edinburgh Review*," and I cite it, in full, in his translation:

> While men contented themselves with their first rustic habitations; while their industry had no object, except to pin together the skins of wild beasts for their original clothing, to adorn themselves with feathers and shells, to paint their bodies with different colors, to perfect or embellish their bows and arrows, to cut out with sharp stones some fishing canoes or some rude instruments of music; while they applied themselves to such works as a single person could execute, and to such arts as required not the concurrence of several hands, they lived free, healthful, humane, and happy, as far as their nature would permit them, and continued to enjoy amongst themselves the sweets of an independent society [*jouir entre eux des douceurs d'un commerce indépendant*]. But from the instant in which one man had occasion for the assistance of another; from the moment that he perceived that it could be advantageous for one person to have provisions for two, equality disappeared, property was introduced, labor became necessary, and the vast forests of nature were changed into agreeable plains, which must be watered with the sweat of mankind, and in which the world beheld slavery and wretchedness begin to grow up and blossom with the harvest.[140]

This passage provides an excellent illustration of the way in which the end of the state of nature (or the beginning of inequality) is continually displaced in the text. Events previously described as already outside of the state of nature—the creation of tools and the use of arts of appearance—here seem to return into it. The expression *commerce indépendant*, an oxymoron from the point of view of the pure state of nature in the first half, shows how pastoral society, where there is *amour-propre* but not division of labor, is now considered as a second state of nature.[141] What marks the end of the state of nature in this case is the appearance, not of agriculture as such (Rousseau says that "its principle was known long before its practice was established" [p. 172]) but of large-scale cultivation, which can be understood only as a function of the division of labor and the relations of dependence that result from it. Without the division of labor, agriculture on this scale is simply unnecessary.

For Rousseau the oxymoron used by Smith—"naturally contrivance," which assumes the possibility of art within nature—is absolutely unacceptable. Rousseau in particular insists that the invention of agriculture is inseparable from that of metallurgy, but, as is so often the case in this text, that only makes the question of causal precedence more difficult to resolve. For Smith, as we have seen, the factors of the accumulation of stock (invention of agriculture) and the division of labor (invention of other arts) were completely interdependent, but Smith's gradualism allows these elements to grow continuously and concurrently out of an original disposition of human nature in minute increments. What is fundamentally natural for Smith is not so much the precedence of agriculture over commerce as the concurrence and interdependence of their growth. Rousseau, however, has carefully excluded any trace of either the accumulation of stock or the division of labor from his description of the state of nature. This means that the order of this development will necessarily be "unnatural" in a much stronger sense.

Rousseau posits metallurgy as the first, or at least the crucial, separate profession, and this choice plays a determining role here. "The invention of the other arts was thus necessary to force the human race to apply itself to that of agriculture. Once men were needed to melt and forge iron, other men were needed to feed them" (p. 173). Once iron tools were invented, the greater agricultural productivity made possible by their use was crucial to fostering the concomitant growth of the two sectors, which would make the relation between the division of labor and the accumulation of stock resemble that described by Smith rather than the relation between language and thought described by Rousseau. But the key moment is the discovery of iron, which is the sudden intervention of a new element and not the result of a developmental process. Metallurgy relies on a completely unnatural and, for Rousseau, properly occult knowledge.[142]

> It is very difficult to conjecture how men came to know and use iron: for it is hardly believable that they imagined on their own to draw the ore from the mine and to prepare it in the necessary way in order to forge it before knowing what the result would be. On the other hand one can all the less attribute this discovery to some accidental fire, in that mines occur only in sites that are arid and lacking in trees and plants, so that one could say that nature took special precautions to hide this fatal secret from us. (p. 172)

The insertion of an occult technology between barbarism (pasturage) and civilization (agriculture) renders this transition properly unimaginable within a developmental framework. Indeed, it is only by means of another recourse to geological catastrophe that Rousseau can keep his story moving. The only hypothesis that remains, he continues, would be "the extraordinary circumstance of some volcano vomiting melted metals."

This sort of impossible transition which has in fact taken place is precisely what the *Discours sur l'inégalité* as a whole designates: the fact that human history is in no way an expression of human nature. Indeed, each of the major transitions we have examined in the second half of the *Discours* recapitulates the relation between the two halves. This structure is also congruent with Rousseau's major methodological criticism of his predecessors in the natural law tradition, who, he says, have constructed their arguments by assuming the presence of the effect within the cause. In the first version of the *Contrat social* Rousseau will summarize this criticism with respect to Thomas Hobbes: "Hobbes's error is thus not to have established the state of war between independent and now sociable men, but to have assumed this state to be natural to the species, and to have given it as the cause of the vices whose effect it is" ("Manuscrit de Genève," p. 288; cf. *Discours sur l'inégalité*, p. 153). Hobbes is criticized by name on this point, but in the Preface to the second *Discours* such an error is attributed to all existing definitions of natural law. Indeed, one might say that Rousseau's own definition of the state of nature is formed primarily by excluding, to as great an extent as possible, any elements of continuity between nature and civilization. If the state of nature is the logical presupposition of human history, if "it is necessary to have a correct understanding" of this fiction "in order to properly evaluate our present condition" (p. 123), that does not mean that nature is in any way the cause of civilization. The concept of the state of nature makes causality and intelligibility radically discontinuous. What effectively happens in the second half of the *Discours* is that this model is generalized to the entire course of human history. History is a process of denaturalization and is thus formed out of a series of "revolutions" that find their intelligibility—that is, their intellectual origins—only in the negation of their own presuppositions.

3. The Author of Nature

[Rousseau] n'est pas, si l'on peut dire, l'arbre des fruits qu'il porte.

—*Anne-Louise-Germaine Necker, 'Lettres sur les ouvrages et le caractère de J.-J. Rousseau'*[1]

Among the many claims concerning Jean-Jacques Rousseau's influence on the French Revolution, Louis-Sébastien Mercier's formulation that he was "one of the first authors of the Revolution" has retained our attention, because, as we saw in the first chapter, it presents a powerful and challenging identification of causality and intelligibility. In the second chapter, however, we saw that Rousseau's own critique of the narrative patterns of eighteenth-century universal history came to bear precisely on the possibility of making an identification of this sort. That is, Rousseau takes up a position conceptually much closer to the one we have identified with Jean-Joseph Mounier's claim that "the Revolution produced [Rousseau's] influence." Rousseau's is a historiography in which the relation between economic, social, cultural, and intellectual factors only becomes thinkable at the cost of accepting narrative discontinuities and even sudden reversals in the order of causality—in other words, revolutions. In order to understand what it might mean to continue to call Rousseau an "author of the Revolution," then, we must examine how Rousseau himself conceived of authorship.

Autobiography and Authorship

THE PERSON OF THE AUTHOR AND THE UNITY OF THE CORPUS

As Michel Foucault pointed out in his notorious essay "What Is an Author?" an author's name (in opposition to other proper names) exists in a necessary relation with a particular set of attributions, namely, the *œuvre*. Foucault describes the link between author and *œuvre* as the "first, solid, and funda-mental unity" of modern criticism. Without the concept of the author the very idea of a corpus would have no sense, and the project of bringing to-gether diverse and sometimes divergent themes into a single object of inter-pretation would be inconceivable.[2] This same unity is an obsessive concern of Rousseau's, most notably in the autobiographical writings. Whatever the hesitations of modern criticism may have been on this score,[3] Rousseau himself continually asserted the fundamental unity of his *œuvre*. In the *Let-tres écrites de la montagne*, for example, he proposes that *Julie* can be inter-preted by *Émile* and vice versa: "The profession of faith of a catholic priest is to be found in *Émile*, and that of a devout woman in the *Héloïse*. These two works are enough in agreement for the one to be explicable by the other" (*Lettres de la montagne*, p. 694). Similarly, Rousseau describes the in-sights gained during the "illumination of Vincennes" as providing a ground of unity for his works: "All that I could retain of the crowd of truths that il-luminated me in that quarter of an hour beneath a tree was weakly spread out in my three principal texts, namely the first discourse, that on inequal-ity, and the treatise on education; these three works are inseparable and to-gether form a whole" (*Lettres à Malesherbes*, p. 1136). The basis on which Rousseau asserts the unity of his corpus, however, is fundamentally not a complementarity of ideas or a repetition of themes. As we shall see, this sort of conceptual coherence is merely a by-product of the true cause. For Rous-seau, the unity of the corpus is ultimately grounded in the unity of the nat-ural person of the author, in much the same way that apologies for monar-chy ground the unity of the state in the natural person of the sovereign.

This relation between an author and his works is in particular the major theme of what has long been agreed to be the most bizarre of Rousseau's works, the one in which his persecution mania reached its fullest flowering, *Rousseau juge de Jean-Jacques*. This text, commonly referred to as the *Dia-logues*, is composed of a series of conversations between an anonymous Frenchman and "Rousseau," a foreigner newly arrived in France, about the conspiracy directed against an author called "J. J." The conspiracy in ques-tion is taken to be universal, and indeed it ranges from the pettiest of per-secutions to systematic calumny, sealed by a pact of silence. Directed by men of letters who "govern public opinions" (*Dialogues*, p. 781), the con-spiracy bears a striking resemblance to the neo-Habermasian view of the Enlightenment.[4]

The epigraph of the *Dialogues* is the same verse from Ovid's *Tristia* that Rousseau had used some twenty years earlier for the first *Discours*: *Barbarus hic ego sum quia non intelligor illis*, "Here it is I who am the barbarian because they do not understand me."[5] The entire development of the *Dialogues*, and the defense of "J. J." against the conspiracy, takes place under the sign of misunderstanding. For Ovid, "barbarian" designates the cruel irony of exile: it is the residents of Tomis, neither Greek nor Roman, who are the true barbarians, even if Ovid is the one who is not understood. Rousseau's own experience of exile, both his life in France generally and his wanderings between 1762 and the composition of the *Dialogues*, gives a new resonance to the motto, and the position of both "J. J." and "Rousseau" as foreigners in France is heavily thematized in the text itself. But the use of "barbarian" to characterize that which is misunderstood echoes even more strongly with the two *Discours*. In the context of universal history the barbarian is the shepherd, midway between savagery and civilization; he is an inhabitant of the golden age and thus still feels pity and *amour de soi* in their natural forms but is already capable of sociability.[6] Like the occupants of the riverbank described in the *Discours sur les sciences et les arts*, or the young people gathered around the oak tree or watering hole in the *Discours sur l'origine de l'inégalité* or the *Essai sur l'origine des langues*, the inhabitants of the ideal world described in the first *Dialogue* are distinguished by the directness and strength of their passions, uncontaminated by *amour-propre*, and by their transparency to one another (pp. 668–73).[7] The central point of misunderstanding can therefore be characterized as the interpretation of the doctrine of the state of nature, and more particularly of the social relations into which natural man can enter. But Rousseau also often uses *barbare* as an adjective to mean "unfeeling" (*insensible*), and he was capable of using it to describe those who did not understand him. The majority of letters written in 1770 (two years before the beginning of the composition of the *Dialogues*) begin with the following quatrain:

Pauvres aveugles que nous sommes!
Ciel, démasque les imposteurs
Et force leurs barbares cœurs
A s'ouvrir aux regards des hommes

Poor blind men that we are! May heaven unmask the impostors and force their barbarous hearts to open themselves to the eyes of men.[8]

Here too, even as the term reveals itself to be completely reversible, what is at stake in barbarism is the transparency of social relations. Rousseau's adversaries have chosen opacity; they make themselves impossible to understand just as they intentionally misunderstand Rousseau.

The most obvious and common form of such a misunderstanding is literalization—Rousseau wants to live in the woods like a bear—and its most eminent practitioner was François-Marie Arouet de Voltaire. The letter he sent in response to the second *Discours* represents a hyperbolic version of this literalistic misinterpretation. "I have received your new book against the human race, sir, and I thank you for it. Never has so much wit been employed in an effort to render us stupid [*bêtes*]. Reading your work, one is seized with the desire to walk on all fours. But since I lost the habit some sixty years ago, I unfortunately feel that it would be impossible for me to start up again."[9] Rousseau always vehemently rejected such literalizations of his methodological fictions.

The conspiracy against Rousseau headed by Denis Diderot and Friedrich Melchior Grimm frequently appears as an exercise in direct persecution, and there are moments when Rousseau will say that the plot is directed entirely against his person, his books being only incidentally involved. "In the storm which has submerged me," he writes in the *Confessions*, "my books served as a pretext, but it was me that they were out to get [*c'était à ma personne qu'on en voulait*]. They cared little about the author but wanted to ruin Jean-Jacques, and the worst thing they were able to find in my writings was the honor that they might do me" (*Confessions*, p. 406). It is in the *Dialogues*, however, that the real significance of the conspiracy for Rousseau becomes most clear. Any hope for a victory over the conspiracy, as held out by "Rousseau" at the end, is based on the possibility of the work's being read correctly in the distant future: "Whatever [his contemporaries] might do, his books, transmitted to posterity, will show that their Author was not as they strive to portray him" (*Dialogues*, p. 956). The Frenchman on the contrary argues that the zenith of the conspiracy will be attained in the massive and total falsification of Rousseau's works, and that its triumph will thus be complete and without appeal. The fundamental signification of the conspiracy is thus the misreading of Rousseau's texts; personal calumny is the most effective way to ensure the spread of such misunderstanding.[10] The text concludes with a prediction that it will itself meet equally complete incomprehension: "I already know what tone everyone will take after reading me. This tone will be the same as before, ingenuous, ingratiating [*patelin*], benevolent; they will pity me for seeing so blackly what is so white, for they are all as spotless as swans [*ils ont tous la candeur des Cygnes*]: but they will understand nothing of what I have said" (pp. 987–88).

The reading of Rousseau's corpus presented by the *Dialogues* is almost entirely concerned with the question of the concordance between the author and his works. Upon being informed of the criminal and vicious nature of "J. J.," "Rousseau," a long-time admirer of the former's works, formulates the hypothesis of a total distinction between "the Author of the books and that of the crimes" (p. 674). "What I do not believe, and will never in my life believe," he exclaims, "is that the *Émile*, and especially the article on taste in the fourth book, is the work of a depraved heart; that the *Héloïse*, and especially the letter on the death of Julie, was written by a scoundrel, that the one to M. d'Alembert on spectacles is the production of a duplicitous soul [*âme double*]" (pp. 689–90). It is this concern, for example, that motivates the lengthy developments on "J. J."'s knowledge of music: if he does not know music, he could not have written the *Devin du village*, which can be recognized as having the same "source" as *La Nouvelle Héloïse*. "Whence does this secret charm that flows thus into hearts draw its source? This unique source into which no one else has dipped is not that of the Hippocrene; it comes from somewhere else. The Author must be as singular as the piece is original. If, already knowing J. J., I had seen the *Devin du village* for the first time without being told the name of the Author, I would have said without wavering that it is the author of *La Nouvelle Héloïse*, it is J. J., and it could only be him" (p. 867). This set of arguments knits together the element of simplicity, the unity of a soul and a discourse without *arrière-pensée*, without a separation between appearance and intention, with singularity, the uniqueness of a soul and a discourse that can be recognized anywhere.

This connection between the author and the person is finally reestablished in a famous passage in which the Frenchman reports on his reading of Rousseau. He begins once again with the question of the singularity of the author and the distinction between authentic and falsified works. "As for myself, even if I did not know that he had abandoned the pen twelve years ago, a glance at the writings that are imputed to him would be sufficient for me to feel that their Author could not be the same as that of the others" (p. 933). From a doctrinal point of view, the authentic texts are perfectly coherent: "It did not take long in reading these books for me to feel that I had been deceived about their content, and that what I had been given to think of as splendid declamations, embellished with beautiful language but disjointed and full of contradictions, were things profoundly thought out and forming a coherent [*lié*] system, which might not be true but which offered nothing contradictory" (p. 930). This judgment is not made on the basis of style ("not that I believe myself to be an infallible judge in questions of style"), which is relatively easy to imitate. Rather, says the Frenchman, "it is the very matter of his writings about which I believe I could not be mistaken [*c'est sur les choses mêmes que je crois ne pouvoir être trompé*]." *Les choses mêmes* here seem to designate above all the author's own personality. "I found J. J.'s writings," the Frenchman continues, "to be full of movements of the soul [*affections d'âme*] that penetrated my own. I found ways of feeling and of seeing that distinguish him easily from all the other writers of his time. . . . His system could be false; but in developing it he has painted himself truly, in so characteristic and so sure a fashion that it would be impossible for me to be mistaken" (pp. 933–34).

The "uniqueness" and "singularity" of the author is thus, for the Frenchman, the strict correlative of the unity of the corpus. The Frenchman imagines the character of the author based on the texts that bear his name. Thus, "in grasping bit by bit this system in all its branches by means of a more reflective reading, at the beginning I lingered less on a direct examination of this doctrine than on its relation with the character of him whose name it bore" (pp. 935–36). The basic methodological principle of this mode of reading is the assertion of an identity between the *dispositions d'âme* of the reader and the author. The text is a medium that transmits these dispositions or affectations from the writer to reader.

> In order to judge the true goal of these books, I did not become attached to picking out here and there a few scattered and separated sentences, but consulting myself both while reading and when I had finished, I examined, as you desired, what dispositions of the soul they put me in and left me in, judging as you do that this was the best way to penetrate the one [i.e., the *disposition d'âme*] in which the Author was while writing them, and the effect he wanted to produce. (p. 930)

The reader's soul is left in the same state that the author's had been in; no gap appears in the transmission from author to reader. The narrative produced by this reading is so continuous as to barely constitute a narrative.

In terms of the question of the relation between Rousseau's literary and political texts, the Frenchman's mode of reading would seem to eliminate the problem entirely. As Jean Starobinski has emphasized, this reading tends to reduce the political works to a series of self-portraits. "In this perspective, the political writings seem to lose their import: They are no more than testimony to the *élans* of a *belle âme*. What had been political theory is henceforth interpreted as self-expression. . . . Everything is absorbed into the poetry of personal confession. Rousseau no longer wants his works to point the way to possible action; they point only to their author, of whom they are an indirect portrait. They paint a generous effervescence, but should not be treated as if they led to real political consequences."[11] There would be no difference between the literary and the political texts insofar as the coherence of the latter would be precisely founded upon their expressive—that is to say, literary—character. Rousseau's political thought, and its foundation in the theory of nature and natural man, is taken to be a displaced self-portrait. The unification of the corpus around the "great principle" disengaged by this reading—"that nature made man happy and good, but that society depraves him and makes him miserable" (p. 934)—is thus a strict reflection of the authorial personality. This identity between an author and his doctrine is most forcefully asserted in a key passage that clearly encapsulates the problems of such a structure:

> Whence could the painter and apologist of nature, today so disfigured and calumniated [*si défigurée et si calomniée*], have drawn his model if not from his own heart? He described nature as he felt himself [*Il l'a décrite comme il se sentait lui-même*]. . . . In a word, only by painting himself could a man have thus shown us primitive man. (p. 936)

The drawing of a model from his own heart would make the state of nature a metaphorical expression for the author's *dispositions d'âme*, even for its *élans*, that is, it expresses precisely the spontaneous expression of the heart. The phrase "today so disfigured and calumniated" is the key moment here. On the one hand, the depth of the metaphorical exchange between the author and nature appears in the transfer of the attribute of being persecuted from "J. J." (in context, the reference can only be to the various lies told by "*nos Messieurs*" about "J. J." and the texts falsely imputed to him) to "*la nature*," the only feminine noun in the sentence and thus the only possible grammatical referent of the phrase "*si défigurée et si calomniée*." This metaphorical movement, however, is not itself based on the expressive or genetic understanding of literary language upon which the Frenchman's argument is based. It is simply the exploitation of a grammatical structure. It neither expresses nor transmits a *disposition d'âme*. It therefore raises the possibility—never explicitly banished by the *Dialogues*—that this author is himself nothing but a construction, the exploitation of a grammatical structure. The *Dialogues* are only too aware of this fact: the Frenchman refuses to the end to meet "J. J." He is thus content to take "Rousseau"'s word about his character and to assume that the correspondence between the author constructed by his reading and the person described by "Rousseau" is sufficiently persuasive. But this does not amount, as "Rousseau" points out, to conviction (pp. 946–47). We remain within the realm of reading—that is, the construction of models of intelligibility—rather than acceding to the realm of judicial proof to which the text constantly appeals.[12] There are even suggestions that the "J. J." whom "Rousseau" describes may be every bit as much a fiction: the correspondence of this character to the doctrine of natural man is established by a development introduced by an expression familiar to all readers of Rousseau. "The better to feel this necessity, let us for a moment set aside all the facts [*écartons un moment tous les faits*] and suppose that the only thing known is the temperament I have described to you. Let us then see what the natural result should be in a fictional being about whom we would have no other idea" (p. 820).[13] Both "J. J." as described in the *Dialogues* and the state of nature are methodological fictions. The character of the author can thus be seen to be an a posteriori construction, a figurative representation (a personification) of the interpretation or understanding of the text.[14]

This interpretation of the function of the figure of the author sheds light on the meaning of the multiple authorial personae presented by the autobiographical writings. In the *Dialogues*, the most evident version of such a multiplication is the split between "J. J." and "Rousseau." Which of the two could be considered to be the author of the *Dialogues* themselves is far from clear. At one moment "Rousseau" describes "J. J." as writing "a sort of judgment of [his persecutors] and himself in the form of a Dialogue quite like that which might result from our talks" (p. 836); the footnotes, however, are clearly in the voice of a Jean-Jacques Rousseau who is neither one of the participants in the dialogue nor its object. The most important relation, however, seems to me to be one within "J. J.," who is persistently split by every explanatory hypothesis offered: between the author of the books and the author of the crimes, between his life before and after forty years of age, and above all between passion and reflection.

This final distinction occurs throughout Rousseau's autobiographical writings. Usually this opposition is treated in terms of sentiment and reason, *l'esprit* and *le cœur*, an analysis that is, for example, applied to Mme de Warens in the *Confessions* (pp. 197–99). Aligned with a temporal opposition between the *l'instant* and *la durée*, it plays, as we shall see, a structural role in *La Nouvelle Héloïse*. Most important, it provides Rousseau's most consistent (or at least most frequent) explanation of the singularity of his own character, and recurs in all the autobiographical works.[15] In the *Confessions*, Rousseau writes, "Two things that are almost impossible to ally are united in me without my being able to see how: a very ardent temperament, lively and impetuous passions, and thoughts [*idées*] that are slow to be born, encumbered, and that present themselves only after the fact. It could be said that my heart and my mind do not belong to the same individual" (p. 113). The second letter to Malesherbes formulates this same opposition in only terms of soul and temperament: "A lazy soul that is frightened by any responsibility [*soin*], and an ardent, bilious temperament, easily perturbed and excessively sensible to all that affects it, seem incapable of being allied in the same character, and yet they form the basis of mine. While I cannot resolve this opposition by principles, it nonetheless exists" (*Lettres à Malesherbes*, p. 1134). This emphasis on a fundamental inconsistency of character recalls Rousseau's extensive reading of Montaigne, particularly as it is reflected in a text such as the early *Persifleur* (pp. 1103–12). But this theme goes far beyond a recognition of the unending variety of human mutability. The opposition between heart and mind, or passion and reflection, plays a fundamental role in the conceptual economy of the *Dialogues*. As Jean Starobinski has pointed out, the extension of the reflexive figure of self-portraiture to the relation between "Rousseau" and "J. J." is formally excluded by the logic of the text.

> The Rousseau who judges and the Jean-Jacques who is unfit for the effort of judgment cannot be the same man. If he were what he thinks himself to be, Rousseau would not have the right to think himself [*Tel qu'il se pense, Rousseau n'aurait pas le droit de se penser*]. The reflective activity by means of which Rousseau claims to prove his innocence is forbidden by the very principles on which good and evil are based. . . . Rousseau is excluded from Jean-Jacques, yet it is on this peculiar exclusion that the portrait of Jean-Jacques is constructed.[16]

The burden of "Rousseau"'s portrait of "J. J." is to demonstrate that he is a creature entirely dominated by beneficent natural passions and in particular by an *amour de soi* entirely uncontaminated by *amour-propre*—that he has a purely reactive (positive) rather than reflective (negative) form of sensibility.[17] "His emotions are prompt and lively but rapid and of short duration, and this is evident. His heart, transparent as crystal, can hide nothing that happens within it; every movement he feels is immediately transmitted in his eyes and on his face" (*Dialogues*, p. 860). His mind, on the other hand, is slow and heavy. For such a creature, reasoned discourse is painful. "The heavy succession of discourse is unbearable [to men like him]; they chaff against its slow progression; in the rapidity of the movements they experience, it seems to them that what they feel should come to light and penetrate from one heart to another without the cold ministry of speech" (p. 862).

Yet "J. J." is an author. Even if the operations of his mind seem to contradict those of his heart they cannot be purely and simply excluded from his character. This contradiction shows up in every aspect of his life and character. "He is active, ardent, hardworking, indefatigable; he is indolent, lazy, without vigor; he is proud, audacious, bold; he is fearful, timid, easily embarrassed; he is cold, disdainful, disagreeable to the point of harshness; he is gentle, affectionate, easygoing to the point of weakness." Indeed, Rousseau presents such a contradiction as the very foundation of "J. J."'s character: "Everything about him follows from a first logical contradiction [*Tout suit en lui d'une première inconséquence*]" (pp. 817–18). Rousseau asserts a division to be the fundamental trait of a character; even more radically, he asserts a break in causality to be the causal or narrative principle from which everything else follows. Such a contradiction is thus primarily a question of a discontinuous relation between narration and logic, of a sequence that is also an *inconséquence*.

In a letter to Dom Léger-Marie Deschamps, Rousseau explicitly poses this *inconséquence* as the principle of his writing.

> You are quite correct to scold me about my imprecisions in matters of reasoning. Have you been able to perceive that I see certain objects very well, but that I do not know how to compare them; that I am fairly fertile in propositions without ever seeing consequences, that order and method which are your Gods are my Furies; that nothing ever offers itself to me except isolated, and that instead of tying my ideas together in my writings I use transitions like a charlatan

[*j'use d'une charlatanerie de transitions*], which impresses you most of all, you great philosophers.[18]

The argument of *Rousseau juge de Jean-Jacques* and the other autobiographical texts that we have arranged around it can be summarized in a series of propositions. First, Rousseau's work is both singular and simple—that is, immediately recognizable on account of its inimitable tone and argument—and profoundly coherent and unified in its inspiration. Secondly, the best possible representation of this singular character is to be found in the equally singular character of the personality of the author. But this character, finally, is fundamentally divided; it is founded upon an original and inexpugnable contradiction. Now, it would certainly be possible to denounce this set of propositions as an example of the logical *inconséquence* that Rousseau himself is the first to recognize. But it would be far more productive, it seems to me, to draw a fairly simple consequence from the way Rousseau counterposes coherence and unity so closely with illogicality and division: the unity of Rousseau's corpus lies precisely in an inimitable and eminently consistent breakdown (to be understood in both active and passive senses) of narrative and causal logic.

THE SYMPATHETIC READER

We can pose the question in the following terms: what would a reading of the *Dialogues* along the lines of the model of reading proposed within the *Dialogues* by the Frenchman look like? It would certainly not be literary-critical in spirit: Rousseau was bitterly disappointed by the reaction of his old friend Étienne Bonnot de Condillac, who "spoke of this text [*écrit*] as he would have about a work of literature that I had asked him to examine in order to know his opinion" (*Dialogues*, p. 982). Rousseau judged this response to be in the spirit of the conspiracy and soon ceased to see Condillac. Rather, it would have to be based on a movement of identification in which the state of the reader's soul would come to reproduce that of the author. As the fan mail Rousseau received after the publication of *La Nouvelle Héloïse* attests, this sort of identification was one of the most common ways Rousseau was read by his contemporaries. But such an identificatory mode of reading is deeply problematic in this case. Even if pity is a natural movement of identification, it would be insufficient and indeed insulting merely to pity Rousseau. Such pity would in fact reproduce the false benevolence of

the gentlemen who direct the conspiracy. It would then perhaps be necessary, whatever our own circumstances, to feel ourselves persecuted like him.
Indeed, the character "Rousseau," if not the Frenchman, consistently describes himself as having suffered great disappointments at the hands of his
fellow men, and Robespierre's reading of Rousseau could easily be described
in these terms. It seems to me, however, that such an identificatory reading
was also generally perceived by Rousseau as part of the *complot*. One can
simply attribute this to paranoia, but our reading of the nature of the conspiracy encourages us to seek a further signification.

Rousseau was certainly capable of responding positively, at least for a
while, to praise. But the universality of the plot, as applied to one of the
most popular writers of the eighteenth century (if not the most popular),
can only indicate that the identificatory reading is as much a persecution as
the literalizing one. Rousseau's discussion of the sale of his portraits, for example (pp. 779–82), or his rage at the popular appropriation of his Christian name (p. 663), indicates that the conspiracy includes the entire gamut
of phenomena that make up literary celebrity. More fundamentally, we can
note that one of the primary characteristics of the conspiracy is that it produces an absurd and contradictory discourse about "J. J.," who is accused of
contrary and incompatible vices. "You have created at your leisure a being
such as never existed, a monster not found in nature, probability [*vraisem-
blance*], or possibility, made up of unalliable, incompatible, mutually exclusive parts" (p. 755). This is in fact a description of the history of Rousseau interpretation, as much that of his admirers as of his detractors. It therefore
seems to me that we can say that if Rousseau is universally misread, it is because he is always partially read. There is no complete reading. It could be
objected that this is true, and banally so, of every great writer. It could further be objected that the empirical absence of a complete interpretation can
never disprove in principle the possibility that one might exist. I would argue, however, that this partiality is not an empirical accident of literary history but rather a necessary effect of the structure of Rousseau's texts. In particular, in terms of the problem with which we are currently concerned, it
can be seen as an implication of the identification of author and work.

If we are correct in arguing that the character of the author is a figurative
representation of the intelligibility of the text, then this *première inconséquence* would represent a pervasive principle of division. It would occur both
within each text and between texts. The division of the corpus into literary

and political works could then be seen as only one possible translation of this division. Another version can be seen to operate within the narrative structure of single texts, such as both *Discours* or the *Confessions*, where the division between two parts is clearly and explicitly marked, or *La Nouvelle Héloïse*, in which it is signaled by means of a major shift of both theme and tone. In both these cases, a highly entertaining first part is followed by a second part so devoted to truth and to the correction of any errors that may have been perpetrated before as to become painfully dull. At the beginning of the second part of the *Confessions*, Rousseau writes, "In any case this second part has only the same truth in common with the first, and the only advantage it has over the previous part is the importance of the material. . . . I thus warn those who will want to begin this reading that, in pursuing it, nothing will preserve them from boredom except the desire to complete their knowledge of a man, and the sincere love of justice and truth" (*Confessions*, p. 279). What is curious is that in this second part the narrative has a greater linear continuity—that is, the *charlatanerie de transitions* is much more successful in this desperate attempt to establish the true facts—whereas in the avowedly fictionalized first part, a highly episodic narrative form allows the development of a series of allegorical mininarratives, fables, and *apologues*. This potentially allegorical character of the *Confessions* was recognized by its earliest readers, although they were not necessarily able to agree on what was truthful autobiography and what fable. Pierre-Louis Ginguené's *Lettres sur les Confessions de J. J. Rousseau* presents the first part of the *Confessions* as a "supplement and appendix to *Émile*" because "everything is a lesson or a temptation for him, a defeat or a victory, everything is a counsel, and, what is worth even more, an example for the reader. There is perhaps less fruit to be drawn from the second part. . . . The difference that can be seen in the moral utility of the two parts also exists, if less noticeably, in their literary merit." Louis-Sébastien Mercier, on the other hand, argued in *De J. J. Rousseau considéré comme l'un des premiers auteurs de la Révolution* that it was the second part of the *Confessions*, and particularly elements such as the story of Rousseau's abandonment of his children, that needed to be read as cautionary fables.[19]

One of these episodes provides an example of a model of reading that would be based precisely on an attention to such divisions. In a well-known passage from the first book of the *Confessions*, the young Jean-Jacques attempts to steal an apple from the pantry of maître Ducommun, in whose engraving shop he was an apprentice. Unable to pull the apple through the lattice of the pantry, he constructs a complicated apparatus to hold the apple and split it in order to be able to remove it in two separate pieces. "But [the two pieces] had hardly been separated when they both fell into the pantry." Forgetting this evidence lying in the bottom of the pantry, Jean-Jacques puts off a second attempt until the following day. But when, having reassembled his apparatus, he begins this second attempt, he is caught redhanded: "All of a sudden the pantry door opens; my master comes out, crosses his arms, looks at me, and says to me: Bravo!" (*Confessions*, p. 34).

This little story may at first seem infertile ground for developing Rousseau's theory of reading. But immediately after the two halves of the apple have fallen away, there is a parabasis, an aside to the reader: "Compassionate reader, share my suffering [*Pitoyable lecteur, partagez mon affliction*]." This injunction can be taken as a definition of the action of the Rousseauist reader. Indeed, Ginguené reacted to this passage in precisely this way, even taking up the crucial verb. "Despite the bad seed that can be seen in this apple-hunt, which was intended to empty out his master-graver's pantry through the bars, he describes it with such a pleasant truth that one shares [*partage*] all his movements, and even momentarily becomes his accomplice."[20] The letters from the readers of *La Nouvelle Héloïse* printed in R. A. Leigh's massive edition of the *Correspondance complète* are the best possible index of just how thoroughly eighteenth-century readers followed it. The marquise de Polignac, for example, wrote to the marquise de Verdelin:

> I have finished M. Rousseau's book. What a book *ma belle*, and what a soul it took to write it. Judge by what one must think of he who is its hero, which everyone assures [me] is the citizen's case, and I like to believe it myself, a soul so sensible, so delicate, so virtuous honors humanity. The first volumes tore tears from me but the sixth! O *ma belle*, I dare not tell you the effect it had on me, no, it was no longer the time of tears, it was a sharp pain that took me over, my heart constricted, this Julie dying was no longer an unknown being to me, I believed myself to be her sister, her friend, her Claire, my seizure mounted to the point that had I not put down the book I would have been just as badly off as all those who surrounded this virtuous woman in her last moments.[21]

This sort of reaction can be found throughout the rest of the century. "I suffer myself when I read him," exclaims Jacques-Pierre Brissot de Warville. "I enter into his suffering, and I say to myself: Why was I not fortunate enough to have known him? How I would have opened up my soul to him!"[22] The future press baron Charles-Joseph Pancoucke was particularly effusive in writing anonymously to Rousseau:

> I must give you an account of the impressions that the reading of your most recent work has made upon me. This is an effusion that your heart must pardon mine. The weight of gratitude overwhelms me; it is necessary for me to find some relief in communicating to you my sentiments, my admiration, and my transports. Your divine writings, Sir, are a devouring fire, they have penetrated my soul, fortified my heart, enlightened my mind. . . . Reading your *Héloïse* has finished what your other works had already begun. How many tears I have shed, how many sighs, how many sorrows! How many times I have seen myself guilty. Since this happy reading, I burn with love for virtue, my heart, which I had thought extinct, is hotter than ever. Sentiment has won back its place: love, pity, virtue, sweet friendship, will forever hold sway in my soul. . . . I adore your person and your sublime writings, all those who will have the good fortune to read your works will find in you a sure guide who will conduct them to perfection and to the love and practice of all the virtues that form the essence of the good man.[23]

This is the same vocabulary we found in the Frenchman's description of his reading in the *Dialogues*: "I found J. J.'s writings to be full of movements of the soul that penetrated my own." Such a sharing participates in the metaphorical totalization that allows the corpus to be united in terms of its relation to its author.

But the context of the fable, in which the young Jean-Jacques has just split an apple in half in order to grasp it, turns our attention to the other sense of *partager* in French: to split or divide. The verb occurs twice in the passage: "*A force d'adresse et de temps je parvins à la* partager, *espérant tirer ensuite les pièces l'une après l'autre. Mais à peine furent-elles séparées qu'elles tombèrent toutes deux dans la dépense. Lecteur pitoyable,* partagez *mon affliction*" (my emphasis). The definition of the reader's action as a *partage*, both a sharing and a splitting, in the context of this story, places the young protagonist, whose action is equally a *partage*, in the position of the reader. From this point of view, the apple could be taken as representing a text, on any level of extension. The moment here called *partager*, this act of differentiation and decision, could be understood on the level of the corpus, for example, as a distinction between political and literary works. Such a distinction could be phrased in a number of different ways, and a single text could be differently distributed according to that phrasing: what is important is the act and not the details of the *partage*. There is no substantive difference between the two halves of the apple. But the text must be split in order to be grasped, in order for an act of understanding or appropriation to occur.

On a more local level of reading this distinction could be stated as the necessity to distinguish between figurative and literal meanings: in the case under consideration here, the decision as to which of the two senses of *partager* is primary and which is derived would be crucial to the understanding of the narrative. In the first instance, "sharing" an apple (with the reader) could be considered only as a metaphor; in the second case it would be the act of "splitting" an affliction that would necessarily be figurative. The two senses are not compatible and the word cannot be simultaneously understood in both ways; a choice is necessary. More precisely, to choose or not to choose is already a choice. If one need not choose, it is because two meanings peacefully share a word; if one need choose, it is because the word is split by its meanings. To read *partager* as an act of reading would seem to exclude the purely sentimental reaction, whereas to read the story in an emotive fashion requires a totalization rather than a division, an identification rather than an understanding. Rousseau's story separates the two senses or two kinds of reading and narrates a movement from the one to the other, mediated by the loss of the apple.

This reading of the two parts of the apple as representing the political and literary aspects of Rousseau's work may seem forced. It is certainly not "sympathetic." It lacks the symbolic richness and integration of detail that is usually taken to make a reading convincing. Symbolic, in fact, is precisely what the reading is not: the apple does not in any way resemble a text; what is the same is the action called *partage*. But this nonsymbolic structure of the reading is precisely what is at stake here. One of the two main literary sources of the passage, the myth of the golden apples of the Hesperides, designated as explicitly as possible in the text of the *Confessions*, clearly points to the necessity of an allegorical approach. Rousseau begins his story by setting it in a *jardin des Hespérides* ("One day when I was alone in the house I climbed on top of the dough trough to look into the garden of the Hesperides at this precious fruit which I could not approach"). It ends with an identification of maître Ducommun with the ever-watchful dragon (Ovid calls him "unsleeping," *insomni*) that guarded the golden apples: "Unhappily the dragon was not asleep. All of a sudden the pantry door opens." The transmission of such mythological themes from antiquity through the Renaissance, and particularly in the case of Ovid, is fraught with allegorical (often Christianizing) interpretations. Hercules, who is probably the hero of this tale, has a long history of allegorical incarnations culminating in Ronsard's "Hercule chrétien."[24]

It is extremely difficult to point with any assurance to the path by which this myth would have reached Rousseau, on account of both the small number of hints given in the text and the variety of ancient sources. Some versions feature Hercules and others Perseus; in some versions the hero steals the apples himself and in others he tricks Atlas into doing it for him. Ovid's brief reference during his account of Hercules' death is the only verbal reminiscence from a classical text that I have been able to find.[25] But a number of Ronsard's love poems deploy the apples of the Hesperides as emblems of beauty, using the same degree of abstraction as the *Confessions*. In "La Charité," a eulogy of the beauty of Marguerite de Valois, celebrating her marriage with Henri de Navarre, in which Venus sends Charity to verify Cupid's report that Marguerite is more beautiful than she, Ronsard writes:

> Au devant d'elle allaient pour sûres guides
> Avec l'honneur, la grave majesté
> Et la vertu, qui gardaient sa beauté,
> Comme un Dragon le fruit des Hespérides.

> Before her she had as sure guides, along with honor, solemn majesty, and virtue, who guarded her beauty as a dragon does the fruit of the Hesperides.[26]

One of the *Sonnets pour Hélène* takes up the same imagery:

> Les Dragons sans dormir, tous pleins de cruauté,
> Gardaient les pommes d'or pour leur seule beauté.

> Sleepless dragons full of cruelty guarded the golden apples for their beauty alone.[27]

These apples are emblems and not symbols, in the post-Coleridgean sense, of beauty. Their significance derives entirely from a textual tradition, as is made particularly clear by sonnet CXLV of the first book of the *Amours*.

> J'avais l'esprit tout morne et tout pesant
> Quand je reçus du lieu qui me tourmente
> L'orange d'or comme moi jaunissante
> Du même mal qui nous est si plaisant.

Les pommes sont de l'Amour le présent:
Tu le sais bien, ô guerrière Athalante,
Et Cydipé qui encore se lamente
De l'écrit d'or, qui lui fut si cuisant.
    Les pommes sont de l'Amour le vrai signe.
Heureux celui qui de la pomme est digne!
Toujours Venus a des pommes au sein,
    Depuis Adam désireux nous en sommes:
Toujours la Grâce en a dedans la main:
Et bref l'Amour n'est qu'un beau jeu de pommes.

My mind was mournful and heavy when, from the place that torments me so, I received the golden orange, which was turning yellow as I am from the ill we both find so pleasant. Apples are the gift of love: You know this well, Atalanta the warrior, and Cydippe who still laments the golden script that burned her so. Apples are the true sign of love. Happy he who is worthy of the apple! Venus always bears apples in her breast, and we desire them since the time of Adam: Grace always bears them in her hand: In short love is nothing but a lovely play with apples.[28]

A poem like this is an elaboration on a rhetorical commonplace or topos, bringing together a variety of references from ancient authors. The game with which Ronsard concludes is primarily that of collating and combining these references. Rousseau's use of the myth of the Hesperides in the *Confessions* calls upon and inserts itself into this tradition, and necessarily refers us to an allegorical model of reading.

Ronsard's reference to the Garden of Eden points us toward the other main literary source of this fable. In the *Dialogues*, Rousseau makes an explicit analogy between stolen fruit and the understanding of literary texts. "Cleverly passing the real falsifications over in silence," says the Frenchman in the *Dialogues*, the conspirators "have made it be understood that ["J. J."] accused of being falsified passages that everyone knew were not, and focusing the public's entire attention on these passages, they have distracted it from checking up on their infidelities. Suppose that a man says to you: J. J. says some pears have been stolen from him, and he is lying: He has the right number of apples, thus no pears have been stolen from him. Their reasoning has been exactly the same as that man's" (*Dialogues*, p. 960). The pears in question belong to St. Augustine, who in the second book of his own *Confessions* recounts the story of a theft of fruit in order to exemplify all the sins of his adolescence.[29] The point of the comparison is a differentiation: apples are not pears; my story and Augustine's are not the same either. The fact that the pears began life as apples—that is, that Augustine himself lifted the story from Genesis—only complicates the question.[30] Furthermore, this pear tree functions in Augustine's text as a negative prefiguration of another tree in another garden, the fig tree in the garden in Milan where his conversion occurred. This prefigurative, even eschatological aspect of allegory forces us to question the temporal structure of the image of the walled garden, one of the most overdetermined in all of Rousseau's work. A study of this topos in relation to the question of natural religion, particularly in *La Nouvelle Héloïse*, will allow the theory of reading and narrative as constituted by an impossible choice between sharing and splitting, presented in such a schematic and enigmatic form in the episode from the *Confessions*, to be developed.

'La Nouvelle Héloïse'

NATURE, LOVE, AND VIRTUE

Rousseau's lengthy epistolary novel, *Julie, ou La Nouvelle Héloïse*, was the great best-seller of the eighteenth century. It begins as a love story between a young noblewoman (Julie d'Étange) and her bourgeois tutor (known throughout the book by the pseudonym Saint-Preux). The beautiful if dated rhetoric of their letters, a combination of heavy breathing and noble intentions, leads to a night of love that of course results in a pregnancy, which in turn results in a miscarriage. Meanwhile the heroine's father has promised her hand to an old friend of his (emphasis on old). Forced into this unwanted marriage by parental pressure and, most effectively, emotional blackmail, Julie enters the church with the intention of not respecting her marriage vows. But once the ceremony begins she experiences what can only be described as a conversion: suddenly conscious of the sanctity (properly speaking) of marriage and aware of the divinity "read[ing] in the depths of [her] heart," she takes a resolution that produces a sudden change in the course of the novel. "When the Pastor asked me if I promised obedience and perfect fidelity to him whom I took as my husband," she writes to her former lover, "my mouth and my heart made this promise together. I will keep it unto death" (*Julie*, p. 354). After Saint-Preux makes a voyage around the world, Julie, at the instigation of her husband, Wolmar, invites him to come to live with them at the family estate.

This rather curious ménage fills the remaining four hundred pages of the novel with passionate speculations on the relation between memory and identity, the theology of prayer, domestic economy, and the education of children, interrupted only by Julie's tragic death.

La Nouvelle Héloïse is not the most exciting of novels. As the interlocutor "N." puts it in the Préface dialoguée, "The interest is spread too thin and is thus nowhere in particular [*Quant à l'intérêt, il est pour tout le monde, il est nul*]." Rousseau even prided himself on having disdained the devices usually employed to sustain interest in such a long novel. "Not an evil deed, not a wicked man who makes us fear for the good ones. Events so natural, so simple that they are too much so" (p. 13). But what is here characterized as naturalism is not in the least equivalent to realism. The few events that we might characterize as amounting to a plot defy conventional notions of verisimilitude. As Thomas Gray put it, "There is no event that might not happen any day of the week (separately taken), in any private family: yet these events are so put together that the series of them are more absurd and improbable than Amadis de Gaul."[31]

Nevertheless, precisely what the majority of Rousseau's contemporary readers felt his novel to be was *true*. One of the most curious phenomena of the novel's early reception was an overwhelming and even obdurate belief on the part of many readers in the truth of the novel, in the existence of Julie, and concomitantly in its autobiographical character. One of Rousseau's readers, Adrien Cuyet, wrote to him, "I am not as incredulous as your man of letters [N. in the Préface dialoguée]. I believe that this charming creature existed and I believe it for the honor of the humanity that I love." Another (anonymous) reader wrote, "I feel myself to be better since reading your novel which, I hope, is not one. I would be truly afflicted if I could believe that this adorable woman, worthy ornament of humanity and of our sex, had not existed." As sophisticated a reader as William Warburton was wholly able to subscribe to this sort of reading: "You judge truly, and you could not but judge so, that there is more of fact than fiction in [*Julie*]. There would never else have been so much of the domestic part. But above all, the inartificial contexture of the story, and the not rounding and completing its parts, shows the author had not a fiction to manage over which he was an absolute master." This sort of literalism reached its entirely logical culmination in the long correspondence of Marie-Madeleine Bernardoni and Marie-Anne Merlet de Franqueville, who proposed themselves as Claire and Julie, with Rousseau. In the letter that initiates this correspondence, Bernardoni ("Claire") presents its basis in the most lucid fashion possible: "Julie exists, Monsieur, do not doubt it; and why would you doubt it? Monsieur Rousseau exists; is the one more surprising than the other?"[32] This form of literalism is almost invariably tied to an enthusiastic response to the particular combination of sentimentality and moralism that makes the novel so difficult for many modern readers to digest.

Such a concentration on the novel's didactic aims entirely overshadows the novel's lack of verisimilitude. "Diderot has highly complimented Richardson on the prodigious variety of his *tableaux* and the multitude of his characters," noted Rousseau in the *Confessions*. "Richardson in fact has the merit of having characterized them all very well: but as for their number it is something he has in common with the most insipid novelists who make up for the sterility of their ideas by adding characters and adventures" (*Confessions*, pp. 546–47).[33] For Rousseau and many of his readers, then, the weakness of plotting and verisimilitude is a strength of conception, a direct function of the didactic success of the novel. Mme de Staël called it "a great moral idea put into action."[34]

Given that among these didactic aims a large place is given to the praise of the countryside and nature, it is curious that relatively little attention was paid in contemporary reactions to the descriptive language of the novel. The enthusiastic response to the hortatory (as opposed to descriptive) discourse on nature, and the way in which it coincided with already-established movements, has been amply documented by Daniel Mornet in his *Sentiment de la nature en France*. Elie Fréron's review in the *Année littéraire*, as Mornet noted, was one of the few to be sensitive to the way in which the two discourses on nature come together in the novel. *La Nouvelle Héloïse*, he wrote, "doubtless has great faults, but it also contains the greatest beauties. The eloquence of the heart, the tone of sentiment, an exquisite taste for physical and moral nature, a vigorous [*mâle*] and flexible genius that can contemplate it in its grandeur and in its details."[35] Fréron gives an extensive citation from the letter on the Valais and paraphrases the Meillerie episode in book IV at length. By the eve of the Revolution, however, these descriptive passages would be considered among the most important in the novel. Their influence on Bernardin de Saint-Pierre and Chateaubriand, and beyond them on the entire development of French romanticism, is well known. Returning to the contrast between *Julie* and *Clarissa*, Bernardin wrote, "But the way in which Rousseau wins out over Richardson is that the latter lacks the diverse sites and natural backdrops for his paintings that create such a strong effect in the *Héloïse*, as they do everywhere."[36] Mme de Staël waxed ecstatic over the descriptions of Switzerland: "How happily the placement of the scene is chosen! Nature in Switzerland is in such harmony with great passions! How it adds to the effect of the touching scene at Meillerie! How new the pictures that Rousseau makes of it are! How far behind him he leaves Gessner's idylls, those meadows dotted with flowers, those arbors laced with roses! How vividly one feels that the heart would be moved, would open itself more to love near these rocks menacing the skies, at the sight of this immense lake, in the depths of these forests of cypresses, on the edge of these rushing torrents, in this abode that seems on the edges of chaos, than in those enchanted spots, as insipid as the shepherds who live in them!"[37] The same year, Louis-Sébastien Mercier echoed this enthusiasm for the Swiss setting. "Love has more force and a greater sway in this wild land. It appears in its proper place on the rocks of Meillerie; the scene that surrounds it is worthy of it; it becomes free and great, impetuous and strong, like the eagle soaring above."[38]

The place in which a reception of these passages appears most strongly is in the literature produced around pilgrimages to the site of Rousseau's tomb in the gardens constructed by the marquis de Girardin at Ermenonville.[39] Girardin clearly constructed these gardens to recall key landscapes from Julie. His *Promenade ou itinéraire des jardins d'Ermenonville* (1788) describes the *Monument des anciennes amours* as a site in which "everything depicts the situation of Meillerie to your eyes; everything recalls the idea of Saint-Preux writing to Julie to your heart."[40] A *Lettre sur la mort de J. J. Rousseau*, clearly inspired by Girardin, repeatedly calls the *île des peupliers* where Rousseau's tomb was located *l'Elysée*.[41] Girardin's efforts seem to have been well received. Pierre Le Tourneur described the site as one "so analogous to his soul and his tastes,"[42] and Jacques-Vincent Delacroix as "a garden in which art has been reconciled with nature. The author who made so many efforts to unite them today rests in their breast."[43]

There are good reasons why these passages took some time to be noted by criticism. "If nature can always be guessed at in *La Nouvelle Héloïse*," writes Mornet, "it does not hold an essential place. If one leaves out the voyage to the Valais and Julie's Elysium, which do not affect the plot itself, then a whole volume of the four original volumes can be read without encountering a corner of countryside."[44] The descriptive passages are relatively limited in number, and, like the novel as a whole, they have a fairly consistent tonality. The vocabulary in which Rousseau paints his landscapes is in fact quite restricted. The bower in which Saint-Preux and Julie first kiss is described only as "natural" and "enchanting [*charmant*]" (*Julie*, pp. 62–63). Certain key terms will recur in all the loco-descriptive letters (most importantly, *sauvage, désert,* and *torrent*). One of the most important questions that an analysis of the descriptive language of the novel needs to resolve is that of their relation to the one major tonal and thematic shift in the novel, separating the love story of the first two sections from the description of life at Clarens in the second half of the book. A reading of this relation will allow us to determine the temporal structure of the garden, the way in which it represents the sharp divide in narrative time we encountered in the *Confessions*.[45]

The best-known description of this division within Rousseau's novel was provided by Gustave Lanson, who in an abrupt and peremptory judgment called it "a voluptuous dream rectified as a moralizing sermon [*un rêve de volupté redressé en instruction morale*]."[46] Numerous critics, seemingly a bit shocked by this renunciation of the canon of unity, have tried to show the underlying unity of the book's two halves. But even to the extent to which the book can be said to have an *unité d'intention*, Lanson's trenchant formulation may be as accurate as we could hope for. Rousseau's own descriptions of the book, both in terms of moral purpose in the Préface dialoguée ("It might be said that [the beginning and the end] are two different books that the same people should not read" [p. 17]) and in terms of its composition in the *Confessions*, focus on this same incongruous juxtaposition of passion and virtue.

If, as has often been asserted, *La Nouvelle Héloïse* is a novel of happiness,[47] then the accordance of the conception of happiness put forward in each of the two parts should provide a good test for the genuine degree of difference between the two. The terms *bonheur* and *félicité* certainly occur with a more or less constant regularity throughout the book. But the different definitions given in the course of the book are not compatible, and the competition between the paths purporting to lead to happiness provides much of what dramatic tension the novel manages to generate. In the first half, happiness is primarily associated with intense but momentary pleasure. Jean-Louis Bellenot has well described the happiness sought by the two lovers as *la jouissance unique d'un instant d'éternité*.[48] Saint-Preux describes his experience of a single night of love with Julie as a "supreme felicity" (p. 317), and he relies on a rhetoric praising the instant from the very opening pages of the novel. "Ah! if one can live a thousand years in a quarter of an hour, what good does it do to sadly count the days one has lived?" (p. 52). But this sort of happiness is in fact presented by the book as a temptation that must be overcome for the true path to be found. The second half of the novel develops a concept of happiness in which the duration of happiness is the only possible index of its reality. "Is not taking pleasure in the duration [*la durée*] of one's state a sign that one lives happily in it?" (p. 553). Julie presents it as one of the primary precepts of her children's education that "one must pay more attention to the duration of well-being than to the well-being of a single moment" (p. 570). Rousseau's final definition of happiness in the fifth *Promenade* will take up these same terms. "These short moments of delirium and passion, however intense [*vifs*] they might be, are nevertheless, by their very intensity, only widely scattered points along the line of life. They are too rare and too rapid to constitute a state, and the happiness that my heart longs for is not at all composed of fleeting moments, but [is] a simple and permanent state, which is not in itself intense, but whose charm increases with time to the point of finding in it supreme felicity" (*Rêveries*, p. 1046). Insofar as true happiness, for Rousseau, is inseparable from virtue, the movement from valorizing the instant to valorizing duration can indeed be described as "moral instruction."

If this distinction between the false charms of the instant and the true happiness that lasts regulates the division of the novel, it is by no means the case that each conception entirely dominates its own half. It is precisely the few key loco-descriptive passages spread throughout the novel, particularly in books I and IV, at the beginning of each part, that maintain the tension between the two. In both parts of the novel, it is the rocks of Meillerie, doubtless the best-remembered of the novel's landscapes, that represent the temptations of passionate love. It is from Meillerie that Saint-Preux writes the plea to which Julie cedes. Surrounded by a "sad and horrible" landscape, finding in nature "the same horror that reigns within [him]" (*Julie*, p. 90), Saint-Preux reproaches Julie for "seeking a chimerical happiness for a time when we will no longer exist. . . . Ah! dear and tender lover, should we be happy for no more than a day, do you want to leave this short life without having tasted happiness [*quitter cette courte vie sans avoir goûté le bonheur*]?" (p. 93). Even more than his being recalled to Clarens (one of the more obscure passages in the book), the response to this letter is the invitation to the night of love that Julie writes him almost a year later. Its beginning very precisely echoes the beginning of the Meillerie letter. Saint-Preux had described himself, an *âme sensible*, as the "lowly plaything of the air and the seasons [*vil jouet de l'air et des saisons*]" (p. 89); Julie describes the two of them as the "lowly playthings of blind fortune [*vils jouets d'une aveugle fortune*]" (p. 144). Whereas the Meillerie letter had ended with a suicide threat ("The rocks are steep, the water deep, and I in despair" [p. 93]), the threat of a death together at her father's hands is not the least of the seductions that Julie holds out to Saint-Preux the following year: "if today your heart fears the point of a sword no more than it once did the chasms of Meillerie . . . This moment is surrounded by the horrors of death." Finally, she responds directly to Saint-Preux's plea: "No, my sweet beloved, no, we shall not leave this short life without having tasted happiness for one moment [*Non, mon doux ami, non, nous ne quitterons point cette courte vie sans avoir un instant goûté le bonheur*]" (p. 145).

All this talk of dying—Saint-Preux begins his letter following the *nuit d'amour* by exclaiming, "Let us die, my sweet beloved, let us die" (p. 17)—is by no means accidental. The second episode at Meillerie (the final letter of part IV and the emotional and rhetorical high point of the book) is equally obsessed with it. After taking Julie to view the *monuments des anciennes amours*, the boat ride back across the lake becomes the occasion of the great temptation that must be renounced. "Soon I began to turn dire [*funestes*] projects over in my mind, and in a transport that I shudder to think of, I was violently tempted to hurl her into the waves along with myself, and to end my life and my long torments in her arms. This horrible temptation eventually became so strong that I was forced to suddenly drop her hand and go up to the front of the boat" (p. 521). A sense of the stakes of this renunciation can be seen in the fact that the temptation existed for Rousseau as an author as well as for Saint-Preux as a lover. A letter to Rousseau from his friend Alexandre Deleyre suggests that the novel at one time was designed to end at this point with a drowning of the two lovers: "Are you at the end of the novel? Are your people drowned? You're doing the right thing by taking this course, for the earth is not worthy to possess them as you have depicted them."[49] Whether they were to have committed suicide or to have been killed off by the author in an accident, the fundamental signification of such a death, and the termination of the novel in four parts, would have been the same: a refusal to renounce the ideal of passionate love, a refusal to accept the course of time and the process of forgetting, an attempt to find eternity in the moment. Eternity has no duration. "Days of pleasure and of glory, no, you were not for a mortal. You were too beautiful to be perishable. A sweet ecstasy absorbed all your duration, and gathered it into a point like that of eternity. Neither past nor future existed for me, and I savored at once the delights of a thousand centuries. Alas! you have disappeared in a flash! This eternity of happiness was only an instant of my life" (p. 317). Eternity is only another word for the instant; both of them are outside of time. Duration, on the contrary, necessarily has a term and implies the acceptance of change and the possibility of forgetting.

When Julie comes to justify her conduct in renouncing her love for Saint-Preux and marrying Wolmar, in letter 20 of part III (the last letter between the two lovers for two hundred pages and seven years), her emphasis falls precisely on this question of temporality. Passionate love and marriage, she argues, are incompatible.[50] "What long deceived me and perhaps still deceives you is the thought that love is necessary to form a happy marriage. . . . Love is accompanied by the continual disquiet of jealousy or privation, which is inappropriate to marriage, a state of peaceful enjoyment [*un état de jouissance et de paix*]." Because marriage is supposed to be a *state*, stability and duration become its most important conditions. A simple "tender attachment . . . is all the more durable for not being love" (p. 372). This stability is the primary characteristic of Wolmar and the economy (*oikos, maison*) he has established at Clarens. "The order that he has established in his house is the image of the one that reigns in the depths of his heart, and seems to imitate in a small household the order established in the governance of the world" (p. 371). The extensive developments in books IV and V—and indeed their very length— on the domestic economy of Clarens, and the emphasis on the autonomy or autarchy of the Wolmar household, are designed to provide evidence for this contention. The paternal position in this autarchy provides the purest form of durable happiness, the abolition of desire by an uninterrupted appropriation and enjoyment of self. "Alone among all mortals he is the master of his own felicity, because he is happy as God himself is, desiring nothing more than what he already enjoys [*sans rien désirer de plus que ce dont il jouit*]" (p. 467). This ideal of pure happiness (which may turn out to be quite boring) is also expressed by Julie in her "swan song." "My imagination has nothing more to do; I have nothing to desire; for me, feeling and enjoyment [*sentir et jouir*] are one and the same thing" (p. 689). Clarens indeed presents the image of a stable, enduring state.[51]

An enduring state is precisely what the passion of love could never be. Time, and above all the forgetting that comes with it, is love's greatest enemy, and of the illusions fostered by love, the temporal one may be the strongest:

> No other passion creates as strong an illusion on us as love does. Its violence is taken as a sign of its duration; the heart, overburdened by such a sweet sentiment, extends it, so to speak, into the future, and as long as the love lasts one believes it will never end. But on the contrary, it is consumed by its very ardor; it is used up along with youth, it is effaced along with beauty, it dies out under the frost of old age. (p. 372)

The function of death in the economy of passionate love is to prevent forgetting. This can occur either by simply eliminating consciousness and thus both memory and forgetting, or by making this single memory the last one. In either case, the instant is thereby rendered eternal. It is for this reason that the alternative solution represented by Clarens and Wolmar's *méthode* places so much emphasis on the role of memory and forgetting.[52] The memory of passionate love haunts Saint-Preux. "One night, a single night changed my soul forever. Take this dangerous memory away from me and I am virtuous. But this fatal night reigns in the depths of my heart and its shadow will cover the rest of my life" (p. 337). If he takes his voyage around the world "to forget," as one says of the Foreign Legion, it is a massive failure. The intensity of the memory has not diminished. "The same image still rules within my heart," he writes to Claire on his return. "Am I the master of the past? . . . How will I distinguish by imagination alone what is from what was?" (p. 415). The "cure" that Saint-Preux undergoes at Wolmar's hand is designed to make this distinction for him. There is a certain resemblance between past and present, but virtue depends on discontinuity. Wolmar expounds his method to Claire:

> It is not Julie de Wolmar that he is in love with, it is Julie d'Étange. . . . Another man's wife is not his lover; the mother of two children is no longer his former pupil. It is true that she resembles her a great deal and often recalls her to him. He loves her in the past: This is the key to the enigma. Take away his memory and he will have no more love. (p. 509)

The risk to be avoided is that of "confusing [different] times and reproaching himself, as if for a current feeling, for what is only the effect of a too-tender memory" (p. 510). Saint-Preux himself relies on this principle in times of temptation. He can do this precisely because the Julie de Wolmar of book VI is not the Julie d'Étange of book I. "When this fearsome Julie pursues me, I seek refuge with Mme de Wolmar" (p. 677). The path of virtue thus consists in maintaining the maximum possible difference between present and past. The past of love must be an absolute past, one with no direct connection to the present. It is above all Wolmar's method that demands that there be such a sharp break between the two halves of the novel. The principle of this method is a retrospective construction of the past as unlike the present, even as without connection with it.

The path of this virtue, in opposition to the temptations of the instant represented by the rocks of Meillerie in both books I and IV, is figured by a different landscape in each book. In book I this function is held by the letter on the Valais (book I, letter 23), in book IV by that on Julie's garden, known as the Elysium (book IV, letter 11). As we shall see, however, these two letters present fundamentally the same landscape, and fundamentally the same problems of interpretation.

HOW TO READ A LANDSCAPE

Meillerie and the Elysium are opposed to one another as the true path of happiness and the way of error, but Rousseau himself still thought of the two letters as being intimately related. "The return of springtime had redoubled my tender delirium, and in my erotic transports I had composed several letters for the final parts of *Julie* in which the rapture in which I wrote them can be felt. I can cite among others the letters on the Elysium and on the outing on the lake. . . . Whoever can read these two letters and not feel his heart soften and melt into the state of tenderness that dictated them to me should shut the book; he is not made to judge matters of sentiment" (*Confessions*, p. 438).

The Meillerie episode in book IV develops the somberness of the landscape at greater length than in book I, but also softens it. It is asserted that "this solitary site formed a wild and deserted recess [*un réduit sauvage et désert*]; but full of those kinds of beauties that please only sensitive souls and seem horrible to others." The "torrent," "inaccessible cliffs," and "forests of dark firs" surrounding them emphasize the horror, but the actual site is specifically called "a cheerful rustic spot [*un séjour riant et champêtre*]," and the fact that it is deserted makes it all the more suited to serving as an "asylum for two lovers" (*Julie*, p. 518).

The Elysium letter uses the same diction. The *torrent* has been replaced by murmuring brooks, but the two key terms of the Meillerie passage, *sauvage* and *désert*, reoccur with an identical importance. When Saint-Preux first enters the garden, he says that he believed himself "to be seeing the most wild, most solitary site [*le lieu le plus sauvage, le plus solitaire*] in all of nature, and it seemed that [he] was the first mortal ever to have penetrated into this deserted place [*le premier mortel qui eut pénétré dans ce désert*]." "O Tinian! O Juan Fernandez!" he cries out, referring to the desert islands he had seen during his voyage around the world (p. 471).[53]

The landscape of the Valais, in letter 23 of book I, also shares this vocabulary. In terms of the development of the plot, this letter constitutes the first and shortest of Saint-Preux's peregrinations; it both gives the lovers a reason to exchange letters and begins the series of comings and goings that culminate in the voyage around the world. Thematically, the primary function of the letter would seem to be the beginning of the polemical developments on the superiority of country to city life. More than half of the letter is occupied with the discussion of Valaisan customs and morals, their hospitality, eating and drinking habits, and dress. But it is in the description of the Valaisan countryside that the true interest of the letter has generally been taken to lie. Daniel Mornet has extensively documented the extent to which this letter served as a revelation of the Alps for the French public, inspiring numerous voyages and, far more than Haller, making the mountains part of the world of French literature.[54]

The letter on the Valais is tied to the series of letters on Paris in book II by a whole network of thematic contrasts. The contrasts often dwell on sociological questions, as when it is a question of the relation between population size and morals (p. 242), or even in the comparison of the necklines favored by *parisiennes* as opposed to *valaisannes* (p. 265). At another level, Julie compares the letters Saint-Preux writes from Paris unfavorably with the one from the Valais: "At the age of twenty-one you wrote grave and judicious descriptions to me from the Valais; at twenty-five you send me letters like trinkets [*des colifichets de lettres*] from Paris, in which good sense and reason are everywhere sacrificed for a pleasant turn of phrase" (p. 302).[55] The letters are even tied together by the use of the same postal system (p. 258).

The letters from Paris, however, are marked by a total lack of descriptive language. They are instead entirely discursive, given over to a series of *lieux communs* about the evils of Parisian society. As Bernard Guyon puts it in his

notes to the Pléiade edition, "There is not the slightest picturesque evoca-
tion (except in the letter on the Opera); not the least place accorded to the
external world, even when it is a question of a reception in the countryside"
(vol. 2, p. 1475). Nevertheless, the metaphorical diction of these letters draws
on the vocabulary of the loco-descriptive passages. The first of the letters
from Paris begins, "It is with a secret horror that I enter the vast desert of society [*ce vaste désert du monde*]. This chaos offers me only an atrocious solitude in which a mournful silence reigns" (p. 231); it ends, "In the meantime,
judge whether I am right to call this crowd a desert" (p. 236). A later letter
begins, "At last I am in the midst of the torrent" (p. 245).

A connection on this level between the Swiss landscape and Paris should
make us attentive to the possible literary sources of Rousseau's descriptive vocabulary. Although Rousseau's Valais, which one can visit, cannot be treated
as entirely fictional, the description of this site incorporates many elements
already familiar to us:

> I wanted to dream, and I was always turned away from dreaming by some
> unexpected spectacle. Sometimes immense rocks hung in ruins above my
> head. Sometimes high and clamorous waterfalls inundated me with their thick
> fog. Sometimes an eternal torrent opened up at my side an abyss whose depth
> my eyes dared not plumb. Now and then I got lost in the obscurity of dense
> woods. Now and then when leaving a chasm an agreeable prairie suddenly
> delighted my sight.

The focus here falls on the unexpectedness of each sight, the abrupt transitions from one type of landscape to another. For Saint-Preux, the Valais offers the spectacle of all of Nature's different aspects brought together in one
place: "Nature even seemed to take pleasure in setting itself in opposition to
itself. . . . It reunited all the seasons in the same instant, all the climates in the
same place." One of the most important forms of this kind of juxtaposition,
however, is not strictly speaking natural. "An astonishing mixture of wild and
cultivated nature [*de la nature sauvage et de la nature cultivée*] showed everywhere the hand of men, where one would have believed they had never penetrated" (p. 77). Despite the way in which Rousseau's reputation would lead
us to expect him to privilege *la nature sauvage* over *la nature cultivée*, this juxtaposition is a consistent element in all of his descriptions of Switzerland.
The seventh *Promenade*, for example, contains an almost identical description in the account of a botanizing expedition during a visit to Switzerland:

I was alone, I plunged into the crevices of the mountain and, from woods to woods, from rock to rock I arrived at a recess so hidden that I have never in my life seen a wilder sight. Black firs mixed with prodigious beeches, several of which had fallen over with age, and interlaced among themselves, closed this recess with impenetrable barriers. The few intervals that this somber enclosure allowed offered beyond them only sheer rocks and horrible precipices that I only dared look at while lying on my stomach. (*Rêveries*, pp. 1070–71)

In this landscape, all the elements of which could be taken from *La Nouvelle Héloïse*, Rousseau's reverie turns to thoughts of asylum and refuge, and he compares himself to one of "those great travelers who discover a desert island . . . : Doubtless I am the first mortal who has penetrated this far." But suddenly hearing a strange clicking noise, Rousseau pushes through the bushes and sees, in a dell only twenty feet away, a stocking factory. Overcoming his amazement, he comments:

In all the world only Switzerland presents this mixture of wild nature and human industry. All of Switzerland, so to speak, is only a large city in which the streets, longer and wider than the Rue Saint-Antoine, are strewn with forests, cut up by mountains, and whose scattered and isolated houses communicate with one another only by English gardens. (p. 1072)[56]

Switzerland is a *jardin anglais*. It appears to be entirely natural but is in fact a pure artifice, its flowers the traditional flowers of rhetoric. The theme of the *jardin anglais* presents the juxtaposition of nature and artifice as temporal, causal, and semiological. "Nature" throughout *La Nouvelle Héloïse* is a text that needs to be deciphered. As in the story of the stocking factory, the reading of the landscape as allegorical necessarily occurs as the correction of a prior, mistaken reading. For this to occur, nature must suddenly cease to resemble itself. The principle of disconnection advanced by Wolmar's method, which we have seen to regulate the overall narrative pattern of the novel, is also operative in the reading and construction of its landscapes. The clearest statement of this principle is to be found in the discussion of Julie's garden.

Like the garden of the Hesperides, Julie's Elysium is both an island at the end of the world and a walled garden, always locked and surrounded by "foliage . . . that does not at all permit the eye to penetrate" (*Julie*, p. 471). Paul de Man, in "The Rhetoric of Temporality," has shown that this dual character is related to the two major literary sources for the passage: Daniel Defoe's *Robinson Crusoe* and Guillaume de Lorris's and Jean de Meun's *Roman de la*

Rose. The influence of the latter text, de Man argues, can be seen in "the close similarity between Julie's garden and the love garden of Deduit. . . . There is hardly a detail of Rousseau's description that does not find its counterpart in the medieval text. . . . Far from being an observed scene or the expression of a personal *état d'âme*, it is clear that Rousseau has deliberately taken all the details of his setting from the medieval literary source, one of the best known versions of the traditional *topos* of the erotic garden."[57] For de Man, it is in "the use of an allegorical diction" that the combination of the two sources is possible. Referring to G. A. Starr's *Defoe and Spiritual Autobiography* and Paul Hunter's *Reluctant Pilgrim*, de Man argues that "Defoe's gardens, far from being realistic natural settings, are stylized emblems, quite similar in structure and detail to the gardens of the *Roman de la Rose*. But they serve primarily a redemptive, ethical function. . . . The same stress on hardship, toil, and virtue is present in Julie's garden."[58]

In terms of the thematic discourse of the letter, the emphasis on an allegorical discourse found in the literary-historical sources appears in the theme of the *jardin anglais*. When Saint-Preux first enters the garden, he remarks on the absence of any signs of culture. "I see no human labor here." "It is true," Julie responds, "that Nature has done everything, but under my direction, and there is nothing there that I have not ordained" (p. 472). This is emphasized a few pages later when, having been shown the whole garden, Saint-Preux reasserts that "nowhere do I see the slightest trace of culture. Everything is verdant, fresh, vigorous, and the gardener's hand does not show [*la main du jardinier ne se montre point*]: nothing belies the idea of a desert island that came to me when I entered, and I see not a single human footprint [*je n'aperçois aucuns pas d'hommes*]. Ah! said M. de Wolmar, that is because great care has been taken to efface them." Saint-Preux, explains Julie, taking up Wolmar's point, is committing the error of "judging the work by the effect" (pp. 478–79). In accordance with Wolmar's method then, the Elysium is representative of Julie's virtue precisely insofar as it is based upon a separation of the gardener and her garden. Nature is revealed to be unnatural. There is a lack of resemblance between cause and effect, a fundamental discontinuity between past and present. The garden is not the image of its creator. It is a dissemblance.

This principle requires that the landscape be read twice. When Saint-Preux returns alone to the Elysium the following day, he learns a lesson that reinforces the point in terms of Wolmar's principle. Upon first reentering the garden, he is looking forward to contemplating Julie's image in it. He expects the garden as a whole to resemble her, and for every detail of this resemblance to be guaranteed by physical contact. "All that will surround me is the work of she who was so dear to me. I will contemplate her all around me. I will see nothing that her hand has not touched; . . . and I will find her everywhere as she exists in the depths of my heart" (p. 486). According to this conception, the relation between Julie and her garden is simultaneously metaphorical and metonymical, that is, symbolic. By the time Saint-Preux leaves, the situation has been entirely reversed. Whereas previously he had seen it as an image assured by physical contact, now her relation to the garden is reduced to the act of giving it its name. "Everything, even this name, Elysium, rectified in me the strayings [*écarts*] of the imagination, and carried into my soul a calm preferable to the agitation of the most seductive passions." The garden has become an allegorical emblem. Thus it is the name rather than the aspect of the garden that "painted for me in some way the interior of she who found it; I thought that no one with a troubled conscience would have chosen that name. I said to myself: Peace reigns in the depths of her heart as it does in the asylum she named" (p. 487).

The movement from the first reading of the garden to the second occurs by way of what, on account of its formal resemblances with Julie's experience in the church as described in letter 18 of part III,[59] can only be called a conversion. The memory of an image is overthrown by the memory of a statement. "While entering the Elysium with such dispositions, I suddenly remembered the last word M. de Wolmar said to me yesterday in more or less the same place" (p. 486). Saint-Preux having made a somewhat *galant* comparison with the bower where he and Julie first kissed, M. de Wolmar had responded, "Learn to respect the places where you are; they were planted by the hands of virtue" (p. 485). "The memory of this single word," continues Saint-Preux, "instantly changed the entire state of my soul [*a changé sur le champ tout l'état de mon âme*]. I believed that I saw [*j'ai cru voir*] the image of virtue where I had been searching for that of pleasure" (p. 486).

This reevaluation of the Elysium is not one that would simply change it from a pleasure garden to one of virtue, from Deduit's garden of love to Crusoe's island of toil. For it is not the garden that Saint-Preux sees at this moment. Instead, he sees in Julie the same figure of Continence that Saint Augustine saw at the moment of his conversion:[60]

> This image merged in my mind with Mme de Wolmar's features, and for the
> first time since my return, I saw Julie, in her absence, not as she was for me and
> as I still love to represent her to myself, but as she appears before my eyes every
> day. Milord, I believed that I saw [*j'ai cru voir*] this woman, so charming, so
> chaste and so virtuous, in the midst of the same retinue that surrounded her
> yesterday. I saw her three lovable children around her, the honorable and
> precious token of conjugal union and tender friendship, giving to her and
> receiving from her a thousand touching caresses. (p. 486)

This vision, for Saint-Preux, marks the moment of maximum discontinuity
between Julie d'Étange and Julie de Wolmar. It is for this reason and this
reason alone that the Elysium is emblematic of Julie's virtue.

A similar moment of rereading occurs in the letter on the Valais. At the
beginning of this letter, Saint-Preux claims that he "will not give a detailed
account of [his] voyage nor of his remarks," as that would be inappropriate
to an amorous correspondence. Instead he will speak only, he says, of the
"situation of [his] soul" (p. 76). The landscape is first described as both an
image of his soul and the cause of its disposition, as both a metaphor and a
metonymy for it. After briefly describing the landscape, Saint-Preux turns
immediately to its effects on himself. "During the first day," he writes, "I attributed the calm that I felt being reborn in me to charms of this sort [i.e.,
those of the countryside]. I admired the sway [*empire*] that the most insensible beings hold on our liveliest passions, and I despised philosophy for
having no more effect on the soul than a succession of inanimate objects"
(p. 78).

But the fact that this "peaceful state" both endures and grows during the
course of the next day leads Saint-Preux to search for a deeper explanation,
to read the landscape a second time. It is after having moved onto the high-
est of the mountains he could climb that he "gradually figured out, in the
purity of the air in which I found myself, the true cause of my change of humor [*je démêlai sensiblement dans la pureté de l'air où je me trouvais, la véri-
table cause du changement de mon humeur*], and of the interior peace that I
had lost so long ago." The true cause is thus not the beauty of the landscape.
Rather it is "in the air," something one cannot see: "On high mountains
where the air is pure and thin [*subtil*], one feels more ease in breathing,
more lightness in the body, more serenity in the mind, pleasures are less ardent there and passions more moderate." In the one moment at which
Saint-Preux includes a specifically visual stimulus, it is marked negatively:

the sight of a mountain showing only its peak through the clouds is "too vain an image of the wise man's soul [*image trop vaine de l'âme du sage*]." The elevation is both physical and spiritual, moving from a terrestrial to a celestial realm. "It seems that in rising above the abode of men one leaves behind all lowly and terrestrial feelings, and as one approaches the ethereal regions the soul contracts something of their unalterable purity" (p. 78). The passage concludes with a citation from Petrarch's sonnet "Gloriosa Columna in cui s'appoggia":

> Qui non palazzi, non teatro o loggia,
> Ma'n lor vece un' abete, un' faggio, un pino
> Trà l'erba verde e'l bel monte vicino
> Levan di terra al Ciel nostr' intelletto.

> Here are no palaces, no theater or gallery, but in their stead a fir tree, a beech, a pine, amid the green grass and the nearby mountain . . . , lift our intellects from earth to Heaven.[61]

Rousseau translated the majority of the citations from the Italian in a copy of the 1763 Duchesne edition belonging to François Coindet, currently in the Bibliothèque de la Chambre des Députés in Paris. His translation of these verses—*Au lieu des pavillons, des palais, des théâtres, les chênes, les noirs sapins, les hêtres s'élancent de l'herbe au sommet des monts et semblent élever au ciel avec leur têtes, les yeux et l'esprit des mortels* (p. 1391)—presents a curious problem. Rousseau makes the structure by which spiritual elevation occurs both more explicit and less certain than Petrarch, adding a movement by the trees that is echoed first by the movement of the eyes of the observer, and only then by his mind, all qualified as "seeming." Rousseau also supplies a whole forest where Petrarch had placed three lone trees—or perhaps only one tree of indeterminate species, while inserting an oak, which for Petrarch, whose use of trees generally lays a great deal of emphasis on their being deciduous or evergreen (the laurel being the most important of the latter category) would have been a symbol of old age and mortality.[62]

The citation of Petrarch at this point in the letter points directly toward the source of this letter, Petrarch's letter to Dionigi da Borgo San Sepolcro known as "The Ascent of Mount Ventoux." Certain elements in Saint-Preux's description, particularly the view of the clouds below him, and the emphasis on the feeling of light-headedness caused by the thin air, are clearly taken from Petrarch. "Moved by a certain unaccustomed quality of the air [*spiritu quodam aeris insolito . . . permotus*] and by the unrestricted spectacle," wrote Petrarch, "I stood there as in a trance. I looked back. Clouds were beneath me."

Petrarch's letter, like the stanza cited from "Gloriosa Columna," is primarily concerned with the relation between physical and spiritual elevation, and indeed with whether the relation between the physical and the spiritual can itself be described in terms of an "elevation." Petrarch undertakes the climb with his younger brother Gherardo, who takes the difficult but direct route (*iter rectius*) up the mountain, while Petrarch himself, searching for a less arduous path, finds himself doubling his efforts and making no progress upward. When the exhausted Petrarch begins to reflect on his experience, his thoughts quickly turn from physical to spiritual matters (*a corporeis ad incorporea volucri cogitatione transiliens*). "The life we call blessed is certainly located on high, and as it is said, a very narrow road leads to it." Petrarch does not, however, simply affirm this analogy. Instead the emphasis falls on the vanity of the comparison (it is an *image trop vaine*, as Rousseau puts it). At the conclusion of the letter, looking back at the mountain after his descent, Petrarch will say that it appeared to be "scarcely a cubit high in comparison with the loftiness of human meditation."[63]

This reversal and refusal of the analogy is brought about by the central event of the "Ascent," Petrarch's reading of a passage from Saint Augustine. Petrarch opens Augustine's *Confessions* at random to seek what amounts to an oracle, and reads the following passage from book X: "Yet men go out and gaze in astonishment at high mountains, the huge waves of the sea, the broad reaches of rivers, the ocean that encircles the world, or the stars in their courses. But they pay no attention to themselves [*et reliquunt se ipsos*, "they abandon themselves"]." Petrarch's conclusion, "that I ought to consider nothing wonderful except the human mind compared to whose greatness nothing is great," is in accordance with the immediate context of the citation from Augustine, a meditation on memory and the unplumbable depths of the human mind. But it hardly seems comparable to the conversion experienced by Augustine in the garden in Milan, when he himself performed a similar random reading of a sacred text.[64] Rousseau's Valais needs to be read as a text referring to a previous text, Petrarch's Ventoux, but that previous text tells the story of its own dissemblance from yet another text, Augustine's garden.

Petrarch, as Robert Durling has pointed out, ironizes Augustinian prefigurative allegory. Analyzing the numerous parallels that can be drawn between Petrarch's ascent and Augustine's conversion, Durling argues that "almost without exception the parallels are negative. In place of the integrative, resynthesizing process of Augustine's experience, we find disjunction, the dissolution of possible connections, negative parallels."[65] John Freccero has likewise opposed Petrarch's laurel, "the emblem both of the lover's enthrallment and of the poet's triumph," with Augustine's fig tree. As Freccero points out, "The fig tree was already a scriptural emblem of conversion." The fig tree takes on its significance from these past uses, taken up in a pattern of prefiguration and refiguration. The laurel, on the other hand, is distinguished by its lack of reference to anything but its own sonority, taken up in the system of puns around the name of Petrarch's beloved, Laura (in addition to the laurel tree, two recurrent key terms in the *Canzoniere* are *l'auro*, "gold," and *l'aura*, "breeze"). "The two emblems," Freccero argues, represent "two different modes of signification: the allegorical and the autoreflexive."[66]

Petrarch follows Augustine's allegorical procedure quite exactly, but puts a disjunction in the place of the fulfillment of a promise. "Figural interpretation," as Erich Auerbach has defined this procedure, "establishes a connection between two events or persons, the first of which signifies not only itself but the second, while the second encompasses or fulfills the first."[67] This movement between promise and fulfillment is almost invariably characterized as a conversion: a movement from blindness to insight, from the letter of the law to its spirit, from carnal to spiritual understanding, etc. In Petrarch's "Ascent," however, this connection is taken apart; physical and spiritual elevation fail to correspond; the image is *trop vaine*. The Petrarch citation intervenes in, and occurs as a confirmation of, Saint-Preux's rereading of the landscape as unable to support the metaphor of elevation. It designates the breakdown of the narrative of conversion.

The concept of conversion, however, occupies a prominent thematic and structural position in *La Nouvelle Héloïse*. It is Julie's conversion in book III that, in many ways, defines the division of the novel into two parts. The hinted-at conversion of Wolmar at the end of book VI is the only major problem to which the novel does not provide a definite resolution, making it an important topic of debate. We have already seen how Saint-Preux's rereading of the Elysium is associated both with Julie's conversion and with the Augustinian model.

GOD THE GARDENER

Julie's conversion is to what the Savoyard vicar, in his *Profession de foi* in book IV of *Émile*, calls "natural religion." God is seen as the author of nature, and it is the grandeur of nature that provides the primary proof of his existence.[68] It is this grandeur that provides the necessary frame for the vicar's discourse: "In the distance, the immense chain of the Alps crowned the landscape. . . . It could have been said that nature was spreading all its magnificence before our eyes in order to provide the text for our discussion [*la nature étalait à nos yeux toute sa magnificence pour en offrir le texte à nos entretiens*]" (*Émile*, p. 565). Earlier manuscript versions of this passage made the Petrarchan inspiration even clearer, reading "in order to lead our souls away from lowly thoughts and lift us to sublime contemplations [*pour écarter de nos âmes les pensées basses et nous élever aux sublimes contemplations*]" (p. 1509). *Émile*'s preceptor, commenting after the end of the *Profession*, describes how his pupil's education has made it "easy for him to raise himself [*s'élever*] from the study of nature to a search for its author" (p. 636). The vicar himself gives only two precepts for the quest for truth in this domain: "See the spectacle of nature, listen to the voice within" (p. 607).

The vicar's primary proof of the existence of God is based on the incomprehensibility of nature without the presumption of a prime mover. This passage is worth citing at length:

> The first causes of movement are not in matter; matter receives and communicates movement but does not produce it. The more I observe the action and reaction of the forces of nature acting upon one another, the more I find that, from effect to effect, it is always necessary to go back [*remonter*] to some will as a first cause, for to suppose an infinite progress of causes is to suppose none whatsoever. In a word every movement that is not produced by another movement can come only from a spontaneous, voluntary act. . . . I thus believe that a will moves the universe and animates nature. . . . How does a will produce a physical and corporal action? I do not know, but I experience in myself that it produces one. I want to act, and I act; I want to move my body, and my body moves; but that an inanimate body at rest should move of itself or produce movement, that is incomprehensible and without example. The will is known to me by its acts and not by its nature. I know this will to be a motor cause, but to conceive of matter as producing movement, is clearly to conceive of an effect without a cause, is to conceive absolutely nothing. (p. 576)[69]

One of Rousseau's most important developments on this theme is his description of an experience of religious ecstasy in the third of the *Lettres à Malesherbes*, which occurred while he was living at the Ermitage, that is, during the composition of *La Nouvelle Héloïse*. He loves best to remember, says Rousseau, his time spent wandering and dreaming in the forest, "those rapid but delicious days that I spent entirely alone with myself, with my good and simple governess, with my beloved dog, my old cat, with the birds of the countryside and the does of the forest, with all of nature and its inconceivable author" (*Lettres à Malesherbes*, p. 1139). The passage ends in a "staggering ecstasy . . . that in the agitation of my transports made me cry out: O great being! O great being! unable to say or think anything else" (p. 1141). Whatever differences there might be between the forest of Montmorency and the rocks at Meillerie, the mountains of the Valais, or an enclosed landscape garden, the structure of the description is the same. "I then went off at a more tranquil pace to seek some wild spot in the forest, some deserted site where, nothing showing the hand of men, nothing announced servitude and domination [*quelque lieu sauvage dans la forêt, quelque lieu désert où rien ne montrant la main des hommes n'annonçât la servitude et la domination*], some asylum where I could believe myself to be the first to have penetrated and where no importunate third party could come between nature and myself" (pp. 1139–40). This forest, like all the other landscapes we have seen, is a *jardin anglais*. It is so precisely because it is considered not as existing in itself, but as a figure for its author, God. The principle and significance of its existence is to be found in its cause. A long description of the beauty of the flowers to be found there culminates in a citation of the Sermon on the Mount: "No, Solomon in all his glory was never dressed like one of these" (p. 1140; cf. Matthew 7:29, Luke 12:27). The beauty of the flowers is a figure for the greater glory of their creator. Such figures construct not only this glory but also the very existence of their author.

La Nouvelle Héloïse most explicitly adopts this rhetoric in a comparison of Julie's faith and Wolmar's unbelief in relation to the spectacle of nature. "Imagine Julie walking in the countryside [*à la promenade*] with her husband," Saint-Preux writes to Milord Edouard. Nature is Julie's temple. Julie will admire "in the rich and brilliant finery displayed by the earth, the work and the gifts of the Author of the universe." Wolmar the atheist, on the contrary, will see "nothing more in all this than a fortuitous combination in which nothing is bound together except by a blind force. . . . Alas!" Saint-

Preux has Julie lamenting her husband's fate, "the spectacle of nature, so alive, so animated for us, is dead to the eyes of the unfortunate Wolmar and in the great harmony of beings, where everything speaks of God with such a sweet voice, he perceives only an eternal silence" (*Julie*, p. 591).[70]

This threat of the eternal silence of a dead nature appears with a surprising regularity in the loco-descriptive passages we have been examining. Saint-Preux at Meillerie, for example, remarks: "I find in every object the same horror that reigns within me. . . . All of nature is dead to my eyes, as hope is in the depths of my heart" (p. 90). One formulation recurs with a particular frequency. The "horror that reigns within" Saint-Preux at Meillerie, the Paris "where a mournful silence reigns" (p. 231), are the same as the "mournful silence [that] reigns in the depths" of Saint-Preux's heart after Wolmar's departure (p. 512). The only difference between Wolmar the atheist, who "carries the atrocious peace of the wicked in the depths of his heart" (p. 588), and the "peace [that] reigns in the depths of [Julie's] heart as it does in the asylum that she named" (p. 487), is the interpretation given to the absence of sound.

The soul or meaning that is to be given to nature, that gives it life, that quite literally *animates* it, has a number of possible sources. As in the discussion of the difference between Wolmar and Julie, it can come from a recognition of the power of the creator in all his works. But it can also come from earthly love. Responding to Julie's suggestion for a *rendez-vous champêtre* at an isolated chalet, Saint-Preux exclaims, "Let us carry the image of pleasure into sites that offer only a vain image of it; let us animate all of nature, it is dead without the fires of love" (p. 117).[71] Finally, it can come from the imposition of an allegorical meaning. Inviting Saint-Preux to see the aviary in her Elysium, Julie says, "Everything you see is only vegetal and inanimate nature, and whatever one might do, it always leaves a saddening idea of solitude. Come see it animated and sensible" (p. 475). "Inanimate nature" here is fundamentally a designation of the landscape of *La Nouvelle Héloïse*—a landscape, as we have seen, that is invariably *sauvage* and *désert*—before the rereading that gives it meaning. There is no difference on the level of the figure between the *sauvage* and *désert* of Meillerie and those of the Valais or the Elysium. Rather, a different interpretation is imposed on them. Moreover, the fact that the landscapes are arranged in an order opposite that of the progression of the book as a whole—Meillerie is in both books I and IV, the second of the two landscapes presented—makes any interpretation that would imply an increase in understanding impossible. The landscapes move from virtue to error. That both earthly and divine love are able to fill the function of organizing the rereading of the landscape, given that they characterize Julie in the two halves of the novel, should give us pause with respect to the success of Wolmar's method.

However much of a *prêcheuse* Julie admits to being, she never waxes quite so philosophical as the vicar. But the traces of a voluntaristic conception of God similar to his can be found throughout *La Nouvelle Héloïse*. When she gathers herself to pray following her conversion and marriage, it is in terms of the submission of her will to God's: "I will, I said to him, the good that thou willest, and of which thou alone art the source" (p. 356). Her definition of God as "the Being existing through himself [*l'Etre existant par lui-même*]" echoes similar formulations of the vicar's (*Julie*, p. 693; *Émile*, p. 581, and citation below). For Julie this question of existence is clearly tied to will. When she tells Saint-Preux that "nothing exists but by he who is" (*Julie*, p. 358), this recalls one of Saint-Preux's first vows to her, in which he puts his will and his existence in her hands: "From this moment on I remit to you for life rule over my wills: dispose of me as of a man who is nothing for himself, and whose entire being exists only with respect to you" (p. 56). The relation of creature and creator in fact is suspiciously close to that between lover and beloved. As "R.," presumably representing Rousseau, puts it in the preface, "Love is only illusion. It makes for itself, so to speak, another universe; it surrounds itself with objects that do not exist, or to which it alone gives being; and as it renders all its sentiments in images, its language is always figurative." This figurative language of love is, according to "R.," equivalent to that of *dévotion*. The figures used by amorous language, continues "R.," "are without exactitude and without consequence [*sans justesse et sans suite*]; love's eloquence is in its disorder; it proves all the more the less it reasons. Enthusiasm is the last degree of passion. At its peak, it sees its object as perfect; it places it in Heaven; and just as the enthusiasm of *dévotion* borrows the language of love, the enthusiasm of love also borrows the language of *dévotion*" (pp. 15–16). Julie struggles greatly with this tendency to anthropomorphize the deity, what Kant called *Schwärmerei*. It is on this basis that she, on more than one occasion, criticizes mystics like Saint Theresa who "willfully mistake their object" (p. 590). "I do not like," she later says, "this mystical and figurative language that nourishes the heart on chimeras of the imagination, and substitutes for the veritable love of God sentiments imitated from earthly love, and too apt to reawaken it" (p. 697).

Nevertheless, it is by such a figurative substitution, a perception of the creator through his works, that natural religion approaches the divinity.

> It is all in vain, she often says, the heart only attaches itself by the intermediary of the senses or of the imagination, which represents them, and how can one see or imagine the immensity of the great Being! . . . What can I do . . . to escape from the phantoms of an erring reason? I substitute a cult that is crude but within my reach for these sublime contemplations that surpass my faculties. Regretfully I lower divine majesty; I interpose between myself and it sensible objects; unable to contemplate it in its essence, I contemplate it in its works, I love it in its beneficence; but however I go at it, instead of the pure love it demands, I have only a self-interested gratitude to present to it. (p. 591)[72]

It thus is not an easy question to answer as to which illusion, that of love or that of religion, Julie is referring to in her final note to Saint-Preux: "I have long been fooling myself [*je me suis longtemps fait illusion*]. This illusion saved me [*me fut salutaire*]; it is destroyed at the moment I no longer need it. . . . Let us give thanks to he who made this illusion last [*durer*] so long as it was useful" (p. 740). The illusion could certainly be that fostered by Wolmar's method, namely, that a strict separation of past and present, cause and effect, is possible. Julie's comment here that "you believed me cured, and I believed it too" would seem to confirm this. In this case illusion becomes the very principle of duration. As Julie had put it not long before,

> In this world the land of chimeras is the only one worthy of being lived in, and such is the nothingness of human affairs that, except for the Being who exists through himself, nothing is beautiful but that which is not [*Le pays des chimères est en ce monde le seul digne d'être habité, et tel est le néant des choses humaines, qu'hors l'Etre existant par lui-même, il n'y a rien de beau que ce qui n'est pas*]. (p. 693)

But for all Wolmar's atheism, his method coincides, as we have seen, with Julie's conversion in defining the separation between the two halves of the novel. It is equally possible to interpret Julie's conversion as the illusion in question here. As she says of her taste for extended prayer and meditation, "Perhaps it is madness, but a gentle and sweet one [*C'est une folie, soit, mais elle est douce*]" (p. 1788).[73]

God is a methodological fiction, a name given to the principle of will. This supposition is particularly clear in the first draft of the *Profession de foi* known as the Manuscrit Favre.[74] This manuscript describes the transition from the necessity of a first cause, from the notions of supreme will and intelligence, to the existence of "God," as the imposition of a name that does not in itself contain any knowledge. "This being who wills and who accomplishes his will [*qui veut et qui peut*], this active being, whatever he may be, who governs the universe and presides over all things, I call God. Does this word allow me to know any better the essence of the being it represents? No. This word expresses only the ideas of power and will that I have brought together in my mind, and expresses nothing more." But this leaves the vicar in a perplexing situation. For what can actually be known of this being?

> I know that God is the author of my existence and of that of all beings. He equally escapes my senses and my understanding. . . . I perceive God everywhere in his works, I sense him in me, I see him all around me, and when I want to know what he is, where he is, what his substance is, he escapes me and my troubled mind perceives no more.

The vicar is therefore forced to resort to analogical reasoning, conceiving the divine on the basis of the human. "I will never know him in his being. I thus can study him only in his attributes, and these attributes themselves are not accurately represented in my understanding [*n'ont point leur idée juste dans mon entendement*]. I cannot even conceive of him well by his attributes, for how would I conceive of them other than by comparison with human faculties?" This analogy can never be assured, and it is the treatment of it as knowledge rather than hypothesis that constitutes mysticism. Rousseau added here what would at first seem to be an extremely optimistic conclusion from this difficulty. "Never has an induction been drawn with more legitimacy, never has a conclusion from what one perceives to what one does not perceive been more reasonable." This is immediately followed, however, by a comparison of human and divine faculties that shows to what extent the comparison is unjustified. "Man is intelligent when he reasons, and the supreme intelligence has no need to reason. Neither premise nor consequence exists for it, there is not even any proposition. It understands at once all that exists and all that can exist. For it the entire truth of things is comprised in a single idea just as all places are comprised in a single point and all time in a single moment."[75] The vicar's analogical argument moves from effect to cause, from the human to the divine. The deity is a figurative representation of the intelligibility of the book of nature.

If God is the author of nature it is because he is a gardener in the English fashion, one whose action is entirely hidden in his creation. "God himself has veiled his face," writes Julie (*Julie*, p. 699). More precisely, his garden is incomprehensible, unreadable without the postulate of his existence, but his relation to that garden is equally incomprehensible.[76] For to argue from the beauty of nature to the existence of the deity is to commit precisely the mistake that Julie criticizes in Saint-Preux's first reading of the Elysium, that of judging the work by the effect. Nature is an *image trop vaine*.

The conception of nature as having an author, in both the *Profession de foi* and the landscape sections of *La Nouvelle Héloïse*, presents the relation between cause and effect as a semiological one. It is perhaps inevitable that Rousseau has recourse to the classic argument according to which the absurdity of the composition of a literary classic by chance occurrence demonstrates the necessity of an intentional structure to the universe as a whole (*Émile*, p. 579; *Lettre à Voltaire*, p. 1071). The fiction of the author banishes chance and assures intelligibility. It is according to this structure, in fact, that the relation between Rousseau and the Revolution functions. This narrative is not a prefigurative, conversionary one according to which Rousseau's political writings would fulfill the promise of his literary works, or the Revolution fulfill the promise of his political writings. The revolutionaries adopted "Rousseau" as the "author" of their experience in order to assure its intelligibility by providing a figurative representation of it. The fiction of an author, whether it be that of Nature or that of the Revolution, simultaneously describes a discontinuity and an identity between a text and its understanding. The narration of this relation in Rousseau's works, however, occurs not as a conversion but as the repetition of an error. In the *Confessions*, Jean-Jacques fails in both attempts to retrieve the apple; the temptation represented by Meillerie is never banished from *La Nouvelle Héloïse* and in fact underlies the final theophany. The *partage* that allows such a narrative must take place for an initial grasp of the text to be possible, but the loss of both parts of the apple can be read only as a failure of understanding. Rousseau's description of causal narratives demonstrates that any reading of his texts that seeks to become effective will necessarily include a constitutive moment of discontinuity and misunderstanding. One might say, then, that it is precisely because Rousseau did exist that the revolutionaries were forced to (re-)invent him. It is in this sense that Rousseau can be considered to be the author of the Revolution.

4.   The Author of the Revolution

> Committee of Public Safety: A group formed during the French
> Revolution to execute Rousseau.
>
> —*Student answer on a European History exam*

'Du contrat social' and Its Vicissitudes

As with the issue of the entire Enlightenment's influence on the Revolution,
there is a long tradition of identifying Rousseau, and in particular the doctrine of *Du contrat social*, with the Revolution in order to glorify or to vilify
them together. Rousseau is equally likely to be characterized as one of the
main inspirations of Western democratic institutions and denounced as the
origin of what J. L. Talmon called "totalitarian democracy."[1] Even in less extreme forms than Talmon's, there is a whole side of liberal thought that sees
in Rousseau's concept of popular sovereignty a dangerously authoritarian
model of the state. In the century following the French Revolution this position was held, in differing degrees, by Edmund Burke, Benjamin Constant, Alexis de Tocqueville, and Hippolyte Taine, among others.[2] Taine reserved a place of honor in his attack on the Enlightenment for Rousseau,
whose *Contrat social* presents, for Taine, the model of the problems caused
by reasoning about the construction of society on the basis of abstract man.
"Practice follows theory, and the dogma of the sovereignty of the people, interpreted by the crowd, will produce complete anarchy until the moment
when, interpreted by the leaders, it will produce complete despotism. . . . It
is Rousseau's doctrine that is repeated in the streets, the *Discours sur l'inégalité*, the *Contrat social* amplified, vulgarized and repeated by its disciples in all
tones and all forms."[3] Opposed to this "liberal" school there is another tradition, beginning with the orators of all the revolutionary assemblies, who
have taken Rousseau to be the source of the ideals of liberty, equality, and

fraternity. Generally, such approaches are dependent upon establishing a parallel between a given passage in the *Contrat social* and a revolutionary event, institution, or discourse, and applying a *post hoc propter hoc* analysis to declare Rousseau the cause of the Revolution's glories or its evils. This sort of analysis remains a necessity. Neither bibliographical data, including types that would provide unhoped-for revelations such as exact press runs, nor explicit statements of influence on the part of the revolutionaries, can substitute for a determination of whether the Declaration of the Rights of Man of 1789 or the Constitution of 1793, to take two important examples, are in full accord with the *Contrat social*, merely compatible with it, or actually opposed to it. Still, a simple accord could be merely fortuitous. Any claim that the Revolution fulfills Rousseau's political theory, for better or for worse, owes itself a patient and careful analysis of the paths by which his reception traveled.

PROBLEMS OF BIBLIOGRAPHY

As in other domains, the work of Daniel Mornet stands at the beginning of the serious study of this problem. Mornet was the first to reject Rousseau's influence on the Revolution neither because he liked Rousseau and not the Revolution, nor vice versa, but because he felt that the political texts were simply not widely read before 1789. For Mornet, Rousseau's influence lay primarily in *La Nouvelle Héloïse* and the sentimental enthusiasm, the *élan du cœur*, it inspired and exalted. His study of private libraries between 1750 and 1780 provided strong evidence for this view. "It is necessary to go through 500 library catalogues from the eighteenth century, in which one finds one hundred eighty-five copies of *La Nouvelle Héloïse*, to encounter a single copy of this book [the *Contrat social*] which was tolerated in France."[4] In terms of the number of editions and counterfeits, the treatise on political institutions was equally overwhelmed by the novel.[5] For Mornet, the primary character of the reception accorded to Rousseau during this period was even opposed to the *Contrat*. "One does not see, between 1770 and 1787, the *Contrat social* and the [other] political writings . . . take on, in public opinion, a real importance," he writes in *Les Origines intellectuelles de la Révolution française*. "These are works in which one does not recognize Rousseau, the Rousseau one loves, the Rousseau who thrills; and they generally seem not to be known."[6]

This position finds no small support in the few documents we have recording reactions to the book. Gabriel Sénac de Meilhan noted the conformity between the *Contrat social* and the work of the National Assembly, but discounted it because "this profound and abstract book was little read, and understood by few people."[7] Louis-Sébastien Mercier, in his book devoted to celebrating Rousseau's influence on the Revolution, draws a sharp line between the way the book was received before and after 1789. "In the past the *Contrat social* was the least read of all of Rousseau's works. Today all citizens meditate upon it and learn it by heart."[8] The *Mémoires secrets*, after having expressed impatience to see a copy of the book, initially very difficult to obtain, saw its subversive character largely diminished by its incomprehensibility for the average reader. "It is of great importance that such a work not ferment in easily exalted heads; great disorders would result. Happily the writer has wrapped himself in a scientific obscurity that renders him impenetrable to the average reader."[9] Generally, scholars have found relatively little evidence in either printed journals or manuscript newsletters of much public discussion in France of the work, particularly in comparison with the large amounts of documentation that exist for the reception of Rousseau's other works.[10]

Mornet's conclusions were long accepted. Samuel Taylor adopted them in his article on "Rousseau's Contemporary Reputation," as did Robert Derathé in his study of refutations of the *Contrat*.[11] They also form the primary documentary evidence for the most sustained attack on Rousseau's influence on the Revolution, Joan McDonald's *Rousseau and the French Revolution*. At the beginning of her conclusion, McDonald summarizes her argument as follows:

> The influence of Rousseau's political theories was by no means a major factor in the history of the first three years of the Revolution. It would appear that the *Social Contract* was not widely read before 1789, or between 1789 and 1791. The majority of speakers who appealed to the authority of Rousseau did so in order to put forward not Rousseau's views but their own, with the result that his name was frequently associated with arguments that were in direct contradiction with those which he had formulated. It is not unusual to find that when revolutionary writers actually studied the *Social Contract* they were critical of some aspects of Rousseau's political theory, particularly of his condemnation of representation.[12]

The first of these points, although treated in a summary form here (and not exposed at that much greater length in the body of the argument), forms the foundation of McDonald's argument. For example, in discussing Achille-Nicolas Isnard's *Le Principe qui a produit les Révolutions de France, de Genève et d'Amérique dans le dix-huitième siècle* (1789), an attack on the principle of the general will, McDonald suggests that Isnard "may have been laboring under the same misapprehension which has misled some later historians," namely, "that the *Social Contract* was widely read in 1789." McDonald cites the following passage from Isnard:

> The *Contrat social* contains the dangerous principle that produced the revolutions of J. J. Rousseau's fatherland, that took America away from England, that can take France away from the Bourbons and that perhaps, for the unhappiness of Europe, will ferment for a long time still in heads agitated by some taint of politics. . . . Here is the fatal principle that led on the Genevans, the Americans, and the French: The law is the act or expression of the general will.[13]

McDonald argues that the expression *volonté générale* could have been derived from many sources. She lists Charles de Secondat, baron de la Brède et de Montesquieu, Paul Thiry, baron d'Holbach, Denis Diderot, and J. V. Gravina as other possibilities. The key element here seems to me to be not the simple expression "general will" but the entire definition, "The law is the expression of the general will." This formulation was given a final and definitive form by Article 6 of the *Déclaration des droits de l'homme et du citoyen* completed on August 27, 1789.

> The law is the expression of the general will. All citizens have the right to contribute personally, or through their representatives, to its formation. It must be the same for all, whether it protects or punishes. All citizens, being equal in its eyes, are equally admissible to all public dignities, positions, and employments, according to their capacities, and without any other distinction than that of their virtues and their talents.[14]

Thanks to Patrick Riley's history of *The General Will before Rousseau*, as well as a number of studies detailing the construction of the *Déclaration*, we are today in a much better position than McDonald was to evaluate this problem.[15] We should note first of all that the definition of the law as the expression of the general will closely links the universality of participation to the necessary egalitarianism of the law in a way that, as we shall see, and making allowances for the problem of representation, is clearly concordant with Rousseau's thought. The text presented by the committee of five that served as the basis of discussion uses a formulation even more clearly derived from

Rousseau: "The law, being the expression of the general will, must be general in its object."[16] The formulation of the second half of the article concerning "capacities" and "distinctions" provoked extensive debate, but the opening definition seems to have been accepted with little or no discussion.[17] It can be found in a particularly large number of the proposals for a declaration that had been circulating both inside and outside the Assembly for the previous month: some variant of it (usually involving the copula, but occasionally substituting "result" for "expression") occurs in texts by François-Louis Legrand de Boislandry; Adam-Philippe, comte de Custine; Arnaud Gouges-Cartou; Honoré-Gabriel Riquetti, marquis de Mirabeau; Jean-Joseph Mounier; Jean-Paul Rabaut Saint-Étienne; Joseph-Michel-Antoine Servan; abbé Emmanuel-Joseph Sieyes; André-Louis-Esprit, comte de Sinety; Guy-Jean-Baptiste Target; and Jacques-Guillaume Thouret, as well as a number of anonymous projects. It does not occur in the earliest projects by Jean-Antoine-Nicolas Caritat, marquis de Condorcet, Jacques-Pierre Brissot de Warville, and Marie-Joseph-Paul-Yves-Roch-Gilbert du Motier, marquis de Lafayette, which give the idea of a declaration impetus, although it can be found in the *Cahier général du Tiers état de la Ville de Paris*, composed in May 1789.[18] The phrase seems to impose itself, beginning with Sieyes's use in his "Reconnaissance et exposition raisonnée des Droits de l'Homme et du Citoyen," read in the Assembly on July 20 and 21 and published immediately afterward: "The law can only be the expression of the general will. Among a great people, it must be the work of a body of representatives chosen for a short time, mediately or immediately, by all citizens who combine interest in and capacity toward the *chose publique*."[19] This hypothesis that it was Sieyes who established the formulation would seem to be confirmed by the way it is taken up by Mounier on July 27, in a proposal that is very much a response to Sieyes, in which he seeks to limit the possible expansiveness of the formulation: "Citizens can be submitted to no laws other than those that have been freely consented either by them or their representatives; and it is in this sense that the law is the expression of the general will."[20]

To my knowledge, the only time Rousseau actually uses the formulation "expression of the general will" is in a passage of the *Discours sur l'économie politique* whose context renders it little susceptible of celebrity.[21] But it is indeed a faithful summary of his doctrine, faithful enough that commentators frequently adopt it without any hesitation. Among Rousseau's definitions of law, the textually closest variant can be found in a passage of the *Lettres écrites de la montagne* summarizing the argument of *Du contrat social,* in which law is defined as "a public and solemn declaration of the general will on an object of common interest" (*Lettres de la montagne,* pp. 807–8). More generally, we can say that Rousseau consistently defines sovereignty as the "exercise" of the general will, and asserts that only laws are to be recognized as acts of sovereignty.[22] For our purposes, what is most important is that contemporaries clearly perceived this formulation as Rousseauist: this is in fact what the passage from Isnard cited by McDonald demonstrates. Similarly, Alexandre-Joseph de Falcoz, comte de La Blache, a noble deputy from Dauphiné who was close to Mounier, wrote in a letter to the marquis de Viennois that the principles of Sieyes's text were "almost entirely drawn from the *Contrat social.*"[23]

As for the other possible sources, I will begin by simply avowing my ignorance of Gravina. Montesquieu does indeed use an opposition between "general will" and "particular will" in an important passage in book XI of *De l'esprit des lois,* and in such a way that the general will is associated with legislation.[24] But the generality with which he is concerned is only that of application. There is no mention of the subjective generality of participation in the formation of the law, whether directly or through representatives. Diderot's case is somewhat complicated by the fact that his discussion in the *Encyclopédie* article on "Droit naturel" served as Rousseau's point of departure in the first draft of *Du contrat social,* known as the "Manuscrit de Genève." But insofar as he is concerned with establishing absolutely universal natural right, and therefore with the "general will" of the species (*genre*) rather than the nation, this same lack of the subjective aspect is equally characteristic of his use of the term, in opposition to what we find in the *Déclaration.*[25] D'Holbach, in a group of texts published anonymously in the early 1770s, would seem to be writing under the influence of Rousseau's usage (however much personal enmity there may have been between these two, they certainly read each other's work with care and attention). But d'Holbach sees the general will as both a direct extension of natural right and as equivalent to the "will of society," a terminological fluctuation that seems to me to be quite significant. "Every legislator," writes d'Holbach, "is the organ of the general will; his laws are just and good when they agree with the nature of man, the goal of the association, the interest of society, and its present circumstances; they are unjust and bad when they are contrary to man's happiness and the good of society, when they favor only particular interest and are opposed to the circumstances in which society finds itself."[26] Montesquieu, Diderot, and d'Holbach all present generality in a purely objective mode. Insofar as the *Déclaration des droits de l'homme* understands the general will as the locus of an encounter between objective and subjective forms of generality in the context of a particular nation, Rousseau is the only source that really matters.

McDonald's reasons for discounting Rousseau as the source of the revolutionary understanding of the general will are thus of necessity primarily bibliographical. "Reasons for doubting that the revolutionaries were familiar with the theories put forward in the *Social Contract* have already been given, and it is not proposed to repeat these in relation to the revolutionary use of the phrase 'la volonté générale.'"[27] In order to dismiss prerevolutionary knowledge of the *Contrat social*, McDonald's main evidence, following Mornet, is the number of editions: "The first edition of the *Social Contract* was published in 1762, by Rey of Amsterdam. There were no further editions until 1772, when one edition was published, again by Rey. After 1772, no edition appeared until 1790."[28]

As R. A. Leigh pointed out in his review of McDonald's book, "All of these statements are wrong, except the first, and even that is somewhat misleading."[29] Leigh devoted a substantial study to the rectification of the bibliography of the *Contrat social*, and his results have been posthumously published under the title *Unsolved Problems in the Bibliography of J.-J. Rousseau*. Two major new elements emerge from this study. First of all, by showing that even if it was not officially condemned in as public a manner as *Émile*, the *Contrat social* was subject to vigorous interdiction by French authorities, Leigh has turned Mornet's study of libraries and the lack of public discussion of the book from evidence of lack of interest into evidence of systematic suppression. Secondly, he has shown that there were far more prerevolutionary editions of the *Contrat social* than had previously been admitted: "Between 1762 and 1783, a period of twenty-one years, we can enumerate twenty-eight separately available texts of the *Contrat social*, at a conservative estimate, plus at least twelve reprints in collective editions, forty in all. Not bad for an unread book."[30] It is manifestly impossible to treat the *Contrat social* as unread before the Revolution because unavailable.

A consideration of some of the details of the editions listed by Leigh may help us to understand the way in which the book might have been received. Leigh provides the following summary breakdown:

1   Rey's two editions, 8° [octavo] and 12° [duodecimo].
2   The thirteen pirate editions of 1762 and 1763.
3   The "Marc-Michel Bousquet" of 1766.
4   Rey's two editions for Guy, 8° and 12°. (Printed in 1764; available
     in 1765.)
5   Guy's four editions, 8° and 12° (c. 1768 and 1771).
6   The four pirate editions of 1772, 1773, 1775, and 1776.
7   Cazin's edition of 1782.
8   At least one identifiable imitation of Cazin, undated ("Londres,
     Œuvres choisies"), probably 1783–85.[31]

The history of the prerevolutionary sets of collected works, as described
by Leigh, is relatively simpler. Marc-Michel Rey produced complete editions
in both octavo and duodecimo in 1769, and in octavo in 1772 (political
works contained in the second volume). In 1774 a bibliophile folio edition
was printed in Bruxelles for Jean-Louis de Boubers, and in 1775 Samuel
Fauche printed an imitation of Rey's 1772 set in Neuchâtel. The Geneva edition of 1782 was printed by the Société Typographique de Genève under the
direction of René-Louis, marquis de Girardin; Paul-Claude Moultou; and
Pierre-Alexandre du Peyrou in four formats, and it was pirated the following
year in Zweibrucken, Berne, and Kehl. This accounts for a total of twelve
printings of the complete works.

Of the editions printed more than a year after the book's first release, the
most interesting cases are Pierre Guy's editions for Nicolas-Bonaventure Duchesne, both the ones printed by Rey and those Guy printed himself. These
form part of what Leigh calls a "tap" edition—that is, an open-ended collected edition of which all the volumes were available individually and were
separately reprinted as sales required. All printings of the volume of Guy's
"tap" containing the *Contrat social* were dated 1764—prior to Guy's run-in
with the law over his importation of the Rey printing—in order to protect
him from charges of continuing to print a book for which he had already
faced legal action. Nevertheless, the existence of two distinct states (called
"Type A" and "Type B" by Leigh) allows a minimum of two separate printings to be postulated.[32] The edition by Hubert-Martin Cazin (and presumably its imitation as well) followed similar principles: "All the works were
sold separately, except that the *Contrat social*, *Inégalité*, and *Considérations*,
though each a separate volume, were at first offered together for 9 livres."[33]

Thus although available separately, these eight editions were in principle parts of collected editions.

Furthermore, of the pirate editions produced between 1772 and 1776, the 1773 edition appears in "Volume II of a cheap set of the complete works," and Leigh describes the 1776 edition as "another inexpensive imitation of Rey's edition of 1772." This in fact leaves only three editions printed after the book's inaugural year that were entirely detached from collected editions: the 1776 edition whose title page reads "A Genève, chez Marc-Michel Bousquet" but was probably printed in Avignon; the 1775 edition with the imprint "A Philadelphie, chez John Robert, imprimeur du Congrès général" (also including the *Discours sur l'économie politique*); and a 1772 edition that resembles the pirates of 1763.[34]

The grouping of these printings in the early 1770s—that is, during the Maupeou crisis—would seem to be significant. The pamphlet literature generated by the struggle between the chancellor René-Nicolas de Maupeou and the parlements provides one of the few documented uses of the *Contrat social* in prerevolutionary France.[35] Guillaume-Joseph Saige's *Le Catéchisme du citoyen* (1775) follows Rousseau quite literally on many key points: the absolute alienation of individual to collective, the inalienability and nonrepresentability of general will, the necessary double generality of general will, and the distinction between sovereign and government. The *Mémoires secrets* commented that the *Catéchisme du citoyen* "marvelously fulfills its title, which is to say that it puts within the grasp of the most simple and inept a doctrine that the *Esprit des lois* and the *Contrat social* have clouded in a metaphysics very difficult to understand."[36] The text was reprinted in 1787 and several times in 1788.[37]

READING THE COMPLETE ROUSSEAU

If we accept the pattern established by the entries in the *Mémoires secrets* for the first year after the publication of the *Contrat social*[38]—intense anticipation of the new work by the author of *Julie* and *Émile*; rarity of the book caused by problems with the importation of Rey's edition, stimulating counterfeiting; followed by disappointment with the book's difficulty—then after this point it would seem that both publishing and purchasing interest in the *Contrat social* was sustained primarily as part of collected editions. Only three of the twenty-five available editions after 1764 are entirely independent of such a format. Furthermore, no independent editions appeared between 1782, when the massive Geneva edition and its pirates first became available, and the Revolution.

The example of the Rochellois merchant and fervent Rousseauist Jean Ranson, whose correspondence with Frédéric-Samuel Ostervald of the Société typographique de Neuchâtel (hereafter STN) has been presented by Robert Darnton, provides a good model for how this sort of interest in Rousseau generally would overflow into any of his works. Darnton's presentation of Ranson's interest in Rousseau focuses on themes derived largely from *Émile* and *Julie* (sentimentalism and parenting, particularly breastfeeding, etc.), but Ranson's desire for everything by Rousseau is quite notable. Ranson possessed (at least) the Fauche edition of the *Œuvres de J. J. Rousseau* (Neuchâtel, 1775), the Geneva edition of 1782, and a twelve-volume edition of the *Œuvres posthumes de J.-J. Rousseau, ou recueil des pièces manuscrites pour servir de supplément aux éditions publiées pendant sa vie* (Neuchâtel and Geneva, 1782–83). This last edition contained all the material published for the first time in the Geneva edition, and probably served Ranson as a supplement to the Fauche until he could obtain the later edition.[39] Ranson, says Darnton, "wanted to know every secret of his mentor's soul, every detail of his past, every product of his pen. . . . He wanted above all to possess the complete Rousseau, to absorb it into his inner world, and to express it in his daily life."[40] Passages in Ranson's correspondence with Ostervald make clear his desire to have an absolutely complete collection of the master's works.

> Even more interesting [works] by this illustrious author might exist, not even counting his memoirs, and I very much desire it. He said some years ago that none of the new editions of his works were correct, but rather that all were full of falsifications, suppressions, and alterations, even Rey's, which he complained about bitterly. I hope that he has left behind some manuscripts that will make it possible for one to have an edition free of all those faults. If you learn anything about that, or anything else concerning Rousseau, you would give me the greatest pleasure by sharing it with me.[41]

Less than a year after Rousseau's death, Ranson was already losing his patience. "I must be as patient as I can until you are able to send me news about your projects for a COMPLETE collection of J. J. R.'s works."[42] Everything written by Rousseau was of interest to him simply because it was by Rousseau.

Guy's correspondence with Rey about the printing and shipping of the version of the *Contrat social* for his 1764 "tap" edition shows a similar concern. Guy had at first addressed himself, in May of 1764, to Hans Caspar Arkstée and Hendrick Merkus, Dutch competitors of Rey's, to produce the edition. Despite Guy's request to keep the commission silent, these two went straight to Rey, who promptly agreed to counterfeit his own book. For unknown reasons, Guy was not to receive Rey's shipment of this curious edition of the *Contrat* until August of 1765.[43] Guy complained about the poor quality of the printing and paper, the excessive number of copies delivered, and the expenses involved in getting the shipment through French customs. But above all he was angered by the delay in shipping. In January of 1765, Guy wrote to Rey,

> I still have no news of the volume containing the *Contrat* by either land or sea. On that subject, what do you expect me to do with such a quantity? I wanted only five hundred of the in-8° and a thousand of the in-12°. Even that was more than I could consume, because these works are printed everywhere, and on the other hand they can't be sold openly. See if you can't sell them in Germany or somewhere else, at least half of them; I will write to M. Boubers to tell him to send me only half. So many precautions will still be required to make sure they come into port safely, and the expenses are so great that to tell the truth you really have to want to complete this author to get involved in it [*il faut bien avoir envie de compléter cet auteur pour s'y exposer*].[44]

The long list of complaints that precede it could make this last statement sound as though it were merely part of a posture adopted for the sake of negotiations. But the desire to *compléter cet auteur* was equally the reason Guy had given to Arkstée and Markus for getting involved in the venture in the first place. "I have a proposition to make to you, gentlemen. I have just produced a beautiful edition of Rousseau's *Œuvres diverses* and of his *Héloïse*, in all ten volumes both in-8° and in-12°. To make all the works of this author available, I am missing only (for I also have his *Émile*), I am missing only his *Contrat social* and the *Lettre* to the Archbishop of Paris."[45] Interest in the *Contrat social* before the Revolution thus appears as driven by the construction of Rousseau's corpus as a totality in which his position as author guarantees the interest of each piece, following much the same logic as has led to the inclusion of his laundry-lists in the Pléiade edition of the *Œuvres complètes*. *Émile* and *La Nouvelle Héloïse*, the two books that can independently be ranked as best-sellers, are the keystones of this construction. But the collected works themselves were a best-seller. Darnton's statistical analysis of the orders for forbidden books preserved in the archives of the STN places the *Œuvres* in the twenty-third position overall, with more than twice as many orders as any other collected set. If we were to add the supplement to the older complete sets, the eleven volume *Œuvres posthumes*, the combination would account for triple the orders of any other complete set. And at over thirty volumes, the *Œuvres complètes* would most likely be at the top of the overall list if calculations were made in terms of the number of volumes.[46]

This situation, in which the *Contrat social* is of interest primarily as an annex to *Julie* and *Émile*, does not, however, survive 1789. The political works, led by the *Contrat social*, acquire an increasingly prominent and in-dependent position within the corpus. Between 1790 and 1795, the *Contrat social* appeared alone at least eleven times, in formats ranging from 32° to fo-lio. It was published an additional eight times along with the *Considérations sur le gouvernement de Pologne* and other of the political writings. Six editions of the complete works appeared during this period. Finally, one of the most curious editions is a 1793 printing in London, the first volume of which con-tains Rousseau's *Contrat social*, and the second Paul-Philippe Gudin de la Brenellerie's *Supplément au Contrat social*, an attempt to reconcile Rousseau's treatise with the system of representative government.[47]

These bibliographical considerations would thus tend to confirm, in the case of Rousseau, Mounier's assertion that "it was not in the least the influ-ence of these principles that produced the Revolution; on the contrary, it was the Revolution that produced their influence."[48] The *Contrat social* was not unknown, but its influence—or at least the feeling that it was influential—dates from 1789. It was neither unavailable nor unknown, but it did occupy a subordinate position within the corpus. Much like the passions in the state of nature, it appears as a potentiality waiting to be actualized. Joseph La-kanal, in his discourse on the occasion of the movement of Rousseau's re-mains from Ermenonville to the Pantheon, noted that "all the publicists who have considered Rousseau in relation to the French Revolution have particularly praised the influence of the *Contrat social* and his other political writings." Lakanal considered this praise to be well founded, for Rousseau had developed in it "the veritable principles of social theory." "The immor-tal author of this work," continued Lakanal, "has in some sense become as-sociated with the glory of the creation of the world, by giving its inhabitants laws as universal and necessary as those of nature; laws which, before you made a present of them to the peoples of the earth, existed only in the writings of this great man." But this did not amount, for Lakanal, to proof of the influence of the *Contrat social* on the origins of the Revolution. "The great maxims developed in the *Contrat social*, however evident and simple they seem to us today, produced little effect then; they were too far above the grasp of average minds [*la portée commune des esprits*], and even above the grasp of those who were or who believed themselves to be superior to vulgar minds. In some sense it was the Revolution that explained the *Contrat social* to us. Another work was needed to lead us to the Revolution, to elevate us, to instruct us, to fashion us for it; this work was *Émile*, the only code of education sanctioned by nature."[49]

The story of the reception of the *Contrat social* is thus structured exactly in the same way as the discontinuous narratives we have seen within Rousseau's work. The moment of the break between the two parts, we might therefore expect, is one in which the experience of a conversion to the truth and the possibility of radical error coincide. It is also a moment that necessarily gives rise to a double reading.

Incomplete Readings

THE DIVERSITY OF ROUSSEAUISMS

If it was indeed, as Lakanal put it, "the Revolution that explained the *Contrat social* to us," it is evident that different people took this explanation in many different ways. The revolutionary figures whose prerevolutionary Rousseauism is well known, from Brissot and Marie-Jeanne Phlipon (Mme Roland) to Jean-Paul Marat, Bertrand Barère de Vieuzac, Marie-Jean Hérault de Séchelles, and Maximilien Robespierre,[50] indicate the way in which Rousseauism cut across the divide between the Montagne and the Gironde. It was Thermidorians such as Lakanal and Jean-Jacques-Régis de Cambacérès who eventually carried out the long-promised granting of the honors of the Pantheon to Rousseau. The pseudonymous Ptivar's *La Vérité, ou J. J. Rousseau montrant à Robespierre le livre des destins* attempts to reclaim Rousseau from the Jacobin legacy for the Thermidorians. "O good Jean-Jacques!" apostrophizes Ptivar. "If you had seen that your name and your immortal words were abused and made into a title of oppression and tyranny; if the writings of the apostle of freedom and gentleness became chains and daggers in the hands of a few men of blood, how much you applaud yourself seeing France become happy from the labors and travails that have prepared its glory and happiness."[51] As has been established beyond dispute by the research of Roger Barny, every period and every party of the Revolution made some claim upon the heritage of Rousseau.[52]

This is true even of the opposition to the Revolution. Particularly in the early days, but continuing throughout the Revolution, there is an aristocratic, counterrevolutionary reading of the *Contrat social* that uses Rousseau's arguments to argue against the National Assembly. Pamphlets such as Charles-François Lenormant's *J. J. Rousseau, aristocrate* (1790) and A.-F. Ferrand's *Adresse d'un citoyen très actif* (1790?) argue that Rousseau's conception of the inalienability of sovereignty rendered the operations of a representative assembly fundamentally illegitimate. It may be questioned how sincere this attempt was. For such authors, it was above all a question of showing how the Assembly's actions were in contradiction with its own avowed principles. But such pamphlets, moreover, demonstrate the extent to which reference to Rousseau had become an obligatory part of political debate at the time.[53]

For McDonald, it is in these attacks on the Revolution that the greatest fidelity to Rousseau's principles is to be found. She claims to have shown "that the most careful analysis of Rousseau's political theory is to be found not in the pamphlets of revolutionary writers, but in those of the aristocratic critics of the Revolution who protested against the use of Rousseau's name to justify the deeds of the revolutionaries."[54] This conclusion is based on her having adopted the rejection of representation as the touchstone by which to judge fidelity to Rousseau. One could, however, propose other criteria. In counterrevolutionary writers, for example, the attack on representation usually goes hand in hand with a defense, if only implicit, of the particularistic institutions Rousseau had rejected with an equal fervor. If the universality of the law were to be our touchstone it would be this counterrevolutionary adaptation of Rousseau that would appear to be unfaithful. The choice of such criteria is neither self-evident nor innocent.

Most scholars would, I think, agree that Rousseau's definition of sovereignty is the key point that might allow a distinction to be made between his influence and that of a more diffuse sense of majority rule. As Robert Derathé put it in his magisterial study of Rousseau's relation to his predecessors in political philosophy,

> It has been said over and over that Rousseau formulated the principle of the sovereignty of the people in the *Contrat social.* . . . But the meaning to be given

to this principle of popular sovereignty must still be specified, for it can signify two very different things. The *origin* and the *exercise* of sovereignty must not be confused. All the thinkers attached to the school of natural right admit that the source of sovereignty is in the people. If Rousseau had limited himself to affirming that sovereignty rested *originally* in the people, he would have said nothing more than Jurieu, Pufendorf, or even Hobbes. . . . What is new in his doctrine is the affirmation that sovereignty must always rest in the people. . . . The only legitimate state is the one in which the people itself exercises sovereignty, that is, the republican state.[55]

The formulation adopted in the 1789 *Déclaration des droits de l'homme et du citoyen* carefully skirts the issue. "The principle of all sovereignty resides essentially in the nation; no body or individual can exercise any authority that does not expressly emanate from it [*Le principe de toute souveraineté réside essentiellement dans la nation: nul corps, nul individu ne peut exercer d'autorité qui n'en émane expressément*]."[56] It is impossible to tell from this statement just what powers the nation can legitimately delegate. "Principle" could perfectly well be another word for "source"; "essentially" could either be opposed to "in practice," or could just as well mean "inalienably."

The strictures Rousseau places on representation are indeed very strong. "Sovereignty, being nothing more than the exercise of the general will, can never be alienated, and the sovereign, which is only a collective being, can only be represented by itself; power can very well be transferred, but will cannot," Rousseau writes at the beginning of book II (*Contrat social*, p. 368). He returns to the charge in a chapter of book III specifically devoted to the issue: "Sovereignty cannot be represented for the same reason that it cannot be alienated; it consists essentially in the general will, and will cannot be represented [*la volonté ne se représente point*]: It is the same or it is other; there is no middle ground" (p. 429). In addition to these statements of principle, Rousseau makes a specific and biting critique of parliamentary systems of the English type:

The people's deputies are not and cannot be its representatives, they are only its agents [*commissaires*]; they can conclude nothing definitively. Any law that the People in person has not ratified is null; it is not a law. The English people believes itself to be free; it is sadly mistaken, it is only free during the election of the members of Parliament; once they are elected, the people is a slave, it is nothing. . . . The instant a people gives itself representatives, it is no longer free; it no longer exists. (pp. 429–31)

To combat the Revolution and defend the Old Regime on the basis of passages like this one, as writers like Lenormant and Ferrand did, is nonetheless equally to exclude major elements of Rousseau's political theory. In particular, such arguments ignore the formal conditions that Rousseau lays down for determining whether what passes for the general will is truly general. The formation of any intermediate body in the state, like the provinces and *pays d'état*, the aristocracy, clergy, or corporations such as the craft guilds of the Old Regime, gives rise to particular wills that interfere with the formation of the general will. Nor can the exclusion of any citizen from deliberation be allowed. For it is not the people taken individually but the "people assembled" that is sovereign. Groups of electors, such as the bailiwicks that elected delegates to the Estates General, would have to be considered intermediate bodies: they express the will of a particular constituency, and not the general will. Thus the imperative mandate, according to which a delegate would have strict orders from his constituents to vote a certain way on certain questions, violates the conditions of generality. This is true even if one considers only the election of the Third Estate; the division of the Estates into Clergy, Nobility, and Commons only exacerbates the problem.

The rejection of representation is an important aspect of Rousseau's theory of sovereignty. But we still must ask whether it occupies a commanding position within that theory, which would make it into the fundamental criterion for determining the faithfulness of a reading, or if, on the contrary, it exists within a conceptual constellation in which other factors are at least equally important.

INALIENABLE, INDIVISIBLE, INFALLIBLE

Rousseau's social contract is a contract of association and not of subjection. "Before examining the act by which a people elects a king," he writes in rejecting Grotius's notion of a contract by which sovereignty would be permanently transferred from people to ruler, "it would be good to examine the act by which a people is a people" (p. 359). The function of the contract is thus to create an association that will be a true "body politic," that is, a moral person endowed with the same unity as a natural individual. The motivation for naturally free and independent individuals to enter into such a pact can only be the state of generalized war that marks the end of the state of nature, in which life, liberty, and property are constantly threatened. But these individuals cannot renounce their liberty without ceasing to be human, which leads Rousseau to formulate the problem in the following terms: "To find a form of association that defends and protects with all the common force the person and goods of each associate, and by which each, uniting himself with all, nevertheless obeys only himself and thus remains as free as before the pact." Rousseau's solution to this problem is the "total alienation of each associate with all his rights to the entire community." The alienation must be total so as to be equal. This equality is what gives us an interest in being just: "The condition being equal for all, no one has an interest in making it onerous for the others" (pp. 360–61). The equality of total alienation (or total dependence) is the defining characteristic of the act of association, for it alone ensures the existence of a truly general interest upon which all can agree. "The engagements that bind us to the social body," Rousseau insists, "are obligatory only because they are mutual, and their nature is such that in fulfilling them one cannot work for others without also working for oneself" (p. 373).

But this total alienation is not, for Rousseau, a loss of freedom. Rather, just as simple (and always precarious) possession is transformed into property, the natural liberty of man in the state of nature, simultaneously allencompassing and severely limited by his individual weakness, is transformed into civil or moral liberty, "which alone renders man truly master of himself, for the impulsion of mere appetite is slavery, and obedience to the law one has prescribed for oneself is freedom" (p. 365). This new form of freedom, however, can never be exercised individually but only collectively. Just as the individual's freedom is exercised through his will, which always relates to his own interest, so civil freedom is exercised through the legislative activity of the general will, whose object is always the general interest. This is what Rousseau calls sovereignty. Rousseau gives three fundamental characterizations of sovereignty, enumerated in the headings to the first three chapters of book II: sovereignty is inalienable, indivisible, and infallible. It is in the relations established between these three terms that we must seek our criteria for evaluating the fidelity of readings of the text.

The inalienability of sovereignty is, as we have already seen, the basis of Rousseau's critique of representation. "Sovereignty, being nothing more than the exercise of the general will, can never be alienated, and the sovereign, which is only a collective being, can only be represented by itself; power can very well be transferred, but will cannot" (p. 368). It is important to note, however, that Rousseau does not discuss this problem here in terms of parliamentary-style constitutional arrangements but rather has in view the more traditional problem of the delegation of sovereignty from the people to an individual (i.e., a king). It is the temporal structure of the promise[57]—that is, the "contract" of subjugation (or any contract whose content goes beyond its own form, which is to say the agreement to have a contract at the present time)—that constitutes the primary object of Rousseau's critique; he thus focuses on the temporal relations between general and particular wills. The general will, Rousseau begins, can agree with a particular will at a given point in time, but this agreement is necessarily the effect of chance; there is no possible guarantee that it will endure. The general will therefore cannot promise that it will agree with a given particular will in the future. "If the people thus simply promises to obey, it is dissolved by this very act; it loses the quality of being a people; from the moment there is a master there is no more sovereign, and henceforth the body politic is destroyed" (p. 369). This analysis has three important implications. The first is that sovereignty inheres in the body politic in the form of the assembly of the people, and that it exists only in this form. "The Sovereign having no force other than the legislative power acts only by laws, and laws being only authentic acts of the general will, the Sovereign can act only when the people is assembled" (p. 425). Secondly, it implies that sovereignty is always and only exercised in the present.[58] Even if the social contract is necessarily represented as a foundational moment in the past, it is equally necessarily reaffirmed in every act of the general will. This is why the social contract is not a constitution in the modern sense.[59] "It is contrary to the nature of the body politic for the sovereign to impose upon itself a law that it cannot break. . . . There neither is nor can be any kind of fundamental law that would be obligatory for the body of the people, not even the social contract" (p. 362). Finally, we can note that the general will maintains a constant relation with the general interest, whose objective existence is always assumed by Rousseau. It is because "particular will tends by nature to preferences, and the general will to equality" that the agreement of these two wills can never be more than accidental (p. 368).

Sovereignty is indivisible, Rousseau proclaims, "for the same reason that [it] is inalienable." This would seem to refer above all to the idea of inherence. "For the will is general, or it is not; it is that of the body of the people, or only of a part" (p. 369). The key point here is that Rousseau defines sovereignty as the exercise of will, not power. He attacks the traditional understanding of the separation of powers, which, since it defines sovereignty as power (*potestas, imperium,* or *dominium*),[60] can attribute different forms or domains of power to different instances within the state.

> But our politicians, unable to divide sovereignty in its principle, divide it in its object; they divide it into force and will, legislative power and executive power, into rights of taxation, justice, and war, into interior administration and power to treat with foreigners: At one point they confuse all these parts and at another they separate them; they make the Sovereign into a fantastic being formed out of borrowed parts [*pièces rapportées*]; it is as if they composed a man out of several bodies one of which would have eyes, another arms, another feet, and nothing else. (p. 369)

Rousseau does have a version of the separation of powers, but it is by no means a division of sovereignty. Even if sovereignty is indivisible, the body politic as a whole is subject to a division into force and will: "Every free action has two causes that come together to produce it, one moral, namely the will that determines the act, the other physical, namely the power that executes it. . . . The body politic has the same motive forces; one distinguishes likewise force and will; the latter under the name of *legislative power*, the former under that of *executive power*" (p. 395).[61] The separation of powers as Rousseau understands it is a direct logical consequence of the distinction between sovereign and government, which is itself a logical consequence of the definition of the law as expression of the general will. If Rousseau distinguishes between executive and legislative powers, it is because the executive power is not part of the sovereign. Only will—that is, the legislative power—is sovereign, and it is so indivisibly, but on condition of maintaining the double generality characteristic of the law. "Executive power cannot belong to the generality as Legislative or Sovereign; because this power consists only in particular acts that do not fall within the competence of the law, nor, in consequence, in that of the Sovereign, all of whose acts can only be laws" (pp. 395–96). Rousseau thus excludes acts traditionally considered to be sovereign from the purview of sovereignty. A declaration of war or peace "is not a law but only the application of the law, a particular act determining the case of the law" (p. 370). Likewise, the execution of criminal sentences is not a sovereign act but "a right that [the Sovereign] can confer without being able to exercise it itself" (p. 377). Perhaps most surprisingly, Rousseau points out that the act of nomination is a particular act par excellence and therefore cannot be a law. "The law can establish privileges but not grant them to individuals; it can establish a monarchy but not name a king" (p. 379). It is thus necessary to distinguish between the sovereign act that establishes the kind of government, and the nomination of a particular government, which is itself an act of government.

> The difficulty is to understand how one can have an act of government before the government exists, and how the people, which is only sovereign or subject, can become prince or magistrate in certain circumstances. It is here that we discover one of these astonishing properties of bodies politic, by which apparently contradictory operations are reconciled. For this operation occurs by means of a sudden conversion of sovereignty into democracy; in such a way that, without any noticeable change, and only by a new relation of all to all, the citizens, become magistrates, pass from general acts to particular acts and from the law to its execution. (pp. 433–34)

This distinction allows Rousseau to insist simultaneously that "every legitimate government is Republican" (that is, ruled by laws in the true sense [pp. 379–80]) and to take in the vast empirical range of existing political institutions considered as forms of government. Monarchy, aristocracy, democracy, and their gradations are governments, not sovereigns. Rousseau's overriding concern with the question of legitimacy is to be resolved entirely at the level of sovereignty. Governments may be more or less good, more or less wise, but if they remain within their competence and do not try to usurp sovereignty (which, however, they inevitably do), they are all possible. Rousseau is thus able to combine a sort of absolutism with respect to the question of legitimacy with a thoroughgoing relativism with respect to governmental forms. "When one asks absolutely what is the best government, one poses an insoluble because indeterminate question; or, if you prefer, a question that has as many correct solutions as there are possible combinations in the absolute and relative positions of peoples" (p. 419). In particular, Rousseau follows Montesquieu closely in granting a large role in determining which form of government would be most appropriate for each people to factors of size, fertility of soil, character of the inhabitants, and above all, climate.

The indivisibility of sovereignty thus depends upon a particular form of limitation of sovereignty. This is particularly clear if we compare Rousseau's definition to that of Jean Bodin, who also insisted on indivisibility. Bodin calls "the power to make and unmake [*donner et casser*] the law" "the first mark of sovereignty." But he goes on to subsume under this general category a whole variety of powers (declaring war and making peace, judging in the last resort, instituting officers, coining money, etc.) that Rousseau ascribes to the executive.[62] For Bodin the indivisibility of sovereignty is the unity of power necessary to maintain public order in the body politic. For Rousseau, too, the unity of the body politic is very much at stake, but indivisibility is even more fundamentally a feature of the nature of law. Indeed, this restriction of sovereignty to the faculty of will and the activity of legislation alone puts us at the heart of Rousseau's reasoning in declaring the general will infallible.

Rousseau in fact never uses the term "infallible," which I have adopted for the sake of symmetry. The heading to chapter 3 of book II of *Du Contrat social* puts it in the form of a question: "Whether the general will can err," which in the body of the chapter turns into the assertion that "the general will is always just [*toujours droite*]." Rousseau begins by declaring that "it follows from what precedes that the general will is always just and always tends toward public utility: But it does not follow that the people's deliberations always have the same rectitude [*droiture*]." Just as it is specifically will that cannot be alienated or divided, so it is only will, and not the means to attain its object, that can be considered infallible. This is because one of Rousseau's constant suppositions is a tautological relation between will and self-interest. "One always wills [*veut*] one's own good, but one does not always see it" (p. 371).[63] But because there is no necessary correspondence between understanding and will, bad legislation is all too possible.

> How can a blind multitude that often does not know what it wants [*veut*], because it rarely knows what is good for it, carry out on its own as great and difficult an enterprise as a system of legislation? On its own the people always wills the good, but it does not always see it by itself. The general will is always just, but the judgment that guides it is not always enlightened. (p. 380)

Now, Rousseau is by no means opposed to more enlightened voters as such. But his solution to this problem does not take the path later taken by Condorcet, for example, of attempting to ensure the conditions of the rationality of majority decision-making in terms of the degree of enlightenment of the body of voters.[64] Rather, his solution is above all formal. It consists primarily in giving a rigorous definition, consequent upon his interpretation of the division of powers, to the notion of law, and laying down stringent formal conditions for determining the generality of the general will. The government issues what Rousseau calls decrees, which establish the application of the law to particular cases. The sovereign only makes laws, which are defined by their absolutely egalitarian, nonparticular character. "When the entire people enacts statutes for the entire people, it considers only itself, and if a relationship is formed, it is between the entire object considered from one point of view and the entire object considered from another point of view. Then the matter the statute concerns is general, like the will that enacts it. It is this act that I call a law" (p. 379).

If the law is the expression of the general will, it is also the only possible expression of the general will. Any will that expresses itself in a form other than that of the law is not general but particular. The generality of the general will is determined not only by its subject (the entire people declaring its will) but just as much by its object, that is, by the formal universality of its application. Rousseau thus lays down that

> the general will to be truly such must be general in its object as in its essence, that it must set forth from all to be applied to all, and that it loses its natural rectitude when it tends toward some individual and determinate object. . . . Just as a particular will cannot represent the general will, the general will in turn changes its nature when it has a particular object, and cannot, as general, pronounce upon either a man or a fact. (pp. 373–74)

Inalienability constitutes the subjective side of generality: representation, which is always the substitution of the will of an individual or group for the will of the whole collectivity, is a clear loss of generality. What is perhaps more surprising is that indivisibility turns out to be the objective side of generality. As soon as it considers a particular object, the general will ceases to be general and becomes particular because this consideration of particulars provokes a division within the body of the citizens:

> I have already said that there was no general will with respect to a particular object. Either this object is within the state or outside of the state. If it is outside of the state, a will that is foreign to it is not general with respect to it; and if this object is in the state, it is part of it: A relation is then formed that makes the state into two separate beings, of which the part is one and the whole minus the part is the other. But the whole minus the part is not the whole, and so long as this relation subsists there is no longer a whole but two unequal parts; whence it follows that the will of the one is no longer general with respect to the other. (pp. 378–79)

In these passages Rousseau explicitly refers back to his previous analyses of inalienability and indivisibility. His three definitions of sovereignty clearly form a coherent system. Indeed, we can say that infallibility—that is, the necessary double generality of the law—is precisely a statement of the unity of inalienability and indivisibility. Just as the general will, the power to make law, cannot be delegated without ceasing to exist, the execution of law (that is, any act that is not characterized by a strict universality and equality) *must* be delegated, again lest the general will cease to exist. The condition of this unity is that the sovereign in fact limit itself to making laws. The analysis of the formal conditions of generality of the general will can also be described in Kantian terms as depending on a rigorous distinction between theoretical and practical reason. For Kant, the categorical imperative requires that the moral individual universalize himself by making maxims susceptible of universal legislation into the principle of his will.[65] For Rousseau, the subjective moment of universality is provided empirically by the assembly of the whole people. But the formal analysis determining what rules are susceptible of universalization in the form of law are the same. As Ernst Cassirer, who has most strongly argued the connection between Rousseau and Kant on this point, puts it, "To [Rousseau] freedom did not mean arbitrariness but the overcoming and elimination of all arbitrariness, the submission to a strict and inviolable law which the individual erects over himself. Not renunciation of and release from this law but free consent to it determines the genuine and true character of freedom."[66]

But this is, we must emphasize, a formal rather than pragmatic analysis, and the system it establishes is fundamentally precarious. Indeed, if Rousseau declares at the outset that he is taking "men as they are and laws as they can be" (p. 351), and insists that one cannot consider "the people assembled" as merely chimerical since it has actually existed,[67] the *Contrat social* as a whole is suffused with a deep pessimism about the possibility of maintaining legitimate political institutions. When Rousseau argues that "if the opposition of particular interests made the establishment of societies necessary, it is the agreement [*accord*] of these same interests that has made it possible" (p. 368), he comes dangerously close to reversing—without refuting—his statement in the second *Discours* that "the vices that make social institutions necessary are the same as the ones that make their abuse inevitable" (*Discours sur l'inégalité*, p. 187). The loss of freedom, which Rousseau seems to view as an inevitable consequence of an organic cycle of life and death that applies as inexorably to states as it does to individuals, is most likely to be the result of the government, which must have a particular will in order to exist at all and have a force of its own.[68] But "as particular will constantly acts against the general will, so the government makes a continual effort against sovereignty" (*Contrat social,* p. 421). The natural inclination of government is to shrink in size, which strengthens its particular will and reinforces the particularity of that will, that is, makes it more sharply distinct from the general will. It is further prone to usurp sovereignty, ceasing to apply the law and aspiring to make the law itself. Democracy degenerates into ochlocracy, aristocracy into oligarchy, monarchy into tyranny.[69] Sooner or later, the government takes itself for the sovereign.

But this same process of dissolution of the social bond—which is essentially the diremption of particular interest and general interest—can also occur among the citizens themselves. Indeed, the concept of ochlocracy (traditionally "mob rule," but here more precisely rule by the whole body of the people that does not respect the formality of law) indicates that governmental usurpation may well depend on the dissolution of the general interest and the subordination of the general will itself in the very process of legislation. While Rousseau is often described as a democrat, "democracy" in the sense that he gives the term—that is, a situation wherein the body of the people as a whole acts alternately in the different capacities of sovereign and government—seems no less destined to ochlocracy than monarchy to tyranny. It is both impossible and necessary: "If there was a people of gods, it would be governed democratically. So perfect a government is not made for men" (p. 406). The difficulty of democratic government partially stems from considerations of size and the necessity of constantly, rather than merely occasionally, assembling the body politic. But these prudential considerations quickly shade into questions of principle. The alternation of functions that democracy presupposes creates confusion, a lack of distinction where distinction is necessary. "It is not good for he who makes the laws to execute them, nor for the body of the people to turn its attention away from general perspectives to devote it to particular objects" (p. 404). The presentation before the body of the people of matters of particular interest can only give it bad habits and eventually corrupt the sovereign. "Were it possible for the sovereign, considered as such, to hold executive power, right and fact would be so confused that one would no longer know what is a law and what is not, and the body politic would soon be prey to the violence against which it was established" (p. 432). The problem is not only how to keep the government from acting as if it were the sovereign but also how to keep the sovereign from acting as if it were the government. This problem is exacerbated in Rousseau's system by the fact that he formally excludes the possibility of a "constitutional" solution that opposes different interests and makes them counterbalance one another. As we shall see, only virtue stands between the state and ruin.

THEORY AND PRACTICE; OR, HOW DOES THE CITIZEN VOTE?

If the conceptual unity of Rousseau's theory of sovereignty resides in an entirely formal definition of generality, the maintenance of this system itself depends in practice upon a relation between general and particular will within the individual citizen that is anything but formal. In a brilliant essay devoted to following the displacement of a series of fault lines in the *Contrat social*, Louis Althusser described this problem as the "very discrepancy [*décalage*] of the theory with respect to the real," and he presents it as resulting in "the transfer of the impossible theoretical solution into the alternative to theory, literature."[70] Indeed, the whole problem of the applicability of the *Contrat social* hinges on this point. The charge of being unrealistic and unrealizable, made by both adversaries and admirers of Rousseau, is perhaps the most frequent characterization of the *Contrat social*. It plays a particularly large role in aristocratic and counterrevolutionary appropriations of Rousseau. During the Revolution, for example, the Belgian-Swiss aristocrat Isabelle de Charrière wrote,

> What did I admire most in Rousseau? It is his *Dreams*. . . . Where will we, surprised and curious, interrogate his art, seek to recognize if it is this word or that word, or such an arrangement of words, which makes of us what he wishes? in projects and chimerical hypotheses; in an impossible education; in a Social Contract that no society has made nor could make; in Dreams, in a word. How lovable these Dreams are![71]

Another example can be found in the rigorously Kantian reading of Rousseau presented by Éric Weil (who goes so far as to say that "it took Kant to *think* Rousseau's *thoughts*"),[72] which forcibly ejects the *Contrat social* from the domain of practical politics. Rousseau's theory, writes Weil, "is, and *intends itself to be*, unrealizable [*Sa théorie est, et se veut, irréalisable*]." Application is therefore impossible, or perhaps, more precisely, application is necessarily partial and deforming. "The man who wants to act," Weil continues, "cannot remain faithful to Rousseau."[73] It would then be precisely the unity of Rousseau's theory that could not survive its enactment. While admitting that certain isolated themes (*"ces aperçus politiques, ces idées brillantes"*) were taken up by the revolutionaries, Weil contends that "what seems sure is that, *if* one searches for—or constructs—the unity of Rousseau's political thought, it found no real representative [during the Revolution], and for good reason: it allows judgment; it does not allow action."[74]

But the separation of the conceptual coherence of Rousseau's thought from its rhetoric that allows Weil to make such a claim is itself a division (if not an impoverishment) of the text. While the formal argumentative structure of the book means that it cannot be divided into two clearly separated halves, as can so many other of his texts, one can in fact describe the existence of a *partage* of the *Contrat social* into two different rhetorical modes, one of which dispassionately defines the criteria by which the legitimacy or illegitimacy of political institutions can be judged, while the other, in powerful and often urgent tones, seeks the conditions of possibility of the construction of a just polity and demands its realization. As a set of canons of judgment, we have seen the theory to be applicable to states of all sizes and governments. This does not prevent Rousseau from telling us, in a prescriptive or hortatory mode, that only in a small state can legitimacy be maintained, and that elective aristocracy is "the best" of governments (p. 406). Indeed, in the *Lettres écrites de la montagne*, Rousseau presents the *Contrat social* as a whole as applicable primarily to Geneva, functioning both as a description of its institutions that holds it up as a model for all of Europe, and a series of warnings about how to maintain the true spirit of those institutions against the usurpations of the Petit Conseil.[75] "I thus took your constitution, finding it beautiful," he writes to a fictive Genevan, "and in proposing it as a model of political institutions, far from seeking to destroy you I exposed the means to preserve you." The last thing his book presents, in this account, is another utopia.

> Since a government existed along the lines of my model, I thus did not tend to destroy all existing governments. Monsieur, if I had only constructed a system, be sure that nothing would have been said against me. It would have been enough to relegate the *Contrat social*, along with Plato's *Republic, Utopia*, and the *Histoire des Sévarambes*, to the land of chimeras. But I painted an existing object, and certain people [*on*] wanted to change the appearance of this object.

My book bore witness against the attack [*attentat*] that was being prepared. For this I could not be pardoned. (*Lettres de la montagne*, pp. 809–10)

The series of chapters in book II, "On the People," that attempt to establish the conditions under which a people is susceptible of foundation, or the detailed discussions of Roman institutions in book IV, clearly reveal a continual preoccupation with pragmatic politics.

Indeed, one of the primary points of interest of Althusser's concentration on the existence of fault lines within the argumentation of *Du contrat social*, confirming the interpretations we have advanced in the preceding chapters, is that it suggests that this sort of division is internal to Rousseau's logic. The analysis of these fault lines, Althusser writes, will "make intelligible the possibility of a number of 'readings' of Rousseau's *Contrat social*, and the subsequent interpretations (Kantian, Hegelian, etc.). These interpretations will no longer seem to us to be simply arbitrary or tendentious but will appear as founded, in their possibility, in Rousseau's text itself."[76] While Althusser focuses on philosophical readings, I would like to present a similar analysis of the "readings" of Rousseau's text that the various attempts to "apply" it in the course of the Revolution constitute. Weil is correct when he writes that "the unity of Rousseau's political thought . . . found no real representative" during the Revolution. What is at stake, however, is to understand how the partial appropriations of that theory, in their very disunity, are founded in a logic that is itself faithful to Rousseau.

Before turning at long last to the Revolution itself, then, I would like to indicate something about how the process of double reading and division that we have seen to be so consistently at work in Rousseau's literary texts plays itself out in the *Contrat social*. It would be possible to pursue other versions of this logic: for example, the question of application and in particular the relation to the Genevan model could be a fruitful path. In terms of source analysis, one might explore the interplay within Rousseau's thought between the civic republican and natural law traditions. But it seems to me that all these concerns come together most forcefully in the question of the psychological process that takes place in voting, since it is there that the relation between particular and general interests and wills is most fully worked out. In fact, and quite characteristically, Rousseau gives two distinct accounts of how voting works in the course of this text.

The first version of the psychological process of voting occurs in the context of the discussion of what we have called the "infallibility" of sovereignty. The key to Rousseau's argument here is not a Kantian morality but a methodological individualism and a notion of enlightened individual self-interest that clearly draws on the natural law tradition. On this account, the key to arriving at a correct decision in voting is precisely that each vote be purely individual. What falsifies elections is the formation of parties, interest groups, or other "partial associations," each of which has a will that is "general with respect to its members, and particular with respect to the state. . . . It is thus important in order to truly have the statement of the general will that there be no partial society in the state and that each citizen give only his own opinion [*n'opine que d'après lui*]" (*Contrat social,* pp. 371–72). A true relation between particular wills and the general will is dependent on a relation between particular interests and the general interest that is not falsified by the existence of intermediate bodies. The relation must be *immediate.* Voting takes place within the immediacy of this identity of particular and general.

> Why is the general will always just [*droite*], and why do all constantly will the happiness of each, if not because there is no one who does not take for himself [*s'approprie*] the word *each,* and think of himself when voting for all? Which proves that the equality of right and the notion of justice that it produces derive from the preference that each gives himself and consequently from the nature of man. (p. 373)

Even if this understanding of voting relies on a sort of psychological subterfuge,[77] it will work under a condition that we can describe in two ways. One would be to say that "each" and "all" are genuinely equivalent, which is the case when the formal conditions of generality are fulfilled, or, as Rousseau puts it in continuing this passage, "The general will to be truly such must be general in its object as in its essence." If the law in fact applies equally to all, then this psychological subterfuge will be entirely innocent. On this account the formulation of the text of the law proposed for voting becomes particularly important. We could also describe this in terms of the real existence of a common interest within particular interests. "What generalizes the will," Rousseau contends, "is less the number of votes than the common interest that unites them" (p. 374). Particular and general wills are convergent so long as particular and general interests are. As Althusser puts it in his forceful characterization of this argument, each individual "will want [*voudra*] for others what he wants for himself, as a function of the equality imposed by the clause of total alienation. But he would not want anything for the others if he did not first want it for himself. The general interest is not the product of a moral conversion that tears the individual away from his interest; it is only individual interest forcibly generalized by equality [*forcé à la généralité de l'égalité*]."[78]

In this respect, the pragmatic existence of the double generality characteristic of the law would seem to hinge on maintaining a real common interest, that is, not allowing a real divergence of interests to develop within the state. Formal equality is insufficient; real equality is necessary.[79] Insofar as this version of voting relies on the category of interest in order to make the double generality of the law pragmatically possible, it also depends on the existence of real conditions that are, to put it mildly, difficult to achieve in practice, as Rousseau himself was quick to recognize. "This equality, they say, is a speculative chimera that cannot exist in practice: but if abuse is inevitable, does it follow that one should not regulate it? It is precisely because the force of things always tends to destroy equality, that the force of legislation should always tend to maintain it" (p. 392). Thus the empirical conditions that allow for just legislation to be possible are themselves the result of wise legislation. Equality is both the structure of the laws and a pragmatic presupposition that needs to be reaffirmed, together with the social pact itself, in every act of sovereignty. If voting takes place according to interest, only an already-existing state of relative equality can produce the spirit of equality that characterizes truly just (that is, egalitarian) laws.

> In order for a nascent people to appreciate healthy maxims of politics, and follow the fundamental rules of reason of state, it would be necessary for the effect to become the cause, for the social spirit that ought to be the product [*ouvrage*] of the institution to preside over the institution itself, and for men to be before the laws what they ought to become by them. (p. 383)

In this logical circle we will find the hand of the legislator. We can recall here the importance, for Scottish gradualism, of the critique of the category of intent in the history of civilization, and thus the rejection of the cult of the great legislators. In the *Essay on the History of Civil Society*, Adam Ferguson writes,

> We are therefore to receive, with caution, the traditionary histories of ancient legislators, and founders of states. Their names have long been celebrated; their

supposed plans have been admired; and what were probably the consequences of an early situation, is, in every instance, considered as an effect of design. An author and a work, like cause and effect, are perpetually coupled together. This is the simplest form under which we can consider the establishment of nations: and we ascribe to a previous design, what came to be known only by experience, what no human wisdom could foresee, and what, without the concurring humor and disposition of his age, no authority could enable an individual to execute.[80]

Rousseau's attachment to the sources of these "traditionary histories," Plutarch in particular, doubtless plays no small role in his attachment to their heroes. But as we have already seen, his general rejection of gradualism is based on very real theoretical disagreements. The figure of the legislator is a theoretical necessity of Rousseau's radical conventionalism. He refuses to consider either political society or civil society (that is, the system of needs and interests) as natural or autofoundational. "It is always necessary to go back to a first convention" (p. 359), which can only be represented as a true first beginning, that is, a cause that does not presuppose its effects. Since this account of voting presents the system of interests that constitutes civil society as self-regulatory, it gives rise to a regression that returns us to such a first moment. It can only sustain itself as a system if it refers to a cause that is outside its system.

Rousseau's second discussion of the psychological structure of voting will lead us back to this same logical circle by a different path. The point of departure of this discussion is the position within the body politic of the dissenting citizen.[81] In book I, following upon his definition of the social pact, Rousseau had noted that "each individual can, as man, have a particular will contrary or dissimilar to the general will he has as Citizen," but the existence of a body politic necessarily implies the existence of a coercive force that can be applied to citizens. "Thus in order that the social pact not be merely a vain formula, it tacitly includes the one engagement that can give force to all the others, namely that whoever refuses to obey the general will, will be constrained to do so by the whole body." As a description of the necessity for criminal law and penal institutions, this is entirely uncontroversial. But Rousseau, in perhaps the most controversial sentence of the entire book, goes on to interpret this coercive force precisely as an expression of liberty: "which means nothing more than that he will be forced to be free" (pp. 363–64). Rousseau's discussion of criminal sentences in book II, however, moves along fairly different lines.[82] Since Rousseau defines civil liberty, in a passage immediately following this one, as "obedience to the law one has prescribed for oneself," the more fundamental question, to which Rousseau returns in book IV, is that of the dissenter in voting. "How can opponents be free and submitted to laws to which they did not consent?" The social contract itself requires unanimity, but subsequent votes are necessarily decided by majority. In what way can we say that the minority is forced to be free?

> I respond that the question is poorly posed. The citizen consents to all laws, even those passed despite him, and even those that punish him when he violates one of them. The constant will of all members of the state is the general will; it is by this will that they are citizens and are free. When a law is proposed in the assembly of the people, what is asked of them is not precisely whether they approve or reject the proposition, but whether or not it is in agreement with the general will which is theirs [*si elle est conforme ou non à la volonté générale qui est la leur*]; in voting everyone gives his view [*avis*] on this question, and the counting of votes gives the general will. Thus when the view contrary to mine is victorious, this proves nothing more than that I was mistaken, and what I thought was the general will was not. If my particular view had won, I would have done something other than what I willed, and it is then that I would not be free. (pp. 440–41)

In this analysis the role of particular interest and particular will have entirely disappeared. The general will exists within each citizen, alongside and separate from his particular will. Rather than voting according to his particular interest, and allowing the general will to be determined by a mathematical combination of particular wills, the citizen becomes an interpreter of the general will: he does not in fact declare his will but rather "gives his view" on what he thinks the general will to be. This is an intellectual operation, however, and is therefore subject to error in a way that pure willing of one's own good is not.

The fact that, in this version of voting, two wills exist within each citizen poses a further problem: it becomes possible for him to vote his particular will, not as his contribution to the mathematical formation of the general will, but precisely instead of the general will. The general will is no longer the result of a self-regulating mechanism inherent in particular will, but a choice that the citizen must make. In this case, the formation of the general will is indeed in some sense "the product of a moral conversion," and voting patterns become a clear indication of the moral health of the state. And it is indeed the *moral* health of the state that is at stake: it is not only possible, it is even likely that the degeneration of public spirit will occur in times of material prosperity. Rousseau argues that a healthy state needs "very few laws" (p. 437) and that those that it does need will be clearly evident to all, producing a marked tendency toward universal consensus in voting. This tendency toward unanimity is a sure sign that morals are good, the state healthy, and the general will dominant. The weakening of the state, on the other hand, is signaled by the emergence of factions, acrimonious debate, and the loss of consensus.

> Finally when the state, near its ruin, subsists only in a vain and illusory form, when the social bond is broken in everyone's heart, when the vilest interest brazenly covers itself with [*se pare de*] the sacred name of public interest, then the general will becomes mute; everyone, guided by secret motives, no more opines as a citizen than if the state had never existed, and iniquitous decrees that serve only private interests are falsely passed under the name of laws.

In this sort of sham voting, the general will is not destroyed. Incapable of "extinguish[ing] the general will within himself," the corrupted citizen "eludes it" by voting according to particular or corporate interest (p. 438). The key phrase here is that "the social bond is broken in everyone's heart." We can name this social bond the identification of particular and general interest, but insofar as it is located in the heart it is an affective link rather than a rational calculation.

The hearts of the citizens are the particular object of the wise legislator's attention. The only defense against the weakening of the state is a kind of law that works on the basis of habit rather than authority because it is "engraved not in marble or bronze, but in the hearts of the citizens."

> I am speaking of morals [*mœurs*], customs, and above all opinion, a part of legislation unknown to our politicians, but upon which the success of all the others depends; the great legislator concerns himself with this part in secret, while he appears to restrict himself to particular regulations that are only the sides of the arch, while morals, slower to be born, at last come to form the unshakable keystone. (p. 394)

The role of the legislator once again marks the necessity of a logical circle, which this time must be formulated in terms of morality rather than interest: only a virtuous people can make good laws, but only good laws can make a virtuous people. The legislator can resolve the paradox of a cause that presupposes its own effects, which so preoccupied Rousseau in the *Discours sur l'inégalité*, only by means of a subterfuge far more devious than thinking of oneself in voting for all. If he uses force his work will be illegitimate, but persuasion is of no avail in the absence of the social spirit that can, again, be the result only of his work. It is this dilemma that forces the legislator to "have recourse to an authority of another order . . . , that from time immemorial has forced the fathers of nations to have recourse to heavenly intervention and to honor the gods with their own wisdom, so that peoples, submitted to the laws of the state as they are to the laws of nature, and recognizing the same power in the formation of man and the formation of the polity, obey with freedom and docilely bear the yoke of public felicity" (p. 383).

Now, it seems to me important that we not read this as an open invitation to clerical deception. While Rousseau calls for unity of church and state in the infamous chapter on Civil Religion, he calls for the dominance of the temporal power over the spiritual one. Here, most importantly, a charlatan will never found a state. Only someone with a true legislative genius will be able to convince the people that he is speaking in the name of the gods; indeed, the legislator is himself a more-or-less divine figure, endowed with "a superior intelligence that sees all human passions but feels none of them. . . . It would take Gods," Rousseau writes, "to give laws to men" (p. 381). The figure of the legislator in *Du contrat social*, all-seeing, impassive, Godlike and yet cynical in his use of religion, closely resembles Wolmar in *La Nouvelle Héloïse*.[83] Like the geological catastrophe that marks the end of the state of nature in the second *Discours*, or Julie in her garden, or the God that we seek in the book of nature in *La Nouvelle Héloïse*, the legislator is above all a necessary hypothesis. This implies that political virtue produces (and is produced by) the same sort of religious (and not merely clerical) illusion that sustained sexual virtue in *La Nouvelle Héloïse*. To put it in more general terms, we can say that if political virtue is in fact a human possibility it is because it is (or can be) a passion: it is the love of the general interest. While such a love allows the citizen to place the general will above his own particular will, the fact that it is a passion implies that the general interest, the object of the general will, is the object of a passion, and is therefore subject to the same set of illusions we have analyzed in the case of both romantic love and *dévotion*. It is produced as a figurative projection rather than as a rational calculation.

The Two Readings in Practice

The political situation of 1788–89 made impossible a reading of the *Contrat social* that would take into account the entirety of Rousseau's strictures. The size of the nation, the monarchy and the traditional form of the Estates General were fundamental givens that had to be accommodated. In particular, no pragmatic response to the situation could bypass the existence of representation in the form of the Estates General. The question was, what powers should it have, and how should the nature and origins of that power be conceptualized? Public reaction to the Parlement's declaration in September 1788 that the Estates should be called according to the forms of 1614, the last time they had met, and the government's subsequent vacillations on these forms, focused debate on the questions of vote by head or by order. In the electoral regulations promulgated on January 24, 1789, Necker's ministry allowed the doubling of the Third Estate, a precedent set in the Provincial Assemblies established by Calonne, but left the question of voting to be decided by the Estates themselves.[84] Without the vote by head, the doubling of the Third would have been meaningless. This situation, I will argue, effectively divided the reading of the *Contrat social* into two separate dogmas: the inalienability of sovereignty and the formal conditions of generality. If one allowed for representation, the united assembly, voting by head without reference to their mandates, could fulfill the conditions of generality. If one remained bound by the mandates or some other form of control by direct constituents, inalienability would in some sense be preserved but indivisibility lost. In the choices posed by this situation, the interpretation given to the interrelations of the theses of the *Contrat social* became one of the major ideological battlegrounds of the Revolution, and was to remain so at least until Thermidor. The interpretations adopted by particular figures varied according to the shifting demands of the political situation, but Rousseau provided the conceptual terms in which the struggle developed.

Given the problems inevitably involved in adapting the reading of *Du contrat social* to these circumstances, one might wonder why it was not bypassed; after all, other political philosophies that did not lead to such difficulties were available. A first set of reasons, attempting to account for the choices made and paths followed by individuals, can be termed subjective. The already established familiarity with Rousseau the sentimental novelist and theorist of education—that is, the author of *La Nouvelle Héloïse* and *Émile*—must have provided a strong motivation for many deputies to turn to the same author's treatise on politics. The experience of subjective regeneration and renewal to which all the accounts of reading Rousseau that we have encountered testify, must have at the very least suggested a powerful analogy to the demands made for a regeneration of the nation, if they were not in fact one of the primary sources for the language of those demands. Carol Blum, in *Rousseau and the Republic of Virtue*, has provided a compelling account of the processes of identification with Rousseau that his texts fostered and that made an exalted sense of virtue available to the revolutionary generation.[85] This explanation would make sense of two well-established sets of facts. First, the belated "discovery" of *Du contrat social* with respect to the great sentimental and novelistic works would appear as a rearrangement of the internal relations of the Rousseauian corpus, an awakening to the political dimension of the vision of virtue presented in those works, in reaction to the changing political situation. In particular, the increasing emphasis on constitutional issues in the course of the summer of 1789 would have given powerful impetus to a careful reading of the technical aspects of the *Contrat*.[86] Furthermore, the equally frequently noted diversity of political positions adopted by avowed Rousseauists suggests that the attachment to Rousseau was most likely formed in the literary and moral spheres, and then carried, as best one could, into the political realm. Lakanal's characterization of the relation between the *Émile* and the *Contrat*, in perfect agreement with Mounier's argument about influence, seems to me to suggest that this is the most likely scenario on the subjective level.

Nevertheless, there are also what can be called objective reasons why Rousseau, rather than Montesquieu (for example), quickly becomes the dominant philosophical reference of the Assembly's majority. Marcel Gauchet, in the Introduction to his *Révolution des droits de l'homme*, suggests that certain conceptual structures of Rousseau's thought are in fact best (and not worst) adapted to the situation. We should therefore, Gauchet proposes, speak of "the Revolution's encounter with Rousseau" rather than his "influence."

> Had Rousseau's thought not existed, it would have been necessary to invent it. . . . It is in fact the thought that most rigorously ensures the plenitude and preeminence of legislative power even as it leaves open the possibility of a monarchical executive. The theoretical model is an exact fit [*s'ajuste*

exactement] for the practical difficulty. The signal seductive virtue of the "general will" is to carefully preserve the king's place, while offering the most radical vision of the engendering of collective legitimacy on the strict basis of the right of individuals.[87]

Rousseau's thought is able to fulfill this function, however, only on the condition of coming to terms with representation in some form. In the immediate historical context, then, the split in the interpretation of Rousseau that occurs in 1789 can be described in terms of different ways of attempting to reconcile the practice of representation with the principles of Rousseau's system. But this split draws on the fault lines already at work within the *Contrat social*, and therefore is itself structured as a Rousseauian dynamic.

THE DEBATE ON THE VETO, SEPTEMBER 1789

One of the clearest examples of the way in which Rousseau's doctrine is divided by its reading during the Revolution, and how this division supplied the terms of debate, is provided by the constitutional debates of September 1789. These debates, on the relation between the legislative and executive branches of government, focused primarily on the question of whether the king should be accorded a veto over legislation, and if so, of what sort.[88] The proposal of the committee on the constitution, presented by Mounier on August 28, included a bicameral legislature, with the upper house to be nominated by the king, and an absolute royal veto.

This proposal was clearly modeled on Montesquieu's interpretation of the government of England in *De l'esprit des lois*. In Montesquieu's conception, the separation of powers is primarily a prudential measure, designed to prevent too much power from accumulating in the hands of any one man or group. "Separation of powers" is actually a misnomer here; "balance of powers," the term developed in the American context, much more accurately characterizes Montesquieu's conception. "In order to prevent the abuse of power," Montesquieu had written in a famous formulation, "things must be arranged so that power checks power [*Pour qu'on ne puisse abuser du pouvoir, il faut que, par la disposition des choses, le pouvoir arrête le pouvoir*]."[89] This conception requires rather than prohibits that each constituted power have some effect on the proper field of action of the other powers. In his series of *Federalist Papers* devoted to this question, James Madison argued that an overlap rather than a strict separation was required: "Unless these departments be so far connected and blended as to give to each a constitutional control over the other, the degree of separation which the maxim requires, as essential to a free government, can never in practice be duly maintained."[90] Both Montesquieu and Madison were far more concerned with the possibility of tyranny of the legislature than of the executive. Montesquieu therefore decisively gave the executive power the upper hand in that it is allowed to "take part in legislation by its faculty of preventing, without which it would soon be stripped of its prerogatives." But the legislative power is to be given no part in execution, for in this case "the executive power would be equally lost." The way in which the House of Lords stands in for the judicial function allows it to prevent a standoff between and to "temper" the other two branches. The three powers are thereby "bound" (Montesquieu uses both *enchaîner* and *lier*) by one another, and thus are "forced to move in concert."[91]

In the defense of this proposal by Trophime-Gérard, comte de Lally-Tollendal, the Montesquieuan and "Anglophile" inspiration of the committee is particularly clear. He referred specifically to the "general principle of the balance of powers" and the necessity that there be three of them because two would "combat each another until one has crushed the other."[92] Mounier's argument in behalf of the veto a week later, at a point when the Monarchiens were already on the defensive, began (in order to combat it) from the more Rousseauist position that dominated the Assembly.

> I know that the principle of sovereignty resides in the nation: Your Declaration of Rights contains this truth. But being the principle of sovereignty and exercising sovereignty are two very different things. . . . [A large nation] must delegate the whole of sovereign power. I do not say that the nation can alienate it; but in any case it confides it. . . . One part of the French nation's sovereignty has been confided to the monarch, and the other should be confided to freely elected representatives.[93]

Mounier was unwilling to admit any distinction between the type of delegation made to the legislature and that made to the executive. "Cannot one say with reason that the deputies chosen by the different departments are not the only representatives of the people; that the king is its first delegate; that he too is the representative of the people in all the parts of authority that have been confided to him, and that the people has charged them jointly to express the general will . . . ?"[94] The two delegations made by the nation would then be thus equally sovereign, or rather, neither of them would be sovereign. For Mounier, the separation of powers was indeed a division of sovereignty.

For the majority of the Assembly, however, the separation of powers was not this Montesquieuan or Madisonian division of sovereignty but an opposition between the sovereign and its agent that was clearly and explicitly derived from Rousseau. They overwhelmingly upheld the unity of the legislative power, voting against the bicameral legislature on September 10 by 490 to 89, with 122 deputies abstaining. The vote on the veto the following day was more ambiguous: the king was accorded a veto easily, but the absolute veto was rejected in favor of a suspensive one by a vote of 673 to 325, with only eleven abstaining.[95] In political terms, the suspensive veto doubtless represented a compromise by which the king's prerogatives could be defended without ceding too much on the principle of national sovereignty represented by the Assembly.

What makes this debate particularly interesting is the extent to which partisans of the suspensive veto and opponents of any veto whatsoever shared the same set of assumptions. As Étienne de Polverel put it,

> The partisans of the royal veto, whether absolute or suspensive, all begin, to accredit their systems, from the same principles that I use to combat them. They all agree: 1. That the law is an act of the general will. 2. That the king cannot have the right of veto against the will of the nation. 3. That the legislative power must be forever separated from the executive power, and that they can never be united in any point.[96]

This agreement in principle is clearly grounded in a Rousseauist rather than a Montesquieuan understanding of the separation of powers. In the debates of September 1789, both supporters of the suspensive veto and opponents of any veto adopted variants of this position. For the majority of the Assembly, the separation of powers was not a division of sovereignty but a functional distinction between legislation as the expression of the general will and execution as the application of law to particular cases. While this conception allowed a continuing place in the constitutional system for the king, this place has now become strictly subordinate. The executive branch has no authority whatsoever in matters of legislation. Monarchy was thus defined in strictly Rousseauist terms by the future director Louis-Marie de La Revellière-Lépeaux:

What is a monarchy? According to this universally admitted principle, that in every legitimate government the expression of the general will is the law, the definition [of monarchy] is simple: It is a government in which a single man is charged with ensuring the execution of the will of all; and the only difference between this government and a republican one, is that in the former, the prince or head of the executive power is an individual, and in the latter it is a collective being. According to this definition, it is easy to see that in this government as in every (*legitimate*) government, only execution is confided to the prince or head of the executive power, and that every act of legislation belongs to the nation or its representatives, without any other will having the right to compete with it against its will, and consequently without anyone having a right to oppose it: for sovereignty resides in the nation. Now if the monarch had, by the Constitution, an absolute veto of such a type that he could legally oppose the known will of the nation, it is clear that he would share, or, better, that he would annihilate the sovereignty of the nation by rendering the effect of its will null.[97]

This set of assumptions was shared by almost all speakers on the question. Robespierre asserted, "Monarchy, in its true signification, means only a State in which the executive power is confided to one man."[98] Legislative power must either remain in the nation or be vested in the assembly; in no case can it be shared with the king. Rabaut Saint-Étienne, for example, distinguished between "the power of self-government [that] belongs to the whole nation, with as much simplicity as it belongs to each individual" and the various authorities that emanate from it.

> Now, if I consider power (and I no longer need to say that it is neither authority, nor the authorities), I distinguish between what the nation distributes and what it keeps. What it distributes is execution and what it keeps is legislation. It keeps what it can do and distributes what it cannot do. It delegates authorities and keeps power, and the power it keeps is the legislative power. . . . But the sovereign is a simple thing, for it is the collection of all without exception; thus the legislative power is one and simple: and if the sovereign cannot be divided, the legislative power cannot be divided.[99]

Jean-Baptiste Salle responded to suggestions that the government of the people needs to be tempered by insisting on the distinction between sovereignty and government. "The people cannot govern without passion! But who speaks of governing here? Government is not sovereignty: To govern is not to make laws." This distinction allowed Salle to appeal to a historical version of Rousseau's argument that the general will cannot err even if peoples are often unenlightened. "When the people of Athens judged its great men," he continued,

> it performed a function of magistrature; it had a particular object in view; it governed, it was capable of being mistaken, and it often was. But when the people of Athens, that of Sparta, of Rome, etc., made use of their sovereignty, that is, legislated, when they stipulated by themselves and about themselves, they were no longer mistaken, they became wise. . . . The general will cannot err, says the greatest publicist of the century. Why? Because when a nation legislates, all stipulate for all: The general interest is necessarily the only one that dominates.[100]

Polverel insisted that "the custodian [*dépositaire*] of the executive power has no judgment to make. His function is limited to employing the public force to ensure the execution of the acts of the legislative power . . . without examining whether they are just or unjust."[101] Sieyes argued that "if you want to consider the king as the custodian of all the branches of executive power, it is evident that nothing in his authority, however great, however immense it may be, can be offered as entering, as an *integral part*, into the formation of the law. . . . The execution of the law is posterior to its formation; the executive power and all that belongs to it is considered to exist only after the law is completely formed."[102] In his version of the Declaration of Rights, Sieyes made the distinction between sovereign and government on a strictly Rousseauian basis. "The public establishment is a sort of political body, which having, like the human body, both needs and means, should be organized in more or less the same way. It must be endowed with the faculty of *willing* and with that of *acting*. The legislative power represents the first and the executive power the second of these two faculties. The *government* is often confused with the action or exercise of both of these powers, but this word is more particularly consecrated to designating the executive power, or its action."[103]

Rabaut Saint-Étienne and Salle supported the suspensive veto; Robespierre, Polverel, and Sieyes opposed it. It was the former position that the vast majority of the assembly adopted. But it conceived of the suspensive veto not as a royal prerogative, nor as an integration of the king into the legislative process, but as a precaution to be taken against the representative system, an *appel au peuple*. Jérome Pétion de Villeneuve provided the most succinct formulation: "It is useful to allow a suspensive veto, and deadly to allow an absolute one. It is an appeal to the people, on the part of the prince: It is up to the nation, from whom all powers emanate, to decide."[104] This phrasing recurred in speech after speech. Charles de Lameth presented the following scenario:

> The representatives make a law and present it to the King; the King rejects it as contrary to the constitution; the representatives persist; who will win out, the King or the representatives? The only judge is the nation. . . . Thus, the appeal to the people becomes indispensable; it gives it the time to become enlightened; passions are appeased, and if the new representatives demand the same law, the King is forced to sanction it. . . . The King can disobey delegates, but not the general will.[105]

It was the possibility of a discordance between the will of the assembly and the true general will that motivated the suspensive veto.

The distrust of the representative assembly shown in the debate on the veto often had a clearly Rousseauist inspiration. The two most elaborated arguments in favor of the suspensive veto, presented by Salle and Rabaut Saint-Étienne, marked this inspiration quite explicitly. Salle, after recalling the distinction between sovereignty and government, concluded that "*if the general will cannot err* when a nation legislates, the assemblies it delegates can be mistaken, for if will cannot be represented, it is because assemblies can, as in England, let themselves be corrupted and prevaricate." Salle went on to cite Rousseau: "The English people believes itself to be free; it is sadly mistaken."[106] Rabaut Saint-Étienne distinguished between representation and substitution, so that "it is not really the representatives who legislate but the people, of which the representatives are merely the organ; thus it is the people who has the legislative power; the General Assembly does not have it." In Rabaut's argument, this distinction was deployed in order to refute Mounier's suggestion that the nation could make a divided delegation of its sovereignty to both king and assembly, giving them both a share of legislative power. "The whole question," Rabaut argued, "comes down to whether the National Assembly has the legislative power, or whether the people keeps it, and must and can keep it; for if the nation keeps legislative power, it cannot be divided."[107] Thus the position of the king could be only that of Rousseau's executive, who can be granted no part of legislation but who can ask the people to verify that the law proposed by the legislature is indeed the expression of the general will. "The king is the executor of the law, and as such, you could accord him the right to stop its execution by refusing the sanction that precedes it. This act of the king would not be an act of legislation, contributing to the law, but an act by the supreme magistrate that delays its sanction. It is . . . an appeal he makes from the representatives of the nation to the nation itself."[108] As an appeal to the nation, the royal veto functions as a safeguard against representation, a way of guaranteeing the real existence of direct popular sovereignty within representative institutions.[109]

Rousseau himself seems to have envisaged the possibility of a body that would propose laws to be submitted to popular ratification. His attack on the English constitution, already cited, includes the specification that "the people's deputies are not nor can they be its representatives, they are only its agents; they can conclude nothing definitively. Any law that the People in person has not *ratified* is null; it is not a law" (*Contrat social*, pp. 429–30; emphasis added). The divinely inspired legislator Rousseau speaks of writes the laws but has no power to impose them, and therefore must submit them for ratification. "It can never be ensured that a particular will is in conformity with the general will until it has been submitted to the free suffrage of the people" (p. 383).[110] Rousseau's espousal of a rigorous form of the imperative mandate in the *Considérations sur le gouvernement de Pologne* (pp. 979–81) notwithstanding, a complete adherence to the system established by the *Contrat social* would continue to require that this ratification be performed by "the people assembled." Otherwise legislative power would be vested in each district assembly. The will of a district assembly is, according to an oft-repeated analysis of Rousseau's, general with respect to its members but particular with respect to the nation. Curiously, Mounier deployed this same logic in support of the absolute veto. "You will doubtless forbid imperative mandates in the constitution," he noted.

> You are thus forced to admit that the electors are not sovereign; and what then becomes of the principle that engages you to submit to them the decision on laws vetoed by the prince? And doubtless they should not be sovereign, for sovereignty can be only in the entire nation, or in the union of its delegates; I have never been able to conceive of a sovereignty divided into forty thousand fractions.[111]

This is the analysis that the opponents of any veto whatsoever use again and again. They are not numerous: garnering few votes, the position was defended (at least within the Assembly) almost exclusively by Robespierre and Sieyes. Nevertheless, the crucial position these two figures held in the development of the Revolution, and even more the role that their argument played in it, requires that attention be devoted to it. Robespierre, posing the sort of brutal alternative that will later become the rhetorical basis of his influence, reduced the question of the suspensive veto to an opposition between direct democracy and representative government. "In a word, either you put legislative power in each district assembly, or you confide it to the National Assembly. In the first case, the latter is superfluous; in the second, instead of taxing [*exercer*] and degrading it, you should give it all the force and authority it needs to defend freedom, whose guardian it is against the always formidable enterprises of the executive power."[112] The district assemblies are themselves representative bodies, but partial and particular ones that will express an infinity of different wishes.

Despite all the distance that was to come to separate the two men and their positions, Sieyes in this instance made fundamentally the same argument, although more rigorously worked out.[113] This greater rigor derives largely from the fact that Robespierre's position was primarily a political one, which would change with the shifting relations of force in the course of the Revolution, whereas Sieyes's position was primarily philosophical. As Patrice Gueniffey puts it, "Sieyes's analysis is the only one compatible with the dogma of the indivisibility of sovereignty."[114] This rigor will also allow us to clearly establish the logic of a partial and deforming, but nonetheless real, reading of Rousseau operative in Sieyes's thought.

SIEYES'S REPRESENTATIVE ROUSSEAUISM

From *Qu'est-ce que le tiers état?* onward, Sieyes argued for the necessity of a unitary representative body, one that would quite precisely represent the unity of the nation. "The general will," he argues, "cannot be *one* as long as you allow three orders and three representations. At most these three assemblies might unite in the same wish, as three allied nations can form a single desire. But you will never make of them *one* nation, *one* representation, and *one* common will."[115] In the opening pages of that pamphlet, Sieyes presented two different but ultimately mutually reinforcing definitions of the nation in order to establish that the Third Estate is a "complete nation" from which the privileged orders are necessarily excluded. The first definition states that a nation is a collective enterprise of useful labor, and goes on to specify that all the genuinely useful forms of labor, whether in private or public sectors (and public service has always been one of the justifications of privilege) are in fact accomplished by members of the third estate.[116] From this point of view, the nobility is not even a body (much less a nation of its own), but merely a parasite upon another body.[117] The nobility's *fainéantise* makes it "foreign" to the nation.

The second definition of the nation is politico-legal in form and is the primary basis for the rest of the pamphlet. In fact, it can be seen as already containing the totality of Sieyes's argument: a nation is "a body of associates living together under a *common* law and represented by the same *legislature.*" This definition brings together an insistence on absolute civic equality with a vision of representation as a process of unification. The mere existence of privilege renders the nobility foreign to the nation on the first count; the traditional structure of the Estates General, with its separate representation of each order, renders it equally foreign on the second count. The representation of the nobility "is essentially distinct and separate: It is foreign to the nation by its principle, since its mission does not come from the people, and by its object, since it consists in defending not the general interest, but particular interest."[118] Even though he is speaking of representation, Sieyes here relies on Rousseau's analysis of the relation between source and object of the general will.

Representation is a historical necessity. We have already noted how the calling of the Estates General made it an unavoidable fact at the beginning of 1789. Sieyes never gave much weight to the sort of historical argument in which tradition confers legitimacy, preferring to ground his discourse in the rational principles of "the veritable science of the state of society."[119] But representation is also the necessary result of a rational—that is, universal—history, in which it appears as the form of government appropriate to the development of enlightenment and commerce. Sieyes presents a very brief version of this history in *Qu'est-ce que le tiers état?* beginning with a first epoch in which citizens come together as a nation but without any determinate form, and moving to a second stage in which they form a true union with a single common will. In Sieyes's third epoch, "the associates are too numerous and spread out over too great a territory to easily exercise their common will themselves. What do they do? They detach from it the part necessary to watch over and provide for public concerns, and confide the exercise of this portion of national will, and consequently of power, to some group of them."[120] While here this historical development of representation is established in an extremely schematic way in terms of population growth alone, it is clear that Sieyes conceived of it as tied less to size as such than to the distinctively modern phenomenon of commercial society. In his discourse on the veto Sieyes makes this quite explicit:

> Modern European peoples are quite unlike ancient peoples. Among us it is only ever a question of commerce, agriculture, manufacturing, etc. The desire for wealth seems to make all the states of Europe into vast workshops, where people think much more of consumption and production than of happiness. Thus today's political systems are founded exclusively on labor.[121]

But since labor occupies all of our time, and we cannot devote ourselves to politics as the Greeks did, representative government is necessary. In his recent study of Sieyes, William Sewell has conclusively demonstrated just how intertwined his economics and his politics are. Specialized politicians and representative government are merely an extension of the general principle of the division of labor. The division of labor, Sieyes writes in his *Observations* on the work leading to the constitution, "applies as much to political labor as to all other types of productive labor. The common interest, the amelioration of the social state itself, cries for us to make of government a distinct profession."[122] But this identification works in the other direction as well. As Sewell puts it, Sieyes "conceptualizes the division of labor as a system of mutual representation."[123] In an early manuscript note, Sieyes characterizes "representative labor" as the source of the "progress of liberty" in modern society.[124] Everything that one individual can get another to do for him makes him more free. Freedom is therefore inseparable from economic cooperation and interdependence. It is in this notion of representative labor that it is possible to reconcile Sieyes's two definitions of the nation at the beginning of *Qu'est-ce que le tiers état?*

As we have seen, the interdependence brought on by the division of labor was the object of Rousseau's bitterest comments in the *Discours sur l'origine de l'inégalité*. And while the complete denaturalization of man proposed by *Du contrat social* would result in political interdependence—perfect legislation is achieved when "each citizen is nothing, and can do nothing, except through all the others" (*Contrat social*, p. 382)—economic independence, even autarchy, remained Rousseau's ideal. Thus we can say that Sieyes's notion of representation combines two factors both of which were anathema to Rousseau. Nevertheless, at least in his speeches and writings of 1789, Sieyes does not so much propose representation as an alternative to Rousseau as insert his notion of representation into Rousseau's system, precisely at one of the points where it is most fragile. As Bronislaw Baczko put it, "Paradoxically it is where Sieyes puts the most distance between himself and Rousseau that he comes closest to him."[125]

First of all, we can say that despite the use of representation, Sieyes accepts the idea that sovereignty inheres in the body politic, which had been the foundation of Rousseau's doctrine of inalienability. At the end of his short history of the development of representation, Sieyes emphasizes that "the community does not give up [*ne se dépouille pas de*] its right to will, which is its inalienable property. It can only commit the exercise of this will. This principle is developed elsewhere."[126] This "elsewhere" seems to me to be a sort of backhanded reference to Rousseau. The remarks that follow establish the difference between constituted legislative power and constituent power. This crucial distinction for Sieyes functions above all as a way of preserving the principle of inherence. While it may not be as strong as the idea of an appeal to the people, this distinction is likewise a form of safeguard against representation. Delegates to a constituted legislature do not exercise the plenitude of power, and cannot change the conditions under which that power was delegated to them. Delegated powers, including legislative power in a representative system, must have a constitution, that is, "an organization, forms, and laws proper to fulfill the functions for which it is destined." But claims that the nation itself already has a constitution (for example, that it is monarchical and divided into three estates) that it cannot alter are vehemently rejected by Sieyes in terms drawn from Rousseau. "Would someone tell me what views and what interest justify the idea of giving a constitution to the *nation* itself? The nation exists before everything, it is the origin of everything. Its will is always legal, it is the law itself."[127] As for Rousseau, there is no law that the nation cannot change because it cannot make a promise binding on itself. "What is a contract with oneself? The two terms being the same will, it can always undo the so-called engagement."[128] Attempts of this sort to distinguish between delegation and alienation were made by numerous speakers in these debates.

Sieyes also insists repeatedly on the necessity of the formal egalitarianism of the law. His proposition for a Declaration of Rights lays this out in great detail.

Art. 14. All citizens are equally submitted to the law. . . . Art. 15. The law has only the common interest as its object, it cannot accord any privilege to anyone whomsoever, and if privileges become established, they must instantly be abolished whatever their origin may be. Art. 16. If men are not equal in *means*, that is, in wealth, intelligence, strength, etc., it does not follow that they are not all equal in *rights*. Before the law, all men have the same worth, the law protects them all without distinction. Art. 17. No man is more free than any other. None has more right to his property than another has to his. All must enjoy the same guarantee and the same security. Art. 18. Since the law obliges citizens equally, it must punish the guilty equally.[129]

Absolute civic equality is thus, for both Sieyes and Rousseau, the only possible basis of political legitimacy. In one of the few passages in which he allows himself a metaphor, Sieyes writes, "I imagine the law in the center of an immense globe; all citizens without exception are at the same distance on the circumference and occupy equal places; all depend equally upon the law, all offer their freedom and their property to it to protect; and this is what I call the *common rights* of the citizens, by which they all resemble one another."[130] Sieyes closely follows Rousseau in this understanding of the objective generality of the law.

Finally, the convergence between Sieyes and Rousseau can be seen most clearly in the definition of the general interest in relation to particular interests. This is closely related to the problem of formal generality, which can be called objective insofar as this generality is derived from its object, the common interest. Sieyes and Rousseau share a conception of the common interest as having an existence independent of particular interests, which implies that there is a single common interest and that the general will is precisely the will of that interest. As Sieyes's version of the Declaration of Rights puts it, "The law, being a common instrument, can have only the common interest as its object. A society can have only *one* general interest."[131] Both of them therefore seek to discount the effect of particular wills relating to individual interests and to abolish what they call corporate wills relating to group interests.

In discussing the structure of the one corporate body he cannot banish— namely, the government—Rousseau set up a division of wills and the interests to which they correspond.

We can distinguish in the person of the magistrate three essentially different wills. First the will proper to the individual, which intends only his particular

advantage; secondly the common will of the magistrates, which is uniquely
related to the advantage of the Prince and which can be called a corporate will
[*volonté de corps*] . . . ; and in the third place, the will of the people or the
sovereign will. . . . In a perfect legislation, particular or individual will should
be null, the corporate will proper to the government very subordinate, and
consequently the general or sovereign will always dominant and the unique
rule of the others. (*Contrat social,* pp. 400–401)

Sieyes entirely adopts the core of this analysis, including the consequent refusal to allow partial bodies of any sort to form. In his analysis of how voting works in the assembly, Sieyes presents a distinction between three sorts
of interest. While he formulates this analysis in terms of interest rather than
will, it is clear at the end that Sieyes has adopted the tautological relation between interest and will that underlay much of Rousseau's argument as well.

First, that by which all citizens are similar [*se ressemblent*]; this presents the
just extent of the common interest; secondly, that by which an individual
allies himself with a few others, which is corporate interest [*l'intérêt du corps*];
finally, that by which each man is isolated, thinking only of himself, which is
personal interest. The interest by which a man agrees [*s'accorde*] with all his
co-associates is evidently the object of the will of all and that of the common
assembly.

Like Rousseau, Sieyes believes that the action of individual interest should
be "null," and he is confident that it will be insofar as genuinely particular
interests are too diverse to have any substantial influence. "The great difficulty," he continues, "comes from the interest by which a citizen agrees with
a few others only. This interest permits concertation and leagues. . . . There
should thus be no astonishment that social order so rigorously requires that
simple citizens not be allowed to form *corporations*. . . . Thus, and not otherwise, the common interest is assured of dominating particular interests."[132]

The clearest example of corporate interest is of course the privileged orders. The inexpugnable opposition between the interest of the nobility and
the interest of the nation is the point Sieyes hammered home most repeatedly in *Qu'est-ce que le tiers état?* For so long as privilege exists, it gives that
difference of interests a status in law that renders it necessary. In justifying
his argument that members of the privileged classes should be disqualified
from being elected as representatives of the third estate, he compares this restriction to the already accepted disqualifications of women, minors, beg-

gars, vagabonds, and foreign nationals. "The comparison is completely favorable" to his proposal, he writes, since "a beggar or a foreigner can have an interest that is not opposed to that of the Third, whereas the noble and the ecclesiastic are, by their estate, friends of the privilege that profits them."[133] This same logic leads him to reject both vote by order and vote by head: "Each order is a distinct nation," no more competent to have a voice in the others' affairs than foreigners would be. Better to elect an Englishman in time of war than a noble.

A similar argument rejecting any form of particular group influence in the formation of the general will is made regarding the primary electoral assemblies. Such assemblies, along with the tiered form of election they implied, were a constant feature of revolutionary electoral practices.[134] But for Sieyes it is crucial that they not be allowed to form independent bodies. They must evaporate before the nation. In his justification of the noneligibility of nobles, he had emphasized that each representative votes for the nation as a whole and therefore truly represents the nation rather than his bailiwick. Even in the supposition that an electoral assembly should want to harm its own interests, argued Sieyes, "does that give it the right to harm the others? . . . The deputies of a district are not only the representatives of the bailiwick that named them, they are further called upon to represent the generality of citizens, to vote for the whole kingdom."[135] The same position recurs in Sieyes's discourse on the veto. "The deputy of a bailiwick is immediately chosen by his bailiwick; but mediately, he is elected by the totality of bailiwicks. This is why every deputy is the representative of the entire nation."[136] It is thus illegitimate for a deputy even to take into consideration the particular will of the primary assembly that elected him.

> A deputy, as we have said, is named by a bailiwick in the name of the totality of bailiwicks; a deputy is one of the entire nation; all citizens are his constituents. Since, in a bailiwick assembly, you would not want for he who has just been elected to be charged with the wish [*vœu*] of the small number against that of the majority, you cannot want, *a forteriori*, a deputy of all the citizens of the nation to listen to the wish of the inhabitants of a single bailiwick or municipality against the will of the entire nation. Thus there is not nor can there be for a deputy an imperative mandate, or even a positive wish, other than the national wish; he is bound to the counsels of his direct constituents only insofar as these counsels are in conformity with the national wish.[137]

Sieyes's construction of legislative power, unlike the version proposed by partisans of the suspensive veto, meets Rousseau's formal conditions for the generality of the law. The fact that he places it in a representative assembly, and that he often polemicizes against Rousseau on the question of representation, should not blind us to this important affinity. What is perhaps most striking about the structure of this affinity is that Sieyes in fact founds the legitimacy and necessity of a representative assembly precisely upon those same formal conditions that for Rousseau had excluded it. Because the true object of the national assembly is the common interest, Sieyes writes near the end of his pamphlet, "the right to be represented belongs to citizens only on account of the qualities that are common to them, and not those that differentiate them."[138] It is precisely this relation between the equality of all citizens, the dimension in which they are all equivalent, and the unity of the general interest, that makes representation possible. "The interests by which the citizens resemble one another are thus the only ones of which they can treat in common, the only ones by which and in the name of which they can claim political rights, that is, an active part in the formation of the social law, consequently the only ones that imprint upon the citizen the quality of being *representable*."[139] The formation of the representative assembly is the primary place in which the citizen exercises his sovereignty.[140]

For Sieyes, the unity of the general will appears only in the unity of the representative assembly. As we have seen, the deputies do not come to the assembly already charged with the wills of their individual constituents. The declaration of June 17 constituting the Third Estate as the National Assembly, whose language was proposed by Sieyes and carried by a vote of 491 to 90, choosing the name of National Assembly, speaks of the Assembly as being the sole body capable of "interpreting and presenting the general will of the nation," and justifies the choice of name by the fact that "representation being one and indivisible, no deputy, whatever order or class may have chosen him, has the right to exercise his functions separate from the present assembly."[141] The subsequent justification of this revolutionary act by the quashing of the imperative mandates was defended by Barère (who two months later supported the suspensive veto) in the following terms:

> Particular constituents cannot be legislators, because it is not their particular
> interest alone with which the Assembly will be concerned, but the general in-
> terest. . . . The legislative power begins only when the general assembly of rep-

resentatives is formed. . . . If the system of imperative and limited powers were to be admitted, the resolutions of the Assembly would evidently be blocked by recognizing a frightening veto to each of the 177 bailiwicks of the kingdom.[142]

The primary assemblies, Sieyes argued in his discourse on the veto, should choose representatives for their ability to "know the general interest, and to interpret in this respect their own will,"[143] that is, the will of the people. The Assembly must be free to debate and to follow the greater enlightenment that may arise from its deliberation. "It is thus incontestable that the deputies are not at the National Assembly to announce the already formed wish of their direct constituents, but to deliberate and vote freely, according to their *current* opinion, informed by all the enlightenment [*éclairé de toutes les lumières*] that the Assembly can give to each. . . . The decision belongs and can only belong to the nation assembled. The people or the nation can have only one voice, that of the national legislature."[144] Exactly like Rousseau's citizen in the assembly, the deputies are charged with interpreting the general will. Indeed, one can describe Sieyes's construction as based on the realization that, in Rousseau's second account of voting, which assumes the independence of general and particular wills within each citizen, the citizen himself already represents the general will. The generalization of the will, that is, takes place within the individual through an act of representation. In his discourse on the veto he warns against thinking of "the national wish as if it could be something other than the wish of the representatives of the nation, as if the nation could speak other than by its representatives. . . . Where can one recognize this wish, if not in the National Assembly itself?"[145] Patrice Gueniffey cites an unpublished note by Sieyes in which he argues that "the people cannot *will in common*, thus it can make no law; it can do nothing in common because it does not exist in that way. . . . Thus, strictly speaking, the representation is not named by the people but by the sections of the people. *It alone is the people united*, for the whole group [*ensemble*] of associates cannot otherwise be united."[146]

In that Sieyes derives the unity of the general will from its representation, his theory can be considered to be a Hobbesian interpretation of Rousseau. Hobbes had described the unity of what he calls a person as deriving from representation: "A Multitude of men, are made *One* Person, when they are by one man, or one Person, Represented; so that it be done with the consent of every one of that Multitude in particular. For it is the *Unity* of the Representer, not the *Unity* of the Represented, that maketh the Person *One*. And it is the Represented that beareth the Person, and but one Person: And *Unity*, cannot otherwise be understood in Multitude."[147] Rousseau grudgingly admired Hobbes's insistence on political unity, if not his identification of the state of war with the state of nature. In a well-known letter to Mirabeau *père*, Rousseau admitted that he saw "no acceptable middle point between the most austere democracy and the most complete Hobbesianism,"[148] and many have felt that his politics represents precisely a combination of the two. In *Du contrat social*, this admiration for Hobbes is most directly stated in the chapter on Civil Religion, that is, with respect to the ideological foundations of the state in belief.[149]

We can therefore suggest that Sieyes has given to representation the role played in Rousseau by *mœurs*. Indeed, in discussing how voting will occur in the assembly, and showing how the general interest should dominate if it is properly constituted, Sieyes had contrasted his vision with that of Rousseau on this point.

> Let us first present this political mechanism in the most advantageous supposition, according to which public spirit, in full force, would permit only the activity of the common interest to be manifested in the assembly. These prodigies are rare in history, and they do not last. To bind the destiny of societies to efforts of virtue would betray a very poor knowledge of men. Even in the decadence of public morals [*mœurs*], when egotism appears to govern every soul, even in these long intervals, it is necessary for a nation's assembly to be so constituted that particular interests remain isolated and that the wish of the plurality is always in agreement with the general good.[150]

This distrust of the effectivity of civic virtue continues to mark Sieyes, in contrast to Rousseau, as one of the moderns, one who is not only fully reconciled but indeed enthusiastic about the development of the division of labor and commercial society. Nevertheless, his vision of political unity is, like Rousseau's, finally grounded in a vision of the objective and independent existence of a common interest. Representation is an institutional arrangement that takes the place of virtue in ensuring the subordination of particular interests to the common interest, and not a means of communicating the diversity of social interests to a common forum. In his rationalism, Sieyes is no more capable than Rousseau of conceiving of politics as a competition of different interests within a society. One of the best measures of this is the extent to which Sieyes's construction of representational legislative sovereignty continued to be active in the later years of the Revolution, when representation came to be conceived more and more as founded in virtue.

The fundamental question is not whether Sieyes (or any other figure of the revolutionary period) was subjectively Rousseauist. It is clear that Sieyes had read Rousseau closely; it is also clear that he thought of himself as a particularly original thinker (his claims of priority over Adam Smith, whether true or not, testify clearly to this self-conception).[151] What is most important, in my view, is the extent to which Sieyes—and most if not all of his colleagues—was *objectively* Rousseauist, that is to say, was led by a combination of available concepts and tactical exigencies to recapitulate certain problems (again, problems rather than doctrines) that Rousseau had laid out with particular force and perspicacity. One of the major implications of this way of posing the problem is that it situates the importance of Rousseau's thought for the Revolution at a theoretical rather than at an ideological level—that is, it is operative by the understanding of the dynamics and aporias of democratic politics that it makes available, and not merely by the "influence" its themes, even its rhetoric and tonality, had on individual revolutionaries. This sort of subjective influence certainly did exist, and on a massive scale. But the inevitability of references to Rousseau in the debates of 1789–94 (which may often have been unconscious) is also tied to a certain predictive value of his thought.

INSURRECTIONAL AND CONSTITUTIONAL DEMOCRACY

In commenting on this debate in the final pages of his admirable *Inventing the French Revolution*, Keith Baker has argued that the "profound defeat" suffered by Sieyes meant that the Assembly had chosen "the most unstable" of the possible choices, and that this instability set them on a path toward the Terror.

> To the extent that their acceptance of the suspensive veto implied a repudiation of Sieyes's arguments for a theory of representation based on the division of labor, the assembly was setting aside a discourse of the social, grounded on the notion of the differential distribution of reason, functions, and interests in modern civil society, in favor of a discourse of the political, grounded on the theory of a unitary general will. In the most general terms, it was opting for a language of political will, rather than of social reason, of unity, rather than of difference; of civic virtue, rather than of commerce; of absolute sovereignty,

rather than of government limited by the rights of man—which is to say that, in the long run, it was opting for the Terror.[152]

The oppositions laid out by Baker can serve as a guide for our understanding of the fate of Rousseauist discourse from 1789 to 1794. The most salient feature of this set of oppositions, however, is that in 1789 they did not appear as oppositions. The revolutionaries themselves often thought they had succeeded in reconciling them. The *Déclaration des droits de l'homme*, to take the most immediate example, carefully juxtaposes the foundation of sovereignty with the limitation of the law: even as the law is the expression of the general will, its function is to give a formal articulation to naturally existing relations of reciprocity. "Liberty consists in being able to do anything that does not harm others: Thus, the only limits to the exercise of the natural rights of each man are those that ensure the other members of society the enjoyment of these same rights. These limits can be determined only by the law."[153] Sieyes himself was perhaps the one who most consistently and forcefully articulated these gestures as the two sides of a single coin. He insists, for example, that the notion of right supposes that men regard one another as means rather than obstacles. This implies that the prototype for all social relations is the "reciprocal utility" of two individuals, who are equally free to do so or not, entering into a contract.[154] In a manuscript probably composed in the Year III, he argued that the fault of all previous declarations was that they assumed the preexistence of a sovereign power with which it was necessary to negotiate. "The general and common character of all [previous] declarations is always the *implicit recognition* of a lord, a suzerain, a master to whom one is naturally obliged, and of a few of the oppressions whose continuance in the future one is no longer willing to bear. . . . A declaration of rights must totally change in spirit and nature; it ceases to be a *composition*, a transaction, a treaty condition, a contract, etc., between two authorities. There is only *one* power, only *one* authority."[155] What this suggests is that the Assembly did not (and perhaps could not) conceive of itself as making a clear choice between "absolute sovereignty and government limited by the rights of man." What is articulated in the summer and early fall of 1789 is a fragile identity between these terms. The instability is not to be found in one of the terms of the opposition, or in one of the choices that could be made, but rather in the synthesis attempted.

What the debates on the veto establish is two different revolutionary readings of a single text, Rousseau's *Contrat social,* that compete for favor throughout the Revolution. One reading insists on the unity of sovereignty, the other on its direct exercise. As separate theses, they can both be found elsewhere. But we have seen them appear in the debates of the summer of 1789 in the language of the one text that attempts to think them together. Because they subsequently appear as two partial readings of a single text, they are henceforth functionally inseparable and appear with predictable regularity in any debate touching on constitutional questions. In the form of a struggle between representative centralism and direct democracy, this division within the reading of Rousseau was to provide the terms in which the major political battles of the Revolution were to be fought. The two possible positions they describe are adopted in turn by different groups and individuals depending on the shifts of the political situation. At least until Thermidor, the positions do not change, only the figures occupying them. In particular, we shall see that moderate constitutionalists and Jacobins, Girondins and Montagnards adopted each side of the question at different moments. If there is a consistency, it is not so much between parties and their ideologies as between the party in power in the Assembly, which necessarily must uphold the legitimacy of representation, and the party out of power, which leans on the activities and aspirations of the Parisian sections.[156] But even this is not completely stable.

Indeed, while Sieyes was a loser in an extremely one-sided vote on the question of the suspensive veto, he may, at least in the medium term, have in fact won on the question of principle.[157] The moderate "patriot" majority in favor of the suspensive veto was probably more concerned to maintain the possibility of a reconciliation with the king than with purity of principle. By the time the constitution is finally implemented in 1791, the majority of the assembly will in fact have returned to an avatar of Sieyes's position. Under pressure from the king's flight to Varennes and the massacre of the petitioners on the Champ-de-Mars, the Assembly voted a revision of the constitution, beginning, "Sovereignty is one, indivisible, inalienable and imprescriptible; it belongs to the nation; no section of the people, nor any individual, can claim its exercise; but the nation, from whom all powers emanate, can exercise them by delegation only."[158] This time it was Robespierre, renouncing his earlier position, who attacked representation in the name of Rousseau. "Allow me to cite the authority of a man whose principles you have adopted. . . . Jean-Jacques Rousseau said the legislative power constituted the essence of sovereignty, because it was the general will, which is the source of all powers; and it is in this sense that Rousseau said that when a nation delegated its powers it was no longer free."[159] Particularly after the law of May 10, 1790, forbidding collective petitions, the juridical organization of elections, strictly separating choice of representative from any form of deliberation, explicitly reflected Sieyes's construction of representation.[160]

The entire policy of the National Assembly with respect to the range of phenomena that can be termed "partial bodies," from the church and the aristocracy to trade guilds, clubs, and popular societies, and even the primary electoral assemblies, seems to have been guided by the language of the analysis Sieyes derived from Rousseau. The most famous and durable piece of this legislation was the law of June 14, 1791, abolishing trade unions.[161] The author of this law, Isaac-René-Guy Le Chapelier, pursued this program in a report on popular societies that justified the proposed restrictions on the activity of the clubs by calling them "corporations" (what was in question was not the right to assemble but the right of clubs to affiliate, communicate with one another, publish proceedings, demand accounting from constituted authorities, and generally act like a political party—it was clearly the Jacobins who were under attack).

> There are no powers except those constituted by the will of the people expressed by its representatives. . . . It is in order to preserve this principle in all its purity that, from one end of the Empire to the other, the constitution has abolished all corporations, and henceforth recognizes only the social body and individuals. As a necessary consequence, it has prohibited any petition or poster appearing under a collective name.[162]

Sieyes's construction of representative sovereignty, founded on the principle of indivisibility and continuously articulated with the universality of the law (and not, we might note, particularly favorable to the expression of local difference and diverse social interests) thus served the majority of the Assembly as its primary argument in its battle with both the increasingly radicalized clubs and agitation in the primary assemblies. A particularly clear statement of the application of this principle to the primary assemblies was made by Mirabeau, responding to Robespierre on the question of the permanence of the Parisian districts: "To demand the permanence of the districts is to want to establish sixty sovereign sections in a great Body, where they can only create an effect of action and reaction capable of destroying our constitution."[163]

The arguments used for the suspensive veto, insisting on the people's direct exercise of its power, in opposition to representational sovereignty, can be seen as underlying the sectional movement and Parisian popular agitation in the months leading to the overthrow of the king on August 10, 1792, by a combination of Parisian national guards and *fédérés* from Marseilles and Brittany. Here it is inalienability rather than indivisibility that is the key term taken over from Rousseau. The most conceptually elaborated justification of this position was provided by Robespierre, no longer a member of the legislature but carefully cultivating his influence at the Jacobin club. In a major speech at the Jacobin Club at the end of July, Robespierre abandoned his position as "Defender of the Constitution" and called not only for the deposition of the king but also for the renewal of the legislature and the establishment of both universal male suffrage and new safeguards on the representative system. In Robespierre's discourse it is no longer the clubs, popular societies, and district assemblies but the legislature itself that is seen as being necessarily expressive of a "corporate" rather than general will: "Where will you seek the love of the *patrie* and the general will, if not in the people itself? Where will you find pride, intrigue, and corruption, if not in the powerful corporations that substitute their particular will for the general will, and that are always tempted to abuse their authority against those who confided it to them?"[164] Taking up the theme of inalienability, Robespierre describes the representative sovereignty of the legislature, characterized by the independence of deputies from their constituents, as a despotic usurpation of sovereignty. "The source of all our ills is the absolute independence from the nation the representatives have given themselves without consultation. They recognized the sovereignty of the people and then destroyed it. By their own avowal, they were only the people's mandataries, and they made themselves sovereign, that is, despots. For despotism is nothing other than the usurpation of sovereignty."[165] But Robespierre, following in this respect the arguments traced out by Pétion, Rabaut Saint-Étienne, and Salle during the debate on the veto, does not advocate an abandonment of the representative system but rather its control by the continuous surveillance of the primary assemblies, institutionalized in the form of a constant possibility of censure and revocation.

> The nation will thus be of the view that, by a fundamental law of the state, at
> determinate and sufficiently close intervals for the exercise of this right not to

be illusory, the primary assemblies can bear judgment upon the conduct of their representatives, or that they can at least revoke, according to the rules to be established, those who will have abused their confidence.[166]

The most direct expression of this principle emanating from the sectional movement itself can be found in an address made by the Mauconseil section to the forty-seven other sections of Paris and read to the Legislative Assembly on August 4. The Mauconseil address asserted that "it [was] impossible to save freedom by constitutional means" and declared that it could thus no longer "recognize the constitution as the expression of the general will." The Mauconseil section,

> considering that Louis XVI has lost the confidence of the nation, that consti-
> tuted powers have force only by means of opinion, and that the manifestation
> of this opinion is thus a rigorous and sacred duty for all citizens, declares to all
> its brothers, in consequence, in the most authentic and solemn manner, that it
> no longer recognizes Louis XVI as king of the French.[167]

What is stated here simply as the force of "opinion" is evidently a claim to the location of sovereignty in the primary assemblies. The Mauconseil petitioners speak of the "noble purpose of taking back their rights." The Legislative Assembly clearly saw this as an attack on the basis of its legitimacy. Without a vote the Assembly adopted the Girondin leader Pierre-Victurnien Vergniaud's motion quashing the Mauconseil petition as unconstitutional, on the basis of the fact that "sovereignty belongs to the whole people and not to a section of the people."[168]

Insurrection is, of course, inseparable from revolutionary legitimacy. The *fête nationale* is July 14, the anniversary of the fall of the Bastille and not of the Tennis Court Oath or the assumption of the title of National Assembly. Without the march on Versailles of October 5 and 6, 1789, the king would not have accepted the *Déclaration* or the decrees of August 10 and 11 destroying the feudal regime. During the period of censitary suffrage, it is the parallel forms of expression of popular sovereignty that allow for the participation of those formally excluded from voting: women and the poor. In fact, the experience of women's clubs and popular societies suggests that claims for the symbolic attributes of insurrectionary citizenship such as wearing the tricolor cockade and bearing arms had a far greater importance than the demand for the right to vote that has made Olympe de Gouges so popular today. The aspirations for citizenship of working-class women, write Darline Gay Levy and Harriet B. Applewhite, took the form of a legitimation of insurrection as "the most authentic embodiment of the general will."[169] Even if the arguments actually emanating from sectional agitators (as opposed to those who, in the Assembly or the press, set themselves up as spokesmen for the *sans-culottes*) seldom show the direct imprint of Rousseau's language, the demands of the Parisian sections, as Albert Soboul has demonstrated, can be seen to be largely compatible with the construction of Rousseau's doctrine that centers on the inalienability of sovereignty at the expense of its indivisibility.[170]

To this point, Baker's reading of the consequences of the debate on the veto seems to hold: even if the majority of the National Assembly came back to Sieyes's position, they had let the genie of this corrosive form of Rousseauism out of the bottle. But this would in the end imply that the Terror was founded unequivocally (although not exclusively) on the suspicion of representation; that, however, is by no means clear. Insofar as it was formed through the purging of the Convention, the revolutionary government was dependent on the intervention of the insurrectionist sections. But if there is one thing the revolutionary government was clearly not, it is a direct democracy. As Soboul and Guérin continually remind us, the hegemony of the "Robespierrists" was also founded on the repression of the popular movement.[171] For the first time in the history of the revolution, a group in power in an assembly was able to strike effectively at its left. In many respects the revolutionary government represents the complete collapse, rather than reconciliation, of Rousseau's distinctions. As the demand for the supremacy of sovereign over government becomes more and more strident, the executive function is in fact entirely absorbed into the legislature. The fundamental principle of revolutionary government, as articulated by Jacques-Nicolas Billaud-Varenne on 14 frimaire II, was "legislative centrality," another word for the location of the general will in the representative assembly. A good Jacobin, Billaud-Varenne also contested the activity of insufficiently disciplined popular societies as incompatible with the indivisibility of sovereignty:

> Once legislative centrality ceases to be the pivot of the government, the principal basis of the edifice becomes faulty and it necessarily crumbles. These congresses [of popular societies inspired by the Cordeliers] have such a baleful

influence, that the popular societies themselves, in lending themselves to such unions, have not been exempt from the tint of federalism that has become the favorite color of intriguers.[172]

Robespierre himself, in the same speech in which he proclaimed terror to be a necessary complement to virtue in times of revolution ("Sur les principes de morale politique"), was careful to maintain the idea of delegated unity. "Democracy is not a state where the people, continually assembled, decides by itself on all public affairs, still less one where a hundred thousand fractions of the people, by isolated, precipitate, and contradictory measures, decide on the fate of an entire society: Such a government has never existed, and could exist only in order to return the people to despotism. Democracy is a state where the sovereign people, guided by laws of its own making, does by itself everything it can do, and by delegates everything it cannot do itself."[173]

As Billaud-Varenne's reference to "federalism" suggests, the struggle with the Gironde was a key turning point.[174] It was during the king's trial that the positions began to be reversed.[175] Louis-Antoine de Saint-Just, the youngest member of the National Convention, first came to prominence with his speech of November 13, 1792, calling for a summary judgment of Louis Capet. Saint-Just argued that the former king "must be judged as an enemy" rather than as a citizen, and that he should be put to death "not for the crimes of his administration, but for the crime of having been king." Saint-Just's position, which stunned the Convention and which, while never adopted by the majority, had a determining effect on the course of the trial, is summed up in a characteristically aphoristic *sentence*: "One cannot reign innocently; the folly of it is too evident [*On ne peut point régner innocemment; la folie en est trop évidente*]."[176] This definition of the king as an enemy takes up the tradition established by Sieyes in excluding the aristocracy from the nation and making it the enemy, by definition, of the public interest, and the category will be crucial in all the justifications of the terror.[177] Saint-Just himself was to declare, in another aphorism, that "between the people and its enemies there is nothing in common but the sword."[178] Curiously, it also echoes a passage of the *Contrat social* in which Rousseau had written:

> Moreover every evil-doer, attacking social right, becomes a rebel and a traitor
> to the fatherland by his evil deeds, and ceases to be a member of it by violating
> its laws, and even declares war upon it. Then the conservation of the state is

incompatible with his own conservation; one of the two must perish, and when the guilty party is put to death, it is less as a citizen than as an enemy. (p. 376)

This passage is found in chapter 5 of book II, "On the Right of Life and Death," which comes between the chapters "On the Limits of Sovereign Power" and "On the Law," in which the doctrine of the objective generality of the general will is most clearly argued. It is there that Rousseau argues that the general will is denatured and loses its rectitude when it attempts to judge or decree on a particular object. In Rousseau's terms, a sovereign judgment, which is what the Convention understood itself to be delivering in the king's trial, is possible only when applied to an object outside the body politic (such a judgment would be legitimate, but subject to a high likelihood of error). This same passage of the *Contrat social* was used during the king's trial by Raymond de Sèze, Louis's defense attorney, in order to contest the Convention's right to function as a sovereign court. If the Convention represents the general will, Sèze argues, it cannot judge a particular.

> Some have asserted that Louis ought to be tried as an enemy. But is he not an enemy who puts himself at the head of an army against his own nation? And yet it is very necessary to repeat it, since it is forgotten, that the constitution did anticipate this case, and fixed the penalty. It has been said that the king was inviolable only for every citizen; but that between a nation and a king, there was no longer any natural relationship. But in this case the republican functionaries themselves could not sue for those guarantees that the law had given them. What an inconceivable system! It has likewise been said, that if there is no law applicable to Louis, the will of the people must take its place. Citizens, here is my response. I read in Rousseau, "Where I see neither the law that ought to be followed, nor the judge who ought to pronounce it, I cannot leave it to the general will. The general will as such cannot decide either on a man, or on a fact." Such a text needs no comment.[179]

Sèze's defense of Louis, it should be said, is impeccable. The trial was manifestly unconstitutional. And whether the Convention or the insurrection of August 10 be taken as the legitimate expression of the general will, his appeal to Rousseau here, regardless of whether he or the king believed in Rousseau at all, is quite to the point.

In order to complete the picture with one last turn of the screw, it was Vergniaud, who the previous summer had defended the Sieyesan principle of the location of indivisibility in the Assembly, who now became the fore-most spokesman of an "appeal to the people." Vergniaud rehearsed arguments we have previously seen coming from Robespierre or sectional militants. In a representative government, he recalled,

> the decisions of the people's representatives are executed as laws: but why?
> Because they are presumed to be the expression of the general will. Their force
> derives from this presumption alone. . . . The people conserves, as an inherent
> right of sovereignty, the right to approve or disapprove. If the presumptive
> will does not agree with the general will, the people conserves, as an inherent
> right of sovereignty, the right to make its wish known, and as soon as this
> manifestation occurs, the presumptive will, that is the decision of the national
> representation, must disappear. To rob the people of this right would be to
> despoil it of sovereignty; it would transfer sovereignty, by a criminal usurpa-
> tion, onto the representatives the people had chosen; it would transform these
> representatives into kings or tyrants.[180]

What is most important about this discourse, from our point of view, is its predictability. Someone had to take up this side of the argument. Indivisibility and inalienability are two terms that cannot appear without the other, but can no longer appear in the same place.

The various constitutional projects of the spring of 1793 represent the moment at which the Revolution came closest to a synthesis of these two positions. The Convention called upon "all friends of liberty and equality" to submit their ideas, and there are in fact a plethora of published plans, most of which were written by members of the Convention.[181] As a group, these projects represent a failed attempt to make insurrection part of the constitution itself. The stakes and difficulties of this enterprise can be seen clearly in the fate of the final articles of the new *Déclaration des droits de l'homme et du citoyen*. The 1789 text had listed "resistance to oppression" as one of the fundamental rights of man, but it had given no content to this notion, no guidance as to when it was and was not legitimate. Condorcet's project, which served as the basis of discussion for the rewriting of the text, stipulated that "men united in society must have a legal means of resisting oppression."[182] In the "Girondin" version adopted on May 29, this was modified, on the motion of Jacques-Antoine Rabaut-Pommier, by the addition of "and when this means is powerless, insurrection is the most holy [*saint*] of duties."[183] Insurrection can be legitimate, but there is a real question as to whether it can be legal. After the expulsion of the Girondins in the "insurrection" of May 31–June 2, 1793, the "Jacobin" version of the *Déclaration* would further spell out the right of "resistance to oppression" in a true glorification—in what is meant to serve as the preamble to the Constitution—of insurrectionary democracy:

> Resistance to oppression is the consequence of the other rights of man. There is oppression of the social body when any one of its members is oppressed; there is oppression against each member when the social body is oppressed. When the government violates the rights of the people, insurrection is, for the people and for every portion of the people, the most sacred of rights and the most indispensable of duties.[184]

While the rhetoric has been considerably inflated, the key conceptual difference is the insertion of the phrase "for every portion of the people."[185] The problem remains the same one we have encountered all along: how can egalitarian insurrection be reconciled with formal equality, that is, inalienability with indivisibility?

Robespierre never presented a full-scale plan for a Constitution, limiting himself to a set of constitutional principles designed to prevent the usurpation of sovereignty by government. "Never do the ills of society come from the people," Robespierre declaimed, "but from the government. How could it be otherwise? The people's interest is the public good; the interest of a man with a position is a private interest. To be good, the people needs only to prefer itself to what it is not; to be good, the magistrate must sacrifice himself to the people."[186] This emphasis on the naturalness and ease of virtue in the people and its difficulty if not impossibility among the government, which is always prone to corruption, was one of the most constant elements of Robespierre's rhetoric.[187] He posed here as an "incontestable maxim" "that the people is good, and that its delegates are corruptible; that it is in virtue and in the sovereignty of the people that a preservative against the vices and despotism of the government must be sought."[188] This implies preventing the "independence" of public functionaries and submitting them to an "imposing responsibility," both physical and moral. Moral responsibility consists primarily in "publicity," to be ensured by the location of the Assembly in a "sumptuous and majestic edifice, open to twelve thousand spectators. . . . Under the eyes of such a large number of spectators, neither intrigue, corruption, nor perfidiousness would dare to show its face; the general will alone would be consulted, the voice of reason and public interest alone would be heard."[189] But government agents must also be made to account publicly for their administration. Moral responsibility needs to be backed up by "physical responsibility, which is, in the last analysis, the surest guardian of freedom: It consists in the punishment of prevaricating public functionaries." Robespierre concluded by asserting that it was only on this condition that Rousseau's rejection of representative government could be surmounted:

> A people, whose mandataries owe account of their administration to no one, has no constitution; a people, whose mandataries owe an account of their administration only to other inviolable mandataries, has no constitution, since it only depends on this second group to betray it with impunity, and to allow it to be betrayed by the first group. If this is the sense to be attached to the idea of representative government, I declare that I adopt all of the anathemas pronounced against it by Jean-Jacques Rousseau.[190]

But this accounting could be done only before each member's constituents. Hérault de Séchelles's penultimate draft presented a similar proposal giving "the section of the people that elected a deputy the charge of judging his conduct." The attraction of such a proposal, in Georges Couthon's words, was its "morality," but it was quickly rejected as incompatible with the indivisibility of sovereignty and likely to encourage rebel departments (Jean-François Delacroix, who made the latter argument, was thinking not only of the Vendée but also of the recently proscribed Girondins).[191]

The concern with giving a practical expression to the indivisibility of sovereignty is perhaps most salient in Saint-Just's proposal. While the theme of virtue, and in particular the attack on an overly "intellectual" approach to the general will at the expense of the heart, play an important role in Saint-Just's rhetoric,[192] the most important pragmatic proposition rejects all earlier systems of representation as merely "federative." Saint-Just in particular sets aside the scheme inherited from Sieyes, in which each representative is chosen by a locality "in the name of all," in favor of a radicalization of the underlying principle.

> I regard as the fundamental principle of our republic, that the national representation should be elected by the people as a body. . . . He who is not named in the simultaneous concourse of the general will only represents the portion of the people that named him, and the various representatives of these fractions, if they assemble to represent the whole, are isolated, without any link

in their suffrages, and cannot form a legitimate majority. The general will is indivisible. . . . This will is not applied only to the laws; it is applied to representation. . . . Representation and the law thus have a common principle.[193]

Each citizen was thus to vote for a single representative, and the 341 names receiving the most votes from the entire nation would constitute the Assembly.[194] But Saint-Just also foresaw an executive council, elected on a departmental basis, that would have the right to provoke an appeal to the people if the law in question "is contrary to the precise text of the declaration of rights, and if the number of votes in the national assembly was fewer than 251." In this case, the law would be approved or rejected by the majority of communes (primary assemblies). The communes would also be able to initiate a recall of deputies who have "betrayed the nation and lost its confidence."[195]

The most radically democratic proposal, and the one that went furthest in the attempt to reconcile the indivisibility and the inalienability of sovereignty, was the initial proposal of the Constitutional Committee, written by Condorcet, and generally known as the "Girondin" constitution. Condorcet's project takes up the whole range of features that we have seen underlying the entire tradition of revolutionary constitutionalism as created in the wake of Rousseau's *Du contrat social*: the unity of the territory, the indivisibility of sovereignty, the unicameral legislature, the distinction between law and decree, and the conception of the separation of powers as a subordination of the executive to the legislative rather than as a system of checks and balances. But its great innovation was the attempt to forge a "legal means of protest [*réclamation*] requiring a new examination of the law" that would emerge from the primary assemblies themselves rather than being set in motion by an "appeal to the people." Any section of the people, that is, would have the right to appeal to the people as a whole. Any law, constitutional or civil, could be contested by a single section of the people, but within the context of a national referendum. The complex formal structure proposed by Condorcet to regulate such claims begins with the action of a single citizen and requires majority support from progressively larger bodies until it becomes the object of a yes or no vote on the national level. By providing an "immediate exercise" of the right of sovereignty, this system allows an outlet for the participatory passion that had fed the Revolution and continuously "remind[s] citizens of the existence and reality" of popular sovereignty.[196] But it also submits this participation to forms, and what is more, to rigorously egalitarian forms. Very much in the spirit of Rousseau, it is precisely this egalitarian aspect that ensures the indivisibility of sovereignty.

> Indeed, each assembly is not sovereign: Sovereignty can belong only to the universality of a people, and this right would be violated if any fraction of this same people did not act, in the exercise of a common function, following a form identical to that followed by the others. In these general functions the individual citizen does not belong to the assembly of which he is a member, but to the people of which he is a part.[197]

This organization will avoid giving too much influence to the Parisian sections, which will no longer be able to immediately represent direct democracy in action but will have to present their case to the whole nation. Thus "regular and legal protests made by assemblies convoked in the name of the law" will replace the turbulent and unregulated activities of the clubs, popular societies, and sectional assemblies.[198] By providing a legal channel for "resistance to oppression," insurrection will be absorbed into the constitution and its violence will cease to be necessary. "If the majority desires a convention, the assembly of representatives will be obliged to indicate it. The refusal of the assembly to convoke the primary assemblies is thus the only case in which the right of insurrection can be legitimately employed."[199]

Condorcet's attempt to legalize insurrection, in what is to my mind the most democratic constitution ever proposed, coincides exactly with Rousseau's attempt, in *Du contrat social*, to think the unity of inalienable and indivisible popular sovereignty. For all the distance that separates Condorcet's rationalism from Rousseau's voluntarism, this text is the closest thing the Revolution produced to a "complete" reading of Rousseau. But it therefore also shares the extreme fragility of Rousseau's theoretical construction. In presenting the final revision of the constitution, Hérault de Séchelles gave an extremely coherent explanation of why this attempt to legalize insurrection had to be abandoned:

> When the social body is oppressed by the legislative body, the only means of resistance is insurrection; but it would be absurd to organize it, for it has different characters. You have experienced this fact: The insurrections of last year [i.e., 1792] differed greatly from the most recent insurrection [i.e., that of May 31–June 2, 1793]. The former were realized by force; the latter began with a petition, the people covered the *Déclaration des droits* with crepe, and finally rose as a mass. It is thus impossible to determine the nature and the character

of insurrections; we must abandon ourselves to the people's genius, and rely upon its justice and its prudence.[200]

Six months later, in November 1793, the constitution was suspended as the government became *révolutionnaire jusqu'à la paix*. The Revolution never succeeded in putting its two readings of Rousseau together.

A Revolutionary Mode of Authorship

In *Politics, Culture, and Class in the French Revolution*, a powerful demonstration of the applicability of literary techniques of reading to the history of the French Revolution that has inspired much of the most important work in the field over the last fifteen years (and played an important role in the inspiration of this project), Lynn Hunt proposes that

> revolutionary rhetoric was in some sense defeated by its inherent contradictions. While being political, it refused to sanction factional politicking. While showing the power of rhetoric, it denied the legitimacy of rhetorical speech. While representing the new community, it pushed toward the effacing of representation (in the name of transparency between citizens). While referring to a mythic present, revolutionary rhetoric also had to explain the failures of the present, which it could only lay at the door of conspiracy-politics. In short, as a text, it was constantly subverting its own basis of authority.

At this point, Hunt refers to Jacques Derrida's *Of Grammatology* and continues in a footnote,

> Derrida's "metaphysics of presence" and threat of the violence of writing have the same relation of tension as the mythic present (the transparency of the community, the fullness of speech) and the violence of conspiracy-politics. In this sense, revolutionary rhetoric was constantly "deconstructing" itself, that is, at once positing the possibility of a community without politics and inventing politics everywhere.[201]

Of Grammatology is, of course, a study of Rousseau. In some sense my entire argument here has been simply to say that this is no accident, and that the relation between Rousseau and the Revolution is to be found not in a logic of linear causality but rather in a shared constitutive instability, in their practice of "deconstruction." Rousseau is the first author of the Revolution precisely because the Revolution could not make its reading of him coincide with itself any more than it could make its political discourse coincide with itself—nor, in fact, than Rousseau himself could. Not any one discourse but what they share in their division, indeed, the combination of a passionate longing for unity and a rigorous experience of division, represent the Revolution's greatest fidelity to Rousseau. To speak of deconstruction in this context does not mean that texts or events are meaningless. Rather it recognizes that the construction of textual significations, like that of historical relations of causality or just political systems, cannot be grounded in nature. Rousseau teaches us what the revolutionaries experienced: that such systems are radically fragile, that is, revolutionary.

Reference Matter

Notes

Chapter 1

1. Discussion following Michel Foucault's presentation of "Qu'est-ce qu'un auteur?" to the Société française de philosophie, in Foucault, *Dits et écrits*, 1:820–21.

2. Furet, *In the Workshop of History*, p. 11.

3. The great dictionaries of the end of the seventeenth century all attest such a sense. Richelet (*Dictionnaire françois*, s.v. "lumière"), gives a neutral version: "ouverture qu'on a pour quelque chose; vue et connaissance qu'on a sur quelque chose. . . . Pénétration, clarté, belles connaissances." But both Furetière and the first edition of the *Dictionnaire de l'Académie française* (1694) run it through an orthodox theological context: "se dit figurément en choses spirituelles et morales. Les *lumières* de la foi, de l'Évangile ont dissipé les ténèbres, l'aveuglement du genre humain. Les Païens n'ont connu Dieu que par la *lumière* naturelle" (Furetière, *Dictionaire universel*, s.v. "lumière"); "sign. fig. Intelligence, connaissance, clarté d'esprit. . . . Il sign. aussi, Tout ce qui éclaire l'âme. Ainsi on dit, *La lumière de la foi*" (*Dictionnaire de l'Académie française*, s.v. "lumière"). See also the discussion of the history of the term in Mortier, *Clarté et ombres au siècle des lumières*, pp. 13–59.

4. Condorcet, "Discours de réception à l'Académie française" (1782), in *Sur les élections et autres textes*, p. 182.

5. Ibid., p. 184. For similar eulogies of the printing press as guarantor of progress and enlightenment, see, among many other possibilities, Malesherbes, *Mémoire sur la liberté de la presse* (1788), p. 223: "It is this art [printing] that spreads upon a whole nation the *lumières* that in the past lit only a small number of wise men"; also Malesherbes's analysis of the relation between the publicity of justice and printing in "Remontrances relatives aux impôts" (1775), in *Les "Remontrances" de Malesherbes*, pp. 269–73.

6. One of the most elaborate versions of this imagery can be found in the following passage from the provincial academician de Pravieux: "The most enlightened academician whose light is spread only in his own atmosphere is one of those imperceptible and indifferent stars that neither cast light nor exert influence on the earth. On the contrary the academician who publishes [*fait part au public*] the fruits of his sleepless nights and his researches takes part in the glory of the visible, luminous, and beneficent celestial bodies. His rays, joined with those of so many other scholars, his precursors or his contemporaries, contribute to dissipating the mists that might still be spread in some regions of the literary sphere; from what each academician harvests must be formed, in the discussion of all, a seed of fire and light, a new star of day for all parts of the scholarly world" (cited by Roche, *Le Siècle des lumières en province*, 1:175–76).

7. See Ozouf, *Festivals and the French Revolution*; and David's "Plan de la Fête de l'Etre suprême" (18 floréal II), in Guillaume, ed., *Procès-verbaux du Comité d'Instruction publique*, 4:347–50. One of the more striking discursive versions of this imagery can be found in a report of November 12, 1793, by Jean-Baptiste Carrier justifying his ultraterrorist measures in Nantes: "The Revolution marches with a giant's steps; prejudices and fanaticism, everything crumbles today before the irresistible force of reason; philosophy's torch casts its light everywhere and burns its enemies" (cited by Gumbrecht, "Who Were the *Philosophes*?" p. 165).

8. Kant, "Beantwortung auf der Frage: Was ist Aufklärung?" (1784), in *Werkausgabe*, 11:53; "An Answer to the Question: What is Enlightenment?" in *Practical Philosophy*, p. 17.

9. Michelet, *Histoire de la Révolution française*, 1:81. My treatment of nineteenth-century historiography in these few pages is very schematic and designed to illustrate simply one point. For the renewed attention that has recently been devoted to these historians, see Orr, *Headless History*; and a series of publications by François Furet: *Interpreting the French Revolution*; *Marx and the French Revolution*; *La Gauche et la Révolution française au milieu du XIXe siècle*; and various entries in the fifth section of Furet and Ozouf, eds., *A Critical Dictionary of the French Revolution*.

10. Taine, *Les Origines de la France contemporaine*, 1:129.

11. See ibid., 1:140–46.

12. Taine, letter to Boutmy (July 31, 1874), cited by François Leger in his introduction, ibid., 1:xxxi. As a statement about revolutionary oratorical style (rather than about the causality of the Revolution), this seems to me to be fundamentally correct.

13. Ibid., 1:139.

14. The founding text of this tradition is Febvre, *The Problem of Unbelief in the Sixteenth Century*; the most systematic attempt to build on Febvre's program

for early modern France is Mandrou, *Introduction to Modern France*. For reviews of the field, its history, structure, and problems, see Le Goff, "Mentalities: A History of Ambiguities"; Ariès, "Histoire des mentalités"; Chartier, "Intellectual History and the History of *Mentalités*," in *Cultural History*, pp. 19–52.

15. See, for example, Taine, *Les Origines de la France contemporaine*, 1:156: "Inherited prejudices constitute a sort of unconscious reason [*Le préjugé héréditaire est une sorte de raison qui s'ignore*]."

16. Tocqueville, *L'Ancien régime et la Révolution*, pp. 83–84.

17. Ibid., p. 194.

18. Ibid., p. 195.

19. Ibid., p. 199.

20. See esp. ibid., p. 212, for the formulation in terms of love and hatred, but also the entirety of book II for the equalizing action of the central administration.

21. Ibid., p. 196.

22. See ibid., p. 209: "Toward the middle of the century there appeared a certain number of writers who treat questions of public administration in particular, and who on account of a number of similar principles were commonly called *economists* or *physiocrats*. The economists made less of a splash in history than the philosophers; perhaps they contributed less than the latter to the coming of the Revolution; but I nevertheless believe that it is in their writings that its true character [*son vrai naturel*] can best be studied."

23. D'Alembert, "Discours préliminaire" (1751), in d'Alembert and Diderot, eds., *Encyclopédie* (1986), 1:117.

24. D'Alembert, "Avertissement des éditeurs" to volume III (1753), ibid., 1:215.

25. D'Alembert, *Essai sur la société des gens de lettres et des grands*, pp. 329–30. D'Alembert's text as a whole is a protest against the practices of patronage, but the positive role conceded to royal (as opposed to aristocratic) favor is characteristic. Good commentaries on the contradictions and evolution of d'Alembert's positions on this problem can be found in Walter, "Sur l'intelligensia des Lumières"; and Hulliung, *The Autocritique of Enlightenment*, pp. 88–94.

26. To take two examples from figures not usually considered to be partisans of "enlightened despotism," see Diderot, "Avertissement des éditeurs" to volume VIII (1766), *Encyclopédie* (1986), 1:224: "Might universal education advance so quickly that in ten years there would be hardly a single line in a thousand of our pages that would not be popular! It is up to the masters of the world to hasten this happy revolution. It is they who extend or shrink the sphere of enlightenment. Happy the age in which they will have learned that their security consists in commanding educated men! Assassinations have only ever been attempted by blind fanatics"; and Condorcet, "Discours de réception," *Sur les élections et autres textes*, p. 189, where he describes "numerous sovereigns" who have seen that their true

interest lies in making of absolute power "the pure and sacred organ of an enlightened and beneficent reason [*l'organe pur et sacré d'une Raison éclairée et bienfaisante*]."

27. Voltaire, *Le Siècle de Louis XIV*, p. 605.

28. Ibid., p. 617.

29. Ibid., pp. 1021–22. See also a passage printed only in the 1753 edition: "This concludes the summary, probably still too long, of the most important events of the century. These great things will one day appear quite small, when they will have been lost among the immense multitude of revolutions that rock the world, and only the faintest memory would be left if the perfecting of the arts did not spread upon this century a unique glory that will never perish" (ibid., p. 1714).

30. Mercier, *L'An deux mille quatre cent quarante*, p. 77. The abolition of absolute monarchy, of course, has occurred peacefully because of the action of a *roi philosophe* (see the chapter entitled "Forme du gouvernement," pp. 328–40).

31. Abbé Claude Fauchet, letter to the editors, *Journal de Paris* 233 (August 21, 1789), cited by Gumbrecht, "Who Were the *Philosophes*?" p. 164.

32. Marat, *Appel à la nation*, in *Œuvres politiques, 1789–1793*, 2:654. Marat cites philosophy as the first of a series of "political circumstances," including the abuse of power by royal agents, the attempts of the courts to check them, and, most important, the action of patriotic writers against the plots of privileged orders. Similarly, in *L'Ami du peuple* 274 (November 8, 1790), ibid., 3:1724, he writes, "Thus, freedom of the press is the great mainspring, the sole highway of civil and political freedom. It is to the enlightenment of philosophy that we owe the revolution, and to the enlightenment of patriotic writers that we owe its triumph. As long as freedom of the press exists, we are sure to triumph." His reference in *L'Ami du peuple* 142 (June 23, 1790), ibid., 2:935, to "cette incroyable révolution, préparée par la philosophie" seems to refer specifically to the abolition of hereditary nobility on June 19, 1790.

33. *Alphabet des sans-culottes* (1793), cited by Gumbrecht, "Who Were the *Philosophes*?" p. 165.

34. Verses cited from Leith, "Les Trois apothéoses de Voltaire," p. 200. For a description of David's contribution, as well as a good sampling of newspaper accounts of the event, see Dowd, *Pageant-Master of the Republic*, pp. 46–54. See also the documentation assembled by Biver, *Fêtes révolutionnaires à Paris*, pp. 37–42, 179–82; and Vercruysse, ed., *Les Voltairiens*, vol. 5.

35. On Ginguené, see Kitchen, *Un Journal "philosophique"*; Hesse, *Publishing and Cultural Politics in Revolutionary Paris*, pp. 151–60.

36. Ginguené et al., *Pétition à l'Assemblée nationale*, pp. 2–3.

37. Ibid., p. 15.

38. On the way in which the translation of Rousseau's remains figured in the

tactical politics of the immediate post-Thermidor situation, see Higgins, "Rousseau and the Pantheon."

39. Cambacérès, *Discours prononcé,* p. 2. See also the sentimental account given by Mercier in *Le Nouveau Paris,* cited by Biver, *Fêtes révolutionnaires à Paris,* pp. 97–98.

40. Mercier, *De J. J. Rousseau,* 2:1–32; and the commentary by Barny, *L'Éclatement révolutionnaire du rousseauisme,* 53–74.

41. Mercier, *De J. J. Rousseau,* 2:306.

42. "Nouvelles littéraires: *Vie de Voltaire,*" 27–28.

43. Mercier, *De J. J. Rousseau,* 1:61. Mercier is very proud of having written along similar lines in *De la littérature* (and with a particularly "happy" choice of words), "The influence of Writers is such that they can today announce their power publicly, and no longer need to disguise the legitimate authority they have over men's minds. Strengthened by public interest and a real knowledge of man, they will direct National ideas; particular wills are in their hands. Morality has become the principle study of all who think [*des esprits*], and literary glory from now on seems destined to belong to he who will most forcefully plead the respective interests of Nations before the Tribunal of Philosophy. . . . One can presume that this general tendency will produce a happy revolution" (p. 9).

44. See Chartier, *The Order of Books,* pp. 40–51.

45. Voltaire, "Gens de lettres," in *Œuvres alphabétiques,* pp. 121–22.

46. Ibid., p. 123.

47. Mercier, *De la littérature,* p. 78. See Walter, "Les Auteurs et le champ littéraire," pp. 392–94.

48. Mercier, *De la littérature,* pp. 38–39. Note that, at least here, Mercier treats the writer as having a vocation rather than a *métier,* in the sense in which the latter would imply deriving income from one's activity. The writer is distinguished by the seriousness, quality, and regularity of his production, and not by its economic reward.

49. D'Alembert and Diderot, eds., *Encyclopédie* (1751–67), s.v. "auteur," 1:894. The first etymology given is the one accepted today; the second had been proposed by Furetière in his *Dictionaire universel.* This order of listing is also maintained in modern French dictionaries.

50. In an influential essay, Michel Foucault proposed that the end of the eighteenth century represented a key transitional moment in the development of the "author-function," insofar as a new legal definition of the author made him or her responsible before the law for the content of his or her texts, and simultaneously made possible a new ideological representation of the author as the hero of subversion. See Foucault, "What Is an Author?" in *Aesthetics, Method, and Epistemology,* pp. 211–12: "Texts, books, and discourses really began to have authors . . . to the

extent that authors became subject to punishment, that is, to the extent that discourses could be transgressive. . . . Once a system of ownership for texts came
into being, once strict rules concerning author's rights, author-publisher relations,
rights of reproduction, and related matters were enacted—at the end of the
eighteenth and the beginning of the nineteenth century—the possibility of trans-
gression attached to the act of writing took on, more and more, the form of an
imperative peculiar to literature." In a recent detailed study of the history of
authorship law in France from 1773 to 1810, Carla Hesse has contested that these
laws ascribed final control of meaning to the author: "The author as a legal
instrument for the regulation of knowledge was created by the absolutist monarchy in 1777, not by the liberal bourgeois democracy inaugurated in 1789. . . .
The revolutionary legislation did redefine the author's 'privilege' as property,
but not as an absolute right. The intention and the result of this redefinition of
the author's claim to his text as property was not to enhance the author's power
to control or determine the uses and meanings of the text. Quite the opposite,
in fact. . . . If the Old Regime first accorded Voltaire, Rousseau, or Mirabeau the
possibility of legal status as privileged authors with perpetual private lineages for
their texts, the Revolution relocated these figures in the public domain, the legal
parallel to the civic rituals that unearthed them from private grave sites and
reposed their bodily remains in the public temple of the Pantheon. By legally
consecrating and protecting the public domain, rather than the private authorial
lineage, the French revolutionary laws on authorship shifted the legal basis of
exclusive commercial claims on the majority of books from the manuscript to
the edition, from the text to the paratext. As a result, the problem of determining
the meaning of a text shifted away from its source, the author, and toward its
destination, its representation and reception by the editor and reader" (*Publishing
and Cultural Politics in Revolutionary Paris*, pp. 121–23). Hesse's conclusion from
the codification of the public domain to a more open regime of meaning seems
to me to be somewhat hasty: that anyone can publish the works of Rousseau
means rather that no *other* individual, even his heir, can lay an exclusive claim to
it. We might say that the representation of author, which remains the source of
meaning, enters into a sphere of contestation. But the creation of such a sphere,
in which, for example, literary criticism ceases to be normative and becomes
increasingly interpretive, is not reducible to changes in the legal status of
authorship.

   51. Gumbrecht, "Who Were the *Philosophes*?" p. 167 (translation modified).

   52. See ibid., p. 168: "By ripping down the old partition between the rulers and
the ruled and opening up chances for political influence and decision making for
intellectuals, the Revolution first of all devalued the game of radical yet noncom-
mittal—because removed from application and without consequences—critique

of authority [*das Spiel radikaler, aber unverbindlicher, weil anwendungsferner und folgenloser Autoritätskritik*]" (translation modified).

53. Chartier, *Cultural Origins*, pp. 87–88. The claim may be slightly overstated in this form: important processes of canon formation (grouping of authors and their texts) were certainly underway long before the Revolution, particularly in the struggle for control of the Académie and in theater polemics set off by Palissot's *Les Philosophes*. See Gumbrecht, "Who Were the *Philosophes?*" pp. 143–55.

54. Mounier, *De l'influence attribuée aux philosophes*, pp. 118–19. On Mounier's political career, see Egret, *La Révolution des notables*.

55. Mercier, *De J. J. Rousseau*, 2:99n. Recent research leads to a more nuanced view of the chronology of reception; see Chapter 4.

56. Chartier, *Cultural Origins*, p. 2.

57. This aspect has been particularly emphasized by Hunt, *Politics, Culture, and Class in the French Revolution*.

58. Tocqueville, *L'Ancien régime et la Révolution*, p. 194; Taine, *Les Origines de la France contemporaine*, 1:235.

59. Darnton, "In Search of the Enlightenment," p. 124. Darnton is primarily referring here to Mornet's "Les Enseignements des bibliothèques privées," a study that provided much of the empirical data for the *Origines intellectuelles*. For other assessments of Mornet's centrality, see Darnton, *The Literary Underground of the Old Regime*, pp. 167–82; Furet, "Avertissement," in Bollème et al., *Livre et société dans la France du XVIIIᵉ siècle*, 1:1; and Chartier, *Cultural Origins*, pp. 1–4.

60. Mornet, *Les Origines intellectuelles*, p. 23.

61. Ibid., p. 24.
62. Ibid., pp. 528–30.
63. Ibid., p. 236.
64. Ibid., p. 259.
65. Ibid., p. 525.
66. Ibid., p. 26.
67. Ibid., p. 525.
68. Ibid., p. 471.
69. Ibid., p. 531.

70. On the growth and decline of the vogue for quantification in the French historiographical tradition, see Le Roy Ladurie, "Quantitative History," in *The Territory of the Historian*, pp. 17–31; Furet, "Quantitative History," in *In the Workshop of History*, pp. 40–53; and Lepetit, "Quantitative History." On the application of quantitative methods to cultural history, see esp. Chaunu, "Un nouveau champ pour l'histoire sérielle"; and Chartier, "Intellectual History and the History of *Mentalités*," in *Cultural History*, pp. 19–52.

71. See Furet and Ozouf, *Reading and Writing*. These measurements are based on Louis Maggiolo's study of signatures in parish marriage registries. Behind these overall figures there is a great deal of local variation, most evident in the division of France into a literate north and northeast and a largely illiterate south and west.

Female literacy in the eighteenth century both began at a lower level and grew at a lower rate.

72. Roche, *The People of Paris*, pp. 199–205.

73. Martin, "Une Croissance séculaire," p. 99. Martin's estimate is based on a study of titles cited in Quérard's *La France littéraire*. For a comparison of different statistical sources for the study of long-term trends in book publication, see Estivals, *La Statistique bibliographique*.

74. Malesherbes, *Mémoires sur la librairie* (1759), p. 209. On *privilèges* and other forms of permission to publish, see Birn, "Profit in Ideas"; and Hesse, *Publishing and Cultural Politics*.

75. Furet, "Book Licensing and Book Production in the Kingdom of France in the Eighteenth Century," in *In the Workshop of History*, p. 117 (a translation of Furet's contribution to *Livre et société*).

76. Ibid., p. 119.

77. Ibid., p. 123 (translation modified).

78. Brancolini and Bouyssy, "La Vie provinciale du livre." The source used for this study includes press runs, and thus allows the percentages to be calculated in terms of volume rather than simply by title.

79. Martin, *Le Livre français sous l'Ancien Régime*, p. 163. Martin cites *L'Ange conducteur dans la dévotion chrétienne* as the most frequently reprinted book (150 times) among these provincial reeditions, with a total of 97,700 copies printed between 1779 and 1789 (ibid., p. 118).

80. Furet, *In the Workshop of History*, p. 117.

81. Malesherbes, *Mémoires sur la librairie*, p. 207.

82. Artier, "Étude sur la production imprimée de l'année 1764."

83. Darnton, *The Great Cat Massacre*, p. 258. See also Darnton, "Intellectual and Cultural History."

84. Darnton, "In Search of the Enlightenment"; Darnton, *The Literary Underground of the Old Regime*, pp. 167–82. A clear example of the way in which a massive statistical corpus relates to an hermeneutic approach can be found in Darnton, "The Facts of Literary Life in Eighteenth-Century France."

85. Chartier, *Cultural Origins*, p. 68.

86. Ibid., pp. 82–85. Chartier refers to Mercier's *Tableau de Paris*, "Placards" (6:85–89), "Estampes licencieuses" (6:92–94), and "Libelles" (7:22–28). Darnton's critique of Chartier's readings of Mercier can be found in *Forbidden Best-Sellers*, pp. 226–33.

87. Engelsing, "Die Perioden der Lesergeschichte in der Neuzeit," discussed by Chartier in *Cultural Origins*, p. 90; see also Chartier, *The Cultural Uses of Print*, pp. 222–25.

88. Chartier, *Cultural Origins*, p. 91.

89. Darnton, *Forbidden Best-Sellers*, p. 6.

90. "Projet de police de la librairie de Normandie donné par M. Rodolphe, subdélégué de M. l'intendant à Caen," cited by Darnton, *Forbidden Best-Sellers*, p. 223.

91. To look at authors rather than titles, the top ten, in order, were Voltaire, d'Holbach, Pidansat de Mairobert, Mercier, Théveneau de Morande, Linguet, du Laurens, Raynal, Rousseau, and Helvétius (table 2.6, ibid., p. 65). Four of the figures derive from the heroic generations of the "high Enlightenment" rather than the "low life of literature." Raynal and Mercier were anthologizers and popularizers, certainly, and neither was a great prose stylist, but it seems excessively tendentious to call them "hacks": in their different ways, both contributed to the formation of the social profile of the enlightened man of letters. Linguet, an *anti-philosophe* whose justifications of absolutism as the best defender of property led him to attack the Bourbon monarchy as a despotism, is perhaps the most difficult to characterize; see Levy, *The Ideas and Careers of Simon-Nicolas-Henri Linguet*. This leaves us then with one outright pornographer and two authors of *chroniques scandaleuses*. In fact, with the exception of Diderot, represented only by his contributions to Raynal's *Histoire philosophique*, we have here that section of the canonical Enlightenment that was forced to circulate in a truly clandestine manner.

92. Darnton, *Forbidden Best-Sellers*, p. 69.

93. Ibid., p. 73.

94. See Cassirer, *The Philosophy of the Enlightenment*, pp. 3–27; Koselleck, *Critique and Crisis*, p. 98–123.

95. Darnton, *Forbidden Best-Sellers*, pp. 85–86.

96. Ibid., pp. 132–33.   97. Ibid., p. 162.

98. Ibid., pp. 189–91.   99. Ibid., pp. 237–38.

100. For other studies of pornographic libels concerning the royal couple, see Revel, "Marie-Antoinette and Her Fictions"; Hunt, *The Family Romance of the French Revolution*, pp. 89–123; Maza, *Private Lives and Public Affairs*, pp. 167–211; Baecque, *The Body Politic*, pp. 29–75.

101. Darnton, *Forbidden Best-Sellers*, pp. 244–46.

102. Ibid., p. 244.

103. See Chartier, "The Practical Impact of Writing," pp. 124–27.

104. In many ways the fundamental impulse of "reader-response criticism" has been to attempt to describe the play between these two positions as a structural feature of the text itself, which would then include both moments of determinacy and moments of indeterminacy, and which would admit of a multiplicity, but not an infinity, of "correct" readings. See the essays collected in Tompkins, ed., *Reader-Response Criticism*, particularly, Poulet, "Criticism and the Experience of Interior-

ity," and Iser, "The Reading Process"; see also Ong, "The Writer's Audience is Always a Fiction"; and above all Iser, *The Act of Reading*.

105. Certeau, *The Practice of Everyday Life*, pp. 165–76; Hoggart, *The Uses of Literacy*.

106. Darnton, *Forbidden Best-Sellers*, p. 186.

107. Fish, *Is There a Text in This Class?*

108. See Paulhan's fascinating study of the logic and effects of the denigration of rhetoric, *Les Fleurs de Tarbes*.

109. Darnton gives a fictional example, drawn from Mercier's *Histoire d'une jeune luthérienne* (1785): "Anyone who had seen me reading would have compared me to a man dying of thirst who was gulping down some fresh, pure water. . . . Lighting my lamp with extraordinary caution, I threw myself hungrily into the reading. An easy eloquence, effortless and animated, carried me from one page to the next without my knowing it. A clock struck off the hours in the silence of the shadows, and I heard nothing. My lamp began to run out of oil and produced only a pale light, but still I read on. I could not even take out time to raise the wick for fear of interrupting my pleasure. How those new ideas rushed into my brain! How my intelligence adopted them!" (cited and translated in *Forbidden Best-Sellers*, pp. 230–31).

110. Darnton, "Readers Respond to Rousseau: The Fabrication of Romantic Sensibility," in *The Great Cat Massacre*, pp. 215–56.

111. For an interpretation presenting Roland's reading as a reconfirmation, see Trouille, *Sexual Politics in the Enlightenment*, pp. 163–92. The studies by May in *De Jean-Jacques Rousseau à Madame Roland*, pp. 76–93, and *Madame Roland and the Age of Revolution*, pp. 55–72, present this reading as a conversion experience.

112. Roland, *Mémoires de Madame Roland*, p. 302.

113. Tackett, *Becoming a Revolutionary*, an exhaustive study of writings by members of the National Assembly, indicates that while the vast majority of deputies were familiar with at least some variant of Enlightenment discourse, it can hardly be described as a dominant cultural framework. In particular, he argues that when a prerevolutionary involvement in the institutions and discourses of the Enlightenment can be identified, this has no predictive value with respect to the political choices the deputies made during the summer of 1789 (see pp. 76 and 304, regarding deputies known to be admirers of Rousseau). Further, Tackett's reading of the testimonies of Third Estate deputies recalls Mounier's claim that the Revolution produced the influence of the Enlightenment. "It was only after the fact, that many deputies began to evolve a coherent ideology—or rather several different ideologies—to explain and justify their actions, ideologies in which diverse elements of eighteenth-century thought were brought together and synthesized. Specific references in deputy testimonies to the ideas of the Enlightenment,

largely absent in May and early June, become more common in the summer and fall of 1789" (p. 308). This finding leads Tackett to reaffirm Mornet's dictum on the division between the origins of the Revolution and the Revolution itself (p. 302). This indeterminacy of the effect of the Enlightenment would seem to be confirmed, in the opposite direction, by a study of libraries confiscated during the Terror, all of which look quite similar in content, regardless of the political choices made by their owners. See Marcetteau-Paul and Varry, "Les Bibliothèques de quelques acteurs de la Révolution."

114. Habermas, *The Structural Transformation of the Public Sphere*, p. 27.

115. See Baker's comments on this point in "Defining the Public Sphere in Eighteenth-Century France," p. 183.

116. Ariès, Introduction to Chartier, ed., *Passions of the Renaissance*, p. 9; Goodman, "Public Sphere and Private Life." A tradition of French scholarship in this field independent of Habermas's influence is represented by a series of works by Maurice Agulhon, most importantly *Pénitents et franc-maçons de l'ancienne Provence*; an excerpt from the Preface to *Le Cercle dans la France bourgeoise, 1810–1848: étude d'une mutation de sociabilité*, in which Agulhon discusses his use of the concept of sociability, has been translated in Revel and Hunt, eds., *Histories: French Constructions of the Past*, pp. 398–407.

117. Habermas, *The Structural Transformation of the Public Sphere*, p. 28.

118. Ibid., pp. 46–47.

119. Ibid., p. 50. See Foisil, "The Literature of Intimacy," and Goulemot, "Literary Practices: Publicizing the Private," both in Chartier, ed., *Passions of the Renaissance*.

120. For a classic statement on the unity of these terms during the reign of Louis XIV, see Auerbach, "La Cour et la Ville," in *Scenes from the Drama of European Literature*, pp. 133–79. For an argument that eighteenth-century notions of civility, politeness, and sociability were formed by aristocratic withdrawal from courtly norms, see Gordon, *Citizens without Sovereignty*, pp. 86–128; and DeJean, *Ancients against Moderns*, pp. 31–77.

121. Most historians today are much less confident about the "bourgeois" character of cultural developments in the eighteenth century than Habermas was in 1962, when his book was first published. I follow a comment by Daniel Roche in viewing this separation as justifying the term: "If [Habermas] characterized this new sphere as essentially 'bourgeois,' it was not so much because it coincided with the interests and ideas of the triumphant bourgeoisie as because it formed outside the traditional spaces for debate and information associated with the public authorities and court society" (*France in the Enlightenment*, p. 423). Neither the participation and even leadership of titular nobility in this movement, nor the near-universal aspiration of nonnoble participants to noble status changes the fact

that claims to distinction more and more have a different foundation ("merit," "virtue," "utility," or even "sentiment"). If the Enlightenment was indeed the shared culture of an "elite" that excluded poorer, provincial nobles as well as most commoners, including merchants, from a cultural point of view this can still be described as an *embourgeoisement* of an important portion of the urban, liberal nobility. We might note that while a key role in the early stages of the Revolution was played by this largely Parisian enlightened nobility, a very different nobility— provincial, military, and reactionary—dominated the second order of the Estates General, with crucial effects for the dynamic of that body (Tackett, *Becoming a Revolutionary*, pp. 28–35). For elements of this debate, see the summary of the development of the "revisionist" interpretation, with an emphasis on the work of anglophone scholars such as Alfred Cobban, G. V. Taylor, Elizabeth Eisenstein, and Colin Lucas, in Doyle, *Origins of the French Revolution.* The most important French contributions, from the point of view that interests us here, are Richet, "Autour des origines idéologiques lointaines de la Révolution française"; Furet, "The Revolutionary Catechism," in *Interpreting the French Revolution,* esp. pp. 100–116; and Chaussinand-Nogaret, *The French Nobility in the Eighteenth Century.* An important and persuasive "postrevisionist" perspective can be found in Jones, "Bourgeois Revolution Revivified"; see also Maza, "Luxury, Morality, and Social Change."

122. Habermas, *The Structural Transformation of the Public Sphere,* p. 32.

123. There is a tremendous amount of recent scholarship on these topics operating within this conceptual framework. On the press, see Sgard, "La Multi-plication des périodiques"; Censer and Popkin, eds., *Press and Politics in Pre-Revolutionary France*; and Censer, *The French Press in the Age of Enlightenment.* Descriptions of individual cafés can be found in Isherwood, *Farce and Fantasy,* but I know of no work that gives a synthetic treatment of café culture in France. On the salons, see Goodman, *The Republic of Letters*; and Kors, *D'Holbach's Coterie.* There is also a large body of important recent research on the seventeenth-century roots of this phenomenon; see esp. Harth, *Cartesian Women*; Lougee, *"Le Paradis des femmes"*; and Viala, *La Naissance de l'écrivain.* On concerts see Johnson, *Listening in Paris*; on the *salon de peinture,* Crow, *Painters and Public Life in Eighteenth-Century Paris*; on theater audiences, Ravel, "Seating the Public." Roche's *Le Siècle des lumières en province* is a definitive study of the provincial academies, and con-tains much information on other forms of sociability in the cities where they were located; see also the essays collected in his *Les Républicains des lettres.* On the masonic lodges, see the opposing perspectives of Halévi, *Les Loges maçonniques dans la France d'Ancien Régime*; and Jacob, *Living the Enlightenment.* Guénot, "Musées et lycées parisiens," is the only recent study I know of devoted entirely to this phenomenon; see also Goodman, *The Republic of Letters,* pp. 233–80.

124. This is more or less self-evident in the cases of cafés, concerts, theaters, and painting exhibitions. The great "philosophical" salons were Parisian, but similar circles existed in provincial cities. For academies, the crucial threshold seems to be a population of twenty thousand (Roche, *Le Siècle des lumières en province*, 1:79). Only three cities with populations above ten thousand did not have lodges, and the majority of cities with population levels between six and ten thousand had lodges. Still, some one hundred towns with population levels below two thousand had lodges in 1789 (Halévi, *Les Loges maçonniques dans la France d'Ancien Régime*, pp. 75–90).

125. Habermas notes that one of the crucial differences between the literary and political modalities of the public sphere was that women and servants were included in the former but excluded from the latter (*The Structural Transformation of the Public Sphere*, p. 56). Landes's influential *Women and the Public Sphere in the Age of the French Revolution* argues that this exclusion was essential to the constitution of the public sphere in the political domain. See Habermas's own comments on this point in "Further Reflections on the Public Sphere," pp. 427–29; an argument that this exclusion is contingent rather than constitutive can be found in Baker, "Defining the Public Sphere," pp. 198–208; see also on these points the debate between Gordon, Bell, and Maza on "The Public Sphere in the Eighteenth Century." For the controversy over women's participation in freemasonry, see Goodman, *The Republic of Letters*, chapter 6; and Burke and Jacob, "French Freemasonry, Women, and Feminist Scholarship."

126. Habermas, *The Structural Transformation of the Public Sphere*, p. 88. No doubt, as Étienne Balibar has argued in a series of recent publications, every ideology contains this moment of universalization. See the essays collected in Balibar, *Masses, Classes, Ideas*; and Balibar, "Ambiguous Universality."

127. Habermas, *The Structural Transformation of the Public Sphere*, p. 51.

128. Ibid., p. 69. Necker's *Compte rendu* is in vol. 2 of his *Œuvres complètes*. On its success, see Egret, *Necker, ministre de Louis XVI*, pp. 169–79.

129. Richelieu, *Testament politique*, p. 332.

130. The most philologically complete study of public opinion, whose broad historical perspective emphasizes the continuing importance of the notion of reputation (and with it how public opinion is as much a tool for ministerial manipulation as for popular control) is Gunn, *Queen of the World*. The most important studies of the vicissitudes of "public opinion" in the last years of the Old Regime are Ozouf, "'Public Opinion' at the End of the Old Regime"; and Baker, "Public Opinion as Political Invention," in *Inventing the French Revolution*, pp. 167–99.

131. Habermas, *The Structural Transformation of the Public Sphere*, pp. 95–96.

132. Ibid., p. 53.

133. Baker, "Defining the Public Sphere," pp. 185–86.

134. Chartier, *Cultural Origins*, pp. 17–18. A more extended grounding of the argument in Foucault's work can be found in Chartier, *On the Edge of the Cliff*, pp. 51–71.

135. Chartier, *Cultural Origins*, pp. 109–10.

136. Ibid., pp. 141–45, 151–54. Chartier's arguments on these points are based on Root, *Peasants and King in Burgundy*, pp. 155–204; and Sonenscher, *Work and Wages*, pp. 244–94.

137. Chartier, *Cultural Origins*, pp. 20–37; 154–68.

138. Ibid., p. 196.

139. Cochin, *L'Esprit du jacobinisme*, p. 36. See also Barruel, *Mémoires pour servir à l'histoire du jacobinisme*; Furet, "Augustin Cochin: The Theory of Jacobinism," in *Interpreting the French Revolution*, pp. 164–204; Halévi, *Les Loges maçonniques dans la France d'Ancien Régime*; Halévi, "L'Idée et l'événement"; Gueniffey and Halévi, "Clubs and Popular Societies." Whatever its influence on Habermas may have been, Koselleck's emphasis in *Critique and Crisis* on the "hypocrisy" of criticism seems to me to place him within this tradition; see Jacob, *Living the Enlightenment*, pp. 9–15.

140. Chartier, *Cultural Origins*, p. 16.

141. Goodman, The *Republic of Letters*, p. 75.

142. See ibid., pp. 54–73. The most interesting moment of her critique of the historiography is probably her discussion of Cassirer, whose detachment of Enlightenment from social context she sees as going hand in hand with his insistence that Rousseau be understood as an integral part of the Enlightenment. "Cassirer made the Enlightenment serious by freeing it from the complex and problematic social reality of which salonnières were an important part, and he used Rousseau to help him do it" (p. 63).

143. Ibid., p. 91. See her account of the role of disputation in eighteenth-century educational practices, pp. 91–96.

144. Ibid., p. 80.

145. *Poli* (literally "polished," the French word for polite) and *policé* are in fact not cognates, although they were often treated as such in eighteenth-century discourse. See Starobinski, "The Word *Civilization*," in *Blessings in Disguise*, pp. 12–17.

146. Goodman, *The Republic of Letters*, p. 6.

147. Ibid., pp. 212–13.

148. Ibid., p. 190. See also the discussion of how Galiani's use of "enthusiastic" indicates religious fanaticism, a theme developed through comparisons with the Jansenist convulsionaries at the tomb of deacon Pâris in the Saint-Médard churchyard, pp. 194–95. The relation of this sort of "wit" based on ridicule to the standards of politeness seems to me to be one of the principal blind spots of Goodman's argument.

149. Gordon, *Citizens without Sovereignty*, p. 19.

150. For the contrast between Delamare and Peuchet, see Gordon, "Philosophy, Sociology, and Gender," pp. 893–99. I discuss Peuchet's account of the civilizing process in relation to public opinion in Chapter 2.

151. Kaplan, *Provisioning Paris*, p. 593. See also Kaplan, *Bread, Politics and Political Economy in the Reign of Louis XV,* the fundamental study of debates around the grain trade in the 1760s and early 1770s.

152. Abbé Fernando Galiani to Louise-Florence-Pétronille Tardieu d'Esclavelles, marquise de Lalive d'Épinay, August 7, 1773, in Galiani and d'Épinay, *Correspondance,* 4:46; translation as given by Kaplan, *Provisioning Paris,* p. 594. Recalling that "commerce" is frequently used for "conversation," I would argue that the distinction between commerce and *police* is one between realms that operate based on self-regulation, or regulation by means of social pressure alone, and realms where the repressive apparatus of the state can and must legitimately intervene.

153. Goodman, *The Republic of Letters*, p. 202.

154. Ibid., pp. 107–11, 126–32. See also the similar treatment of Morellet in Gordon, *Citizens without Sovereignty*, pp. 177–241; and Gordon, "'Public Opinion' and the Civilizing Process in France."

155. Goodman, *The Republic of Letters*, p. 185. See also a number of related passages—for example: "Discourse could not be controlled once it moved out of the well-governed precincts of the salons any more than it could be outside of the confines of the court" (p. 152). For a statement that "anarchy" is essential to the Republic of Letters, see d'Alembert, *Essai sur la société des gens de lettres et des grands,* p. 346: "Anarchy, which destroys political states, on the contrary sustains the Republic of Letters and guarantees its subsistence; a few Magistrates may have to be suffered, but no Kings are wanted."

156. Goodman, *The Republic of Letters*, p. 280.

157. Ibid., p. 234.

158. Ibid., pp. 9, 234n3.

159. Ibid., p. 2.

160. I have attempted to give a historical account of this functioning of the term in Swenson, "A Small Change in Terminology or a Great Leap Forward?"

161. See Kernan's comments comparing Rousseau and Samuel Johnson in *Samuel Johnson and the Impact of Print,* pp. 299–301. On Rousseau's views on literary property and his negotiations with his publishers, see Birn, "Rousseau et ses éditeurs"; and Birn, "Rousseau and Literary Property." The most extensive treatment of Rousseau's conflictual relations with patronage can be found in Mély, *Jean-Jacques Rousseau.*

162. I owe this point to the work of Joseph Chaves (Department of Compara-

tive Literature, Rutgers University) in his doctoral dissertation, currently under preparation. The reflections that follow are indebted to our conversations.

163. Kant, "Was ist Aufklärung?" *Werkausgabe*, 12:55; "What is Enlightenment?" *Practical Philosophy*, p. 18.

164. Baker, *Inventing the French Revolution*, pp. 4–5.

165. Baker's use of "discourse" draws on both Foucault and the "Cambridge School" of intellectual history. For methodological discussions, see Foucault, *The Archaeology of Knowledge and the Discourse on Language*; Pocock, *Virtue, Commerce, and History*, pp. 1–34; Skinner, *Meaning and Context*.

166. Baker, Introduction to *The French Revolution and the Creation of Modern Political Culture*, 1:xiii.

167. Baker, *Inventing the French Revolution*, p. 25.

168. Montesquieu, *De l'esprit des lois*, p. 247: "Intermediate, subordinate, and dependent powers constitute the nature of monarchical government, that is, one in which a single man governs according to fundamental laws. . . . The most natural intermediate, subordinated power is that of the nobility, which in some sense enters into the essence of monarchy, whose fundamental maxim is: *no monarch, no nobility; no nobility, no monarch.*"

169. Baker discusses Malesherbes in *Inventing the French Revolution*, pp. 117–20. See Richet, "Autour des origines idéologiques lointaines de la Révolution française"; Carcasonne, *Montesquieu et le problème de la constitution française*; and Egret, *Louis XV et l'opposition parlementaire*. On the relations between Jansenism and parlementary constitutionalism, see Van Kley, "Church, State, and the Ideological Origins of the French Revolution"; and Van Kley, "The Jansenist Constitutional Legacy in the French Prerevolution."

170. Baker, *Inventing the French Revolution*, p. 86.

171. See esp. ibid., pp. 123–27, 143–46.

172. Ibid., p. 26. In addition to the discussions of Turgot and the essay on "Science and Politics at the End of the Old Regime" in *Inventing the French Revolution*, see also Baker, *Condorcet*.

173. Baker, *Inventing the French Revolution*, p. 127.

174. Necker, *De l'administration des finances de la France* (1784), in *Œuvres complètes*, 4:56; as cited and translated by Baker, *Inventing the French Revolution*, p. 194.

175. Baker, "Defining the Public Sphere in Eighteenth-Century France," p. 197.

176. Baker, *Inventing the French Revolution*, p. 198.

177. Ibid., p. 172.

178. Ibid., p. 186. Habermas seems to me to misread Rousseau badly on this point in *The Structural Transformation of the Public Sphere*, pp. 96–99, conflating *opinion publique* with *volonté générale*.

179. Baker, "Defining the Public Sphere in Eighteenth-Century France," p. 193. This position is strikingly reiterated at the end of the same essay in an effort to dispute Landes's use of Rousseau in *Women and the Public Sphere* to characterize the late eighteenth-century public sphere as essentially masculinist: "Moreover, Landes fails to grasp the extent to which republican and rationalist conceptions of the public sphere derive from radically competing discourses in the eighteenth-century context. Rousseau's reworking of the discourse of classical republicanism, fundamentally concerned with the recovery of sovereignty by a community of autonomous citizens, was couched in quite different terms than the rationalist discourse of the social, grounded on notions of the rights of man, the division of labor, and the apolitical rule of reason" (p. 202). Baker argues that the examples of both Condorcet and Wollstonecraft show that this latter conception is not essentially masculinist.

180. Baker, *Inventing the French Revolution*, p. 27.

181. For reasons of economy, I have chosen to give an account here of Maza's argument but not Crow's, but I think that the demonstration would be substantially the same. In part this has to do with their common concentration on the Kornmann affair, for which both draw extensively on the unpublished portions of Robert Darnton's 1964 Oxford doctoral dissertation, "Trends in Radical Propaganda on the Eve of the French Revolution (1782–1788)." But both draw even greater strength from their concrete analyses of texts and, in Crow's case, paintings. Crow's analysis centers on the way in which the success of Jacques-Louis David's paintings of the 1780s, particularly *Le Serment des Horaces* and *Brutus*, allowed a convincing representation of a "public" in the Salon to come into being. Of particular importance in these paintings by David is the depiction of masculine, republican virtue counterposed in highly discontinuous compositions to feminine emotionality within a domestic setting. But even more important, in Crow's account, is David's use of the painterly equivalent of a rhetoric of sincerity, what he calls an "anti-style" that "made dissonance and discontinuity into elementary constituents of picture-making" and that grounds the appeal to an "oppositional public" within artistic practice itself (Crow, *Painters and Public Life in Eighteenth-Century Paris*, citations from pp. 253–54).

182. Maza, *Private Lives and Public Affairs*, pp. 59–60.

183. Ibid., pp. 66–67.

184. Ibid., p. 315.

185. Ibid., p. 269.

186. Maza would appear to have a somewhat more sanguine view of Rousseau's relation to the advancement of women than Goodman and most other contemporary writers on the question. See Maza, "Women, the Bourgeoisie, and the Public Sphere," p. 949: "Undoubtedly, as Dena Goodman has argued, the salons did of-

fer a small number of intelligent and ambitious women an outlet they would not have had in another time and place. But the role of *salonnière* was available to only a very small number of women and perhaps not attractive to many. The philosophers put a handful of *salonnières* on pedestals for subordinating themselves to the social and intellectual needs of men. Rousseau, on the other hand, presented all women with the promise of total empowerment within the home and emotional control over their husbands and children. Rousseau was influential because, within the parameters of eighteenth-century culture, he offered women the better deal."

187. Maza, *Private Lives and Public Affairs*, pp. 261–62.

188. Ibid., p. 321.

189. Blum, *Rousseau and the Republic of Virtue*, esp. pp. 133–52. The extent of my debt to Blum's book may not always be apparent in these pages, since key decisions about the shape of the argument were determined in part by a desire not to repeat what she so convincingly establishes.

Chapter 2

1. "Here it is I who am the barbarian because they do not understand me." Latin given as cited by Rousseau in the epigraphs for both the *Discours sur les sciences et les arts* (p. 1) and the *Dialogues* (p. 657). The Loeb edition gives a slightly different reading: *barbarus hic ego sum, qui non intellegor ulli* ("here it is I who am a barbarian, understood by nobody").

2. Robespierre, "Sur les rapports des idées religieuses et morales avec les principes républicains et sur les fêtes nationales" (18 floréal II), *Œuvres*, 10:458. On Robespierre's religious project, see Mathiez, "Robespierre and the Cult of the Supreme Being."

3. Robespierre, "Sur les rapports," *Œuvres*, 10:456.

4. Condorcet was arrested on March 27, 1794, and died in prison two days later (by suicide, according to legend, but more likely from exhaustion). See Badinter and Badinter, *Condorcet*, pp. 577–79, 613–18.

5. Robespierre, "Sur les rapports," *Œuvres*, 10:454. On Robespierre's attacks on the encyclopedists and invocations of Rousseau, see Blum, *Rousseau and the Republic of Virtue*, pp. 231–46; and Huet, *Mourning Glory*, pp. 9–31.

6. Robespierre, "Sur les rapports," *Œuvres*, 10:455.

7. Ibid., p. 443.

8. Ibid., p. 444.

9. Condorcet, *Esquisse d'un tableau historique des progrès de l'esprit humain*, p. 86.

10. We will examine the structure of stadial theory in the second section of this chapter. Condorcet gives an extremely condensed version of it in the second epoch of the *Esquisse*, pp. 97–103, but it plays no organizing role in his thought.

11. Condorcet, "Discours préliminaire" to the *Essai sur l'application de l'analyse à la probabilité des décisions rendues à la pluralité des voix* (1785), in *Sur les élections et autres textes*, p. 9. On the textual history of the *Esquisse*, and in particular on the existence of a draft dating from before the Revolution, see Baker, *Condorcet*, pp. 346–47.

12. Condorcet, *Esquisse*, p. 265.

13. Kintzler, *Condorcet*, p. 37: "The passage of time permits us to employ today a Kantian vocabulary which Condorcet could not have known, but which is contemporary to him; we will propose the formulation: in order to measure the legitimacy of a decision, it is always necessary to make use of a minimum amount of knowledge, truth is not a pure form. The only foundation of justice is the theoretical use of reason; there is no practical reason." Crampe-Casnabet, *Condorcet, lecteur des lumières*, also draws a comparison between Kant and Condorcet, one but that tends to bring them together.

14. Kant, *Kritik der praktischen Vernunft* (1788), *Werkausgabe*, 7:190; *Critique of Practical Reason*, in *Practical Philosophy*, p. 197: "Mysticism of practical reason . . . makes what served only as a symbol into a schema, that is, puts under the application of moral concepts real but not sensible intuitions (of an invisible kingdom of God) and strays into the transcendent." The explanation of this distinction between symbol and schema is to be found in §59 of the *Kritik der Urteilskraft* (1790), *Werkausgabe*, 10:295–97; *Critique of Judgment*, pp. 221–23.

15. Condorcet, *Esquisse*, p. 80.

16. Cited and translated by Baker, *Condorcet*, p. 346, from a manuscript in the Bibliothèque de l'Institut, MS 855(1), f. 3.

17. Condorcet, *Esquisse*, p. 209.

18. Ibid., p. 181.

19. Ibid., p. 211. On Descartes, see Voltaire, *Le Siècle de Louis XIV*, pp. 997–98, as well as *Lettres philosophiques*, p. 76. D'Alembert's version of this topos in the "Discours préliminaire" to the *Encyclopédie* (1986, 1:142) is well worth quoting: "[Descartes] can be regarded as the head of a band of conspirators [*un chef de conjurés*] who first had the courage to rise up against a despotic and arbitrary power and who, preparing an astonishing revolution, laid the foundations for a more just and happy government, which he did not live to see established."

20. Condorcet, *Esquisse*, pp. 206–7. Again, compare d'Alembert, who is less sanguine about this development, which, he says, "has helped make enlightenment more general, if stretching its surface can really be considered to extend the spirit of a people" (*Encyclopédie* [1986], 1:153).

21. Condorcet, *Esquisse*, p. 253.

22. Baker, *Condorcet*, p. 358.

23. Condorcet, *Esquisse*, p. 95.

24. Ibid., pp. 119–20. As allegorism is one of the fundamental resources of
sacerdotal tyranny, the progress of science, as well as that of equality, is necessarily
accompanied by a continual reduction of the figurative dimension of language.
See Condorcet's "Discours de réception," *Sur les élections et autres textes,* p. 190
(languages will become "less bold and less figurative [*moins hardies et moins
figurées*]"), and Baker's analysis in *Condorcet,* pp. 361–67.

25. It should be noted here that Condorcet uses the term "progress" neither
absolutely (that is, without a complement) nor in the singular; he always speaks
of the "progresses of" something. Brunot, *Histoire de la langue française des origines
à nos jours,* 6:109–10, gives the following comment: "*Progrès* was applied, before
the eighteenth century, to all sorts of forward movements: *progrès* of a military
operation, of an illness, of a science. What is new is to say *progrès* and nothing
more, and to resume, in this one word, the entire ascension of humanity toward
the ideal." For all the modernity of Condorcet's concept of progress—it differs
little if at all from the one we still struggle with today—this usage gives it a
somewhat archaic tone and renders the translation somewhat awkward. It is the
argument rather than the grammar that totalizes "progress."

26. Condorcet, *Esquisse,* p. 235.

27. Ibid., p. 188.

28. Ibid., p. 225.

29. Ibid., p. 216. See also p. 215, where French absolutism is characterized as
"the type of despotism . . . in which almost arbitrary authority—contained by
opinion, regulated by enlightenment, softened by its own interests—has often
contributed to the progresses of wealth, industry, education, and sometimes even
to those of civil liberty."

30. Ibid., p. 195.

31. Ibid., p. 216.

32. Ibid., pp. 229–30.

33. Ibid., p. 233.

34. Ibid., p. 235.

35. Ibid., p. 236.

36. Saint-Just, "Rapport sur la nécessité de déclarer le gouvernement révolutionnaire jusqu'à la paix" (October 10, 1793), *Œuvres complètes,* p. 529.

37. Ibid., p. 525.

38. Robespierre, "Rapport sur les principes du gouvernement révolutionnaire"
(5 nivôse II), *Œuvres,* 10:274.

39. Marx, *Das Kapital,* 1:779; *Capital,* 1:915–16.

40. Condorcet, "Sur le sens du mot 'révolutionnaire'" (June 1, 1793), *Œuvres,*
12:616.

41. Ibid., p. 623.

42. Condorcet, *Essai sur la constitution et les fonctions des Assemblées provinciales*
(1788), *Œuvres,* 8:497, cited and translated by Baker, *Condorcet,* p. 352.

43. Condorcet, *Esquisse,* p. 86.

44. See ibid., p. 219: "These principles, for which the noble Sydney paid with his blood, and to which Locke attached the authority of his name, have since been developed with more precision, breadth and force by Rousseau, and he deserves the glory of having placed them among the number of truths that can never again be forgotten or contested."

45. Ibid., p. 137.

46. In the polemical writings following upon the *Discours*, this relation becomes clearer because of the introduction of a more specifically economic discourse. See, for example, the "Réponse à Stanislas," p. 50: "From riches were born luxury and idleness; from luxury came the fine arts and from leisure the sciences." For summary discussion of eighteenth-century debates on luxury, see Berry, *The Idea of Luxury*, pp. 126–76; and Perrot, *Le Luxe*.

47. La Harpe, "De J. J. Rousseau," pp. 10–11.

48. I borrow the notion of expressive causality from Althusser, "The Object of *Capital*," in Althusser and Balibar, *Reading Capital*, pp. 186–87.

49. "Culture" is today the most common name for this sort of expressive totality. One of the most fascinating deployments of this sort of logic in contemporary scholarship is the relation between historical anecdote, literary text, and "regime of power" in new historicist literary criticism. See esp. the most brilliant example of this school, Greenblatt's *Shakespearean Negotiations*.

50. Horace, *Ars Poetica*, v. 25. "Right" here concerns not justice but poetics.

51. La Rochefoucauld, *Réflexions ou sentences et maximes morales*, Maxim 128.

52. Starobinski, *Jean-Jacques Rousseau: Transparency and Obstruction*, pp. 3–5 (hereafter cited as *Transparency and Obstruction*). See also François Bouchardy's notes to the Pléiade edition, vol. 3, pp. 1237–56.

53. Rousseau to Marie-Charlotte-Hippolyte de Campet de Saujon, comtesse de Boufflers-Rouverel, April 5, 1766, *Correspondance complète*, Letter 5146, 29:93. Cf. Cajot, *Les Plagiats de M. J. J. R. de Genève sur l'éducation*, particularly the chapter on his borrowings from Montaigne, pp. 119–58, and the appendix entitled "Observations touchant le discours de M. J. J. Rousseau de Genève, Sur le rétablissement des Sciences et des Arts," pp. 357–76.

54. Diderot, *Réfutation suivie de l'ouvrage d'Helvétius intitulé l'Homme*, p. 475. The anecdote occurs in a discussion of Helvétius's treatment of chance, where Rousseau's literary career is taken as the primary example, and continues on pp. 475–76, 482, 506–7. See also Diderot, *Essai sur les règnes de Claude et de Néron* (1779), in *Œuvres complètes*, 25:128. Rousseau recounted his own version of the origin of the first *Discours* in the second of the *Lettres à Malesherbes* (pp. 1135–36), and in book 8 of the *Confessions* (pp. 350–53, 356, 365–67); he also discusses it tangentially in the third promenade of the *Rêveries du promeneur solitaire* (p. 1015).

55. Taylor, "Rousseau's Contemporary Reputation in France," pp. 1548–49.

56. Stanislas Leszczynski, roi de Pologne et duc de Lorraine, "Réponse au discours qui a remporté le prix de l'Académie de Dijon" (1751), and *Journal encyclopédique*, February 1, 1758, both cited by Taylor, "Rousseau's Contemporary Reputation in France," pp. 1549, 1548, respectively.

57. This tendency draws support from Rousseau's explicit statement. Describing the "illumination of Vincennes," he writes, "All that I could retain of the crowd of truths that illuminated me in that quarter of an hour beneath a tree was weakly spread out in my three principal texts, namely the first discourse, that on inequality, and the treatise on education; these three works are inseparable and together form a whole" (*Lettres à Malesherbes*, p. 1136).

58. This interpretation of the fictionality of the state of nature has been most rigorously advanced by Weil, "J. J. Rousseau et sa politique." See also Starobinski's comments in his introduction to the second *Discours* in the Pléiade edition, 3:lvii.

59. See *Discours sur les sciences et les arts*, pp. 16–17: "Let us thus consider the arts and sciences in themselves. Let us see what should result from their progress, and let us no longer hesitate to agree on all points where our reasoning should turn out to be in accord with historical inductions. . . . In fact, whether one leafs through the annals of the world or supplements uncertain chronicles with philosophical speculations [*soit qu'on supplée à des chroniques incertaines par des recherches philosophiques*] . . . "

60. Machiavelli, *Discorsi sopra la prima deca di Tito Livio* (1531), I.2 and II.proemio, in *Tutte le opere*, pp. 78–81, 144–46; *Discourses on Livy*, pp. 10–14, 123–25; see also *Istorie fiorentine* (1525), V.1, in *Tutte le opere*, pp. 738–39; *Florentine Histories*, pp. 185–86. There are no direct references to Machiavelli in the first *Discours*, but he is referred to and extensively cited in the *Contrat social* (pp. 372, 384, 409 [and variant (a)], 420, 422). The best general treatment of Rousseau's relation to Machiavelli is to be found in Viroli, *Jean-Jacques Rousseau and the "Well-Ordered Society"*; see also Shklar, "Montesquieu and the New Republicanism."

61. Skinner, *The Foundations of Modern Political Thought*, 1:128–35, 182–85.

62. Montesquieu, *De l'esprit des lois*, p. 227.

63. Pocock, *The Machiavellian Moment*.

64. See Machiavelli, *Discorsi*, I.3–6, in *Tutte le opere*, pp. 81–87; *Discourses on Livy*, pp. 15–23; and Montesquieu, *De l'esprit des lois*, pp. 393–430 (book XI, which discusses Roman institutions as extensively as it does English ones). I will return to the difference between Montesquieu's and Rousseau's versions of the "separation of powers" in discussing *Du contrat social* in Chapter 4.

65. It is significant in this respect that Rousseau comes closest to developing his critique in positive terms at the points that open onto the economic problems of the *Discours sur l'inégalité*. The problematic of luxury that Rousseau places at the juncture of his two metaphorical systems is no longer that of the unhistorical

moralist and his critique of hypocrisy from which our reading began: "The first source of the evil is inequality; from inequality came riches. The words rich and poor are relative, and wherever men are equal there will be neither rich nor poor" ("Réponse à Stanislas," pp. 49–50). See the excellent account of the role of the polemics between the two *Discours* in the formation of Rousseau's mature thought in Rosenblatt, *Rousseau and Geneva*, pp. 60–76.

66. Stewart, *Account of the Life and Writings of Adam Smith*, pp. 292–96.

67. Meek, *Social Science and the Ignoble Savage*, which is the fullest account of the different versions of stadial discourse, even if many of its orientations, and particularly its concern with a "pure" version of the theory, seem somewhat dated. The question of priority is not essential to my argument here.

68. Smith, *Lectures on Jurisprudence*, LJ(A) i.28.

69. Ibid., LJ(A) i.28–32.

70. Turgot, "Plan d'un ouvrage sur la géographie politique" and "Plan de deux discours sur l'histoire universelle," in *Œuvres*, 1:255–323.

71. Both texts were probably written in 1751, after Turgot had left the theology faculty of the Sorbonne, but it should be recalled that the first text of the sequence to which they belong dealt with the benefits Christianity has brought to the human race as a civilizing factor. See Turgot, "Discours sur les avantages que l'établissement du christianisme a procurés au genre humain" (July 3, 1750), ibid., 1:194–214.

72. Smith, *Lectures on Jurisprudence*, LJ(A) iv.56.

73. Turgot, "Histoire universelle," *Œuvres*, 1:278.

74. Ibid., p. 279.

75. Ibid., p. 282.

76. See Helvétius, *De l'esprit*, p. 291; Helvétius, *De l'homme*, 2:904. I have based my attempts to figure out the relative importance of different schemes on the corpus of authors discussed by Meek in *Social Science and the Ignoble Savage*. Even if Smith's position can be considered orthodox it is by no means dominant. One also finds important texts where no single factor can be considered the main causal principle (Montesquieu, de Pauw, Ferguson, Herder), or where the question of subsistence occurs within (and not as the base of) a general progress of knowledge or the passions. Perhaps the best example of this sort of position can be seen in the Introduction to Millar, *The Origin of the Distinction of Ranks*. For Millar, rather than being driven by expanding population and needs, the changes in stages of society are primarily made possible by an expanding mental outlook and thus have to be considered as part of "a natural progress from ignorance to knowledge" (see esp. p. 176).

77. Hume, "Of Commerce" (1752), in *Political Essays*, p. 104; citation from Virgil, *Georgics*, 1.123, "sharpening men's wits with care."

78. See Buffon, *Histoire naturelle* ("Animaux communs aux deux continents"

[1761]), in *Œuvres complètes*, 11:370–71: "As for his generative organs, [the American male] is weak and small; he has neither body hair nor beard, and no passion for his female. . . . One needs go no further to find the cause of the dispersed life of the savages and their distance from society: the most precious spark of nature's fire has been denied them: they lack passion for their female, and consequently lack love for their fellow man." This theme was taken up by Kames, *Sketches of the History of Man*, 3:144–49.

79. Ferguson, *An Essay on the History of Civil Society*, p. 96.

80. Ibid., pp. 137–38.

81. On the relation between the seventeenth-century Augustinian moralists and eighteenth-century economic thought, see Raymond, "Du jansénisme à la morale de l'intérêt"; Van Kley, "Pierre Nicole, Jansenism, and the Morality of Enlightened Self-Interest"; Dickey, "Pride, Hypocrisy and Civility in Mandeville's Social and Historical Theory"; and Force, "Self-Love, Identification, and the Origin of Political Economy."

82. Smith, *Wealth of Nations*, I.xi.c.7; see also Smith, *Theory of Moral Sentiments*, IV.i.10 (the "invisible hand" passage).

83. See the discussion of seventeenth- and eighteenth-century dictionary definitions of "society" in Baker, "Enlightenment and the Institution of Society." A clear example can be found in Furetière (1694): "Assembly of many men in one place to come to one another's aide [*s'entrecourir*] in their needs" (cited on p. 99); the *Encyclopédie* describes the members of "civil or political society" as "tied together by their mutual needs and by the relations they have with one another" (cited on p. 101).

84. Smith, *Wealth of Nations*, Introduction and Plan, 4–6.

85. Ibid., I.ii.1–2.

86. Hont, "The Language of Sociability and Commerce," p. 264; Smith, *Theory of Moral Sentiments*, II.ii.3.2. On the definition of commercial society, see also *Wealth of Nations*, I.iv.1; and Hont, "Commercial Society and Political Theory in the Eighteenth Century," pp. 60–72. The primary source in Pufendorf for the issues discussed here is *De officio hominis et civilis juxta legem naturalem libri duo* (1673), I.2, edited by Gerald Hartung, in *Gesammelte Werke*, 2:18–21; *On the Duty of Man and Citizen*, pp. 27–32. A passage from Barbeyrac's influential translation of Pufendorf, *Droit de la nature et des gens* (1712), 2.3.18, seems to me particularly telling on this point: "Car la Nature en nous ordonnant d'être sociables, ne prétend pas que nous nous oubliions nous-mêmes. Le but de la Sociabilité est, au contraire, que par un commerce de secours et de services, chacun puisse mieux pourvoir à ses propres intérêts" (cited in Derathé, *Rousseau et la science politique de son temps*, p. 143; for the original, see *De jure naturae et gentium* [1672], edited by Frank Böhling, in *Gesammelte Werke*, 4[1]:152).

87. Smith, *Lectures on Jurisprudence*, LJ(A) iv.7; the argument is repeated in LJ(A) iv.21–22; in both cases the context is the origin of government at this stage as a defense of private property.

88. Smith, *Wealth of Nations*, I.ii.3.

89. See most importantly Hume, "Of the First Principles of Government," "Of the Origin of Government" (both 1742), and "Of the Original Contract" (1752), *Political Essays*, pp. 16–19, 20–23, 186–201.

90. Smith, *Lectures on Jurisprudence*, LJ(A) iv.21–23.

91. Ibid., LJ(A) iv.15.

92. Enlightening comparisons of the relevant passages (Smith, *The Theory of Moral Sentiments*, IV.i.10; *Wealth of Nations*, IV.ii.10; and "History of Astronomy" (1795), III.2, in *Essays on Philosophical Subjects*) have been made by Taieb, "Tours de mains"; and Macfie, "The Invisible Hand of Jupiter." Let us recall here, in addition to the mythological context of the "Astronomy," the explicitly providentialist turn of the passage in the *Theory of Moral Sentiments*: "The rich . . . are led by an invisible hand to make nearly the same distribution of the necessaries of life, which would have been made, had the earth been divided into equal portions among all its inhabitants, and thus without intending it, without knowing it, advance the multiplication of the species. When Providence divided the earth among a few lordly masters, it neither forgot nor abandoned those who seemed to have been left out in the partition."

93. See the important passage from Ferguson, *An Essay on the History of Civil Society*, p. 120, cited and discussed in Chapter 4.

94. Smith, *Wealth of Nations*, I.ii.1. The process by which this occurs is made even clearer by Ferguson, even though the concept does not occupy the systematic place in his thought that it does in Smith's. See *An Essay on the History of Civil Society*, p. 174: "But the establishments of men, like those of every animal, are suggested by nature, and are the result of instinct, directed by the variety of situations in which mankind are placed. Those establishments arose from successive improvements that were made, without any sense of their general effect. . . . Who could anticipate, or even enumerate, the separate occupations and professions by which the members of any commercial state are distinguished; the variety of devices which are practiced in separate cells, and which the artist, attentive to his own affair, has invented, to abridge or facilitate his separate task? . . . Human ingenuity, whatever heights it may have gained in a succession of ages, continues to move with an equal pace, and to creep in making the last as well as the first step of commercial or civil improvement."

95. See Smith, *Wealth of Nations*, I.i.5–8.

96. Ibid., III.i.1.

97. Binoche, *Les Trois sources des philosophies de l'histoire*, pp. 54–60.

98. Diderot, "Avertissement des éditeurs (Vol. VIII)," *Encyclopédie* (1986), 1:223–24. See also d'Alembert, "Discours préliminaire," ibid., 1:176; and Diderot, "Encyclopédie" (1755), ibid., 2:49–51.

99. The theme of barbarism in the Revolution began its career in the reactionary camp (Burke, Mallet du Pan) before moving into the republican one. See Baczko, *Ending the Terror*, pp. 192–202.

100. Smith, *Wealth of Nations*, III.i.2.

101. See ibid., III.i.3, 7: "Upon equal, or nearly equal profits, most men will choose to employ their capitals rather in the improvement and cultivation of land, than either in manufactures or in foreign trade. The man who employs his capital in land, has it more under his view and command, and his fortune is much less liable to accidents than that of the trader. . . . In seeking for employment to a capital, manufactures are, upon equal or nearly equal profits, naturally preferred to foreign commerce, for the same reason that agriculture is naturally preferred to manufactures." See the argument that these passages demonstrate Smith's "agrarian bias" in McNally, *Political Economy and the Rise of Capitalism*, esp. 234–50; and Dickey's comments in the appendices to his abridged edition of Smith, *Wealth of Nations*, pp. 221–23, 239–41.

102. Smith, *Wealth of Nations*, III.i.9.

103. See Robertson, *The Progress of Society in Europe*; and Hume, "Of Commerce," in *Political Essays*, pp. 93–104. Smith himself calls Hume "the only writer" to have noticed the connection between commerce and civil liberty, which has given rise to much speculation on Smith's feelings that he had been plagiarized; see the editor's note to *Wealth of Nations*, III.iv.4. For an account of accusations specifically directed against Robertson, see Scott, *Adam Smith as Student and Professor*, pp. 55–56, 118–20.

104. See Smith, *Wealth of Nations*, III.iv.5–6, 10–15; *Lectures on Jurisprudence*, LJ(A) i.116–121, iv.9, 157; LJ(B) 21, 51. The analysis is repeated with respect to ecclesiastical domains in *Wealth of Nations*, V.i.g.25.

105. Condorcet, Peysonnel, and Le Chapelier, *Bibliothèque de l'homme public*, 3:206–7. The abridgment of book III is, to my sense, remarkably complete: most of the omitted sections are excursions in the history of positive jurisprudence, whereas almost all the key economic aspects of the historical argument seem to be included. The exception to this appears to me to be the question of the extent of the market in III.i.1 and 4; in both cases the beginning but not the end of the paragraph is included. Diatkine ("A French Reading of the *Wealth of Nations* in 1790"), from whom I have taken the attribution to Condorcet, sees this as a general conceptual weakness of the abridged text.

106. This can be seen clearly in comparison with Hume in "Of Commerce," who sees agriculture as having a natural priority ("As soon as men quit their savage

state, where they live chiefly by hunting and fishing, they must fall into these two classes [husbandmen and manufacturers]; though the arts of agriculture employ *at first* the most numerous part of the society" [*Political Essays*, p. 95]). But he sees commerce as having a universal-historical priority with respect to manufacturing ("If we consult history, we shall find, that, in most nations, foreign trade has preceded any refinement in home manufacturers, and given birth to domestic luxury" [p. 101]).

107. Smith, *Wealth of Nations*, IV.ix.48–51. See also Stewart's citation of a no longer extant manuscript dated 1755, in *Account of the Life and Writings of Adam Smith*, pp. 321–22.

108. Hont, "The Political Economy of the 'Unnatural and Retrograde' Order," p. 138. My thanks to John Robertson for directing my attention to this essay.

109. Cf. Hont and Ignatieff, "Needs and Justice in the *Wealth of Nations*," pp. 21–22: "The adequate subsistence of the poor, like everything else in the Smithian system, depended on growth led by increasing productivity in manufacturing. The only way agricultural surplus could be induced was if the manufacturing sectors of the town produced goods which would serve as an incentive for the production of food for sale. . . . The Smithian solution to agricultural productivity, therefore, was profoundly counterintuitive—to expand the manufacturing sector and to induce the agricultural sector to produce surpluses in exchange for finished goods."

110. We might note that the Crusades, in both Smith's and Robertson's accounts of the transition from feudalism to commercial society, play a role not unlike that of fortuitous, external causes in Rousseau, in that the key element is the exposure to an already civilized society.

111. Hirschman, *The Passions and the Interests*, p. 61. The most canonical statement of this thesis can be found in Montesquieu, *De l'esprit des lois*, p. 585: "Commerce cures destructive prejudices; and it is a more or less general rule, that wherever there are gentle manners [*mœurs douces*], there is commerce; and wherever there is commerce, there are gentle manners."

112. Robertson, *The Progress of Society in Europe*, pp. 63, 67. See also pp. 26–32.

113. Gordon, *Citizens without Sovereignty*, pp. 155, 159.

114. Gordon cites Pancoucke, the publishing magnate and director of the *Encyclopédie méthodique*, on the crucial place Peuchet's "Discours" held in the project: "In the 'Prospectus' to the entire encyclopedia, the editor Pancoucke declared that Peuchet would 'bring together all the sciences, general and particular, philosophical, historical and practical' so as to reveal what was most important 'for the happiness of society and public prosperity'" ("Philosophy, Sociology, and Gender," pp. 893–94). No substantial information on Peuchet is to be found in the available studies of the *Encyclopédie méthodique*. Braunrot and Doig, "The

Encyclopédie méthodique," state merely that he was "a lawyer who had long worked as one of Pancoucke's hack journalists, . . . was a moderate in the Revolution and filled a post in the city administration for several years" (p. 93). Likewise, Darnton refers to Peuchet as a "garret type" (*The Business of Enlightenment,* p. 433), which may simply mean that Darnton doesn't know anything more about him, although the sort of compilation by which this text is constructed would lend support to this description. But he would seem to have been a particularly accomplished compiler. Perrot (*Une Histoire intellectuelle de l'économie politique,* pp. 74, 124) describes him as having been Morellet's secretary during his youth and the inheritor of his archives, which he used in the publication of a number of later-Revolutionary or Napoleonic-era books on economics and statistics: *Dictionnaire universel de la géographie commerçante* (Year VII–VIII), 5 vols.; *Vocabulaire des termes de commerce, banque, manufactures, navigation marchande, finance mercantile et statistique* (Year IX); *Essai d'une statistique générale de la France* (Year IX); *Statistique élémentaire de la France* (1805).

115. Peuchet, "Discours préliminaire," p. ciii. Compare Smith, *Wealth of Nations,* III.iv.17: "To gratify the most childish vanity was the sole motive of the great proprietors. The merchants and artificers, much less ridiculous, acted merely from a view to their own interest, and in pursuit of their own pedlar principle of turning a penny wherever a penny was to be got. Neither of them had either knowledge or foresight of that great revolution which the folly of the one, and the industry of the other, was gradually bringing about." My thanks to Keith Baker for introducing me to this text.

116. Peuchet, "Discours préliminaire," p. xliii, drawn from Robertson, *The Progress of Society in Europe,* pp. 60–61: "Among nations, as well as individuals, the powers of imagination attain some degree of vigor before the intellectual faculties are much exercised in speculative or abstract disquisition. Men are poets before they are philosophers. They feel with sensibility, and describe with force, when they have made but little progress in investigation or reasoning. . . . But, unhappily for our literature, our ancestors deviating from this course which nature points out, plunged at once into the depths of abstruse and metaphysical inquiry."

117. Peuchet, "Discours préliminaire," p. lxxxiv.

118. Ibid., p. cxv. For a similar perspective on the urban origins of civilization, see Volney, *Tableau du climat et du sol des États-unis,* pp. 359–60: "If, in order to define *civilization,* [Rousseau] had sought the meaning of the thing in that of the root word itself (*civitas*), he would have shown that by *civilization* should be understood the union of these very men in a city, that is, an enclosure of dwellings provided with a common defense against external pillaging and internal disorder." In the *Lectures on Jurisprudence,* Smith also introduced "regular government" with the foundation of the Greek city.

119. Peuchet, "Discours préliminaire," p. x. Peuchet thus conceives of precommercial society as frozen, fixed in its customs, unable to reform itself. The equilibrium between ideas and government is perfect, indeed too perfect. In a sense, this means that precommercial societies have no history.

120. Ibid., p. ix.

121. On Constant's education in Edinburgh and his possible personal relations with various figures of the Scottish Enlightenment, see Wood, *Benjamin Constant*, pp. 43–62; and Courtney, "An Eighteenth-Century Education." Constant's father originally "left him under the protection of the historian William Robertson, Principal of the University, who seems to have taken a personal interest in Benjamin's progress" (Wood, *Benjamin Constant*, p. 45). He studied in particular with Andrew Dalzel (Greek) and Alexander Tytler Fraser (history), and participated actively in the debates of the Speculative Society. His later introduction to Paris society was arranged through Suard, the translator of Richardson. Some indications on Constant's intellectual relations to Scottish thought can be found in Fontana, "The Shaping of Modern Liberty."

122. Constant, "De la liberté des anciens comparée à celle des modernes" (1819), in *De la liberté chez les modernes*, p. 501.

123. Constant, *De l'esprit de conquête et de l'usurpation dans leurs rapports avec la civilisation européenne* (1814), in *De la liberté chez les modernes*, p. 118.

124. Ibid., p. 177.

125. On the development of the concept of public opinion, in addition to sources cited in the previous chapter, see Staël, *Des circonstances actuelles qui peuvent terminer la Révolution*, particularly pp. 22, 42, 106–7. Constant attempted to help Staël edit this text for publication.

126. Constant, *Des réactions politiques*, p. 95.

127. Ibid., p. 96.

128. Constant, *De l'esprit de conquête*, in *De la liberté chez les modernes*, p. 246.

129. See esp. Rousseau's note IV to the *Discours sur l'inégalité* (p. 198), where he argues, on the authority of Buffon, that forestation contributes to the fertility of the soil and that forests provide the greatest quantity of subsistence, whereas the deforestation necessary for either concentrated human populations or for agriculture leads to an impoverishment of the soil. It should be noted, however, that in other texts Rousseau implies that agricultural labor is capable of reinvesting the fertility of the soil, so that the returns of farming are always in direct proportion to the labor invested in the land. Wolmar, for example, "claims that the earth produces in proportion to the number of hands that cultivate it: Better cultivated, it gives greater returns; this overabundance of production makes it possible to cultivate it better yet. The more men and beasts are set to working it, the more of a surplus it supplies for their subsistence. No one knows just how far this

continual and reciprocal augmentation of product and cultivator can go" (*Julie*, p. 442). In both cases, however, the key to maintaining or reestablishing natural fertility is the even dispersal of the human population. See the texts by Rousseau, as well as other writers, in particular Mirabeau *père*, cited by Rétat, "L'Économie rustique de Clarens." See also notes V and VIII to the second *Discours* on the fundamental vegetarianism of natural man. Gathering the fruits and nuts of the forest, unlike hunting, is best done alone. Moreover, carnivorous animals have frequent conflicts but frugivorous animals live in peace with one another.

130. Montesquieu, *De l'esprit des lois*, p. 232. Rousseau refers to "the expression of the general relations established by nature among all animate beings for their common conservation" (*Discours sur l'inégalité*, p. 124).

131. See, on England and France respectively, Crane, "Suggestions Towards a Genealogy of the 'Man of Feeling'"; and Baasner, "The Changing Meaning of 'Sensibilité.'"

132. In both cases the influence of Lockian psychology and new developments in the physiology of the nervous system (from Willis to Haller, Whytt and Bordeu) is particularly important. On the physiological side, see, among many other studies, Carlson and Simpson, "Models of the Nervous System"; Figlio, "Theories of Perception and the Physiology of Mind"; Rousseau, "Nerves, Spirits, and Fibres"; and Lawrence, "The Nervous System and Society in the Scottish Enlightenment." For literary and social developments in Britain see Todd, *Sensibility*; Van Sant, *Eighteenth-Century Sensibility and the Novel*; and Barker-Benfield, *The Culture of Sensibility*. A synthesis of the physiological and literary aspects of the question in France has just been presented by Vila, *Enlightenment and Pathology*; see also Trahard's classic *Les Maîtres de la sensibilité française au dix-huitième siècle*; and Denby, *Sentimental Narrative and the Social Order in France*.

133. In theological terms, here as elsewhere in the literature of sensibility, the crucial step is the abandonment of the idea of human nature as essentially corrupted by original sin. It should be noted that Rousseau is pointedly unwilling to extend this analysis to the question of sexual morality.

134. The relation between Rousseau's doctrine of pity in the second *Discours*, the *Essai sur l'origine des langues*, and the *Émile* has been the object of a particularly important (and much contested) commentary by Derrida, *Of Grammatology*, pp. 171–92.

135. For a clear example of this sort of argument, see the discussion of why pity for criminals is misdirected in Helvétius, *De l'esprit*, p. 23.

136. An extremely compressed version of the same reversal can even be seen in the *Contrat social* itself, the first chapter of which begins: "Man is born free, and everywhere he is in chains. Such a man believes himself to be the master of the others, who does not cease to be any less a slave than they are. How did this

change come about? I do not know. What can make it legitimate? I believe that I can resolve this question" (p. 351).

137. Cf. Derathé, *Rousseau et la science politique de son temps*, p. 174: "The political problem thus in reality is composed of both a question of fact and a question of right, or, if one prefers, a psychological problem, that of the origin of societies, and a juridical problem, that of the foundation of authority."

138. Cf., for example, *Discours sur l'inégalité*, p. 135, where Rousseau sets aside one sort of tool in order to describe the use of another: "If he had a slingshot, would he throw a rock by hand so straight?"

139. Rousseau's theory of the origin of languages has been a particularly vital topic since the publication of Derrida's *Of Grammatology*. See esp. de Man, *Allegories of Reading*, pp. 135–59.

140. Rousseau, *Discours sur l'inégalité*, p. 171; translation taken from Smith, "Letter to the Editors of the *Edinburgh Review*" (1756), §13, in *Essays on Philosophical Subjects*.

141. When Rousseau speaks of the *douceurs d'un commerce indépendant* this is both a direct reference to and an overturning of the *doux commerce* thesis, which emphasizes precisely the role of interdependence in the civilizing process. See Rosenblatt, *Rousseau and Geneva*, pp. 76–87.

142. See the related criticisms of mineralogy in the *Rêveries du promeneur solitaire*, pp. 1066–67.

Chapter 3

1. Staël, *Lettres sur les ouvrages et le caractère de J. J. Rousseau*, p. 107.

2. Foucault, "What Is an Author?" in *Aesthetics, Method, and Epistemology*, p. 205 (translation modified). For Foucault's discussion of the particular status of the authorial name, see pp. 209–11, and on procedures of unification, pp. 214–15.

3. Traditionally, the question of the unity of Rousseau's *œuvre* has concentrated on the conceptual compatibility or coherence of the political texts. In particular, the question to be resolved has been whether *Du contrat social* finds its place within the system established by the two *Discours* and the *Émile*, centered around the complementary concepts of the state of nature and of natural man, or whether it is, on the contrary, radically opposed to that system. In his classic essay on "L'Unité de la pensée de Jean-Jacques Rousseau," Lanson describes this objection as "the general incompatibility established between the authoritarian socialism of the *Contrat* and the anarchic individualism of the other works," or more generally as "the antinomy of freedom and equality" (p. 25). In a fashion that has since become classic, Lanson accounts for this apparent incompatibility by the different problems posed by each work. Thus, whereas *Émile* and *La Nouvelle Héloïse* "concern the private man in his conscience and his domestic relationships," *Du*

contrat social "concerns the citizen and the relations established between the members of the same state" (p. 20).

4. Citton, "Fabrique de l'opinion et folie de la dissidence dans le complot selon Rousseau."

5. Ovid, *Tristia* 5.10.37. See note 1 to Chapter 2.

6. This tripartite classification was first established by Montesquieu in *De l'esprit des lois*, pp. 536–40. The clearest example in Rousseau's work is to be found in the *Essai sur l'origine des langues*, p. 385. This point was suggested to me by Alain Grosrichard in discussion following my presentation of a portion of this chapter at the Rousseau Association colloquium on the *Dialogues*, Université Laval, Québec, May–June 1997.

7. See Chapter 2 for discussions of the relevant passages from Rousseau's two *Discours*. The passage on the inhabitants of the ideal world is the first of a series of hypothetical descriptions allowing one to understand the principles of "J. J."'s character.

8. See Rousseau, *Correspondance complète*, vols. 37, 38, particularly Leigh's note (a) to letter 6653 (Rousseau to Julie-Anne-Marie Boy de La Tour, née Roguin, January 22, 1770), 37:210–11.

9. François-Marie Arouet de Voltaire to Rousseau, August 30, 1755, ibid., Letter 317, 3:156–57. See also Palissot, *Les Philosophes*.

10. For a similar interpretation of the conspiracy, see the Introduction by Masters and Kelly to their recent edition of the *Dialogues* in *The Collected Writings of Rousseau*, 1:xiii–xxvii; and Kelly, *Rousseau's Exemplary Life*, pp. 210–18. See also de Man's comment in "The Rhetoric of Blindness," in *Blindness and Insight*, p. 112: "It is as if the conspiracy that Rousseau's paranoia imagined during his lifetime came into being after his death, uniting friend and foe alike in a concerted effort to misrepresent his thoughts."

11. Starobinski, *Transparency and Obstruction*, p. 382n20 (translation modified).

12. The most important of the appeals to judicial canons of proof in this respect is "Rousseau"'s determination "to reject in this affair all human authority, all proof that depends on the testimony of others, and to make up my mind solely on the basis of what I can see with my own eyes and know on my own account" (*Dialogues*, p. 769).

13. Cf. *Discours sur l'inégalité*, p. 132: "Let us thus begin by setting aside all the facts, as they do not affect the question [*Commençons donc par écarter tous les faits, car ils ne touchent point à la question*]." On the role of hypothesis in the *Dialogues*, see McDonald, *The Dialogue of Writing*, pp. 33–46.

14. Cf. de Man, "Autobiography as De-Facement," in *The Rhetoric of Romanticism*, p. 70: "Autobiography, then, is not a genre or a mode, but a figure of reading or of understanding that occurs, to some degree, in all texts. The autobiographical

moment happens as an alignment between the two subjects involved in the process of reading in which they determine each other by mutual reflexive substitution. . . . This specular structure is interiorized in a text in which the author declares himself the subject of his own understanding, but this merely makes explicit the wider claim to authorship that takes place whenever a text is stated to be *by* someone and assumed to be understandable to the extent that this is the case." In *Allegories of Reading*, p. 202, de Man applies this interpretation of the author as a "metaphor for readability in general" to the "Préface dialoguée" to *La Nouvelle Héloïse*, where the terms deployed are strikingly similar to those in the passage under consideration here.

15. On the problem of the two sides of Rousseau, see Raymond, "Aspects de la vie intérieure," in *Jean-Jacques Rousseau: La Quête de soi et la rêverie*, pp. 13–87; and Starobinski, *Transparency and Obstruction*, pp. 47–58.

16. Starobinski, *Transparency and Obstruction*, pp. 253–54 (translation modified).

17. See the extended discussion of different forms of sensibility and their relations to *amour-propre* and *amour de soi, Dialogues*, pp. 804–11.

18. Rousseau to Dom Léger-Marie Deschamps, September 12, 1761, *Correspondance complète*, Letter 1490, 9:120–21.

19. Ginguené, *Lettres sur les Confessions de J. J. Rousseau*, pp. 21–26; Mercier, *De J. J. Rousseau*, 2:258–69. On the problems caused by the necessity of reconciling Rousseau's reputation as an apostle of virtue with the scandalous character of some of the revelations of the *Confessions*, see Gagnebin, "L'Étrange accueil fait aux *Confessions* de Rousseau"; and Barny, *Rousseau dans la Révolution: Le Personnage de Jean-Jacques*, pp. 9–78. A thoroughly allegorical reading of the *Confessions* has been presented by Kelly in *Rousseau's Exemplary Life*.

20. Ginguené, *Lettres sur les Confessions de J. J. Rousseau*, p. 29.

21. Diane-Marie-Zéphyrine-Adelaïde Mazarini-Mancini, marquise de Polignac, to Marie-Madeleine de Brémond d'Ars, marquise de Verdelin, February 3, 1761, *Correspondance complète*, Letter 1258, 8:56. Cf. *Confessions*, pp. 547–48. I will discuss other aspects of the reception of *Julie* in part 2 of this chapter. For an overview, see Attridge, "The Reception of *La Nouvelle Héloïse*." An extensive reading of the correspondence received by Rousseau can be found in Labrousse, *Lire au XVIIIe siècle*.

22. Brissot, *Journal du Licée de Londres* (1784), cited and translated by Darnton, *The Literary Underground of the Old Regime*, p. 68.

23. Charles-Joseph Pancoucke to Rousseau, [about February 10, 1761], *Correspondance complète*, Letter 1278, 8:77–78.

24. For the theoretical background for the allegorical transmission of classical mythology, see, among a number of other possibilities, Seznec, *The Survival of the*

Pagan Gods; and Curtius, *European Literature and the Latin Middle Ages.* On the figure of Hercules, see Trousson, "Ronsard et la légende d'Hercule"; and, more generally, Jung, *Hercule dans la littérature française du 16ᵉ siècle.* Ronsard often compares Henri II with Hercules, but he was more commonly associated with François Iᵉʳ, the "Hercule françois." On the continued use of Hercules during the Revolution, see Hunt, *Politics, Culture, and Class in the French Revolution,* pp. 87–119.

25. Ovid, in the *Metamorphoses* (iv.621–62), gives an account starring Perseus, but focusing on the transformation of the giant Atlas into Mount Atlas. He also makes an extremely brief reference to the episode during his account of Hercules' death: "Are these the hands . . . thanks to whose strength I brought home . . . the apples that the unsleeping dragon guarded closely [*pomaque ab insomni concus-todita dracone*]" (ix.186–91).

26. Ronsard, "La Charité," vv. 169–72, *Œuvres complètes,* 1:580.

27. Ronsard, *Sonnets pour Hélène,* I, xlvi, ibid., 1:366. See also I, lxi, 1:373, where the golden apples are compared to the beloved's breasts, to the disadvantage of the former, and *Odes,* III, 5, "A Monseigneur le duc d'Alençon," vv. 153–54, where the allegorical figure of Africa predicts the slaughter of all her inhabitants by the new-born prince, including *ceux qui gardent le verger / Des Hespérides dépouillés* (1:749).

28. Ronsard, *Les Amours,* I, cxlv, ibid., 1:98–99. Text of 1584 edition of *Œuvres;* earlier editions of *Les Amours* read *la pomme d'or* rather than *l'orange d'or* in v. 3. See also the commentary by Rémi Belleau, first published in the 1571 edition: "The golden fruit [*pomme*], the orange, all sorts of fruits [*pommes*], and particu-larly oranges, are dedicated to Voluptuousness, to the Graces and to Love. See Philostrates, *de Imaginibus,* and Pierius' Hieroglyphics: and the true sign and symbol of Venus and Cupid [*Amour*] is the *pomme,* which signifies voluptuous-ness." The apple is the symbol of love because "all that is most delicate and precious in love draws on the round form" (commentary cited from text of 1578 edition, in Ronsard, *Les Amours,* p. 240).

29. See Augustine, *Confessiones,* p. 30; *Confessions,* p. 47: "There was a pear tree near our vineyard, loaded with fruit [*pomis*] that was attractive neither to look at nor to taste. Late one night a band of ruffians, myself included, went off to shake down the fruit and carry it away, for we had continued our games out of doors until well after dark, as was our pernicious habit. We took an enormous quantity of pears, not to eat them ourselves, but simply to throw them to the pigs [*sed vel proicienda porcis*]. Perhaps we ate some of them, but our real pleasure consisted in doing something that was forbidden. . . . I loved my own perdition and my own faults, not the things for which I committed wrong, but the wrong itself." On Rousseau's relation to Augustine, see Hartle, *The Modern Self in Rousseau's Confessions.*

30. *Pomum,* the generic term in Latin for fruit that grows on trees, is also the term used to describe the Hesperidean apples.

31. Thomas Gray to Pastor William Mason, January 22, 1761, *Correspondance complète,* Letter 1229, 8:20. Gray continues, commenting on the passage just cited, "The *dramatis personae* (as the author says) are all of them good people; I am sorry to hear it, for had they all been hanged at the end of the third volume nobody (I believe) would have cared."

32. Adrien Cuyret, seigneur de Margency, to Rousseau, February 23, 1761, ibid., Letter 1317, 8:159; a reader of *La Nouvelle Héloïse* to Rousseau, [March 1761], ibid., Letter 1364, 8:257; William Warburton to Richard Hurd, March 24, 1761, ibid., Appendix A239b, 8:355; Marie-Madeleine Bernardoni, née Bernard, to Rousseau, September 28, 1761, ibid., Letter 1496, 9:133.

33. Diderot's "Éloge de Richardson" (*Œuvres complètes,* 13:181–208) was first published in January 1762, about a year after the appearance of *La Nouvelle Héloïse* on the French market. See also Suard, "Parallèle entre la Clarice de Richardson et la nouvelle Eloïse de M. Rousseau."

34. Staël, *Lettres sur les ouvrages et le caractère de J. J. Rousseau,* p. 19.

35. Fréron, *Année littéraire,* April 5, 1761, 2:314. See Mornet, *Le Sentiment de la nature,* pp. 199–201.

36. Bernardin de Saint-Pierre, *La Vie et les ouvrages de Jean-Jacques Rousseau,* p. 140. My translation here is somewhat loose, given the highly elliptical structure of Bernardin's sentence: "*Mais en quoi il l'emporte, c'est qu'il n'y a point de sites divers ni de fonds naturels à ses tableaux qui font un si grand effet dans l'Héloïse, et partout.*"

37. Staël, *Lettres sur les ouvrages et le caractère de J. J. Rousseau,* p. 44.

38. Mercier, editorial note to *La Nouvelle Héloïse* in Rousseau, *Œuvres complètes* (Paris: Poinçot, 1788–93), 4:457.

39. See Ridehalgh, "Preromantic Attitudes and the Birth of a Legend." Ridehalgh summarizes her study of the discourse about Ermenonville as follows: "The main interest of this literature is that it offers a glimpse of the relationship between Rousseau and a certain group of his readers: a restricted group, of relatively easy means and some progressive literary influence. As a generalization, it can be said that in their eyes, Rousseau's most important works were *La Nouvelle Héloïse* and *Émile*; that Ermenonville was important to them because it seemed to embody the combination of intellect and emotion which Rousseau had proposed to them in these works; that for them, Rousseau the individual was hardly distinguishable from the ideas propounded in his works, and that out of the fusion of the individual, the works and the physical surroundings, there grew an Ermenonville legend which illustrates as much the dreams and aspirations of the visitors as any reality connected with Rousseau" (p. 231).

40. Cited in ibid., p. 234.

41. *Lettre sur la mort de J. J. Rousseau écrite par un de ses amis, aux auteurs du J.ᵃˡ de Paris,* in *Correspondance complète,* Appendix 682, 40:359–62.

42. Pierre Le Tourneur, "Voyage à Ermenonville," in Rousseau, *Œuvres complètes* (Paris: Poinçot, 1788–93), 1:166.

43. Delacroix, *Éloge de Jean-Jacques Rousseau,* p. 42.

44. Mornet, *Le Sentiment de la nature,* p. 324.

45. The existing literature on the use of landscapes in *La Nouvelle Héloïse* is generally disappointing in this respect. Most treatments of the subject are concerned either with the relation between Rousseau's landscapes and the real ones he is presumably describing, or else tend toward the construction of pseudo-Jungian archetypes. See Behbahani, *Paysage rêvés*; Kusch, "Landscape and Literary Form"; Kusch, "The Garden, the City, and Language"; Lecercle, *Rousseau et l'art du roman,* pp. 215–24; and Marin, "L'Effet Sharawadgi ou le jardin de Julie."

46. Lanson, "L'Unité de la pensée de Jean-Jacques Rousseau," p. 17.

47. I have taken the formulation *le roman du bonheur* from Bernard Guyon's introduction to the Pléiade edition (2:xli), but the idea appears in almost all Rousseau criticism.

48. Bellenot, "Les Formes de l'amour dans la *Nouvelle Héloïse*," p. 190. See also Osmont, "Remarques sur la genèse et la composition de la *Nouvelle Héloïse*," p. 100: "To give in to the vertigo of passing time, to give in to desire, to give in to despair, in a word, to believe that life should take on its entire meaning in the instant, such is the temptation for souls in this first part of the *Héloïse*."

49. Alexandre Deleyre to Rousseau, November 23, 1756, *Correspondance complète,* Letter 449, 4:123.

50. This would seem to have been Rousseau's personal opinion as well. A letter to Deleyre counsels him against marrying his mistress for reasons parallel to those put forward by Julie here, concluding, "*Songez que l'amour n'est qu'illusion*" (Rousseau to Alexandre Deleyre, November 10, 1759, ibid., Letter 884, 6:192).

51. See the analysis of Clarens as a political ideal in Shklar, *Men and Citizens,* pp. 150–54. On Rousseau's treatment of economics in *La Nouvelle Héloïse,* see Rétat, "L'Économie rustique de Clarens"; and Starobinski, *Transparency and Obstruction,* pp. 104–13.

52. See Gilson, "La Méthode de M. de Wolmar," in *Les Idées et les lettres,* pp. 275–98.

53. See *Julie,* pp. 413–14, for the voyage around the world: "I stayed three months in a delicious and deserted island, a sweet and touching image of the ancient beauty of nature, and which seems to have been confined at the end of the world to serve as an asylum for innocent and persecuted love. . . . I came upon a second desert island, even more unknown and more charming than the

first, and where the cruelest accident almost confined us forever. I was perhaps the only one who was not terrified by so sweet an exile." Rousseau's descriptions of Tinian and Juan Fernandez are based on Walter's *A Voyage Round the World in the Years 1740–1744.* As Mornet pointed out in the notes to his edition of *La Nouvelle Héloïse,* Rousseau's descriptions are by no means embellishments of Walter's, who is significantly more "romantic" than Rousseau. See, for example, his description of Juan Fernandez: "The irregularities of the hills and precipices, in the northern part of the island, necessarily traced out by their various combinations a great number of romantic valleys, most of which had a stream of the clearest water running through them, that tumbled in cascades from rock to rock, as the bottom of the valley, by the course of the neighboring hills, was at any time broken into a sudden sharp descent. Some particular spots occurred in these valleys where the shade and fragrance of the contiguous woods, the loftiness of the overhanging rocks, and the transparency and frequent falls of the neighboring streams, presented scenes of such elegance and dignity as would with difficulty be rivaled in any other part of the globe" (p. 115).

54. Mornet, *Le Sentiment de la nature,* p. 260.

55. Cf. *Julie,* p. 243, where Saint-Preux responds to the critique of his first letter from Paris by Julie (or Claire), once again on the subject of the abuse of rhetoric: "You were not displeased by [the letters] that I wrote you from Meillerie and the Valais." On the discussion of rhetoric in the letters from Paris, see McDonald Vance, *The Extravagant Shepherd,* pp. 95–120.

56. My use of this passage is indebted to Burt, "Mapping City Walks." Burt emphasizes the overlay of the Swiss landscape with Parisian topography in connection with other of the *Les Rêveries du promeneur solitaire,* particularly the second and fifth, but does not mention *La Nouvelle Héloïse.* A closely related passage can be found in a letter to the maréchal de Luxembourg: "All of Switzerland is like a great city divided into thirteen quarters, some of which are in valleys, some on hillsides, and some on mountains. Geneva, Saint-Gal and Neuchatel are the *faubourgs*: Some quarters are more or less populated, but all of them are sufficiently so to mark that one is still in the city: Only the houses, instead of being lined up, are dispersed without symmetry and without order as those of ancient Rome are said to have been. One no longer believes oneself to be traversing deserted spots [*parcourir des déserts*] when one finds steeples among the firs, flocks on the rocks, factories in precipices, and workshops in torrents. This bizarre mixture has an undefinable quality of animation, of life that breathes freedom and well-being" (Rousseau to Charles-François-Frédéric de Montmorency-Luxembourg, maréchal-duc de Luxembourg, January 20, 1763, *Correspondance complète,* Letter 2440, 15:49).

57. De Man, "The Rhetoric of Temporality," in *Blindness and Insight,* pp. 202–3.

De Man cites the following details shared by the two texts: "the self-enclosed, isolated space of the '*asile*'; the privilege reserved to the happy few who possess a key that unlocks the gate; the traditional enumeration of natural attributes—a catalogue of the various flowers, trees, fruits, perfumes, and, above all, of the birds, culminating in the description of their song. Most revealing of all is the emphasis on water, on fountains and pools that, in *Julie* as in the *Roman de la Rose*, are controlled not by nature but by the ingenuity of the inhabitants."

58. Ibid., pp. 203–4.

59. Two elements in particular mark this similarity: the emphasis on the suddenness of the conversion, and the repetition of the formula *je crus* (or *j'ai cru*) *voir* to mark the unreal aspects of the visions. Compare the citations given here with *Julie*, pp. 353–54.

60. Cf. Augustine, *Confessiones*, p. 176; *Confessions*, p. 176: "While I stood trembling on the barrier, on the other side I could see the chaste beauty of Continence in all her serene, unsullied joy, as she modestly beckoned me to cross over and to hesitate no more. She stretched out loving hands to welcome and embrace me, holding up a host of good examples to my sight. With her were countless boys and girls, great numbers of the young and people of all ages, staid widows and women still virgins in old age. And in their midst was Continence herself, not barren but a fruitful mother of children, of joys born of you, O Lord, her Spouse."

61. Italian cited as given by Rousseau, *Julie*, p. 79, citing verses 5, 6, 7 and 9; I have adapted Durling's translation (*Petrarch's Lyric Poems*, pp. 44–45) to fit around the line skipped by Rousseau.

62. Thus he portrays his old age and loss as "my laurels are faded, are oaks and elms [*spenti son I miei lauri, or querce et olmi*]" (*Rime* 363, *Petrarch's Lyric Poems*, pp. 572–73).

63. Petrarca, *Le Familiari*, 1:156–57, 160; *Rerum familiarium*, pp. 175–76, 179. For the reference to the Sermon on the Mount, see Matthew 7:14. Petrarch's brother Gherardo became a Carthusian monk in 1343; this fact, usually taken as the reference of his "direct path," is one of the primary reasons why scholars generally reject Petrarch's dating of his letter as having been written in 1336, and treated it as at least fictionalized, if not wholly invented.

64. Petrarch emphasizes the comparison, citing both the passage from Augustine's *Confessions* (book VIII, chapter 12) and the story from the life of Saint Anthony that had served as a model for Augustine himself. See Courcelle, *Les Confessions de saint Augustin dans la tradition littéraire*, pp. 329–51.

65. Durling, "The Ascent of Mount Ventoux and the Crisis of Allegory," p. 21. Durling suggests that this negative form of allegory be called irony: "If allegory joins two events in a proposition that seeks fulfillment, irony disjoins two events by denying or frustrating fulfillment."

66. Freccero, "The Fig Tree and the Laurel." For the signification of the fig tree, Freccero refers to Micah 4:4 and John 1:48–50.

67. Auerbach, "Figura," in *Scenes from the Drama of European Literature*, p. 53. Both Durling and Freccero are working with a concept of allegory based largely on Auerbach's "figura," designed primarily to deal with the use of allegorical typology in Dante. See also Freccero's essays in *Dante: The Poetics of Conversion*.

68. I have found Burgelin, *La Philosophie de l'existence de J.-J. Rousseau*, pp. 406–34, to be the most useful introduction to Rousseau's religious thought. The most extensive discussion is still Masson, *La Religion de J. J. Rousseau*; on *La Nouvelle Héloïse*, see esp. 2:65–80. See also Grimsley, *Rousseau and the Religious Quest*; and Derathé, *Le Rationalisme de Jean-Jacques Rousseau*.

69. On the Cartesian roots of the dualism that organizes Rousseau's argument here, see Gouhier, *Les Méditations métaphysiques de Jean-Jacques Rousseau*, p. 49–83.

70. God is referred to as an "author" five other times in the course of *La Nouvelle Héloïse*, in the expressions *l'auteur de mon être* (p. 332); *l'auteur de toute vérité* (p. 356); *l'auteur de tout bien* (p. 362); *la nature . . . son Auteur* (p. 482n); and *l'Auteur de son être* (p. 588). On a further occasion Milord Edouard tells Wolmar he needs to learn to read in the book of Nature (p. 655). The simple literary sense of *auteur* is used seven times, all in the course of the letters on Paris (pp. 235, 241, 252, 253, 254, 266, and 277), and Saint-Preux is referred to as an author of his letters (p. 305). On seven occasions Julie refers to her parents as the *auteurs de mes jours* (pp. 39, 72, 96, 202, 208, 319, 335). There are a number of other usages along these lines: Julie calls Saint-Preux *l'auteur de ma faute* (p. 139); Saint-Preux calls Julie's father *l'auteur de tous mes maux* (p. 326); finally, Saint-Preux describes Wolmar, in his unbelief, in relation to Julie, as *l'unique auteur de toute sa peine* (p. 588). For the ordering of these different senses of *auteur* by contemporary dictionaries, see Chapter 1.

71. Both letters (book I, letters 36 and 38) concerning the possibility of a sexual encounter in a chalet contain citations from Petrarch, and the repetition of the phrase *vaine image* here accentuates the connection with the rhetorical structure of the letter on the Valais. Mornet argued, with respect to Julie's citation in letter 36 from "Standomi un giorno solo a la fenestra" (*Rime* 323, *Petrarch's Lyric Poems*, pp. 502–4), that "between the allegories in which Petrarch sings the virtues of Laura and the landscape in which Julie dreams of finding Saint-Preux there is, in reality, no connection outside of these two verses" (*La Nouvelle Héloïse*, ed. Mornet, 2:132n3). Taking up the same argument with respect to Saint-Preux's citation in letter 38 from "A la dolce ombra de le belle frondi" (*Rime* 142, *Petrarch's Lyric Poems*, pp. 285–89), Mornet wrote, "There is no resemblance at all between the amorous impatience of Saint-Preux and the allegorical poem in which Petrarch seeks to raise himself from human to divine love. In any case in Petrarch the

268 Notes to Chapter 4

bushes and shrubs have a symbolic significance" (*La Nouvelle Héloïse*, ed. Mornet, 2:138n1). Mornet clearly saw what was at stake in Rousseau's use of Petrarch but was unable to accept it.

72. The vicar also describes his mode of reasoning as that of "contemplating God in his works and studying him in those of his attributes that it matters most to me to know [*qu'il m'importait de connaître*]" (*Émile*, p. 592).

73. This passage occurs in the Copie personnelle but was not retained in the final version of the text. The final version is toned down a bit but makes the same point: "I do not claim that this taste is wise, only that it is sweet [*doux*], that it supplements the sentiment of happiness that dries up. . . . Who is happier even in this world, the wise man with his reason or the *dévot* with his delirium?" (*Julie*, p. 695). This position is not fundamentally different from what she had much earlier said of earthly love: "How lovable are love's illusions!" (p. 129). A similar emphasis on the *douceur* of natural religion being what makes it the correct choice in a situation where reason cannot adjudicate is developed in the third Promenade (*Rêveries*, pp. 1011–23).

74. The edition of the Manuscrit Favre in the Pléiade edition leaves out f° 160 of the manuscript. I have thus used the transcription by Masson, *La "Profession de foi du vicaire savoyard,"* pp. 144, 146, 148. All citations from the manuscript are taken from these three pages. I have made no attempt to duplicate the system by which Masson distinguishes between levels of the manuscript, and simply translated his base text.

75. This final point is taken up almost word for word in *Julie*, p. 673.

76. It is the incomprehensibility of the relation between will and action that the vicar makes into his explanatory principle. See *Émile*, p. 576: "It is no more possible for me to conceive of how my will moves my body than of how my sensations affect my soul. . . . Whether I am passive or active, the means of unity between the two substances seems to me to be equally incomprehensible."

Chapter 4

1. Talmon, *The Origins of Totalitarian Democracy.*

2. The positions of Constant, Tocqueville, and Taine are discussed in Chapters 1 and 2. Burke's attack in the *Letter to a Member of the National Assembly* is particularly interesting in that it bases its attack not on the *Contrat social* but on *La Nouvelle Héloïse*: "Through Rousseau, your masters are resolved to destroy these aristocratic prejudices. The passion called love, has so general and powerful an influence . . . that the mode and the principles on which it engages the sympathy, and strikes the imagination, become of the utmost importance to the morals and manners of society. . . . Instead of this passion, naturally allied to grace and manners, they infuse into their youth an unfashioned, indelicate, sour, gloomy,

ferocious medley of pedantry and lewdness; of metaphysical speculations, blended with the coarsest sensuality. Such is the general morality of the passions to be found in their famous philosopher, in his famous work of philosophical gallantry, the *Nouvelle Eloise.* When the fence from the gallantry of preceptors is broken down, and your families are no longer protected by decent pride, and salutary domestic prejudice, there is but one step to frightful corruption. The rulers in the National Assembly are in good hopes that the females in the first families in France may become an easy prey to dancing-masters, fiddlers, pattern-drawers, friseurs, and valets de chambre, and other active citizens of that description. . . . By a law, they have made these people your equals. By adopting the sentiments of Rousseau, they have made them your rivals. In this manner, these great legislators complete their plan of levelling, and establish their rights of man on a sure foundation. I am certain that the writings of Rousseau lead directly to this kind of shameful evil" (pp. 39–41).

3. Taine, *Les Origines de la France contemporaine,* 1:182, 235. Taine cites for support of his point Mallet du Pan, whom he describes as an "ocular witness": "In the middling and lower classes, Rousseau had a hundred times more readers than Voltaire. It is he alone who injected the French with the doctrine of the sovereignty of the people and its most extreme consequences."

4. Mornet, "L'Influence de J. J. Rousseau au XVIIIe siècle," p. 44.

5. Mornet counted seventy-two editions of *Julie* between 1761 and 1801, both separate and in collected editions, in the introduction to his edition of *La Nouvelle Héloïse* (1:167–235). Nowhere that I have encountered does Mornet specify the number of eighteenth-century editions of the *Contrat social* with which he was familiar.

6. Mornet, *Les Origines intellectuelles de la Révolution française,* p. 265.

7. Sénac de Meilhan, *Du gouvernement, des mœurs et des conditions en France,* p. 364.

8. Mercier, *De J. J. Rousseau,* 2:99n.

9. [Bachaumont et al.], *Mémoires secrets,* September 3, 1762, 1:122. The author of the *Mémoires secrets* showed that he could be included in the *commun des lecteurs* for whom the book is too obscure by giving the following summary of the book: "It results from the *Contrat social* that any authority whatsoever is only the collective representation of all the particular wills, reunited in a single one. Whence, all power collapses as soon as unanimity ceases, at least with respect to the members of the republic, who demand their freedom."

10. See Trenard, "La Diffusion du *Contrat social.*" Important correctives to this argument are to be found in Tatin-Gourier, *Le Contrat social en question.*

11. Taylor, "Rousseau's Contemporary Reputation in France," pp. 1563–65; Derathé, "Les Réfutations du *Contrat social,*" pp. 7–8.

12. McDonald, *Rousseau and the French Revolution*, p. 155.

13. Isnard, *Le Principe qui a produit les Révolutions de France, de Genève et d'Amérique dans le dix-huitième siècle* (1789), cited by McDonald, *Rousseau and the French Revolution*, p. 71.

14. *Déclaration des droits de l'homme et du citoyen*, article 6, in Rials, *La Déclaration des droits de l'homme et du citoyen*, p. 23.

15. Riley, *The General Will before Rousseau*; Rials, *La Déclaration des droits de l'homme et du citoyen*; Gauchet, *La Révolution des droits de l'homme*; Van Kley, ed., *The French Idea of Freedom*, esp. the essay by Wright, "National Sovereignty and the General Will"; *Droits* 2 (1985), special issue on *La Déclaration de 1789*.

16. *Projet de déclaration des droits de l'homme en société*, presented by Mirabeau in the name of the Committee of Five, August 17, 1789, in Rials, *La Déclaration des droits de l'homme et du citoyen*, p. 748.

17. See Gauchet, *La Révolution des droits de l'homme*, p. 162.

18. I have based this survey on the collection of texts presented by Rials, *La Déclaration des droits de l'homme et du citoyen*, "Dossier."

19. Sieyes, "Préliminaire de la Constitution," p. 1018.

20. *Projet des premiers articles de la constitution*, presented by Mounier in the name of the Committee on the Constitution, July 27, 1789, in Rials, *La Déclaration des droits de l'homme et du citoyen*, p. 613.

21. See Rousseau, *Discours sur l'économie politique*, pp. 250–51: "How, I will be asked, can the general will be known in cases where it has not expressed itself? Must the whole nation be assembled at each unforeseen event? Such an assembly is all the less necessary because it is not sure its decision would be the expression of the general will; because this means is impractical for a large people; and because it is rarely necessary when the government is well intentioned."

22. A detailed explication of *Du contrat social* follows.

23. Cited by Rials, *La Déclaration des droits de l'homme et du citoyen*, p. 37. Like McDonald, Rials emphasizes the multiplicity of possible sources of the expression "general will." More generally, he sees the Declaration as having a primarily Lockean rather than Rousseauian inspiration. Thus he says that La Blache's observation "discredits his understanding of the question," and he adds in a note, "There are a few turns of phrase borrowed from Rousseau but . . . defining Sieyes's thought on this subject as Rousseauist is out of the question" (ibid., p. 298n77). This is of course one of the most controversial points in the literature. A detailed defense of my view that Sieyes's thought on the subject can indeed be seen as Rousseauist follows.

24. Montesquieu, *De l'esprit des lois*, p. 399: "The two other powers [i.e., legislative and executive] could instead be given to permanent magistrates or bodies, since they are not exercised upon particulars, the first being only the general will

of the state and the second the execution of that general will." See Riley, *General Will before Rousseau*, pp. 138–80.

25. Diderot, "Droit naturel" (1755), *Œuvres complètes*, 7:28–29. See Wokler, "The Influence of Diderot on the Political Theory of Rousseau"; and Riley, *General Will before Rousseau*, pp. 202–11.

26. D'Holbach, *Système social*, p. 236; see also p. 246, and d'Holbach, *La Politique naturelle*, 1:89–91. On d'Holbach's reading of Rousseau, see Hulliung, *The Autocritique of Enlightenment*.

27. McDonald, *Rousseau and the French Revolution*, pp. 87–88.

28. Ibid., p. 44.

29. Leigh, "Review Article: Jean-Jacques Rousseau," p. 561.

30. Leigh, *Unsolved Problems*, p. 77. *Unsolved Problems* is silent on the question of editions between 1784 and the Revolution, despite Leigh's own assertion that the final decade of the prerevolutionary period is the critical one for the study of this question. In "Rousseau, His Publishers, and the *Contrat social*," a preliminary report on his research that listed only twenty-one separate editions, Leigh makes this figure cover the entire prerevolutionary period (p. 227). These figures, however impressive they may be, still do not even begin to compare with those of *La Nouvelle Héloïse*. McEachern's recent bibliography of *Julie* (*Bibliography of the Writings of Jean-Jacques Rousseau*, vol. 1) enumerates seventy-two editions, and forty-two variant states or separate issues of these editions (including printings in collected editions). See also McEachern's earlier "Publication of *La Nouvelle Héloïse*," which gives slightly lower figures, but is more explicit on the significance of her work. This is more of an increase over Mornet's figure of seventy-two than might otherwise be thought in that McEachern has shown that, because of double listings, only fifty-one true editions and six variant states had been listed. For further comparison, *Bibliography of the Writings of Rousseau*, vol. 2, lists fifty-nine editions and twenty-six variant states.

31. Leigh, *Unsolved Problems*, p. 76.   32. Ibid., pp. 78–113.

33. Ibid., p. 75.   34. Ibid., pp. 67, 70.

35. In January 1771, chancellor Maupeou exiled the Parlement of Paris and replaced it with a new set of courts, which presumably would be less recalcitrant about enforcing the royal will. This event was variously referred to as a "coup" (a coup d'état originally being an act of force by the state rather than against it) and a "revolution." The new courts were abolished and the Parlement recalled shortly after Louis XVI's accession to the throne in 1775. See Egret, *Louis XV et l'opposition parlementaire*; Doyle, "The Parlements of France and the Breakdown of the Old Regime"; Echeverria, *The Maupeou Revolution*.

36. [Bachaumont et al.], *Mémoires secrets*, June 15, 1776, 9:133–34.

37. See Echeverria, "The Pre-Revolutionary Influence of Rousseau's *Contrat*

social"; Baker, "A Classical Republican in Eighteenth-Century Bordeaux," in *Inventing the French Revolution*, pp. 128–52; Barny, *Prélude idéologique à la Révolution française*, pp. 90–120; Tatin-Gourier, *Le Contrat social en question*, pp. 47–64.

38. In addition to the entry for September 3, see the entries in [Bachaumont et al.], *Mémoires secrets*, for June 25, 1762, 1:96 ("There is much talk [*On parle beaucoup*] of Rousseau's book which should serve as a fifth volume for his Treatise on Education, the *Contrat social*. It is claimed [*On prétend*] that there are copies in Paris, but very few of them. It is said to be [*On le dit*] extremely abstract") and July 12, 1762, 1:106 ("The *Contrat social* is slowly getting around [*se répand peu-à-peu*]. People have them sent by mail from Holland. Only the names of those to whom the copies are addressed are written down").

39. Darnton, *The Great Cat Massacre*, p. 222. See also the complete table of Ranson's orders from the STN, pp. 253–56.

40. Ibid., p. 239.

41. Jean Ranson to Frédéric-Samuel Ostervald, August 1, 1778, *Correspondance complète de Rousseau*, Letter 7228, 41:108–9. See also the letters from Ranson to Ostervald of January 25 and March 8, 1777: "Since you do not have the [complete] works of *l'Ami* Jean-Jacques I will get them elsewhere. One thing that makes me hesitate to buy them [*en faire l'emplette*] is the disavowal that great unhappy man made two or three years ago of all the editions being sold then, acknowledging only the first edition, which he helped to produce himself and which has been out of print for years" (ibid., remark to Letter 7119, 40:126–27); "No doubt you will see *l'Ami* Jean-Jacques. Please find out from him whether we might be able to have a good edition of his works" (ibid., remark to Letter 7122, 40:130). I have largely followed Darnton's translations.

42. Ranson to Ostervald, February 9, 1779, ibid., Letter 7466, 43:105.

43. See Leigh, *Unsolved Problems*, pp. 105–7. Rey's half of this correspondence has not been preserved, rendering both his attitudes and the reasons for the delay opaque.

44. Pierre Guy à Marc-Michel Rey, January 28, [1765], *Correspondance complète*, Letter 3934, 23:212.

45. Pierre Guy to Hans Caspar Arkstée and Hendrick Merkus, May 10, 1764, ibid., Letter 3264, 20:39. For the publishing history of the various complete editions, see Birn, "Les 'Œuvres complètes' de Rousseau sous l'Ancien Régime."

46. See Darnton, *The Forbidden Best-Sellers of Prerevolutionary France*, pp. 64, 68, and 403n93, and the companion volume of documentation, *The Corpus of Clandestine Literature in France*. A precise count of per-volume figures is impossible because the STN trafficked in a number of editions. The 240 sets of Rousseau ordered would give a minimum of eight thousand separate volumes. The only possible competitor is Mercier's *Tableau de Paris*, whose first edition was only

two volumes but that grew to a dozen. With 689 orders, this would likely mean about four thousand individual volumes, but possibly more. It should be remembered that the STN was only one of many distributors of clandestine books, so that meaning can be ascribed only to the relative figures, not their absolute magnitude.

47. My account of revolutionary editions of the *Contrat social* is based on Monglond, *La France révolutionnaire et impériale*, 1:1033–35, 2:275–77, 621–22, 909–38, 3:83, 373–75. As it is often based on catalogue descriptions and other secondary sources, Monglond's bibliography does not have the reliability of Leigh's work. But it does provide the most detailed breakdown of editions that I have been able to find. The separate editions of the *Contrat social* listed by Monglond include Geneva, 1791; Paris: Cazin, 1791; Strasbourg, 1791; Paris: Didot, 1792, 2 vols.; Nîmes: J. Gaude, 1792; N.p., 1792; Angers: Pavie, 1793; Paris, 1793; Paris: Louis, an II [1794]; Paris: Didot jeune, an IV [1795]; and Hamburg, 1795. The editions combined with the *Considérations* include Paris: Defer de Maisonneuve, 1790; Evreux: J.-J.-L. Ancelle, 1790; Lyon: J.-B. Delamollière, 1790.; N.p., 1792, 2 vols.; Paris: Josse, an III [1795]; Angers: Mame, an III [1795]; as well as an *Œuvres politiques* (Geneva and Paris, 1792), 4 vols. This list is certainly incomplete. I myself have seen a one-volume edition published in Rouen in 1792 by Veuve Pierre Dumesnil (in the School of Historical Sciences/School of Social Sciences Library of the Institute for Advanced Study, Princeton). The complete works editions include *Collection complète des œuvres de J. J. Rousseau* (Geneva and Paris: Volland, 1790), 4 vols.; *Collection complète des œuvres de J.-J. Rousseau, citoyen de Genève* (Paris: Bossange, and Bruxelles: J.-L. de Boubers, 1791); *Œuvres complètes* (Paris: Poinçot, 1788–93), 39 vols.; *Œuvres complettes de J. J. Rousseau, citoyen de Genève* (Paris: Bélin, Caille, Grégoire, and Volland, 1793), 37 vols.; *Œuvres de J. J. Rousseau, citoyen de Genève* (Paris: Defer de Maisonneuve, 1793), 18 vols.; *Œuvres* (Bâle: Tourneisen, 1793–95), 23 vols.

48. Mounier, *De l'influence attribuée aux philosophes*, pp. 118–19.

49. Lakanal, "Rapport sur J. J. Rousseau," pp. 5–6. There are important personal and institutional reasons for Lakanal to single out *Émile*. He is speaking here as chairman of the Committee of Public Instruction, responsible for educational policy as well as the various revolutionary *fêtes*, of which the *translation des cendres* of Rousseau is one example. Educational policy was Lakanal's specialty; it was he who wrote the decree founding the École normale later that year. A great deal of information on Lakanal's prethermidorian career, particularly as a *représentant en mission*, can be found in Gross, *Fair Shares for All*.

50. For general discussions of the abundant documentation on this subject, see Mornet, *Les Origines intellectuelles*, pp. 456–69; Katz, "Le Rousseauisme avant la Révolution"; and Hampson, *Will and Circumstance*.

51. Ptivar, *La Vérité, ou J. J. Rousseau montrant à Robespierre le livre des destins,* p. 7.

52. See the following works by Barny: "Jean-Jacques Rousseau dans la Révolution"; "Les Aristocrates et J. J. Rousseau dans la Révolution française"; *Prélude idéologique à la Révolution française*; *Rousseau dans la Révolution: Le Personnage de Jean-Jacques*; *L'Éclatement révolutionnaire du rousseauisme*; *Le Comte d'Antraigues.*

53. McDonald, *Rousseau and the French Revolution,* pp. 115–51; Sozzi, "Interprétations de Rousseau pendant la Révolution"; Barny, "Les Aristocrates et J. J. Rousseau dans la Révolution française"; Barny, *Le Comte d'Antraigues.*

54. McDonald, *Rousseau and the French Revolution,* p. 155.

55. Derathé, *Rousseau et la science politique de son temps,* pp. 48–49.

56. *Déclaration des droits de l'homme et du citoyen,* article 3, in Rials, *La Déclaration des droits de l'homme et du citoyen,* p. 22. For a clear example of how these ambivalences can be exploited, see Mounier, "Discours sur la sanction royale," p. 895.

57. Cf. de Man, *Allegories of Reading,* pp. 265–67, 275–77. These highly suggestive passages are marred by a key error, somewhat incomprehensibly identifying sovereign and executive.

58. Cf. "Manuscrit de Genève," p. 296: "The general will which should direct the state is not that of a past time, but that of the present moment, and the true characteristic of sovereignty is that there always be an agreement of time, place, and effect, between the direction of the general will and the employment of public force, an agreement that cannot be counted on as soon as another will, whatever it may be, disposes of this force."

59. Rousseau's use of the word "constitution" invariably designates the "health" of the body politic (in the same sense in which we say that individuals owe their health to a "good constitution"), rather than a foundational body of law. In the chapter on "Division of the Laws" (book II, chapter 12) he admits a distinction between fundamental, civil, and criminal laws, but this is a classification of purposes and not of institutional statuses: Fundamental laws are made and repealed in the same way as all other laws.

60. On the diversity of Latin terms translated by "sovereignty," see the terminological remarks in the Appendix to Derathé, *Rousseau et la science politique de son temps,* pp. 382–84.

61. The most extensive development of this bodily metaphor with respect to the separation of powers occurs in the *Discours sur l'économie politique,* p. 244: "If I may be permitted for a moment to make use of a common and inexact comparison, but which will help me be understood, the political body, taken individually, can be considered as an organized, living body comparable to that of a man. The sovereign power represents the head; the law and customs are the brain, principle

of the nerves and seat of the understanding, the will, and the senses, whose organs are the judges and magistrates; commerce, industry, and agriculture are the mouth and stomach that prepares the common subsistence; the public finances are the blood by which a wise *economy*, performing the functions of the heart, distributes nourishment and life throughout the body; the citizens are the body and the members, which make the machine move, live, and work, and which cannot be injured in any part, without a painful impression being immediately borne to the brain, if the animal is in a state of health." In this passage, as in most uses of the term, the emphasis falls on the relation between the head (government) and the members (citizens or subjects). The famous engraving that serves as a frontispiece for Hobbes's *Leviathan* provides a classic expression of this metaphor. In the *Contrat social*, however, this relation is actually reversed: it is the government that becomes the organ of the people. Rousseau's later use of such metaphors generally explicitly characterizes the different functions as *faculties* rather than as body parts. The starting point for the study of the bodily metaphor remains Kantorowicz, *The King's Two Bodies*.

62. Bodin, *Les Six livres de la République*, 1:308–9. Derathé's remark (*Rousseau et la science politique de son temps*, p. 100n2) that "Rousseau had also read Bodin, whom he cites three times in the *Économie politique*," but that Bodin did not "exercise enough influence on Rousseau" to need discussion, seems to me impossible to sustain.

63. Cf. "Manuscrit de Genève," p. 295: "Now, as will always tends toward the good of the being that wills, particular will always has private interest as its object, and the general will the common interest, it follows that the general will is or ought to be the only motive force [*mobile*] of the social body."

64. See the texts collected in Condorcet, *Sur les élections*; Baker, *Condorcet*, esp. pp. 225–44.

65. Kant, *Kritik der praktischen Vernunft*, in *Werkausgabe*, 7:135–46; *Critique of Practical Reason*, in *Practical Philosophy*, pp. 160–72. See the commentary in Balibar, "Ce qui fait qu'un peuple est un peuple."

66. Cassirer, *The Question of Jean-Jacques Rousseau*, p. 55.

67. See *Contrat social*, pp. 425–26: "The people assembled, it will be said! What a chimera! It is a chimera today, but it was not one two thousand years ago: has human nature changed? . . . The consequence from the existing to the possible seems well founded to me."

68. Cf. ibid., p. 399: "Nonetheless, for the body of the government to have an existence, a real life that distinguishes it from the body of the state, for all its members to be able to act in concert and to fulfill the goal for which government is instituted, the government must have a particular self [*moi*], a sensibility common to its members, a force and a will of its own that tends toward its preservation."

69. The terminology and analysis stem from Polybius, *The Rise of the Roman Empire*, book VI, particularly 303–5.

70. Althusser, "The Social Contract (The Discrepancies)," pp. 153, 160.

71. Charrière, *Éloge de Jean-Jacques Rousseau*, p. 204.

72. Weil, "J. J. Rousseau et sa politique," p. 125.

73. Ibid., pp. 134–35.

74. Ibid., p. 143n5.

75. Rosenblatt, *Rousseau and Geneva*, pp. 241–80.

76. Althusser, "The Social Contract (The Discrepancies)," p. 115 (translation modified).

77. De Man, *Allegories of Reading*, p. 269, points out that the version of this passage in the "Manuscrit de Genève," p. 306, is textually identical except for the qualification of this appropriation as taking place "in secret."

78. Althusser, "The Social Contract (The Discrepancies)," p. 143 (translation modified).

79. Rousseau is careful to define real equality as requiring not "that the degrees of power and wealth be absolutely the same, but that, with respect to power, it stop short of violence and only ever be exercised by virtue of rank and the laws, and with respect to wealth, that no citizen be sufficiently opulent to be able to buy another one, nor so poor as to be constrained to sell himself" (*Contrat social*, pp. 391–92).

80. Ferguson, *Essay on the History of Civil Society*, p. 120.

81. My presentation of the problem in these terms is inspired by the comparison of Condorcet and Rousseau in Baker, *Condorcet*, pp. 229–31.

82. We will discuss these passages with respect to the use of Rousseau by both prosecution and defense during the king's trial in 1792.

83. On the comparison between Wolmar and God, see Starobinski, *Transparency and Obstruction*, pp. 111–13; Shklar, *Men and Citizens*, pp. 135–36.

84. The texts of both the Parlement's proclamation (September 25, 1788) and Necker's *règlement* (January 24, 1789) are available in Brette, ed., *Recueil de documents relatifs à la convocation des États-généraux*, 1:28, 64–87. See Furet, "La Monarchie et le règlement électoral de 1789"; Halévi, "La Révolution constituante."

85. Blum, *Rousseau and the Republic of Virtue*. See also Roussel, "Le Phénomène d'identification dans la lecture de Rousseau"; Barny, *Rousseau dans la Révolution: Le Personnage de Jean-Jacques*.

86. This sense of the timing of the importance of a "technical" reading, at least as far as the members of the Assembly are concerned, is substantiated by Tackett's reading of the testimonies of Third Estate deputies. "Specific references in deputy testimonies to the ideas of the enlightenment," he notes, "largely absent in May

and early June, become more common in the summer and fall of 1789" (*Becoming a Revolutionary*, p. 308).

87. Gauchet, *La Révolution des droits de l'homme*, pp. xii–xiii; see also pp. 28–35.

88. I have been guided in my work on this topic by Grange, "Idéologie et action politique"; Barny, "Les Aventures de la théorie de souveraineté en 1789"; Baczko, "Le Contrat social des français"; Richet, "L'Esprit de la constitution, 1789–1791"; Gueniffey, "Les Assemblées et la représentation"; Baker, "Representation Redefined" and "Fixing the French Constitution," in *Inventing the French Revolution*, pp. 224–305.

89. Montesquieu, *De l'esprit des lois*, p. 395.

90. Madison, Hamilton, and Jay, *Federalist Papers*, XLVIII (Madison), p. 308. See Manin, "Checks, Balances and Boundaries."

91. Montesquieu, *De l'esprit des lois*, pp. 404–5. Montesquieu clearly has problems with the definition of the judicial function, which appears with far greater clarity in the American context. He begins his examination of the English constitution by distinguishing, along with the legislative power, between two kinds of executive power, "executive power with respect to things that depend on international law and executive power with respect to things that depend on civil law." The former "makes peace or war, sends and receives ambassadors, establishes security, prevents invasions," whereas the latter "punishes crimes, or judges disputes between particulars" (pp. 396–97). Most of his discussion, however, turns on the relation between executive power in the first sense and the legislature. "Among the three powers of which we have spoken, that of judging is in some sense null" (p. 401). This requires the House of Lords to function as a court of peers and as a court of last appeal.

92. Lally-Tollendal, "Premier discours sur l'organisation du pouvoir législatif et la sanction royale," pp. 368–69.

93. Mounier, "Discours sur la sanction royale," pp. 895–96.

94. Ibid., p. 900.

95. For the votes, see Mavidal et al., eds., *Archives parlementaires*, 8:608, 612. The *Archives parlementaires* do not specify the first vote on the question of whether there should be any veto at all, saying only that "the veto passed by a very large majority."

96. Polverel, "Développement des observations sur la sanction royale et sur le droit de veto," ibid., 9:72.

97. La Revellière-Lépeaux, "Opinion sur la sanction royale," ibid., 9:65. La Revellière-Lépeaux declared himself in favor of the suspensive veto.

98. Robespierre, "Dire contre le veto royal, soit absolu, soit suspensif" (September 1789) in *Œuvres*, 6:88.

99. *Archives parlementaires*, 8:569 (September 4, 1789).

100. Ibid., 8:530–31 (September 1, 1789).

101. Polverel, "Observations sur la sanction royale et sur le droit de veto," ibid., 9:71.

102. Sieyes, "Sur l'organisation du pouvoir législatif et la sanction royale," p. 1021.

103. Sieyes, "Préliminaire de la Constitution," p. 1012.

104. *Archives parlementaires*, 8:537 (September 1, 1789).

105. Ibid., 8:552 (September 3, 1789). Likewise, the suspensive veto was defined by Jean Meyniel as "the King's right to appeal to the nation" ("Opinion sur le veto et la sanction royale," ibid., 9:67), and by Salle as "a sort of appeal to the Nation, which makes it intervene as judge between the King and its representatives" (8:529). Similar positions were adopted by such important figures as Antoine Barnave, Barère, abbé Henri-Baptiste Grégoire, Alexandre de Lameth, Pierre-Samuel Dupont de Nemours, Louis-Alexandre, duc de la Rochefoucauld d'Enville, and Jean-Denis Lanjuinais. Even supporters of the absolute veto, such as Malouet, admitted that "the royal veto is effective only insofar as it signifies that the proposed law is not the expression of the general will; if the law in question is important, it is a true appeal to the people" (Malouet, "Discours sur la sanction royale," p. 460).

106. *Archives parlementaires*, 8:533.

107. Ibid., 8:570n.

108. Ibid., 8:571.

109. Baker, *Inventing the French Revolution*, pp. 289–95, provides a number of powerful formulations of this point.

110. On the separation between proposing laws and voting on them, with particular reference to the situation in Geneva, see Derathé, *Rousseau et la science politique de son temps*, p. 297n2.

111. Mounier, "Discours sur la sanction royale," p. 897.

112. Robespierre, "Dire contre le veto royal," *Œuvres*, 6:93–94.

113. See Gauchet, *La Révolution des pouvoirs*, pp. 63–64.

114. Gueniffey, "Les Assemblées et la représentation," p. 237.

115. Sieyes, *Qu'est-ce que le tiers état?* pp. 198–99.

116. Ibid., pp. 28–31.

117. See Baecque, *The Body Politic*, pp. 76–128.

118. Sieyes, *Qu'est-ce que le tiers état?* 31.

119. Ibid., p. 64.

120. Ibid., p. 66.

121. Sieyes, "Sur l'organisation du pouvoir législatif et la sanction royale," pp. 1024–25.

122. Sieyes, *Observations sur le rapport du comité de Constitution*, pp. 34–35.

123. Sewell, *A Rhetoric of Bourgeois Revolution*, p. 93.

124. Sieyes, *Écrits politiques*, p. 62.

125. Baczko, "Le Contrat social des français," p. 511.

126. Sieyes, *Qu'est-ce que le tiers état?* p. 66.

127. Ibid., p. 67.

128. Ibid., p. 69.

129. Sieyes, "Préliminaire de la Constitution," p. 1017.

130. Sieyes, *Qu'est-ce que le tiers état?* p. 209.

131. Sieyes, "Préliminaire de la Constitution," p. 1014.

132. Sieyes, *Qu'est-ce que le tiers état?* pp. 86–87.

133. Ibid., p. 41.

134. Gueniffey, *Le Nombre et la raison*, pp. 273–322.

135. Sieyes, *Qu'est-ce que le tiers état?* p. 43.

136. Sieyes, "Sur l'organisation du pouvoir législatif et la sanction royale," p. 1021.

137. Ibid., p. 1026.

138. Sieyes, *Qu'est-ce que le tiers état?* p. 88.

139. Ibid., p. 89.

140. Cf. Balibar, "Citizen Subject," p. 47: "The *representation of the sovereign* in its deputies, inasmuch as the sovereign is the people, . . . is the act of sovereignty *par excellence.* . . . To elect representatives is to act and to make possible all political action, which draws its legitimacy from this election. . . . It *singularizes* each citizen, responsible for his vote (his choice), at the same time as it *unifies* the 'moral' body of the citizens."

141. *Archives parlementaires*, 8:127 (June 17, 1789).

142. Ibid., 8:205 (July 7, 1789). See Halévi, "La Révolution constituante."

143. Sieyes, "Sur l'organisation du pouvoir législatif et la sanction royale," p. 1022.

144. Ibid., p. 1027.

145. Ibid., pp. 1022, 1026.

146. Cited from Archives Nationales 284 AP 5, dossier 1, by Gueniffey, "Les Assemblées et la représentation," pp. 235–36. Emphasis added.

147. Hobbes, *Leviathan*, p. 114. Hobbes's definition of "person" should be kept in mind: "A Person, is he, *whose words or actions are considered, either as his own, or as representing the words of actions of an other man, or of any other thing to whom they are attributed, whether Truly or by Fiction*" (ibid., p. 111). On the relation between Hobbes and Rousseau, see Derathé, *Rousseau et la science politique de son temps*; and for the comparison with Sieyes, Jaume, *Hobbes et l'état représentatif moderne*.

148. Rousseau to Victor Riquetti, marquis de Mirabeau, July 26, 1767, *Correspondance complète*, Letter 5991, 33:240.

149. See *Contrat social*, p. 463: "Of all Christian authors the philosopher

Hobbes is the only one to have seen both the evil and its remedy, who dared to propose uniting the two heads of the eagle, and to bring everything back to political unity, without which no state or government will ever be well constituted. . . . It is not so much what is horrible and false in his politics as what is just and true in it that has made it odious."

150. Sieyes, *Qu'est-ce que le tiers état?* p. 86.

151. Étienne Dumont said of Sieyes that "he read little and meditated much; the works he liked the most were Rousseau's *Social Contract*, the writings of Condillac and Smith's *Wealth of Nations*" (*Souvenirs sur Mirabeau et sur les deux premières Assemblées législatives* [1832],as cited and translated by Forsyth, *Reason and Revolution*, p. 41). Forsyth sees Rousseau as providing a subordinate element in Sieyes's intellectual formation; at least for the writings of 1788–90, he seems to me to provide the framework.

152. Baker, *Inventing the French Revolution*, p. 305.

153. *Déclaration des droits de l'homme et du citoyen*, article 3, in Rials, *La Déclaration des droits de l'homme et du citoyen*, p. 22.

154. Sieyes, "Préliminaire de la Constitution," pp. 1006–7.

155. Sieyes, "Sur les Déclarations des droits en général, sur celle de 1789 en particulier, et sur leurs bases générales" (Year III), manuscript in Archives nationales 284 AP 5 dossier 1 (5), in Fauré, ed., *Les Déclarations de droits de l'homme de 1789*, pp. 321–22.

156. Cf. Furet, *Interpreting the French Revolution*, p. 50: "The history of the Revolution is marked throughout by a fundamental dichotomy. The deputies made laws in the name of the people, whom they were presumed to *represent*, but the members of the sections and of the clubs acted as the *embodiment* of the people. . . . As regards domestic politics, the salient feature of the period between May–June 1789 and 9 Thermidor 1794 was not the conflict between Revolution and counter-revolution, but the struggle between the representatives of the successive Assemblies and the club militants for the dominant symbolic position, the people's will." From a very different perspective, Balibar speaks of the equation of liberty and equality in the founding moment of the Revolution as giving rise to "an indefinite oscillation, . . . a structural equivocation between two obviously antinomical forms of 'politics': an *insurrectional politics* and a *constitutional politics*," whose antinomy has been characteristic of modernity (*Masses, Classes, Ideas*, p. 51).

157. See Gauchet, *La Révolution des pouvoirs*, p. 79. It seems to me to be characteristic of revolutionary politics that the "losing" side in a vote often sets the terms of future debate.

158. *Archives parlementaires*, 29:322–23 (August 10, 1791). An even stronger version of this can be found in a decree on the respect due to the law, proposed by Le Chapelier and adopted with some amendment on February 28, 1791 (ibid.,

23:564): "Sovereignty being one, indivisible, and belonging to the entire nation, no departmental or district administration, no municipality, no tribunal, no commune or section of a commune, no primary or electoral assembly, nor any section of the people or the empire, under any denomination whatsoever, has the right to exercise any act of sovereignty."

159. Robespierre, "Sur les principes de la souveraineté" (August 10, 1791), *Œuvres*, 7:612.

160. Gueniffey, *Le Nombre et la raison*, pp. 17–19, 146–50. For the law on collective petitions, see Le Chapelier, "Rapport sur le droit de pétition et d'affiche."

161. See Le Chapelier, "Rapport sur les assemblées de citoyens de même état de profession."

162. Le Chapelier, "Rapport sur les sociétés populaires," p. 434. This decree was the occasion of an important debate between Le Chapelier and Robespierre on whether, in a phrase Furet has made famous, "the Revolution is over." Both admit that the clubs keep the Revolution going; for Le Chapelier the end of the Revolution is marked by the Constitution, for Robespierre the Revolution cannot be over so long as "discourses and exterior signs have changed, while actions remain the same, and hearts can only have been changed by a miracle" (Robespierre, "Sur les droits des sociétés et des clubs" [September 29, 1791], *Œuvres*, 7:746).

163. *Archives parlementaires*, 15:381 (May 3, 1790).

164. Robespierre, "Des maux et des ressources de l'état" (July 29, 1792), *Œuvres*, 8:414.

165. Ibid., p. 416. On the relation between *représentants, commissaires* (the term preferred by Rousseau in *Contrat social*, book III, chapter 15), and *mandataires* (the term used most frequently in sectional petitions and resolutions, as well as by Robespierre here), see Genty, *Paris 1789–1795*, pp. 49–54, 188–91.

166. Robespierre, "Des maux et des ressources de l'état," *Œuvres*, 8:417.

167. "Extrait des registres de la section Mauconseil," dated July 31, 1792, presented to the Legislative Assembly on August 4, 1792, *Archives parlementaires*, 47:457–58.

168. Ibid., 47:475–76 (August 4, 1792). A second response by the Committee of Twelve, composed by Condorcet, was read to the Assembly on the afternoon of August 9, too late to be acted upon before the insurrection began (ibid., 47:615–16). This remarkable text, which recognizes the people's right to peaceful insurrection but attempts to determine how such a repudiation of the constitution could be submitted to forms that would make possible a true expression of the general will, prefigures the spirit of Condorcet's constitutional proposal.

169. Levy and Applewhite, "Women and Militant Citizenship in Revolutionary Paris," p. 85; for a similar perspective, see Godineau, *The Women of Paris and Their French Revolution*.

170. Soboul, "Audience des lumières"; Soboul, *The Sans-Culottes*, pp. 95–134. Soboul's work has been much criticized over the past twenty years for its assumptions about the social status of the *sans-culottes* and the continuity he sees between certain journalists and popular activists. On these points, see Andrews, "Social Structures, Political Elites, and Ideology in Revolutionary Paris"; and Sewell, "The Sans-Culotte Rhetoric of Subsistence." Nonetheless, Soboul's documentation of the discourse of the sectional movement remains unsurpassed.

171. Soboul, *The Sans-Culottes*; Guérin, *Class Struggle in the First French Republic*.

172. Billaud-Varenne, "Rapport au nom du Comité de Salut public, sur un mode de gouvernement provisoire et révolutionnaire," *Archives parlementaires*, 79:455 (28 brumaire II). The work of Françoise Brunel has given a whole new light on the place of Billaud-Varenne in the Montagnard group. See Brunel, *Thermidor*; Brunel, "L'Acculturation d'un révolutionnaire"; and her critical edition of Billaud-Varenne, *Principes régénérateurs du système social.*

173. Robespierre, "Sur les principes de morale politique qui doivent guider la Convention nationale dans l'administration intérieure de la République" (17 pluviôse II), *Œuvres*, 10:357, 352–53.

174. On the split between the Montagne and the Gironde, see Patrick, *The Men of the First French Republic*; and Higonnet, "The Social and Cultural Antecedents of Revolutionary Discontinuity." Higonnet argues, convincingly to my mind, that the Girondins and Montagnards cannot be distinguished in a significant way on a class basis. He attributes the split between them to "their staggered access to power in 1792–1793; and with that, their staggered disillusionment" ("The Social and Cultural Antecedents of Revolutionary Discontinuity," p. 515). In many ways such an analysis amounts, as Higonnet recognizes, to an attribution of the split to the internal divisions of their shared ideological position, which Higonnet characterizes in Marxist terms as "the dilemma of [being] at once a particularist and a universal class" (p. 535).

175. See Jordan, *The King's Trial*; Walzer, *Regicide and Revolution.*

176. Saint-Just, "Discours sur le jugement de Louis XVI" (November 13, 1792), *Œuvres complètes*, p. 379.

177. See, among hundreds of possible examples, Robespierre, "Sur les principes de morale politique," *Œuvres*, 10:356: "We must smother the interior and exterior enemies of the Republic, or perish with it; in this situation, the first maxim of your policy must be to lead the people by reason, and the people's enemies by terror."

178. Saint-Just, "Rapport sur la nécessité de déclarer le gouvernement révolutionnaire jusqu'à la paix," *Œuvres complètes*, p. 521.

179. Sèze, *Défense de Louis*, p. 14–15.

180. *Archives parlementaires*, 56:90 (December 31, 1792).

181. The collection of projects published and bound together by the Constitutional Committee are preserved in the Archives nationales, series AD XVIII^c. For a discussion of the corpus, see Pertué, "Les Projets constitutionnels de 1793." I have been guided to a great extent by Jaume, *Le Discours jacobin et la démocratie*.

182. Condorcet, "Projet de Déclaration des droits naturels, civils et politiques des hommes" (February 15–16, 1793), *Œuvres*, 12:422.

183. *Archives parlementaires*, 65:580 (May 29, 1793).

184. *Déclaration des droits de l'homme et du citoyen* (known as the "Jacobin" version), articles 33–35, ibid., 67:145 (June 24, 1793).

185. See also the differences in treatment of the indivisibility of sovereignty in Condorcet's articles 26–27 (*Œuvres*, 12:421), the "Girondin" articles 26–28 (*Archives parlementaires*, 65:580), and the "Jacobin" articles 25–27 (ibid., 67:144).

186. Robespierre, "Discours sur la Constitution" (May 10, 1793), *Œuvres*, 9:496.

187. See esp. Robespierre, "Sur les principes de morale politique," ibid., 10:355–56: "Happily virtue is natural to the people. . . . To love justice and equality, the people does not need any great virtue; it is enough for the people to love itself. But the magistrate is obliged to sacrifice his interest to the people's interest, and the pridefulness of power to equality."

188. Robespierre, "Discours sur la Constitution," ibid., 9:498.

189. Ibid., p. 503.

190. Ibid., pp. 504–5.

191. *Archives parlementaires*, 67:140–41 (June 24, 1793).

192. Saint-Just, "Discours sur la constitution de la France" (April 24, 1793), *Œuvres complètes*, pp. 422–23: "It seems to me that the committee considered the general will from an intellectual point of view, in such a way that, the general will being purely speculative, the combination of intellectual calculations [*les vues de l'esprit*] rather than of the interest of the social body, laws would be the expression of taste rather than of the general will. . . . Rousseau, who wrote with his heart, and who wished the world all the good that he could only say, never dreamed that in establishing the general will as the principle of the laws, the general will could ever come to have a foreign principle." This should be contrasted with his statement in the manuscript *De la nature* (ibid., p. 951) that "the law is thus not the expression of will but that of nature."

193. Saint-Just, "Discours sur la constitution," ibid., p. 424.

194. Ibid., p. 428 (chapter V, articles 7 and 12). Gueniffey (*Le Nombre et la raison*, p. 154n135) argues that the motivation was primarily political, as this system would give the greatest weight to "organized minorities," particularly the Jacobins. Even if this is true, the proposal continues to express the *passage à la limite* of Sieyes's logic.

195. Saint-Just, "Discours sur la constitution," *Œuvres complètes*, pp. 431, 433–35 (chapters IX, XIII, XIV).

196. Condorcet, *Plan de Constitution, présenté à la Convention nationale les 15 et 16 février 1793*, *Œuvres*, 12:341.

197. Ibid., p. 347.

198. Ibid., p. 349.

199. Ibid., pp. 352–53.

200. *Archives parlementaires*, 67:139 (June 24, 1793).

201. Hunt, *Politics, Culture, and Class in the French Revolution*, pp. 48–49 and n85.

Bibliography

I. Works by Jean-Jacques Rousseau

I. EDITION OF REFERENCE

Œuvres complètes. Edited by Bernard Gagnebin and Marcel Raymond. 5 vols. Paris: Gallimard, Bibliothèque de la Pléiade, 1959–95.

Citations from the following works in the *Œuvres complètes* are given parethentically in the text, with notation of short title where appropriate:

Les Confessions de J. J. Rousseau. Books I–VI, 1782; Books VII–XII, 1789. Vol. 1.

Considérations sur le gouvernement de Pologne et sur sa réformation projetée. 1782. Vol. 3.

Discours sur l'économie politique. 1755. Vol. 3.

Discours qui a remporté le prix à l'Académie de Dijon en l'année 1750. Sur cette question proposée par la même Académie: Si le rétablissement des sciences et des arts a contribué à épurer les mœurs. 1751. Vol. 3. (*Discours sur les sciences et les arts.*)

Discours sur l'origine et les fondements de l'inégalité parmi les hommes. 1754. Vol. 3.

Du contrat social, ou Essai sur la forme de la République. Vol. 3. ("Manuscrit de Genève.")

Du contrat social, ou Principes du droit politique. 1762. Vol. 3. (*Contrat social.*)

Émile, ou de l'éducation. 1762. Vol. 4.

Essai sur l'origine du langage, où il est parlé de la mélodie et de l'imitation musicale. 1781. Vol. 5. (*Essai.*)

Julie, ou La Nouvelle Héloïse. Lettres de deux amants habitants d'une petite ville au pied des Alpes. 1761. Vol. 2.

Lettre de J. J. Rousseau à M. de Voltaire. August 18, 1756. Vol. 4.

Lettres écrites de la montagne. 1764. Vol. 3.

Observations de J. J. Rousseau, sur la Réponse qui a été faite à son Discours. 1751. Vol. 3. ("Réponse à Stanislas.")

Le Persifleur. 1781. Vol. 1.

Quatre lettres à M. le président de Malesherbes, contenant le vrai tableau de mon caractère et les vrais motifs de toute ma conduite. January 1762. Vol. 1. (*Lettres à Malesherbes.*)

Les Rêveries du promeneur solitaire. 1782. Vol. 1.

Rousseau juge de Jean-Jacques. Dialogues. First Dialogue, 1780; Second and third Dialogues, 1782. Vol. 1. (*Dialogues.*)

II. OTHER EDITIONS AND TRANSLATIONS

Œuvres complètes. 39 vols. Paris: Poinçot, 1788–93.

La *"Profession de foi du vicaire savoyard" de Jean-Jacques Rousseau.* Edited by Pierre-Maurice Masson. Fribourg: Librairie de l'université; Paris: Hachette, 1914.

La Nouvelle Héloïse. Edited by Daniel Mornet. 4 vols. Paris: Hachette, 1925.

Correspondance complète de Jean-Jacques Rousseau. Edited by R. A. Leigh. 51 vols. Oxford and Geneva: Voltaire Foundation, 1965–95.

The Collected Writings of Rousseau. Edited by Roger D. Masters and Christopher Kelly. 7 vols. to date. Hanover, N.H.: University Press of New England, 1990–.

The Discourses and Other Early Political Writings. Edited and translated by Victor Gourevitch. Cambridge: Cambridge University Press, 1997.

The Social Contract and Other Later Political Writings. Edited and translated by Victor Gourevitch. Cambridge: Cambridge University Press, 1997.

II. Other Works Written before 1820

Alembert, Jean Lerond d'. *Essai sur la société des gens de lettres et des grands.* 1753. In *Mélanges de littérature, d'histoire, et de philosophie,* vol. 1. Nouvelle édition. 5 vols. Amsterdam: Zacharie Chatelain et fils, 1773.

Alembert, Jean Lerond d', and Denis Diderot, eds. *Encyclopédie, ou Dictionnaire raisonné des sciences, des arts et des métiers, par une société de gens de lettres.* 35 vols. Paris and Lyon: Briasson, David l'aîné, Le Breton, and Durand, 1751–67.

———. *Encyclopédie, ou Dictionnaire raisonné des sciences, des arts et des métiers, par une société de gens de lettres.* Articles choisis. Edited by Alan Pons. 2 vols. Paris: Flammarion, 1986.

Augustine (Saint). *Confessiones.* Edited by Martinus Skutella. Stuttgard: Teubner, 1981.

———. *Confessions.* Translated by R. S. Pine-Coffin. Harmondsworth: Penguin, 1961.

[Bachaumont, Louis Petit de, et al.] *Mémoires secrets pour servir à l'histoire de la République des lettres en France, depuis MDCCLXII jusqu'à nos jours; ou Journal d'un observateur.* 36 vols. London: John Adamson, 1780–89.

Barruel, Augustin (abbé). *Mémoires pour servir à l'histoire du jacobinisme.* 1797. 2 vols. Vouillé: Diffusion de la pensée française, 1974.

Bernardin de Saint-Pierre, Jacques-Henri. *La Vie et les ouvrages de Jean-Jacques Rousseau.* Edited by Maurice Souriau. Paris: Cornély, 1907.

Billaud-Varenne, Jacques-Nicolas. *Principes régénérateurs du système social.* 1795. Edited by Françoise Brunel. Paris: Publications de la Sorbonne, 1992.

Bodin, Jean. *Les Six livres de la République.* 1576. 6 vols. Paris: Fayard, 1986.

Brette, Armand, ed. *Recueil de documents relatifs à la convocation des États-généraux de 1789.* 4 vols. Paris: Imprimerie Nationale, 1894–95.

Buffon, Georges-Louis Leclerc, comte de. *Œuvres complètes.* 22 vols. Paris: Pourrat frères, 1833–34.

Burke, Edmund. *A Letter to a Member of the National Assembly.* 1791. Oxford and New York: Woodstock Books, 1990.

Cajot, Dom Joseph. *Les Plagiats de M. J. J. R. de Genève sur l'éducation.* The Hague and Paris: Durand, 1766.

[Cambacérès, Jean-Jacques-Régis de.] *Discours prononcé par le Président de la Convention nationale, lors de la translation des cendres de Jean-Jacques Rousseau au Panthéon, le 20 vendémiaire de l'an troisième de la République.* Paris: Imprimerie nationale, Year III. Reprinted in *Jean-Jacques Rousseau dans la Révolution française, 1789–1801.* Paris: Edhis, 1977.

Charrière, Isabelle de. *Éloge de Jean-Jacques Rousseau.* 1790. In *Œuvres complètes,* edited by Jean-Daniel Candaux et al., vol. 10. 10 vols. Amsterdam: G. A. van Oorschot, 1981.

Condorcet, Jean-Antoine-Nicolas Caritat, marquis de. *Esquisse d'un tableau historique des progrès de l'esprit humain.* 1795. Edited by Alan Pons. Paris: Flammarion, 1988.

———. *Œuvres de Condorcet.* Edited by A. Condorcet-O'Connor and M. F. Arago. 12 vols. Paris: Didot, 1847.

———. *Sur les élections et autres textes.* Paris: Fayard, 1986.

Condorcet, Jean-Antoine-Nicolas Caritat, marquis de, Charles de Peysonnel, Isaac-René-Guy Le Chapelier, et al. *Bibliothèque de l'homme public, ou Analyse raisonnée des principaux ouvrages françois et étrangers, sur la Politique en général, la Législation, les Finances, la Police, l'Agriculture, et le Commerce en particulier, et sur le Droit naturel et public,* par M. le Marquis de Condorcet, Secrétaire perpétuelle de l'Académie des

Sciences, l'un des Quarante de l'Académie Françoise, de la Société Royale de Londres; M. de Peysonnel, ancien Consul-général de la France à Smirne, etc.; M. Le Chapelier, Député de l'Assemblée Nationale, et autres Gens de Lettres. 28 vols. Paris: Buisson, 1790–92.

Constant, Benjamin. *De la liberté chez les modernes: Écrits politiques.* Edited by Marcel Gauchet. Paris: Le Livre de poche, 1980.

———. *Des réactions politiques.* 1797. In *De la force du gouvernement actuel de la France et de la nécessité de s'y rallier; Des réactions politiques; Des effets de la terreur,* edited by Philippe Reynaud. Paris: Flammarion, 1988.

Delacroix, Jacques-Vincent. *Éloge de Jean-Jacques Rousseau.* Amsterdam and Paris: Lejay, 1778.

Dictionnaire de l'Académie française. Paris: Coignard, 1694.

Diderot, Denis. *Œuvres complètes.* Edited by Herbert Dieckmann, Jacques Proust, Jean Varloot, et al. 33 vols. projected. Paris: Hermann, 1975–.

———. *Réfutation suivie de l'ouvrage d'Helvétius intitulé l'Homme.* In *Œuvres complètes,* edited by Roger Lewinter, vol. 11. 15 vols. Paris: Le Club français du livre, 1969–73.

Fauré, Christine, ed. *Les Déclarations de droits de l'homme de 1789.* Paris: Payot, 1988.

Ferguson, Adam. *An Essay on the History of Civil Society.* 1767. Edited by Fania Oz-Salzberger. Cambridge: Cambridge University Press, 1995.

Fréron, Elie. "Julie ou La Nouvelle Héloïse." *L'Année littéraire,* 1761, no. 2:289–330.

Furet, François, and Ran Halévi, eds. *Orateurs de la Révolution française.* Vol. 1. Paris: Gallimard, Bibliothèque de la Pléiade, 1989.

Furetière, Antoine. *Dictionaire universel contenant généralement tous les mots françois.* The Hague and Rotterdam: Arnout and Reinier Leers, 1690. Reprint, 3 vols. Paris: SNL-Le Robert, 1978.

Galiani, Ferndando (abbé), and Louise-Florence-Pétronille Tardieu d'Esclavelles, marquise de Lalive d'Épinay. *Correspondance.* Edited by Georges Dulac and Daniel Maggetti. 5 vols. Paris: Éditions Desjonquères, 1996.

Ginguené, Pierre-Louis. *Lettres sur les Confessions de J. J. Rousseau.* Paris: Barois l'aîné, 1791.

[Ginguené, Pierre-Louis, et al.] *Pétition à l'Assemblée nationale, contenant demande de la translation des cendres de J. J. Rousseau, au Panthéon français; Pétition des citoyens de la ville et du canton de Montmorency, à l'Assemblée nationale; Réponse de Monsieur le Président de l'Assemblée nationale.* Paris: Imprimerie nationale, [1791]. Reprinted in *Jean-Jacques Rousseau dans la Révolution française, 1789–1801.* Paris: Edhis, 1977.

Guillaume, James, ed. *Procès-verbaux du Comité d'Instruction publique de la Convention nationale.* 6 vols. Paris: Imprimerie nationale, 1891–1907.

Helvétius, Claude-Adrien. *De l'esprit.* 1758. Edited by Jacques Moutaux. Paris: Fayard, 1988.

————. *De l'homme.* 1773. Edited by Geneviève Moutaux and Jacques Moutaux. 2 vols. Paris: Fayard, 1989.

Hobbes, Thomas. *Leviathan, or the Matter, Forme, and Power of a Common-wealth, Ecclesiaticall and Civill.* 1651. Edited by Richard Tuck. Rev. ed. Cambridge: Cambridge University Press, 1996.

Holbach, Paul Thiry, baron d'. *La Politique naturelle, ou discours sur les vrais principes du gouvernement.* 1773. 2 vols. in 1. Hildesheim: Georg Olds, 1971.

————. *Système social.* 1770. Paris: Fayard, 1994.

Horace. *Ars Poetica.* In *Opera,* edited by D. R. Shackleton Bailey. Stuttgard: Teubner, 1985.

————. *On the Art of Poetry.* In Aristotle, Horace, and Longinus, *Classical Literary Criticism,* translated by T. S. Dorsch. Harmondsworth: Penguin, 1965.

Hume, David. *Political Essays.* Edited by Knud Haakonssen. Cambridge: Cambridge University Press, 1994.

Jean-Jacques Rousseau dans la Révolution française, 1789–1801. Paris: Edhis, 1977.

Kames, Henry Home (Lord). *Sketches of the History of Man.* 2d ed. London and Edinburgh, 1778. Reprint, 4 vols. London: Routledge/Thoemmes Press, 1993.

Kant, Immanuel. *Critique of Judgment.* Translated by James Creed Meredith. Oxford: Clarendon Press, 1952.

————. *Practical Philosophy.* Edited and translated by Mary J. Gregor. In *The Cambridge Edition of the Works of Immanuel Kant,* edited by Paul Guyer and Allen W. Wood. 14 vols. projected. Cambridge: Cambridge University Press, 1992–.

————. *Werkausgabe.* Edited by Wilhelm Weischedel. 12 vols. Frankfurt a.M.: Suhrkamp, 1977.

La Harpe, Jean-François de. "De J. J. Rousseau." *Mercure de France,* October 5, 1778, pp. 7–28.

Lakanal, Joseph. "Rapport sur J. J. Rousseau, fait au nom du Comité d'Instruction publique, dans la séance du 29 fructidor." Paris: Imprimerie nationale, [Year II]. Reprinted in *Jean-Jacques Rousseau dans la Révolution française, 1789–1801.* Paris: Edhis, 1977.

Lally-Tollendal, Trophime-Gérard, comte de. "Premier discours sur l'organisation du pouvoir législatif et la sanction royale" (August 31, 1789). In *Orateurs de la Révolution française,* edited by François Furet and Ran Halévi, 1:364–88. Paris: Gallimard, Bibliothèque de la Pléiade, 1989.

La Rochefoucauld, François, duc de. *Réflexions ou sentences et maximes morales.* 1662. In *Œuvres complètes,* edited by L. Martin-Chauffier. Paris: Gallimard, Bibliothèque de la Pléiade, 1935.

Le Chapelier, Isaac-Guy-René. "Rapport sur le droit de pétition et d'affiche" (May 9, 1791). In *Orateurs de la Révolution française,* edited by François Furet and Ran Halévi, 1:415–28. Paris: Gallimard, Bibliothèque de la Pléiade, 1989.

———. "Rapport sur les assemblées de citoyens de même état de profession" (June 14, 1791). In *Orateurs de la Révolution française,* edited by François Furet and Ran Halévi, 1:428–32. Paris: Gallimard, Bibliothèque de la Pléiade, 1989.

———. "Rapport sur les sociétés populaires" (September 29, 1791). In *Orateurs de la Révolution française,* edited by François Furet and Ran Halévi, 1:432–39. Paris: Gallimard, Bibliothèque de la Pléiade, 1989.

Machiavelli, Niccolò. *Discourses on Livy.* Translated by Harvey C. Mansfield and Nathan Tarcov. Chicago: University of Chicago Press, 1996.

———. *Florentine Histories.* Translated by Laura F. Banfield and Harvey C. Mansfield. Princeton: Princeton University Press, 1988.

———. *Tutte le opere.* Edited by Mario Martelli. Florence: Sansoni, 1971.

Madison, James, Alexander Hamilton, and John Jay. *The Federalist Papers.* 1788. Edited by Isaac Kramnick. Harmondsworth: Penguin, 1987.

Malesherbes, Guillaume-Chrétien Lamoignon de. *Les "Remontrances" de Malesherbes, 1771–1775.* Edited by Élisabeth Badinter. Paris: Flammarion, 1985.

———. *Mémoires sur la librairie et sur la liberté de la presse.* Edited by Graham E. Rodmell. Chapel Hill: University of North Carolina Press, 1979.

Malouet, Pierre-Victor. "Discours sur la sanction royale" (September 1, 1789). In *Orateurs de la Révolution française,* edited by François Furet and Ran Halévi, 1:456–63. Paris: Gallimard, Bibliothèque de la Pléiade, 1989.

Marat, Jean-Paul. *Œuvres politiques 1789–1793.* Edited by Jacques de Cock and Charlotte Goetz. 10 vols. Bruxelles: Pôle Nord, 1989–95.

Mavidal, J., E. Laurent, et al., eds. *Archives parlementaires de 1787 à 1860. Première série (1789 à 1799).* 99 vols. to date. Paris: Paul Dupont, 1867–1913; Paris: Centre national de la recherche scientifique, 1961–.

Mercier, Louis-Sébastien. *L'An deux mille quatre cent quarante, rêve s'il en fut jamais.* 1771. Edited by Raymond Trousson. Bordeaux: Ducros, 1971.

———. *De J. J. Rousseau considéré comme l'un des premiers auteurs de la Révolution.* 2 vols. Paris: Buisson, 1791.

———. *De la littérature et des littérateurs, suivi d'un nouvel examen de la tragédie françoise.* 1778. Geneva: Slatkine Reprints, 1970.

————. *Le Tableau de Paris*. 1782–88. Reprint, 12 vols. Geneva: Slatkine Reprints, 1989.

Millar, John. *The Origin of the Distinction of Ranks*. 1771. In William C. Lehmann, *John Millar of Glasgow, 1735–1801: His Life and Thought and His Contributions to Sociological Analysis*. Cambridge: Cambridge University Press, 1960.

Montesquieu, Charles de Secondat, baron de la Brède et de. *De l'esprit des lois*. 1748. In *Œuvres complètes*, edited by Roger Caillois, vol. 2. 2 vols. Paris: Gallimard, Bibliothèque de la Pléiade, 1966.

Mounier, Jean-Joseph. *De l'influence attribuée aux philosophes, aux francs-maçons, et aux Illuminés sur la Révolution de France*. 1801. Reprint, Paris: Gutenberg, 1980.

————. "Discours sur la sanction royale" (September 5, 1789). In *Orateurs de la Révolution française*, edited by François Furet and Ran Halévi, 1:880–907. Paris: Gallimard, Bibliothèque de la Pléiade, 1989.

Necker, Jacques. *Œuvres complètes*. Edited by Auguste-Louis de Staël-Holstein. 15 vols. Paris: Treuttel and Würtz, 1820–21. Reprint, Aalen: Scientia Verlag, 1970.

"Nouvelles littéraires: *Vie de Voltaire*, par le Marquis de Condorcet . . . " *Mercure de France*, August 7, 1790, pp. 26–43.

Ovid. *Metamorphoses*. Edited by G. P. Goold. 2d ed. Loeb Classical Library. 2 vols. Cambridge, Mass.: Harvard University Press, 1984.

————. *Metamorphoses*. Translated by Mary M. Innes. Harmondsworth: Penguin, 1955.

————. *Tristia, Ex Ponte*. Edited by G. P. Goold. 2d ed. Loeb Classical Library. Cambridge, Mass.: Harvard University Press, 1988.

Palissot de Montenoy, Charles. *Les Philosophes, comédie, en trois actes, en vers*. Paris: Duchesne, 1760.

Petrarca, Francesco. *Le Familiari*. Edited by Vittorio Rossi. 4 vols. Florence: Sansoni, 1933–42.

————. *Petrarch's Lyric Poems: The Rime Sparse and Other Lyrics*. Translated by Robert Durling. Cambridge, Mass.: Harvard University Press, 1976.

————. *Rerum familiarium libri I–VIII*. Translated by Aldo S. Bernardo. Albany: State University of New York Press, 1975.

Peuchet, Jacques. "Discours préliminaire." *Encyclopédie méthodique. Jurisprudence*. Vol. 9: *Police et municipalités*. Paris: Pancoucke, 1789.

Polybius. *The Rise of the Roman Empire*. Edited by F. W. Walbank. Translated by Ian Scott-Kilvert. Harmondsworth: Penguin, 1979.

Ptivar. *La Vérité, ou J. J. Rousseau montrant à Robespierre le livre des destins*. N.p., n.d. Reprinted in *Jean-Jacques Rousseau dans la Révolution française, 1789–1801*. Paris: Edhis, 1977.

Pufendorf, Samuel. *Gesammelte Werke.* Edited by Wilhelm Schmidt-Biggemann. 4 vols. to date. Berlin: Akademie Verlag, 1996–.

————. *On the Duty of Man and Citizen According to Natural Law.* Edited by James Tully. Translated by Michael Silverthorne. Cambridge: Cambridge University Press, 1991.

Rials, Stéphane. *La Déclaration des droits de l'homme et du citoyen.* Paris: Hachette, 1988.

Richelet, Pierre. *Dictionnaire françois contenant les mots et les choses.* 1680. Geneva: Slatkine Reprints, 1994.

Richelieu, Jean-Armand du Plessis, cardinal duc de. *Testament politique.* Edited by Louis André. Paris: Robert Laffont, 1947.

Robertson, William. *The Progress of Society in Europe: A Historical Outline from the Subversion of the Roman Empire to the Beginning of the Sixteenth Century.* 1769. Edited by Felix Gilbert. Chicago: University of Chicago Press, 1972.

Robespierre, Maximilien. *Œuvres de Maximilien Robespierre.* Edited by Marc Bouloiseau, Jean Dautry, Eugène Desprez, Gustave Laurent, Georges Lefebvre, Émile Lesueur, Georges Michon, and Albert Soboul. 10 vols. Paris: Ernest Leroux, Félix Alcan; Nancy: G. Thomas; Gap: Louis-Jean; and Paris: Presses universitaires de France, 1912–67.

Roland de la Platrière, Marie-Jeanne (née Phlipon). *Mémoires de Madame Roland.* 1795. Edited by Paul de Roux. Paris: Mercure de France, 1966.

Ronsard, Pierre de. *Les Amours.* Commentées par Marc-Antoine Muret. Nouvelle édition publiée d'après le texte de 1578. Edited by Hugues Vaganay. Geneva: Slatkine Reprints, 1970.

————. *Œuvres complètes.* Edited by Jean Céard, Daniel Ménager, and Michel Simonin. 2 vols. Paris: Gallimard, Bibliothèque de la Pléiade, 1993–94.

Saint-Just, Louis-Antoine de. *Œuvres complètes.* Edited by Michèle Duval. Paris: Gérard Lebovici, 1984.

Sénac de Meilhan, Gabriel. *Du gouvernement, des mœurs et des conditions en France, avant la révolution.* 1795. In Pierre Escoube, *Sénac de Meilhan (1736–1803): De la France de Louis XV à l'Europe des émigrés.* Paris: Librairie académique Perrin, 1984.

Sèze, Raymond de. *Défense de Louis.* Paris: Imprimerie Nationale, 1792.

Sieyes, Emmanuel-Joseph (abbé). *Écrits politiques.* Edited by Roberto Zapperi. Paris: Éditions des archives contemporaines, 1985.

————. *Observations sur le rapport du comité de Constitution concernant la nouvelle organisation de la France.* Paris: Baudoin, 1789. In *Œuvres de Sieyes,* edited by Marcel Dorigny, vol. 2. 3 vols. Paris: Edhis, 1989.

————. "Préliminaire de la Constitution. Reconnaissance et exposition raisonnée des Droits de l'Homme et du Citoyen" (July 20–21, 1789). In *Orateurs de la Révolution française*, edited by François Furet and Ran Halévi, 1:1004–18. Paris: Gallimard, Bibliothèque de la Pléiade, 1989.

———. *Qu'est-ce que le tiers état?* 1789. Edited by Edme Champion. Paris: Presses universitaires de France, 1982.

———. "Sur l'organisation du pouvoir législatif et la sanction royale" (September 7, 1789). In *Orateurs de la Révolution française*, edited by François Furet and Ran Halévi, 1:1019–35. Paris: Gallimard, Bibliothèque de la Pléiade, 1989.

Smith, Adam. *The Glasgow Edition of the Works and Correspondence of Adam Smith.* 6 vols. Oxford: Clarendon Press, 1976–82. (Individual works listed below. Citations from this edition use the book/chapter/paragraph system developed by the editors.)

———. *Essays on Philosophical Subjects.* Edited by W. P. D. Wightman and J. C. Bryce. *Glasgow Edition*, vol. 3.

———. *An Inquiry into the Nature and Causes of the Wealth of Nations.* 1776. Edited by R. H. Campbell, A. S. Skinner, and W. B. Todd. *Glasgow Edition*, vol. 2.

———. *Lectures on Jurisprudence.* Edited by R. L. Meek, D. D. Raphael, and P. G. Stein. *Glasgow Edition*, vol. 5. ["Report of 1762–1763" designated as "LJ(A)" and "Report dated 1766" as "LJ(B)."]

———. *The Theory of Moral Sentiments.* 1759. Edited by A. L. Macfie and D. D. Raphael. *Glasgow Edition*, vol. 1.

———. *Wealth of Nations.* Edited by Lawrence Dickey. Abr. ed. Indianapolis, Ind.: Hackett, 1993.

Staël, Anne-Louise-Germaine Necker, baronne de. *Des circonstances actuelles qui peuvent terminer la Révolution et des principes qui peuvent fonder la République en France.* 1798. Edited by Lucia Omacini. Geneva: Droz, 1979.

———. *Lettres sur les ouvrages et le caractère de J.-J. Rousseau.* 1788. Geneva: Slatkine Reprints, 1979.

Stewart, Dugald. *Account of the Life and Writings of Adam Smith.* 1794. In Adam Smith, *Essays on Philosophical Subjects*, edited by W. P. D. Wightman and J. C. Bryce. *Glasgow Edition*, vol. 3. Oxford: Clarendon Press, 1976–82.

Suard, Jean-Baptiste. "Parallèle entre la Clarice de Richardson et la nouvelle Eloïse de M. Rousseau." *Journal étranger* (December 1761): 184–94.

Turgot, Anne-Robert-Jacques. *Œuvres de Turgot et documents le concernant.* Edited by Gustave Schelle. 5 vols. Paris: Félix Alcan, 1913–23.

Vercruysse, Jeroom, ed. *Les Voltairiens.* 8 vols. Nendeln, Liechtenstein: KTO Press, 1978.

Virgil. *Georgics.* Edited by Richard F. Thomas. 2 vols. Cambridge: Cambridge
  University Press, 1988.
———. *The Georgics.* Translated by L. P. Wilkinson. Harmondsworth: Penguin,
  1982.
Volney, Constantin-François. *Tableau du climat et du sol des États-unis, suivi
  d'éclaircissements.* 1803. In *Œuvres,* edited by Anne and Henry Deneys,
  vol. 2. 2 vols. Paris: Fayard, 1989.
Voltaire, François-Marie Arouet de. *Lettres philosophiques.* 1734. Edited by
  R. Naves. Paris: Garnier, 1988.
———. *Œuvres alphabétiques.* Edited by Jeroom Vercruysse. In *Œuvres complètes
  de Voltaire,* edited by W. H. Barber, vol. 33. 80 vols. projected. Geneva
  and Oxford: Voltaire Foundation, 1968–.
———. *Le Siècle de Louis XIV.* 1751. In *Œuvres historiques,* edited by René
  Pomeau. Paris: Gallimard, Bibliothèque de la Pléiade, 1957.
Walter, Richard. *A Voyage Round the World in the Years 1740–1744, by George
  Anson.* 1748. London: J. M. Dent, 1911.

III. Secondary Works

Agulhon, Maurice. *Pénitents et franc-maçons de l'ancienne Provence: Essai sur la
  sociabilité méridionale.* 2d ed. Paris: Fayard, 1968.
———. Preface to *Le Cercle dans la France bourgeoise, 1810–1848: Étude d'une
  mutation de sociabilité.* Translated by Arthur Goldhammer. In *Histories:
  French Constructions of the Past,* edited by Jacques Revel and Lynn Hunt,
  pp. 398–407. New York: New Press, 1995.
Althusser, Louis. "Rousseau: The Social Contract (The Discrepancies)." In
  Montesquieu, Rousseau, Marx: Politics and History, translated by Ben
  Brewster, pp. 113–60. London: Verso, 1982.
Althusser, Louis, and Étienne Balibar. *Reading Capital.* Translated by Ben
  Brewster. London: Verso, 1979.
Andrews, Richard Mowery. "Social Structures, Political Elites, and Ideology in
  Revolutionary Paris, 1792–1794: A Critical Evaluation of Albert Soboul's
  Les Sans-culottes parisiens en l'an II." *Journal of Social History* 19 (1985):
  71–112.
Ariès, Philippe. "Histoire des mentalités." In *La Nouvelle histoire,* edited by
  Jacques Le Goff, Roger Chartier, and Jacques Revel, pp. 402–23. Paris:
  CEPL/Retz, 1978.
Artier, Jacqueline. "Étude sur la production imprimée de l'année 1764." In *École
  nationale des Chartes: Positions des thèses soutenues par les élèves de la
  promotion de 1981,* pp. 9–18. Paris: École des Chartes, 1981.

Attridge, Anna. "The Reception of *La Nouvelle Héloïse.*" *Studies on Voltaire and the Eighteenth Century* 120 (1974): 227–67.

Auerbach, Erich. *Scenes from the Drama of European Literature.* 2d ed. Minneapolis: University of Minnesota Press, 1984.

Baasner, Frank. "The Changing Meaning of 'Sensibilité': 1654–1704." *Studies in Eighteenth-Century Culture* 15 (1986): 77–96.

Baczko, Bronislaw. "Le Contrat social des français: Sieyes et Rousseau." In *The French Revolution and the Creation of Modern Political Culture,* edited by Keith Michael Baker, Colin Lucas, and François Furet, 1:493–513. Oxford: Pergamon Press, 1987–94.

———. *Ending the Terror: The French Revolution after Robespierre.* Translated by Michel Petheram. Cambridge: Cambridge University Press, 1994.

Badinter, Élisabeth, and Robert Badinter. *Condorcet (1743–1794): Un Intellectuel en politique.* Paris: Fayard, 1988.

Baecque, Antoine de. *The Body Politic: Corporeal Metaphor in Revolutionary France, 1770–1800.* Translated by Charlotte Mandell. Stanford: Stanford University Press, 1997.

Baker, Keith Michael. *Condorcet: From Natural Philosophy to Social Mathematics.* Chicago: University of Chicago Press, 1975.

———. "Defining the Public Sphere in Eighteenth-Century France: Variations on a Theme by Habermas." In *Habermas and the Public Sphere,* edited by Craig Calhoun, pp. 181–211. Cambridge, Mass.: MIT Press, 1992.

———. "Enlightenment and the Institution of Society: Notes for a Conceptual History." In *Main Trends in Cultural History,* edited by Willem Melching and Wyger Velema, pp. 95–120. Amsterdam: Rodopi, 1994.

———. *Inventing the French Revolution: Essays on French Political Culture in the Eighteenth Century.* Cambridge: Cambridge University Press, 1990.

Baker, Keith Michael, Colin Lucas, and François Furet, eds. *The French Revolution and the Creation of Modern Political Culture.* 4 vols. Oxford: Pergamon Press, 1987–94.

Balibar, Étienne. "Ambiguous Universality." *Differences* 7, no. 1 (spring 1995): 48–74.

———. "Ce qui fait qu'un peuple est un peuple: Rousseau et Kant." *Revue de synthèse* 110 (1989): 391–417.

———. "Citizen Subject." In *Who Comes after the Subject?* edited by Eduardo Cadava, pp. 33–57. London: Routledge, 1990.

———. *Masses, Classes, Ideas: Studies on Politics and Philosophy before and after Marx.* Translated by James Swenson. New York: Routledge, 1994.

Barker-Benfield, G. J. *The Culture of Sensibility: Sex and Society in Eighteenth-Century Britain.* Chicago: University of Chicago Press, 1993.

Barny, Roger. "Les Aristocrates et J. J. Rousseau dans la Révolution française."
     Annales historiques de la Révolution française 234 (1978): 534–64.

————. "Les Aventures de la théorie de souveraineté en 1789 (la discussion sur
     le droit de veto)." In *La Révision des valeurs sociales dans la littérature
     européenne à la lumière des idées de la Révolution française*, pp. 65–93.
     Paris: Les Belles lettres, 1970.

————. *Le Comte d'Antraigues, un disciple aristocrate de J.-J. Rousseau: De la
     fascination au reniement, 1782–1797. Studies on Voltaire and the Eighteenth
     Century* 281. Oxford: Voltaire Foundation, 1991.

————. *L'Éclatement révolutionnaire du rousseauisme. Annales littéraires de
     l'université de Besançon* 378. Paris: Les Belles lettres, 1988.

————. "Jean-Jacques Rousseau dans la Révolution." *Dix-huitième siècle* 6 (1974):
     59–98.

————. *Prélude idéologique à la Révolution française: Le Rousseauisme avant 1789.
     Annales littéraires de l'université de Besançon* 315. Paris: Les Belles lettres,
     1985.

————. *Rousseau dans la Révolution: Le Personnage de Jean-Jacques et les débuts du
     culte révolutionnaire (1787–1791). Studies on Voltaire and the Eighteenth
     Century* 246. Oxford: Voltaire Foundation, 1986.

Behbahani, Nouchine. *Paysage rêvés, paysages vécus dans La Nouvelle Héloïse de
     J. J. Rousseau. Studies on Voltaire and the Eighteenth Century* 271. Oxford:
     Voltaire Foundation, 1989.

Bellenot, Jean-Louis. "Les Formes de l'amour dans la *Nouvelle Héloïse* et la
     signification symbolique des personnages de Julie et de Saint-Preux."
     Annales de la Société Jean-Jacques Rousseau 33 (1953–55): 149–207.

Berry, Christopher J. *The Idea of Luxury: A Conceptual and Historical Investigation.*
     Cambridge: Cambridge University Press, 1994.

Binoche, Bertrand. *Les Trois sources des philosophies de l'histoire.* Paris: Presses
     universitaires de France, 1994.

Birn, Raymond. "Les 'Œuvres complètes' de Rousseau sous l'Ancien Régime."
     Annales de la Société Jean-Jacques Rousseau 41 (1997): 231–64.

————. "Profit in Ideas: Privilèges en librairie in Eighteenth-Century France."
     Eighteenth-Century Studies 4 (1970–71): 131–68.

————. "Rousseau and Literary Property: From the *Discours sur l'inégalité* to
     Émile." *Leipziger Jahrbuch zur Buchgeschichte* 3 (1993): 13–37.

————. "Rousseau et ses éditeurs." *Revue d'histoire moderne et contemporaine* 40
     (1993): 120–36.

Biver, Marie-Louise. *Fêtes révolutionnaires à Paris.* Paris: Presses universitaires de
     France, 1979.

Blum, Carol. *Rousseau and the Republic of Virtue: The Language of Politics in the French Revolution.* Ithaca, N.Y.: Cornell University Press, 1986.

Bollème, Geneviève, et al. *Livre et société dans la France du XVIIIᵉ siècle.* 2 vols. Paris and The Hague: Mouton, 1965–70.

Brancolini, Julien, and Marie-Thérèse Bouyssy. "La Vie provinciale du livre à la fin de l'Ancien Régime." In Geneviève Bollème et al., *Livre et société dans la France du XVIIIᵉ siècle,* 2:3–37. Paris and The Hague: Mouton, 1965–70.

Braunrot, Christabel P., and Kathleen Hardesty Doig. "The *Encyclopédie méthodique*: An Introduction." *Studies on Voltaire and the Eighteenth Century* 327 (1995): 1–152.

Brunel, Françoise. *Thermidor: La Chute de Robespierre.* Bruxelles: Éditions complexe, 1989.

———. "L'Acculturation d'un révolutionnaire: L'Exemple de Billaud-Varenne (1786–1791)." *Dix-huitième siècle* 23 (1991): 261–74.

Brunot, Ferdinand. *Histoire de la langue française des origines à nos jours.* 13 vols. Paris: Armand Colin, 1966.

Burgelin, Pierre. *La Philosophie de l'existence de J.-J. Rousseau.* Paris: Presses universitaires de France, 1952.

Burke, Janet M., and Margaret C. Jacob. "French Freemasonry, Women, and Feminist Scholarship." *Journal of Modern History* 68 (1996): 513–49.

Burt, E. S. "Mapping City Walks: The Topography of Memory in Rousseau's *Second* and *Seventh Promenades.*" *Yale French Studies* 74 (1988): 231–47.

Calhoun, Craig, ed. *Habermas and the Public Sphere.* Cambridge, Mass.: MIT Press, 1992.

Carcasonne, Elie. *Montesquieu et le problème de la constitution française au XVIIIᵉ siècle.* Geneva: Slatkine Reprints, 1970.

Carlson, Eric T., and Meribeth M. Simpson. "Models of the Nervous System in Eighteenth-Century Psychiatry." *Bulletin of the History of Medicine* 43 (1969): 101–15.

Cassirer, Ernst. *The Philosophy of the Enlightenment.* Translated by Fritz C. A. Koelln and James P. Pettegrove. Princeton: Princeton University Press, 1951.

———. *The Question of Jean-Jacques Rousseau.* Translated by Peter Gay. 2d ed. New Haven: Yale University Press, 1989.

Censer, Jack R. *The French Press in the Age of Enlightenment.* London: Routledge, 1994.

Censer, Jack R., and Jeremy D. Popkin, eds. *Press and Politics in Pre-Revolutionary France.* Berkeley: University of California Press, 1987.

Certeau, Michel de. *The Practice of Everyday Life.* Translated by Steven Rendall. Berkeley: University of California Press, 1984.

Chartier, Roger. *Cultural History: Between Practices and Representations.* Translated by Lydia G. Cochrane. Ithaca, N.Y.: Cornell University Press, 1988.

———. *The Cultural Origins of the French Revolution.* Translated by Lydia G. Cochrane. Durham, N.C.: Duke University Press, 1991.

———. *The Cultural Uses of Print in Early Modern France.* Translated by Lydia G. Cochrane. Princeton: Princeton University Press, 1987.

———. *On the Edge of the Cliff: History, Language, and Practices.* Translated by Lydia G. Cochrane. Baltimore: Johns Hopkins University Press, 1997.

———. *The Order of Books: Readers, Authors, and Libraries in Europe between the Fourteenth and Eighteenth Centuries.* Translated by Lydia G. Cochrane. Stanford: Stanford University Press, 1994.

———. "The Practical Impact of Writing." In *Passions of the Renaissance*, edited by Roger Chartier, pp. 111–59. In *A History of Private Life*, edited by Philippe Ariès and Georges Duby. Cambridge, Mass.: Harvard University Press, 1989.

Chartier, Roger, ed. *Passions of the Renaissance.* Translated by Arthur Goldhammer. In *A History of Private Life*, edited by Philippe Ariès and Georges Duby, vol. 3. 5 vols. Cambridge, Mass.: Harvard University Press, 1989.

Chaunu, Pierre. "Un Nouveau champ pour l'histoire sérielle: Le Quantitatif au troisième niveau." In *Mélanges en l'honneur de Fernand Braudel*, 2:105–25. 2 vols. Toulouse: Privat, 1973.

Chaussinand-Nogaret, Guy. *The French Nobility in the Eighteenth Century: From Feudalism to Enlightenment.* Translated by William Doyle. Cambridge: Cambridge University Press, 1985.

Citton, Yves. "Fabrique de l'opinion et folie de la dissidence dans le complot selon Rousseau." In *Rousseau juge de Jean-Jacques: Études sur les Dialogues/Studies on the Dialogues*, edited by Philip Knee and Gérald Allard, 104–14. *Pensée libre* 7. Ottawa, Ontario: North American Association for the Study of Jean-Jacques Rousseau, 1998.

Cochin, Augustin. *L'Esprit du jacobinisme.* Paris: Presses universitaires de France, 1979. [First published in 1921 as *Les Sociétés de pensée et la démocratie.*]

Courcelle, Pierre. *Les Confessions de saint Augustin dans la tradition littéraire: Antécédents et postérité.* Paris: Études augustiniennes, 1963.

Courtney, C. P. "An Eighteenth-Century Education: Constant at Erlangen and Edinburgh." In *Rousseau et le dix-huitième siècle: Essays in Memory of R. A. Leigh*, edited by Marian Hobson, J. T. A. Leigh, and Robert Wokler, pp. 295–324. Oxford: Voltaire Foundation, 1992.

Crampe-Casnabet, Michèle. *Condorcet, lecteur des lumières.* Paris: Presses universitaires de France, 1985.

Crane, R. S. "Suggestions Towards a Genealogy of the 'Man of Feeling.'" In *The*

Idea of the Humanities, 1:188–213. 2 vols. Chicago: University of Chicago Press, 1967.

Crow, Thomas. *Painters and Public Life in Eighteenth-Century Paris.* New Haven: Yale University Press, 1985.

Curtius, Ernst Robert. *European Literature and the Latin Middle Ages.* Translated by Willard R. Trask. Princeton: Princeton University Press, 1953.

Darnton, Robert. *The Business of Enlightenment: A Publishing History of the Encyclopédie, 1775–1800.* Cambridge, Mass.: Harvard University Press, 1979.

———. *The Corpus of Clandestine Literature in France, 1769–1789.* New York: W. W. Norton, 1995.

———. "The Facts of Literary Life in Eighteenth-Century France." In *The French Revolution and the Creation of Modern Political Culture,* edited by Keith Michael Baker, Colin Lucas, and François Furet, 1:261–91. Oxford: Pergamon Press, 1987–94.

———. *The Forbidden Best-Sellers of Pre-Revolutionary France.* New York: W. W. Norton, 1995.

———. *The Great Cat Massacre and Other Episodes in French Cultural History.* New York: Basic Books, 1984.

———. "In Search of the Enlightenment: Recent Attempts to Create a Social History of Ideas." *Journal of Modern History* 43 (1971): 113–32.

———. "Intellectual and Cultural History." In *The Past before Us: Contemporary Historical Writing in the United States,* edited by Michael Kammen, pp. 327–54. Ithaca, N.Y.: Cornell University Press, 1980.

———. *The Literary Underground of the Old Regime.* Cambridge, Mass.: Harvard University Press, 1982.

DeJean, Joan. *Ancients against Moderns: Culture Wars and the Making of a Fin de Siècle.* Chicago: University of Chicago Press, 1997.

De Man, Paul. *Allegories of Reading: Figural Language in Rousseau, Nietzsche, Rilke, and Proust.* New Haven: Yale University Press, 1979.

———. *Blindness and Insight: Essays in the Rhetoric of Contemporary Criticism.* 2d ed. Minneapolis: University of Minnesota Press, 1983.

———. *The Rhetoric of Romanticism.* New York: Columbia University Press, 1984.

Denby, David J. *Sentimental Narrative and the Social Order in France, 1760–1820.* Cambridge: Cambridge University Press, 1994.

Derathé, Robert. *Jean-Jacques Rousseau et la science politique de son temps.* 2d ed. Paris: J. Vrin, 1988.

———. *Le Rationalisme de Jean-Jacques Rousseau.* Paris: Presses universitaires de France, 1948.

———. "Les Réfutations du *Contrat social* au XVIIIe siècle." *Annales de la Société Jean-Jacques Rousseau* 32 (1950–52): 7–54.

Derrida, Jacques. *Of Grammatology.* Translated by Gayatri Chakravorty Spivak. Baltimore: Johns Hopkins University Press, 1976.

Diatkine, Daniel. "A French Reading of the *Wealth of Nations* in 1790." In *Adam Smith: International Perspectives*, edited by Hiroshi Mizuta and Chuhei Sugiyama, pp. 213–23. New York: St. Martin's Press, 1993.

Dickey, Laurence. "Pride, Hypocrisy and Civility in Mandeville's Social and Historical Theory." *Critical Review* (1990): 387–431.

Dowd, David Lloyd. *Pageant-Master of the Republic: Jacques-Louis David and the French Revolution.* Lincoln: University of Nebraska Press, 1948.

Doyle, William. *Origins of the French Revolution.* 2d ed. Oxford: Oxford University Press, 1988.

———. "The Parlements of France and the Breakdown of the Old Regime, 1771–1788." *French Historical Studies* 6 (1970): 415–58.

Droits 2 (1985). Special issue on *La Déclaration de 1789.*

Durling, Robert M. "The Ascent of Mount Ventoux and the Crisis of Allegory." *Italian Quarterly* 69 (1974): 7–28.

Echeverria, Durand. *The Maupeou Revolution.* Baton Rouge: Louisiana State University Press, 1985.

———. "The Pre-Revolutionary Influence of Rousseau's *Contrat social.*" *Journal of the History of Ideas* 33 (1972): 543–60.

Egret, Jean. *Louis XV et l'opposition parlementaire, 1715–1774.* Paris: Armand Colin, 1970.

———. *Necker, ministre de Louis XVI (1776–1790).* Paris: Honoré Champion, 1975.

———. *La Révolution des notables: Mounier et les monarchiens, 1789.* Paris: Armand Colin, 1950.

Engelsing, Rolf. "Die Perioden der Lesergeschichte in der Neuzeit. Das statistische Ausmaß und die soziokulturelle Bedeutung der Lektüre." *Archiv für Geschichte des Buchwesens* 10 (1970): 946–1002.

Estivals, Robert. *La Statistique bibliographique de la France sous la monarchie au XVIIIe siècle.* Paris: Imprimerie nationale, 1965.

Febvre, Lucien. *The Problem of Unbelief in the Sixteenth Century: The Religion of Rabelais.* Translated by Beatrice Gottlieb. Cambridge, Mass.: Harvard University Press, 1982.

Figlio, Karl M. "Theories of Perception and the Physiology of Mind in the Late Eighteenth Century." *History of Science* 12 (1975): 177–212.

Fish, Stanley. *Is There a Text in This Class? The Authority of Interpretive Communities.* Cambridge, Mass.: Harvard University Press, 1980.

Foisil, Madelaine. "The Literature of Intimacy." In *Passions of the Renaissance,* edited by Roger Chartier, pp. 327–61. In *A History of Private Life*, edited by Philippe Ariès and Georges Duby. Cambridge, Mass.: Harvard University Press, 1989.

Fontana, Biancamaria. "The Shaping of Modern Liberty: Commerce and Civilisation in the Writings of Benjamin Constant." *Annales Benjamin Constant* 5 (1985): 3–15.

Force, Pierre. "Self-Love, Identification, and the Origin of Political Economy." *Yale French Studies* 92 (1997): 46–64.

Forsyth, Murray. *Reason and Revolution: The Political Thought of the Abbé Sieyes.* Leicester: Leicester University Press; New York: Holmes & Meier, 1987.

Foucault, Michel. *Aesthetics, Method, and Epistemology.* Edited by James D. Faubion. In *The Essential Works of Foucault, 1954–1984,* edited by Paul Rabinow, vol. 2. 2 vols. New York: New Press, 1997–98.

———. *The Archaeology of Knowledge and the Discourse on Language.* Translated by A. M. Sheridan Smith. New York: Pantheon, 1972.

———. *Dits et écrits.* Edited by Daniel Defert and François Ewald. 4 vols. Paris: Gallimard, 1994.

Freccero, John. *Dante: The Poetics of Conversion.* Edited by Rachel Jacoff. Cambridge, Mass.: Harvard University Press, 1986.

———. "The Fig Tree and the Laurel: Petrarch's Poetics." In *Literary Theory/Renaissance Texts*, edited by Patricia Parker and David Quint, pp. 20–32. Baltimore: Johns Hopkins University Press, 1986.

Furet, François. *La Gauche et la Révolution française au milieu du XIXᵉ siècle: Edgar Quinet et la question du Jacobinisme, 1865–1870.* Paris: Hachette, 1986.

———. *In the Workshop of History.* Translated by Jonathan Mandelbaum. Chicago: University of Chicago Press, 1984.

———. *Interpreting the French Revolution.* Translated by Elborg Forster. Cambridge: Cambridge University Press, 1981.

———. *Marx and the French Revolution.* Translated by Deborah Kan Furet. Chicago: University of Chicago Press, 1988.

———. "La Monarchie et le règlement électoral de 1789." In *The French Revolution and the Creation of Modern Political Culture*, edited by Keith Michael Baker, Colin Lucas, and François Furet, 1:375–86. Oxford: Pergamon Press, 1987–94.

Furet, François, and Jacques Ozouf. *Reading and Writing: Literacy in France from Calvin to Jules Ferry.* Cambridge: Cambridge University Press, 1982.

Furet, François, and Mona Ozouf, eds. *A Critical Dictionary of the French Revolution.* Translated by Arthur Goldhammer. Cambridge, Mass.: Harvard University Press, 1989.

Gagnebin, Bernard. "L'Étrange accueil fait aux *Confessions* de Rousseau au XVIIIᵉ siècle." *Annales de la Société Jean-Jacques Rousseau* 38 (1969–71): 105–26.

Gauchet, Marcel. *La Révolution des droits de l'homme*. Paris: Gallimard, 1989.

———. *La Révolution des pouvoirs: La Souveraineté, le peuple et la représentation, 1789–1799*. Paris: Gallimard, 1995.

Genty, Maurice. *Paris 1789–1795: L'Apprentissage de la citoyenneté*. Paris: Messidor-Éditions sociales, 1987.

Gilson, Étienne. *Les Idées et les lettres*. 2d ed. Paris: J. Vrin, 1955.

Godineau, Dominique. *The Women of Paris and Their French Revolution*. Translated by Katherine Streip. Berkeley: University of California Press, 1998.

Goodman, Dena. "Public Sphere and Private Life: Toward a Synthesis of Current Historiographical Approaches to the Old Regime." *History and Theory* 31 (1992): 1–20.

———. *The Republic of Letters: A Cultural History of the French Enlightenment*. Ithaca, N.Y.: Cornell University Press, 1994.

Gordon, Daniel. *Citizens without Sovereignty: Equality and Sociability in French Thought, 1670–1789*. Princeton: Princeton University Press, 1994.

———. "Philosophy, Sociology, and Gender in the Enlightenment Conception of Public Opinion." *French Historical Studies* 17 (1992): 882–911.

———. "'Public Opinion' and the Civilizing Process in France: The Example of Morellet." *Eighteenth-Century Studies* 22 (1989): 302–28.

Gordon, Daniel, David Bell, and Sarah Maza. "Forum: The Public Sphere in the Eighteenth Century." *French Historical Studies* 17 (1992): 882–956. [See also individual entries for Gordon and Maza.]

Gouhier, Henri. *Les Méditations métaphysiques de Jean-Jacques Rousseau*. Paris: J. Vrin, 1970.

Goulemot, Jean-Marie. "Literary Practices: Publicizing the Private." In *Passions of the Renaissance*, edited by Roger Chartier, pp. 363–95. In *A History of Private Life*, edited by Philippe Ariès and Georges Duby. Cambridge, Mass.: Harvard University Press, 1989.

Grange, Henri. "Idéologie et action politique: Le Débat sur le veto à l'Assemblée constituante." *Dix-huitième siècle* 1 (1969): 107–21.

Greenblatt, Stephen. *Shakespearean Negotiations: The Circulation of Social Energy in Renaissance England*. Berkeley: University of California Press, 1988.

Grimsley, Ronald. *Rousseau and the Religious Quest*. Oxford: Clarendon Press, 1968.

Gross, Jean-Pierre. *Fair Shares for All: Jacobin Egalitarianism in Practice*. Cambridge: Cambridge University Press, 1997.

Gueniffey, Patrice. "Les Assemblées et la représentation." In *The French Revolution and the Creation of Modern Political Culture*, edited by Keith Michael Baker, Colin Lucas, and François Furet, 2:233–57. Oxford: Pergamon Press, 1987–94.

———. *Le Nombre et la raison: La Révolution française et les élections.* Paris: Éditions de l'École des hautes études en sciences sociales, 1993.

Gueniffey, Patrice, and Ran Halévi. "Clubs and Popular Societies." In *A Critical Dictionary of the French Revolution*, edited by François Furet and Mona Ozouf, pp. 458–73. Cambridge, Mass.: Harvard University Press, 1989.

Guénot, Hervé. "Musées et lycées parisiens (1780–1830)." *Dix-huitième siècle* 18 (1986): 249–67.

Guérin, Daniel. *Class Struggle in the First French Republic: Bourgeois and Bras Nus, 1793–1795.* Translated by Ian Patterson. London: Pluto Press, 1977.

Gumbrecht, Hans-Ulrich. "Who Were the *Philosophes?*" Translated by Glen Burns. In *Making Sense in Life and Literature*, pp. 133–77. Minneapolis: University of Minnesota Press, 1992.

Gunn, J. A. W. *Queen of the World: Opinion in the Public Life of France from the Renaissance to the Revolution. Studies on Voltaire and the Eighteenth Century* 328. Oxford: Voltaire Foundation, 1995.

Habermas, Jürgen. "Further Reflections on the Public Sphere." In *Habermas and the Public Sphere*, edited by Craig Calhoun, pp. 421–61. Cambridge, Mass.: MIT Press, 1992.

———. *The Structural Transformation of the Public Sphere: An Inquiry into a Category of Bourgeois Society.* Translated by Thomas Burger and Frederick Lawrence. Cambridge, Mass.: MIT Press, 1989.

Halévi, Ran. "L'Idée et l'événement: Sur les origines intellectuelles de la Révolution française." *Le Débat* 38 (1986): 145–63.

———. *Les Loges maçonniques dans la France d'Ancien Régime: Aux origines de la sociabilité démocratique.* Paris: Armand Colin, 1984.

———. "La Révolution constituante: Les Ambiguïtés politiques." In *The French Revolution and the Creation of Modern Political Culture*, edited by Keith Michael Baker, Colin Lucas, and François Furet, 2:69–85. Oxford: Pergamon Press, 1987–94.

Hampson, Norman. *Will and Circumstance: Montesquieu, Rousseau, and the French Revolution.* London: Duckworth, 1983.

Harth, Erica. *Cartesian Women: Versions and Subversions of Rational Discourse in the Old Regime.* Ithaca, N.Y.: Cornell University Press, 1992.

Hartle, Ann. *The Modern Self in Rousseau's Confessions: A Reply to St. Augustine.* Notre Dame, Ind.: University of Notre Dame Press, 1983.

Hesse, Carla. *Publishing and Cultural Politics in Revolutionary Paris, 1789–1810.* Berkeley: University of California Press, 1991.

Higgins, D. "Rousseau and the Pantheon: The Background and Implications of the Ceremony of 20 vendémiaire Year III." *Modern Language Review* 50 (1955): 272–80.

Higonnet, Patrice L.-R. "The Social and Cultural Antecedents of Revolutionary Discontinuity: Montagnards and Girondins." *English Historical Review* 100 (1985): 513–44.

Hirschman, Albert O. *The Passions and the Interests: Political Arguments for Capitalism before Its Triumph.* Princeton: Princeton University Press, 1977.

Hoggart, Richard. *The Uses of Literacy: Changing Patterns in English Mass Culture.* Fairlawn, N.J.: Essential Books, 1957.

Hont, Istvan. "Commercial Society and Political Theory in the Eighteenth Century: The Problem of Authority in David Hume and Adam Smith." In *Main Trends in Cultural History,* edited by Willem Melching and Wyger Velema, pp. 54–94. Amsterdam: Rodopi, 1994.

———. "The Language of Sociability and Commerce: Samuel Pufendorf and the Theoretical Foundations of the 'Four-Stages Theory.'" In *The Languages of Political Theory in Early-Modern Europe,* edited by Anthony Pagden, pp. 253–76. Cambridge: Cambridge University Press, 1987.

———. "The Political Economy of the 'Unnatural and Retrograde' Order: Adam Smith and Natural Liberty." In Maxine Berg et al., *Französische Revolution und politische Ökonomie,* pp. 122–49. Trier: Schriften aus dem Karl-Marx-Haus, 1989.

Hont, Istvan, and Michael Ignatieff. "Needs and Justice in the *Wealth of Nations*: An Introductory Essay." In *Wealth and Virtue: The Shaping of Political Economy in the Scottish Enlightenment,* edited by Istvan Hont and Michael Ignatieff, pp. 1–44. Cambridge: Cambridge University Press, 1983.

Huet, Marie-Hélène. *Mourning Glory: The Will of the French Revolution.* Philadelphia: University of Pennsylvania Press, 1997.

Hulliung, Mark. *The Autocritique of Enlightenment: Rousseau and the Philosophes.* Cambridge, Mass.: Harvard University Press, 1994.

Hunt, Lynn. *The Family Romance of the French Revolution.* Berkeley: University of California Press, 1992.

———. *Politics, Culture, and Class in the French Revolution.* Berkeley: University of California Press, 1984.

Iser, Wolfgang. *The Act of Reading: A Theory of Aesthetic Response.* Baltimore: Johns Hopkins University Press, 1978.

———. "The Reading Process: A Phenomenological Approach." In *Reader-*

Response Criticism, edited by Jane Tompkins, pp. 50–69. Baltimore: Johns Hopkins University Press, 1980.

Isherwood, Robert. *Farce and Fantasy: Popular Entertainment in Eighteenth-Century Paris*. New York: Oxford University Press, 1986.

Jacob, Margaret C. *Living the Enlightenment: Freemasonry and Politics in Eighteenth-Century Europe*. New York: Oxford University Press, 1991.

Jaume, Lucien. *Le Discours jacobin et la démocratie*. Paris: Fayard, 1989.

———. *Hobbes et l'état représentatif moderne*. Paris: Presses universitaires de France, 1986.

Johnson, James H. *Listening in Paris: A Cultural History*. Berkeley: University of California Press, 1995.

Jones, Colin. "Bourgeois Revolution Revivified: 1789 and Social Change." In *Rewriting the French Revolution: The Andrew Browning Lectures 1989*, edited by Colin Lucas, pp. 69–118. Oxford: Clarendon Press, 1991.

Jordan, David P. *The King's Trial: Louis XVI versus the French Revolution*. Berkeley: University of California Press, 1979.

Jung, Marc-René. *Hercule dans la littérature française du 16ᵉ siècle*. Geneva: Droz, 1966.

Kantorowicz, Ernst H. *The King's Two Bodies: A Study in Medieval Political Philosophy*. Princeton: Princeton University Press, 1957.

Kaplan, Steven Laurence. *Bread, Politics and Political Economy in the Reign of Louis XV*. 2 vols. The Hague: Martinus Nijhoff, 1976.

———. *Provisioning Paris: Merchants and Millers in the Grain and Flour Trade during the Eighteenth Century*. Ithaca, N.Y.: Cornell University Press, 1984.

Katz, Wallace. "Le Rousseauisme avant la Révolution." *Dix-huitième siècle* 3 (1971): 205–22.

Kelly, Christopher. *Rousseau's Exemplary Life: The Confessions as Political Philosophy*. Ithaca, N.Y.: Cornell University Press, 1987.

Kernan, Alvin. *Samuel Johnson and the Impact of Print*. Princeton: Princeton University Press, 1987.

Kintzler, Catherine. *Condorcet: L'Instruction publique et la naissance du citoyen*. 2d ed. Paris: Gallimard (Folio), 1987.

Kitchen, Joanna. *Un Journal "philosophique": "La Décade," 1794–1807*. Paris: Minard, 1965.

Kors, Charles Alan. *D'Holbach's Coterie: An Enlightenment in Paris*. Princeton: Princeton University Press, 1976.

Koselleck, Reinhart. *Critique and Crisis: Enlightenment and the Pathogenesis of Modern Society*. Cambridge, Mass.: MIT Press, 1988.

Kusch, Manfred. "The Garden, the City, and Language in Rousseau's *La Nouvelle Héloïse*." *French Studies* 40 (1986): 45–54.

———. "Landscape and Literary Form: Structural Parallels in *La Nouvelle Héloïse*." *L'Esprit créateur* 17 (1977): 349–60.

Labrousse, Claude. *Lire au XVIIIᵉ siècle: La Nouvelle Héloïse et ses lecteurs*. Lyon: Presses universitaires de Lyon, 1985.

Landes, Joan. *Women and the Public Sphere in the Age of the French Revolution*. Ithaca, N.Y.: Cornell University Press, 1988.

Lanson, Gustave. "L'Unité de la pensée de Jean-Jacques Rousseau." *Annales de la Société Jean-Jacques Rousseau* 8 (1912): 1–31.

Lawrence, Christopher. "The Nervous System and Society in the Scottish Enlightenment." In *Natural Order: Historical Studies of Scientific Culture*, edited by Barry Barnes and Steven Shapin, pp. 19–40. Beverly Hills, Calif.: Sage Publications, 1979.

Lecercle, Jean-Louis. *Rousseau et l'art du roman*. Geneva: Slatkine Reprints, 1979.

Le Goff, Jacques. "Mentalities: A History of Ambiguities." In *Constructing the Past: Essays in Historical Methodology*, edited by Jacques Le Goff and Pierre Nora, pp. 166–80. Cambridge: Cambridge University Press, 1985.

Leigh, R. A. "Review Article: Jean-Jacques Rousseau." *Historical Journal* 12 (1969): 549–65.

———. "Rousseau, His Publishers, and the *Contrat social*." *Bulletin of the John Ryland University Library of Manchester* 66 (1984): 204–27.

———. *Unsolved Problems in the Bibliography of J.-J. Rousseau*. Edited by J. T. A. Leigh. Cambridge: Cambridge University Press, 1990.

Leith, James. "Les Trois apothéoses de Voltaire." *Annales historiques de la Révolution française* 236 (1979): 161–209.

Lepetit, Bernard. "Quantitative History: Another Approach." Translated by Arthur Goldhammer. In *Histories: French Constructions of the Past*, edited by Jacques Revel and Lynn Hunt, pp. 503–12. New York: New Press, 1995.

Le Roy Ladurie, Emmanuel. *The Territory of the Historian*. Translated by Ben and Siân Reynolds. Chicago: University of Chicago Press, 1979.

Levy, Darline Gay. *The Ideas and Careers of Simon-Nicolas-Henri Linguet: A Study in Eighteenth-Century French Politics*. Urbana: University of Illinois Press, 1980.

Levy, Darline Gay, and Harriet B. Applewhite. "Women and Militant Citizenship in Revolutionary Paris." In *Rebel Daughters: Women and the French Revolution*, edited by Sara E. Melzer and Leslie W. Rabine, pp. 79–101. New York: Oxford University Press, 1992.

Lougee, Carolyn C. *"Le Paradis des femmes": Women, Salons, and Social Stratifica-*

tion in Seventeenth-Century France. Princeton: Princeton University Press, 1976.

McDonald, Christie V. *The Dialogue of Writing: Essays in Eighteenth-Century French Literature*. Waterloo, Ontario: Wilfred Laurier University Press, 1984.

McDonald, Joan. *Rousseau and the French Revolution (1762–1791)*. London: Athlone Press, 1965.

McDonald Vance, Christie. *The Extravagant Shepherd: A Study of the Pastoral Vision in Rousseau's La Nouvelle Héloïse. Studies on Voltaire and the Eighteenth Century* 105. Banbury, Oxfordshire: Voltaire Foundation, 1973.

McEachern, Jo-Ann E. *Bibliography of the Writings of Jean-Jacques Rousseau to 1800*. 2 vols. to date. Oxford: Voltaire Foundation, 1989–.

———. "The Publication of *La Nouvelle Héloïse*." *Studies on Voltaire and the Eighteenth Century* 265 (1989): 1710–11.

Macfie, Alec. "The Invisible Hand of Jupiter." *Journal of the History of Ideas* 32 (1971): 595–99.

McNally, David. *Political Economy and the Rise of Capitalism: A Reinterpretation*. Berkeley: University of California Press, 1988.

Mandrou, Robert. *Introduction to Modern France, 1500–1640: An Essay in Historical Psychology*. Translated by R. E. Hallmark. New York: Holmes & Meier, 1976.

Manin, Bernard. "Checks, Balances and Boundaries: The Separation of Powers in the Constitutional Debate of 1787." In *The Invention of the Modern Republic*, edited by Biancamaria Fontana, pp. 27–62. Cambridge: Cambridge University Press, 1994.

Marcetteau-Paul, Agnès, and Dominique Varry. "Les Bibliothèques de quelques acteurs de la Révolution." *Mélanges de la Bibliothèque de la Sorbonne* 9 (1989): 189–207.

Marin, Louis. "L'Effet Sharawadgi ou le jardin de Julie: Notes sur un jardin et un texte (Lettre XI, 4ᵉ partie, *La Nouvelle Héloïse*)." *Traverses* 5/6 (1976): 114–31.

Martin, Henri-Jean. "Une Croissance séculaire." In *Histoire de l'édition française*, edited by Henri-Jean Martin and Roger Chartier, 2:95–103. Paris: Promodis, 1984.

———. *Le Livre français sous l'Ancien Régime*. Paris: Promodis, 1987.

Martin, Henri-Jean, and Roger Chartier, eds. *Histoire de l'édition française*. 4 vols. Paris: Promodis, 1984.

Marx, Karl. *Capital*. Translated by Ben Fowkes and David Fernbach. 3 vols. New York: Vintage, 1977.

———. *Das Kapital*. 3 vols. Berlin: Dietz Verlag, 1962.

Masson, Pierre-Maurice. *La Religion de J. J. Rousseau.* 2d ed. 3 vols. Paris: Hachette, 1916.

Mathiez, Albert. "Robespierre and the Cult of the Supreme Being." In *The Fall of Robespierre and Other Essays,* pp. 84–118. New York: Augustus M. Kelley, 1968.

May, Gita. *De Jean-Jacques Rousseau à Madame Roland.* Geneva: Droz, 1964.

————. *Madame Roland and the Age of Revolution.* New York: Columbia University Press, 1970.

Maza, Sarah. "Luxury, Morality, and Social Change: Why There Was No Middle-Class Consciousness in Prerevolutionary France." *Journal of Modern History* 69 (1997): 199–229.

————. *Private Lives and Public Affairs: The Causes Célèbres of Prerevolutionary France.* Berkeley: University of California Press, 1993.

————. "Women, the Bourgeoisie, and the Public Sphere: Response to Daniel Gordon and David Bell." *French Historical Studies* 17 (1992): 935–50.

Meek, Ronald. *Social Science and the Ignoble Savage.* Cambridge: Cambridge University Press, 1976.

Melching, Willem, and Wyger Velema, eds. *Main Trends in Cultural History.* Amsterdam: Rodopi, 1994.

Mély, Benoît. *Jean-Jacques Rousseau: Un Intellectuel en rupture.* Paris: Minerve, 1985.

Michelet, Jules. *Histoire de la Révolution française.* 2 vols. Paris: Robert Laffont, 1979.

Monglond, André. *La France révolutionnaire et impériale: Annales de bibliographie méthodique et description des livres illustrés.* Grenoble: Arthaud, 1933.

Mornet, Daniel. "Les Enseignements des bibliothèques privées, 1750–1780." *Revue d'histoire littéraire de la France* 17 (1910): 449–96.

————. "L'Influence de J. J. Rousseau au XVIIIᵉ siècle." *Annales de la Société Jean-Jacques Rousseau* 8 (1912): 33–67.

————. *Les Origines intellectuelles de la Révolution française, 1715–1787.* Lyon: La Manufacture, 1989.

————. *Le Sentiment de la nature en France de Jean-Jacques Rousseau à Bernardin de Saint-Pierre.* Paris: Hachette, 1907.

Mortier, Roland. *Clarté et ombres au siècle des lumières.* Geneva: Droz, 1969.

Ong, Walter J. "The Writer's Audience is Always a Fiction." *PMLA* 90 (1975): 9–21.

Orr, Linda. *Headless History: Nineteenth-Century French Historiography of the Revolution.* Ithaca, N.Y.: Cornell University Press, 1990.

Osmont, Robert. "Remarques sur la genèse et la composition de la *Nouvelle Héloïse.*" *Annales de la Société Jean-Jacques Rousseau* 33 (1953–55): 93–148.

Ozouf, Mona. *Festivals and the French Revolution.* Translated by Alan Sheridan. Cambridge, Mass.: Harvard University Press, 1988.

———. "'Public Opinion' at the End of the Old Regime." *Journal of Modern History* 60, supplement (1988): S1–S21.

Patrick, Alison. *The Men of the First French Republic: Political Alignments in the National Convention of 1792.* Baltimore: Johns Hopkins University Press, 1972.

Paulhan, Jean. *Les Fleurs de Tarbes, ou, la terreur dans les lettres.* Paris: Gallimard, 1943.

Perrot, Jean-Claude. *Une Histoire intellectuelle de l'économie politique, XVIIᵉ–XVIIIᵉ siècle.* Paris: Éditions de l'École des hautes études en sciences sociales, 1992.

Perrot, Philippe. *Le Luxe: Une Richesse entre faste et confort, XVIIIᵉ–XIXᵉ siècle.* Paris: Éditions du Seuil, 1995.

Pertué, Michel. "Les Projets constitutionnels de 1793." In *Révolution et république: L'Exception française,* edited by Michel Vovelle, pp. 174–99. Paris: Kimé, 1994.

Pocock, J. G. A. *The Machiavellian Moment: Florentine Political Thought and the Atlantic Republican Tradition.* Princeton: Princeton University Press, 1975.

———. *Virtue, Commerce, and History.* Cambridge: Cambridge University Press, 1985.

Poulet, Georges. "Criticism and the Experience of Interiority." In *Reader-Response Criticism,* edited by Jane Tompkins, pp. 41–49. Baltimore: Johns Hopkins University Press, 1980.

Ravel, Jeffrey S. "Seating the Public: Spheres and Loathing in the Paris Theaters, 1777–1788." *French Historical Studies* 18 (1993): 173–210.

Raymond, Marcel. "Du jansénisme à la morale de l'intérêt." *Mercure de France* 1126 (1957): 238–55.

———. *Jean-Jacques Rousseau: La Quête de soi et la rêverie.* Paris: José Corti, 1962.

Rétat, Pierre. "L'Économie rustique de Clarens." *Littératures* 21 (1989): 59–68.

Revel, Jacques. "Marie-Antoinette and Her Fictions: The Staging of Hatred." In *Fictions of the French Revolution,* edited by Bernadette Fort, pp. 111–29. Evanston, Ill.: Northwestern University Press, 1991.

Revel, Jacques, and Lynn Hunt, eds. *Histories: French Constructions of the Past.* New York: New Press, 1995.

Richet, Denis. "Autour des origines idéologiques lointaines de la Révolution française: Élites et despotisme." *Annales E.S.C.* 24 (1969): 1–23.

———. "L'Esprit de la constitution, 1789–1791." In *The French Revolution and the Creation of Modern Political Culture,* edited by Keith Michael Baker,

Colin Lucas, and François Furet, 2:63–68. Oxford: Pergamon Press, 1987–94.

Ridehalgh, Anna. "Preromantic Attitudes and the Birth of a Legend: French Pilgrimages to Ermenonville, 1778–1789." *Studies on Voltaire and the Eighteenth Century* 215 (1982): 231–52.

Riley, Patrick. *The General Will before Rousseau: The Transformation of the Divine into the Civic.* Princeton: Princeton University Press, 1986.

Roche, Daniel. *France in the Enlightenment.* Translated by Arthur Goldhammer. Cambridge, Mass.: Harvard University Press, 1998.

———. *The People of Paris: An Essay in Popular Culture in the Eighteenth Century.* Translated by Marie Evans. Berkeley: University of California Press, 1987.

———. *Les Républicains des lettres: Gens de culture et Lumières aux XVIIIᵉ siècle.* Paris: Fayard, 1988.

———. *Le Siècle des lumières en province: Académies et académiciens provinciaux, 1680–1789.* 2 vols. Paris and The Hague: Mouton, 1978.

Root, Hilton L. *Peasants and King in Burgundy: Agrarian Foundations of French Absolutism.* Berkeley: University of California Press, 1987.

Rosenblatt, Helena. *Rousseau and Geneva: From the First Discourse to the Social Contract, 1749–1762.* Cambridge: Cambridge University Press, 1997.

Rousseau, G. S. "Nerves, Spirits, and Fibres: Towards Defining the Origins of Sensibility." In *Studies in the Eighteenth Century III*, edited by R. F. Brissenden and J. C. Eade, pp. 137–57. Toronto: University of Toronto Press, 1976.

Roussel, Jean. "Le Phénomène d'identification dans la lecture de Rousseau." *Annales de la Société Jean-Jacques Rousseau* 39 (1972–77): 65–77.

Scott, William Robert. *Adam Smith as Student and Professor.* Glasgow: Jackson, Son & Co., 1937.

Sewell, William H., Jr. *A Rhetoric of Bourgeois Revolution: The Abbé Sieyes and "What is the Third Estate?"* Durham, N.C.: Duke University Press, 1994.

———. "The Sans-Culotte Rhetoric of Subsistence." In *The French Revolution and the Creation of Modern Political Culture,* edited by Keith Michael Baker, Colin Lucas, and François Furet, 4:249–69. Oxford: Pergamon Press, 1987–94.

Seznec, Jean. *The Survival of the Pagan Gods: The Mythological Tradition and Its Place in Renaissance Humanism and Art.* Translated by Barbara F. Sessions. New York: Pantheon, 1953.

Sgard, Jean. "La Multiplication des périodiques." In *Histoire de l'édition française,* edited by Henri-Jean Martin and Roger Chartier, 2:198–205. Paris: Promodis, 1984.

Shklar, Judith N. *Men and Citizens: A Study of Rousseau's Social Theory.* Cambridge: Cambridge University Press, 1969.

———. "Montesquieu and the New Republicanism." In *Machiavelli and Republicanism,* edited by Gisela Bock, Quentin Skinner, and Maurizio Viroli, pp. 265–79. Cambridge: Cambridge University Press, 1990.

Skinner, Quentin. *The Foundations of Modern Political Thought.* 2 vols. Cambridge: Cambridge University Press, 1978.

———. *Meaning and Context: Quentin Skinner and His Critics.* Edited by James Tully. Princeton: Princeton University Press, 1988.

Soboul, Albert. "Audience des Lumières: Classes populaires et rousseauisme sous la Révolution." *Annales historiques de la Révolution française* 170 (1962): 421–38.

———. *The Sans-Culottes: The Popular Movement and Revolutionary Government, 1793–1794.* Translated by Remy Inglis Hall. Princeton: Princeton University Press, 1980.

Sonenscher, Michael. *Work and Wages: Natural Law, Politics, and Eighteenth-Century French Trades.* Cambridge: Cambridge University Press, 1989.

Sozzi, Lionello. "Interprétations de Rousseau pendant la Révolution." *Studies on Voltaire and the Eighteenth Century* 64 (1968): 187–223.

Starobinski, Jean. *Blessings in Disguise, or, The Morality of Evil.* Translated by Arthur Goldhammer. Cambridge, Mass.: Harvard University Press, 1993.

———. *Jean-Jacques Rousseau: Transparency and Obstruction.* Translated by Arthur Goldhammer. Chicago: University of Chicago Press, 1988.

Swenson, James. "A Small Change in Terminology or a Great Leap Forward? Culture and Civilization in Revolution." *MLN* 112 (1997): 322–48.

Tackett, Timothy. *Becoming a Revolutionary: The Deputies of the French National Assembly and the Emergence of a Revolutionary Culture, 1789–1790.* Princeton: Princeton University Press, 1996.

Taieb, Paulette. "Tours de mains." *Revue de synthèse* 110 (1989): 189–203.

Taine, Hippolyte. *Les Origines de la France contemporaine.* 2 vols. Paris: Robert Laffont, 1986.

Talmon, J. L. *The Origins of Totalitarian Democracy.* London: Secker and Warburg, 1952.

Tatin-Gourier, Jean-Jacques. *Le Contrat social en question: Échos et interprétations du Contrat social de 1762 à la Révolution.* Lille: Presses universitaires de Lille, 1989.

Taylor, Samuel S. B. "Rousseau's Contemporary Reputation in France." *Studies on Voltaire and the Eighteenth Century* 27 (1963): 1545–74.

Tocqueville, Alexis de. *L'Ancien régime et la Révolution.* In *Œuvres complètes,* edited by J.-P. Mayer, vol. 2, pt. 1. 18 vols. to date. Paris: Gallimard, 1951–.

Todd, Janet. *Sensibility: An Introduction.* London: Methuen, 1986.

Tompkins, Jane, ed. *Reader-Response Criticism: From Formalism to Post-Structuralism.* Baltimore: Johns Hopkins University Press, 1980.

Trahard, Pierre. *Les Maîtres de la sensibilité française au dix-huitième siècle.* 4 vols. Paris: Boivin, 1931–33.

Trenard, Louis. "La Diffusion du *Contrat social,* 1762–1832." In *Études sur le Contrat social de J.-J. Rousseau,* pp. 432–38. Colloque de Dijon, May 3–6, 1962. Paris: Les Belles lettres, 1964.

Trouille, Mary. *Sexual Politics in the Enlightenment: Women Writers Read Rousseau.* Albany: State University of New York Press, 1997.

Trousson, Raymond. "Ronsard et la légende d'Hercule." *Bibliothèque d'humanisme et de renaissance* 24 (1962): 77–87.

Van Kley, Dale K. "Church, State, and the Ideological Origins of the French Revolution: The Debate over the General Assembly of the Gallican Clergy in 1765." *Journal of Modern History* 51 (1979): 629–66.

———. "The Jansenist Constitutional Legacy in the French Prerevolution." In *The French Revolution and the Creation of Modern Political Culture,* edited by Keith Michael Baker, Colin Lucas, and François Furet, 1:169–201. Oxford: Pergamon Press, 1987–94.

———. "Pierre Nicole, Jansenism, and the Morality of Enlightened Self-Interest." In *Anticipations of the Enlightenment in England, France, and Germany,* edited by A. Kors and J. Korshin, pp. 69–85. Philadelphia: University of Pennsylvania Press, 1987.

Van Kley, Dale K., ed. *The French Idea of Freedom: The Old Regime and the Declaration of Rights of 1789.* Stanford: Stanford University Press, 1994.

Van Sant, Ann Jessie. *Eighteenth-Century Sensibility and the Novel: The Senses in Social Context.* Cambridge: Cambridge University Press, 1993.

Viala, Alain. *La Naissance de l'écrivain: Sociologie de la littérature à l'âge classique.* Paris: Éditions de Minuit, 1985.

Vila, Anne C. *Enlightenment and Pathology: Sensibility in the Literature and Medicine of Eighteenth-Century France.* Baltimore: Johns Hopkins University Press, 1998.

Viroli, Maurizio. *Jean-Jacques Rousseau and the "Well-Ordered Society."* Translated by D. Hanson. Cambridge: Cambridge University Press, 1988.

Walter, Éric. "Les Auteurs et le champ littéraire." In *Histoire de l'édition française,* edited by Henri-Jean Martin and Roger Chartier, 2:383–99. Paris: Promodis, 1984.

———. "Sur l'intelligensia des Lumières." *Dix-huitième siècle* 5 (1973): 173–201.

Walzer, Michael, ed. *Regicide and Revolution: Speeches at the Trial of Louis XVI.* Cambridge: Cambridge University Press, 1974.

Weil, Éric. "J. J. Rousseau et sa politique." In *Essais et conférences*, 2:114–48. 2 vols. Paris: J. Vrin, 1991.

Wokler, Robert. "The Influence of Diderot on the Political Theory of Rousseau." *Studies on Voltaire and the Eighteenth Century* 132 (1975): 55–111.

Wood, Dennis. *Benjamin Constant: A Biography*. London: Routledge, 1993.

Wright, J. K. "National Sovereignty and the General Will: The Political Program of the Declaration of Rights." In *The French Idea of Freedom*, edited by Dale K. Van Kley, pp. 199–233. Stanford: Stanford University Press, 1994.

Index

Boldface indicates the work is the exclusive or primary focus of an extended discussion.

Library of Congress Cataloging-in-Publication Data

Swenson, James.
    On Jean-Jacques Rousseau : considered as one of the first authors of the
Revolution / James Swenson.
        p.   cm. — (Atopia)
    Includes bibliographical references and index.
    ISBN 0-8047-3555-7 (cloth : alk. paper). — ISBN 0-8047-3864-5 (pbk. : alk. paper)
    1. France—History—Revolution, 1789–1799 Literature and the revolution.
2. France—History—Revolution, 1789–1799 Historiography.   3. Rousseau,
Jean-Jacques, 1712–1778—Criticism and interpretation.   4. Rousseau, Jean-Jacques,
1712–1778—Political and social views.   5. Politics and literature—France—
History—18th century.   I. Title.   II. Series: Atopia (Stanford, Calif.)
DC138.S94   1999
944.04—dc21   99-39445

Original printing 2000

Last figure below indicates the year of this printing:
09   08   07   06   05   04   03   02   01   00

Designed by Janet Wood
Typeset by James P. Brommer in 11/14 Garamond